The presumption of non-conformity in European consumer sales law

The presumption of non-conformity in European consumer sales law

Karolina Sikorska

eleven international publishing

Published, sold and distributed by Eleven International Publishing
P.O. Box 85576
2508 CG The Hague
The Netherlands
Tel.: +31 70 33 070 33
Fax: +31 70 33 070 30
e-mail: sales@budh.nl
www.elevenpub.com

Sold and distributed in USA and Canada
International Specialized Book Services
920 NE 58th Avenue, Suite 300
Portland, OR 97213-3786, USA
Tel.: 1-800-944-6190 (toll-free)
Fax: +1 503 280-8832
orders@isbs.com
www.isbs.com

Eleven International Publishing is an imprint of Boom uitgevers Den Haag.

ISBN 978-94-6236-557-5
ISBN 978-94-6274-270-3 (E-book)

Printed in The Netherlands

Table of Contents

Abbreviations **xiii**

1 Introduction **1**
1.1 Research questions 2
1.2 Approach 3

2 Burden of proof **7**
2.1 Introduction 7
2.1.1 Burden of proof – European perspective 8
2.1.2 Functions of the burden of proof in the civil proceedings 9
2.2 Burden of proof in Polish law 10
2.2.1 Introduction 10
2.2.2 Definitions 10
2.2.2.1 Material aspect 11
2.2.2.2 Procedural aspect 12
2.2.3 Allocation of the burden of proof 14
2.2.3.1 General rule of Article 6 of the Civil Code 14
2.2.3.2 Presumptions 15
2.2.4 Standard of proof 17
2.2.5 Conclusions 17
2.3 Burden of proof in German law 18
2.3.1 Introduction 18
2.3.2 Definitions 19
2.3.2.1 *Objektive Beweislast* 19
2.3.2.2 *Subjektive Beweislast* 20
2.3.3 Allocation of the burden of proof 23
2.3.3.1 *Normentheorie* 23
2.3.3.2 Presumptions 24
2.3.4 Standard of proof 25
2.3.5 Conclusions 26
2.4 Burden of proof in English and Welsh law 27
2.4.1 Introduction 27
2.4.2 Definitions 28
2.4.2.1 Persuasive burden 28
2.4.2.2 Evidential burden 30

2.4.3 Allocation of the burden of proof 31
2.4.3.1 Allocation of the burden of persuasion 32
2.4.3.2 Allocation of the evidential burden 32
2.4.3.3 Presumptions 33
2.4.4 Standard of proof 33
2.4.5 Conclusions 35
2.5 Burden of proof in Dutch law 36
2.5.1 Introduction 36
2.5.2 Definitions 36
2.5.3 Allocation of the burden of proof 40
2.5.3.1 General rule of Article 150 Rv 40
2.5.3.2 Presumptions 41
2.5.4 Standard of proof 43
2.5.5 Conclusions 44
2.6 Conclusions 45

3 Consumer Sales Directive and its national implementations 49
3.1 Introduction 49
3.2 Information about the Consumer Sales Directive 49
3.2.1 Legislative process 49
3.2.2 Objectives 50
3.2.3 Implementation methods 51
3.3 Consumer sale in Polish law 52
3.3.1 General information 52
3.3.1.1 Method of implementation 53
3.3.1.2 Characterisation of the implementing act 54
3.3.1.3 Systematics of sales law 55
3.3.2 Legislative changes as a result of the implementation of the Consumer Sales Directive 56
3.3.3 Current issues regarding the law of consumer sale 60
3.3.3.1 Implementation of the Directive on Consumer Rights 61
3.3.3.2 Existence of the case law 61
3.3.3.3 ADR 62
3.3.3.4 Consequences for consumer protection 64
3.3.4 Conclusions 65
3.4 Consumer sale in German law 66
3.4.1 General information 66
3.4.1.1 Method of implementation 67
3.4.1.2 Characterisation of the implementing act 67

3.4.1.3 Systematics of sales law 68
3.4.2 Legislative changes as a result of the implementation of the Consumer Sales Directive 69
3.4.3 Current issues regarding the law of consumer sale 72
3.4.3.1 Implementation of the Directive on Consumer Rights 72
3.4.3.2 Interpretation of German provisions on consumer sales in conformity with the Directive 73
3.4.3.3 ADR 77
3.4.4 Conclusions 78
3.5 Consumer sale in English and Welsh law 79
3.5.1 General information 79
3.5.1.1 Method of implementation 81
3.5.1.2 Characterisation of the implementing act 82
3.5.1.3 Systematics of sales law 83
3.5.2 Legislative changes as a result of the implementation of the Consumer Sales Directive 84
3.5.2.1 Remedies 84
3.5.2.2 Non-conformity 88
3.5.2.3 Limitation and the burden of proof 88
3.5.2.4 Conclusions 89
3.5.3 Current issues regarding the law of consumer sale 89
3.5.3.1 Implementation of the Directive on Consumer Rights 90
3.5.3.2 Substantive law 90
3.5.3.3 Court proceedings 92
3.5.3.4 ADR 92
3.5.4 Conclusions 94
3.6 Consumer sale in Dutch law 95
3.6.1 General information 95
3.6.1.1 Method of implementation 96
3.6.1.2 Characterisation of the implementing act 96
3.6.1.3 Systematics of sales law 98
3.6.2 Legislative changes as a result of the implementation of the Consumer Sales Directive 99
3.6.3 Current issues regarding the law of consumer sale 101
3.6.3.1 Implementation of the Directive on Consumer Rights 102
3.6.3.2 Preliminary questions for the ECJ: *ex officio* application of consumer sales law and specificity of the burden of proof 103
3.6.3.3 ADR (*de Geschillencommissie*) 107
3.6.4 Conclusions 109

3.7 Conclusions 110

4 Non-conformity 113
4.1 Introduction 113
4.2 Non-conformity in the Consumer Sales Directive 113
4.3 Non-conformity in Polish law 115
4.3.1 Introduction 115
4.3.2 Non-conformity: definitions 116
4.3.2.1 Physical defects of Article 556 (1) of the Civil Code (before implementation of the Consumer Sales Directive) 116
4.3.2.2 Legal defects of Article 556 (2) of the Civil Code (before implementation of the Consumer Sales Directive) 117
4.3.2.3 Non-conformity of Article 4 (2) and 4 (3) of the Consumer Sale Act 119
4.3.2.4 Defects of Article 556[1] of the Civil Code (amendments introduced in 2014) 125
4.3.2.5 Conclusions 127
4.3.3 Buyer's knowledge of the non-conformity 128
4.3.4 Burden of proof of the non-conformity 130
4.3.5 Conclusions 136
4.4 Non-conformity in German law 137
4.4.1 Introduction 137
4.4.2 Defects: definitions 138
4.4.2.1 Material defects 139
4.4.2.2 Incorrect installation 142
4.4.2.3 Legal defects 143
4.4.2.4 Conclusions 143
4.4.3 Buyer's knowledge of the defects 144
4.4.4 Burden of proof of the defects 145
4.4.5 Conclusions 147
4.5 Non-conformity in English and Welsh law 148
4.5.1 Introduction 148
4.5.2 Non-conformity: definitions 150
4.5.2.1 Satisfactory quality 150
4.5.2.2 Correspondence with the description, sample or model 151
4.5.2.3 Fitness for purpose (ordinary and specific) 154
4.5.2.4 Correspondence with the characteristics based on the public statements 156
4.5.2.5 Incorrect installation 157

4.5.2.6	Legal defects	159
4.5.2.7	Conclusions	160
4.5.3	Buyer's knowledge of the non-conformity	161
4.5.4	Burden of proof of the non-conformity	162
4.5.5	Conclusions	163
4.6	Non-conformity in Dutch law	165
4.6.1	Introduction	165
4.6.2	Non-conformity: definitions	166
4.6.2.1	Quality	167
4.6.2.2	Identity and quantity	170
4.6.2.3	Incorrect installation	170
4.6.2.4	Legal defects	171
4.6.2.5	Conclusions	172
4.6.3	Buyer's knowledge of the non-conformity	173
4.6.4	Burden of proof of the non-conformity	174
4.6.5	Conclusions	175
4.7	Conclusions	176
5	**Presumption of non-conformity**	**179**
5.1	Introduction	179
5.2	The presumption of Article 5 (3) of the Consumer Sales Directive	180
5.2.1	Introduction	180
5.2.2	General information	180
5.2.3	Conditions for the application of the presumption	183
5.2.3.1	Non-conformity	183
5.2.3.2	Six-month period	183
5.2.4	Construction of Article 5 (3) of the Consumer Sales Directive	184
5.2.5	Conclusions	188
5.3	Presumption of non-conformity in Polish law	188
5.3.1	Introduction	188
5.3.2	Scope of the application of the presumption	189
5.3.3	Conditions for the application of the presumption	191
5.3.3.1	Non-conformity	191
5.3.3.2	Six-month period	196
5.3.3.3	Conclusions	202
5.3.4	Rebuttal of the presumption	204
5.3.5	Exclusion of the application of the presumption	205
5.3.6	Road map of the presumption	208
5.3.7	Conclusions	210

5.4 Presumption of non-conformity in German law 211
5.4.1 Introduction 211
5.4.2 Scope of the application of the presumption 212
5.4.3 Conditions for the application of the presumption 215
5.4.3.1 Non-conformity (*Sachliche Komponente*) 215
5.4.3.2 Six-month period (*Zeitliche Komponente*) 222
5.4.3.3 Conclusions 227
5.4.4 Rebuttal of the presumption 228
5.4.5 Exclusion of the application of the presumption 230
5.4.5.1 Incompatibility with the nature of the goods 231
5.4.5.2 Incompatibility with the nature of the defects 235
5.4.5.3 Conclusions 239
5.4.6 Road map of the presumption 240
5.4.7 Conclusions 242
5.5 Presumption of non-conformity in English and Welsh law 244
5.5.1 Introduction 244
5.5.2 Scope of the application of the presumption 245
5.5.3 Conditions for the application of the presumption 249
5.5.3.1 Non-conformity 249
5.5.3.2 Six-month period 250
5.5.3.3 Conclusions 252
5.5.4 Rebuttal of the presumption 253
5.5.5 Exclusion of the application of the presumption 254
5.5.6 Road map of the presumption 255
5.5.7 Conclusions 256
5.6 Presumption of non-conformity in Dutch law 257
5.6.1 Introduction 257
5.6.2 Scope of the application of the presumption 257
5.6.3 Conditions for the application of the presumption 260
5.6.3.1 Non-conformity 261
5.6.3.2 Six-month period 265
5.6.3.3 Conclusions 267
5.6.4 Rebuttal of the presumption 268
5.6.5 Exclusion of the application of the presumption 271
5.6.5.1 Incompatibility with the nature of the goods 273
5.6.5.2 Incompatibility with the nature of the non-conformity 276
5.6.5.3 Conclusions 281
5.6.6 Road map of the presumption 282
5.6.7 Conclusions 284

5.7 Conclusions 285

6 Comparative conclusions 289
6.1 Aims and objectives of the presumption of Article 5 (3) of the Consumer Sales Directive 289
6.2 Conditions for the application of the presumption 291
6.2.1 Non-conformity 291
6.2.1.1 Poland 292
6.2.1.2 Germany 293
6.2.1.3 England and Wales 294
6.2.1.4 The Netherlands 295
6.2.1.5 Comparative remarks 296
6.2.2 Six-month period 297
6.2.2.1 Poland 297
6.2.2.2 Germany 298
6.2.2.3 England and Wales 299
6.2.2.4 The Netherlands 299
6.2.2.5 Comparative remarks 300
6.3 Rebuttal 301
6.3.1 Poland 301
6.3.2 Germany 302
6.3.3 England and Wales 302
6.3.4 The Netherlands 302
6.3.5 Comparative remarks 303
6.4 Exclusion 304
6.4.1 Poland 304
6.4.2 Germany 305
6.4.2.1 Incompatibility with the nature of the goods 305
6.4.2.2 Incompatibility with the nature of the defects 306
6.4.2.3 Relationship between rebuttal and exclusion of the presumption 307
6.4.3 England and Wales 308
6.4.4 The Netherlands 309
6.4.4.1 Incompatibility with the nature of the goods 310
6.4.4.2 Incompatibility with the nature of the non-conformity 310
6.4.4.3 Relationship between rebuttal and exclusion of the presumption 312
6.4.5 Comparative remarks 312
6.5 Final remarks 313

Literature 315

Legislation 343

Table of Cases 351

Index 359

Abbreviations

AA	Ars Aequi
aant.	Aantekening
ADR	Alternative Dispute Resolution
AG	Amtsgericht
AG.	Aktiengesellschaft
All ER	All England Law Reports
ANWB	Algemene Nederlandse Wielrijdersbond
APK	Algemene Periodieke Keuring
App Cas	Law Reports Appeal Cases
approx.	Approximately
ATW	Algemene Termijnenwet
BGB	Bürgerliches Gesetzbuch
BGBl.	Bundesgesetzblatt
BGH	Bundesgerichtshof
BIS	Department for Business, Innovation and Skills
BJu	Boom Juridische uitgevers
BW	Burgerlijk Wetboek
CC	Civil Code
CESL	Common European Sales Law
CISG	United Nations Convention on Contracts for the International Sale of Goods
CJEU	Court of Justice of the European Union
CSIH	Court of Session, Inner House
DCFR	Draft Common Frame of Reference
diss.	Dissertation
DTI	Department of Trade and Industry
Dz. U.	Dziennik Ustaw
ECLI	European Case Law Identifier
ECR	European Court Reports
EEC	European Economic Community
et seq.	et sequentia
EU	European Union
EWCA Civ	England and Wales Court of Appeal Civil Division
GPR	Zeitschrift für Gemeinschaftsprivatrecht
HL	House of Lords

Hof	Gerechtshof
HR	Hoge Raad
JZ	Juristen Zeitung
k.p.c.	Kodeks Postępowania Cywilnego
km.	Kilometre
LG	Landgericht
Lloyd's Rep	Lloyd's Law Reports
LMCLQ	Lloyd's Maritime and Commercial Law Quarterly
MOT	Ministry of Transport
MvA	Memorie van Antwoord
MvT	Memorie van Toelichting
NBW	Nieuw Burgerlijk Wetboek
NGO	Non-governmental organization
NJ	Nederlandse Jurisprudentie
NMvA	Nadere Memorie van Antwoord
NP	Nowe Prawo
Nr.	Number
OBW	Overgangswet Nieuw Burgerlijk Wetboek
OFT	Office of Fair Trading
OJ	Official Journal
OLG	Oberlandesgericht
p.	page
Parl. gesch.	Parlementaire geschiedenis
PiP	Prokuratura i Prawo
pln	Polski Nowy Złoty
PP	Praktisch Procederen
QB	Queen's Bench Reports
R.T.R.	Road Traffic Reports
Rabels	Rabels Zeitschrift für ausländisches und internationales Privatrecht
Rb	Rechtbank
Rn.	Randnummer
RP	Rzeczpospolita Polska
RPEiS	Ruch Prawniczy, Ekonomiczny i Socjologiczny
Rv	Wetboek van Burgerlijke Rechtsvordering
s.	sentence
S.L.T.	Scots Law Times
SER	Sociaal-Economische Raad
SI	Statutory Instrument

SN	Sąd Najwyższy
SO	Sąd Okregowy
SOGA 1979	Sale of Goods Act 1979
SR	Sąd Rejonowy
SSGCR 2002	Sale and Supply of Goods to Consumers Regulations 2002
Stb.	Staatsblad
sygn.	sygnatura
T&C	Tekst en Commentaar
T.M.	Toelichting Meijers
TvPP	Tijdschrift voor de Procespraktijk
U	Urteil
UCTA 1977	Unfair Contract Terms Act 1977
UOKiK	Urząd Ochrony Konkurencji i Konsumentów
UTCCR 1999	Unfair Terms in Consumer Contracts Regulations 1999
WLR	Weekly Law Reports
ZIP	Zeitschrift für Wirtschaftsrecht
ZPO	Zivilprozessordnug
ZR	Zivilregister

1 Introduction

1. A sale of consumer goods is probably one of the most frequently concluded contracts in Europe. To enhance the functioning of the internal market, the European legislator harmonised the most important matters of consumer sales in the Consumer Sales Directive.[1] The Directive was enacted in 1999 and in 2002 and 2003 entered into force in the legal systems explored in this book. The Directive regulates the issues of non-conformity, buyer's remedies in case of the delivery of non-conforming goods, and consumer guarantees. The Directive also regulates the burden of proof in consumer sale cases and introduces the presumption of non-conformity.

2. One of the principles of European consumer law is to provide for the fair and equal treatment of consumers in all Member States in the context of domestic and cross-border transactions. The uniform simplification in the allocation of the burden of proof in consumer sales law is considered as one of the means for improving consumer protection and boosting consumers' confidence in participating in the internal market. The latter is indispensable for ensuring the balanced growth and development of the internal market.

3. Generally, to be able to receive remedies for the delivery of non-conforming goods, a buyer is required to prove the existence of non-conformity at the time of delivery. It is often difficult to establish whether the non-conformity of goods existed already at the time of the conclusion of the contract, whether it occurred at the time of the delivery of the goods, or whether the non-conformity came into being only after the goods left the seller's control.

The European legislator has recognised that the traditional rules on the burden of proof are too burdensome for a consumer and in Article 5 (3) of the Consumer Sales Directive introduced the presumption of non-conformity. Article 5 (3) of the Consumer Sales Directive provides that '*unless proved otherwise, any lack of conformity which becomes apparent within six months of delivery of the goods shall be presumed to have existed at the time of delivery unless this presumption is incompatible with the nature of the goods or the nature of the lack of conformity.*' The presumption of non-conformity aims to simplify the supply of evidence and to ease the process of receiving remedies in case of the delivery of

1 Directive 1999/44/EC of the European Parliament and of the Council of 25 May 1999 on certain aspects of the sale of consumer goods and associated guarantees, Official Journal L 171, 07/07/1999 P. 0012 – 0016, further referred to as the Consumer Sales Directive.

non-conforming goods in order to encourage consumers to participate in cross-border sales, which should foster integration of the common market.[2]

4. The substance and impact of the presumption of non-conformity has not been entirely foreseen by the European legislator. What initially was considered to be a measure for easing the burden of proof lying with the consumer transpired to be a complex legal construction whose interpretation and application, more than a decade after the implementation to the domestic systems, still causes considerable difficulties.

The provision introducing the presumption required an immediate alteration of the national rules on the allocation of the burden of proof in (consumer) sales law. The change prompted many questions on the conditions and precise legal consequences of a new tool of consumer protection. The questions that arrived considered also whether the presumption of non-conformity is in fact a proper measure to facilitate the balance between the parties. In some cases it disturbed the well-established application of other substantive and procedural measures of protection available to consumers.

5. The Consumer Sales Directive contains provisions which go to the core of the systems of private law found in the Member States. In particular, the impact of Article 5 (3) of the Consumer Sales Directive is far reaching. The implementation of this provision alters the allocation of the burden of proof regarding the moment of the existence of non-conformity, having implications in all the Member States. This is the first European provision which does so on such a large scale. Having that said, the operation of the presumption of non-conformity still depends on the national concepts, notions and practices regarding the burden of proof. To be able to assess the role and function of the presumption of non-conformity in the Member States, it is necessary to analyse the influence the national concepts and practices regarding the burden of proof have on the presumption.

1.1 Research questions

6. To date there is no comprehensive work analysing the role and function of the presumption of non-conformity, its actual influence on consumers' position in litigation and their chances of receiving remedies for the delivery of non-conforming goods, and its influence on the application of substantive law in general. Given the importance of the topic and

2 The importance of the presumption of non-conformity goes beyond the European borders, the Consumer Protection (Fair Trading) Act of Singapore amended in 9 March 2012 contains in Section 12B of Part III the same presumption as found in Article 5 (3) of the Consumer Sales Directive, including the prerequisites, rebuttal and the exclusion criteria.

the frequency with which it is applied, there is a necessity to analyse and clarify the operation of the most crucial provisions of consumer sales law in the Member States.

7. The main question of this research regards the role the presumption of non-conformity has in the facilitation of the burden of proof lying with the consumer, in order to receive remedies for the delivery of non-conforming goods. Answering the above question has several objectives. The first is to identify how the presumption of non-conformity has been implemented into domestic systems. The second is to identify how the presumption operates within the national legal frameworks. And finally, whether the presumption of non-conformity meets the expectations and objectives set out for it by the European legislator.

Reaching the above-mentioned aims will allow the determination of whether the allocation of the burden of proof in consumer cases is similar in the jurisdictions investigated, whether the presumption eases the burden of proof that lies with the consumer and whether (and how) the national rules of the burden of proof affect the application of (European) consumer sales law.

8. The importance of this research is multi-faceted. It investigates how the presumption of non-conformity is implemented in four legal systems: Poland, Germany, England and Wales, and the Netherlands. It shows how this presumption operates in different legal systems and what its importance for the consumers is. It presents the relationship between the different systems in the context of the presumption of non-conformity. Finally, it allows for an evaluation of whether the goal of the Consumer Sales Directive in the context of the presumption of non-conformity has been achieved and if so, whether it has been done in the same way in the different jurisdictions.

1.2 Approach

9. To achieve the goals set for this study several topics will be investigated. The first necessary task will be to explain the main definitions and general rules on the burden of proof existing in the four jurisdictions examined: Poland, Germany, England and Wales, and the Netherlands. The matters such as allocation of the burden of proof and standard of proof will be discussed. Moreover, a brief explanation of the concepts of the burden of proof of four Member States is necessary to identify what is a general rule of the burden of proof and how the presumption of non-conformity alters (if at all) this general rule. Consequently, there will be an examination of how the presumption of non-conformity affects the consumer's position with regard to evidence in relation to the traditional allo-

cation of the burden of proof when no simplifications regarding the supply of evidence apply.

It should be observed that in chapters 5 and 6 the expressions: 'presumption', 'reversed burden of proof' and 'shift of the burden of proof' are used repeatedly, often not explaining precise legal consequences. In such cases it should be understood that the general duty to provide evidence and prove the particular fact has been altered. The precise legal consequences thereof will be discussed only where necessary.

10. Another important matter to be analysed is the notion of non-conformity. There are at least two reasons why the notion of non-conformity could be considered as the core element of the Consumer Sales Directive. First of all, the existence of non-conformity is a condition for seller's liability. Without this element the consumer is not entitled to claim remedies. Second of all, the successfully proven existence of non-conformity is a requirement for the application of the presumption of non-conformity. In this book, the notion of non-conformity will first be briefly discussed from the perspective of the Consumer Sales Directive. Subsequently, a relatively detailed analysis from the perspective of national implementations will be provided. The main focus will be placed on the differences in understanding what the non-conformity is and whether the national concepts include all the criteria of non-conformity found in the Consumer Sales Directive. The questions of what facts and circumstances constitute non-conformity in different jurisdictions and who has to prove these facts and circumstances will take a central place in the discussion.

11. After presenting the matters of national rules on the burden of proof and the analysis of the topics of non-conformity, the main research topics will be analysed. How the presumption of non-conformity has been implemented into domestic laws, how it operates, what are the legal consequences of its application, does it facilitate a similar allocation of the burden of proof among the Member States in question and finally, whether the presumption of non-conformity in fact provides simplifications in the supply of evidence. Another issue regards the potential and actual factors that may hinder the expected or desired functioning of the presumption of non-conformity. This includes the question of the role of national rules on the burden of proof, or rules of another character, for the application of substantive law having its origin in the Consumer Sales Directive.

12. As already stated, this book will compare the law of four jurisdictions: Poland, Germany, England and Wales, and the Netherlands. The selection of legal systems was made based on legal and practical factors. To obtain as broad picture of the application and the role of the presumption of non-conformity as possible, it was important to compare legal systems coming from different legal families, civil law and common law systems. These systems are characterised by different weight of the national and European legislation and the

importance of judiciary in the creation, application and interpretation of legal rules. It was also important to include systems of different civil procedure principles and different practices in terms of resolving consumer disputes. Furthermore, it was desirable to include legal systems having different (initial) approaches to consumer protection, systems where the consumer protection already developed before the promulgation of European measures, and systems where the consumer (sales) law is a new discipline. Finally, in the selection of legal systems investigated one will find systems that were reluctant to implement the European consumer directives, and the systems that duly and timely complied with the implementation duties. The practical reasons to choose these legal systems considered mainly the language abilities to read and understand legal concepts.

13. The analysis of the domestic law of Member States was based mainly on the exploration of national legislation and policy documents, literature study, and a review of the selection of case law regarding the matters at issue.

At this point, there are major amendments of the consumer sales law in two of the jurisdictions. On 9 May 2014 the Polish Parliament passed the statute amending Polish sales law and on 30 May 2014 President signed the new Consumer Rights Act. The new law entered into force on 25 December 2014.

The English Parliament is in an advanced stage of the legislative process of a new Consumer Rights Bill, amending, inter alia, the provisions of consumer sales. At this point Lords amendments to the Bill are under consideration of the House of Commons.[3] Regarding the Polish amendment, this book considers changes passed on 9 May 2014 that entered into force on 25 December 2014, regarding the English amendment, it considers the version of the Consumer Rights Bill as presented to Parliament on 21 January 2014. Throughout this book, often for the sake of convenience the direct reference is made to English law, however it should be understood as English and Welsh law.

14. Comparing European legislation and the legislation of four different legal systems in the context of consumer sales generates several practical problems. The first problem regards the issues of language and terminology. The most problematic notion described in this book is the notion of non-conformity. Different systems use of different terms to describe similar legal constructions. Throughout this book several terms will be used to discuss the topics of non-conformity. Defects, physical defects, material defects, satisfactory quality and fitness for purpose, *(Sach)mangel, Grundmangel, Folgemangel*, all these terms will be used to describe and explain the elements of non-conformity in various jurisdictions. They may have different scopes at times, but what they have in common is to be a counterpart of the notion of non-conformity from Article 2 (2) of the Consumer Sales Directive,

3 http://services.parliament.uk/bills/2014-15/consumerrights.html (23.01.2015).

including the criteria therein, and to be a requirement for the application of the presumption of non-conformity from Article 5 (3) of the Directive. In having to deal with such rich terminology some simplifications and (minor) inaccuracies were inevitable.

Another matter which has proven to be problematic in the comparison of the four jurisdictions in the context of the burden of proof in consumer sales regards the practices and customs of each jurisdiction which do not necessarily have their explanation in the legal provisions. In particular, when it comes to the topics regarding the theories of the burden of proof, the function these rules have in litigation and the capacity of particular terms that must be invoked and proven to win the case were difficult to grasp and compare.

Despite these difficulties, this book provides a comprehensive analysis of the operation of the presumption of non-conformity in four jurisdictions, showing the potential weaknesses and advantages of the presumption of non-conformity as such and the importance of the rules on the burden of proof in solving consumer disputes.

2 Burden of proof

2.1 Introduction

15. This chapter provides information necessary for understanding exactly what the burden of proof means. It explains the scope of burden of proof in four jurisdictions: Poland (2.2), Germany (2.3), England and Wales (2.4) and the Netherlands (2.5). It also presents the different national theories and general rules on the burden of proof. The discussion surrounding the burden of proof can be approached from two perspectives, that of European law and from the perspective of national law.

It is only relatively recently that the law of evidence in civil cases, and in particular rules on the burden of proof have become matters of interests to the European legislator.[1] In 2001 the Regulation on cooperation between the courts of the Member States in the taking of evidence in civil or commercial matters was enacted.[2] There are also many examples of European provisions found mainly in the directives that regulate issues of the burden of proof.[3] Although it shows the rising importance of this field of law for the Member States and for the functioning of the internal market, it is arguable that there is a common European notion of the burden of proof and there is uncertainty what a 'European' understanding of burden of proof entails.

16. The national rules on the burden of proof developed alongside the progress of procedural and substantive law. The national dimensions to this matter regard general theories of the burden of proof, rules on the allocation of the burden of proof and the procedural and material consequences for the parties. They also cover standard of proof, that is, the certainty that must be achieved regarding the existence of essential facts.

17. Below, a short introduction, including the European rules and concepts of the burden of proof as well as current principles and interpretations thereof, will be presented. Subsequently, the focus will be on the national notions of the burden of proof. The general theories, existing exceptions, rules on the allocation of the burden of proof and established practices regarding the distribution of the burden of proof will be briefly discussed. The

1 Comparing to the law of evidence in criminal cases.

2 Council Regulation (EC) No 1206/2001 of 28 May 2001 on cooperation between the courts of the Member States in the taking of evidence in civil or commercial matters.

3 For example: Article 4 (1) of the Council Directive 97/80/EC of 15 December 1997 on the burden of proof in cases of discrimination based on sex; Article 6 (a) the Directive on misleading advertising, 97/55/EC, OJ L 290/18, 23.10.97, amending the Directive of 1984.

short analysis of rules concerning the issues of the burden of proof will demonstrate the specific characteristics of these rules, their role in litigation and importance for the outcome of the dispute, as well as their potential effect on the application of substantive law in general, and consumer law in particular.

2.1.1 *Burden of proof – European perspective*

18. The European Community relies on the Member States to provide the legal means to permit consumers to enforce their rights.[4] The ECJ has established the principle of procedural autonomy, which entails that the substantive rights and obligations may be governed by EU law while the procedures within which these rights are to be made effective are left to the national legislators.[5] There is uncertainty over the scope of national procedural autonomy. First of all, there are legal issues that are difficult to classify, such as the issues of the burden of proof. Secondly, the scope of the principle of autonomy of national procedure seems to be gradually reduced in order to ensure that the objectives of substantive EU rights can be met. The area of consumer law is the field in which a number of provisions on procedure have been identified, and where national procedural autonomy seems to be increasingly limited.[6]

19. European legislation does not provide for a definition or any general theory on the burden of proof. When regulating a particular matter concerning the burden of proof, the European legislator employs terminology derived from the national systems of Member States. On the other hand, in cases where there is a national rule of the burden of proof that makes the application of the EU law impossible or is contrary to particular provisions of the EU law, the ECJ may decide on the (non) admissibility of this particular rule.[7]

The ECJ does not establish essential facts or examine evidence which the national court accepted in support of those facts.[8] There are no general rules on the burden of proof at the European level, however it is said that the classic allocation of the burden of proof, where a party has a duty to prove the facts which lead to the legal consequences he or she

4 Lenaerts and Arts 2003, p. 89-93; Bussani and Werro 2009, p. 280; Kakauris 1997, p. 1386; Storskrubb 2008, p. 14 *et seq.*; De Witte and Micklitz 2011, p. 306, Galetta 2010, p. 34 *et seq.*

5 See *inter alia*: ECJ 27.02.2014, C-470/12, *Pohotovost' s.r.o. v M. Vasuta*, 2014 not yet published, para 46; ECJ 05.12.2013, C-413/12, *Associacion de Consumidores Independedienties de Castilla y Leon v Anuntis Segundamano Espana S.L.*, 2013 not yet published, para 30; ECJ 30.05.2013, C-397/11, *E. Joros v Aegon Magyarorszag Hitel Zrt.*, 2013 not yet published, para 29.

6 Storskrubb 2008, p. 28.

7 ECJ 09.11.1983, *Amministrazione delle Finanze dello Stato v SpA San Giorgio*, C-199/82, ECR (1983) I-03595.

8 See *inter alia*: ECJ 08.05.2008, *Danske Svineproducenter v Justitsministeriet*, (2008) ECR I-3343, para 23; ECJ 05.06.2005 Joined Cases C-211/03, C-299/03 and C-316/03 to C-318/03 *HLH Warenvertrieb, Orthica v Bundesrepublik Deutschland*, (2005) ECR I-5141, para 96; ECJ 18.07.2007, C-119/05, *Lucchini*, (2007) ECR I-6199, para 43.

relies on, counts also in the context of community law.[9] The national legislation and legal practice together with the case law of a particular Member State apply where the issues of the burden of proof are concerned, also when European law is applicable.

Having said that, many European pieces of legislation, mainly Directives, in particular regarding consumer protection, contain special rules on the burden of proof. They often provide an instrument for shifting the burden of proof. Consequently, the allocation of the burden of proof under EU legislation may often differ from the burden established in accordance with the general national rules on the burden of proof. These special rules regarding the burden of proof are to be transposed into national laws to ensure the proper application of rights that the reversed burden facilitates (and to meet implementation duties). An example of such a provision is the presumption of non-conformity of Article 5 (3) of the Consumer Sales Directive, a central topic of this study. Accordingly, the European legislator has influence over legal notions, which are normally reserved for the national legislators and domestic courts.

2.1.2 Functions of the burden of proof in the civil proceedings

20. The burden of proof plays an important role in determining the outcome of disputes. It is difficult to establish the exact meaning and scope of the burden of proof. It can be agreed that the rules on the burden of proof at the same time belong to substantive law as they are a part of procedural law, governing any dispute regarding the application of substantive law. The rules on the burden of proof actuate the process of taking evidence, especially in strictly adversarial systems. They organise the proceedings and may determine the order of presenting evidence.[10] The burden of proof is said to be the most important part of litigation because the final decision is based on what has been established during that time.[11]

21. Regarding the particular functions of the rules of the burden of proof, their two-fold character (material and procedural aspect) must be borne in mind. The rules on the burden of proof allow the occurrence of particular facts to be claimed, from which a party derives an individual right. It is closely connected to the process of assuming evidence that supports the statement that essential facts occurred. This is followed by an assessment of whether the evidence has been sufficiently convincing to be able to state that the alleged facts occurred. This assessment of facts regards the question of whether a party satisfied the

9 Lenaerts and Arts 2003, p. 443, Lasok 1994, p. 344 *et seq.*

10 Piasecki 2010, p. 59.

11 Dolecki 1998, p. 76.

burden of proof. Finally, the rules on the burden of proof determine the consequences of the non-discovery of facts necessary for delivery of a judgement.

The above-mentioned functions of the burden of proof and their importance will be discussed separately for every jurisdiction. The definitions of particular dimensions of the burden of proof will also be explained in the context of national law. In the latter part of this book, the role of the rules on burden of proof will be also discussed from the perspective of consumer sales law and its objective of protecting the weaker party. Finally, the relationship between the issues of how the burden of proof of essential facts is allocated (who has to prove the essential facts) and the successful application of the consumer sales law will be analysed.

22. Due to the fact that the topics surrounding the burden of proof can be complex and multidimensional it is not possible to discuss all aspects of the burden of proof in depth. Another obstacle in covering the issues of the burden of proof in a comprehensible manner is terminology. The translation of particular national theories on the burden of proof leads to the danger that identical terms will have a different scope or meaning in various jurisdictions. Taking the purpose of this dissertation into account, this chapter provides a short overview of general rules on the burden of proof in four jurisdictions: Poland, Germany, England and Wales, and the Netherlands. This overview is necessary for a further analysis of requirements and consequences of the application of the presumption of non-conformity in consumer sales.

2.2 Burden of proof in Polish law

2.2.1 Introduction

23. This section describes the issues of the burden of proof in Polish civil proceedings. Initially, different aspects of the burden of proof will be explained (2.2.2). Subsequently, the rules on the allocation of the burden of proof will be presented, including the application of the general rule of Article 6 of the Civil Code and the applicable exceptions (2.2.3). Additionally, matters of the standard of proof and the evaluation of evidence will be presented (2.2.4).

2.2.2 Definitions

24. According to Article 227 k.p.c., the process of taking evidence regards only the facts which are essential for the resolution of a dispute. The burden of proof regarding these

facts exists in the Polish law in two parallel senses. The burden of proof is an important constituent of the law of evidence and at the same time it corresponds with the substantive rights and their protection.[12] The matters of the burden of proof are regulated in substantive law as well as in procedural law, depending on its role and function. There are two main functions of the burden of proof. First, it actuates the process of taking evidence in the civil proceedings based on Articles 228-309 k.p.c. Second, it determines the outcome of the dispute when the essential facts remain unproven.[13]

2.2.2.1 Material aspect

25. The material aspect of the burden of proof in the Polish legal system considers the negative consequences of a failed process of taking evidence. The rules on the burden of proof establish what the outcome of a dispute is where there is a lack of evidence supporting the statement of the occurrence of essential facts, on which a party relies.[14] According to Article 6 of the Civil Code, the judge is required to rule in the dispute against the person who relies on the (legal) consequences of the occurrence of facts, which have not been proven.[15] The only receiver of the norm of Article 6 of the Civil Code is the court.[16] The provision of Article 6 of the Civil Code does not constitute any obligation or a right of a party to the proceedings. An incorrect application of the rules on the burden of proof based on Article 6 of the Civil Code constitutes an infringement of substantive law and in principle can form a ground for an appeal or cassation.[17]

The application of Article 6 of the Civil Code does not depend on the process of taking evidence as such. The only condition of its application is the court's lack of conviction that the statements about the alleged facts are true. The court's lack of conviction can be caused by the parties' passive behaviour or inefficient actions, for example insufficient evidence or lack of sufficient credentials. Ultimately, it is not important why the court has not been convinced by the parties' statements and evidence. For the material aspect of the burden of proof only the final result counts, namely, what has and what has not been successfully established.[18]

26. The determination of the outcome is the most important function of the burden of proof. It allows for the substantive resolution of the dispute even when the essential facts could not have been established. To be able to decide on the case without essential facts being identified, the principle of *non liquet* must be applied. *Non liquet* literally means 'it

---

12 Piasecki 2010, p. 58.
13 Piasecki 2010, p. 59.
14 Dolecki 1998, p. 69; Piasecki 2010, p. 59.
15 Machnikowski 2011, p. 34.
16 Kmiecik 2008, p. 96.
17 Dolecki 1998, p. 190-198.
18 Dolecki 1998, p. 53.

is not clear'.[19] As long as the procedural requirements have been met, it is an obligation of the court to deliver a judgment. The court cannot dismiss the case only because there is a lack of factual grounds for the decision. In practice, when the essential facts have not been proven, only a party who did not have to prove them can obtain a positive result from the proceedings.[20] This matter has been discussed and approved by Polish Supreme Court, which has confirmed that the rules on allocation of burden of proof do not always provide a clear solution.[21]

Summing up, if the facts important for the final decision remain unproven, the decision will depend on which of the parties bears the burden of proving these facts. The party who bears the burden of proof bears the negative consequences of a non-discovery of essential facts.

2.2.2.2 Procedural aspect

27. The procedural aspect of the burden of proof regards an 'obligation', or a 'duty' on the party to the proceedings to provide evidence. Article 3 and Article 232 k.p.c. provide for the regulation of the burden of proof in the procedural sense. Article 3 k.p.c. contains a general rule requiring parties to the proceedings to fully and honestly present facts and their explanations before the court. Furthermore, Article 232 k.p.c. states that '*parties are required to adduce evidence to establish facts from which they derive legal consequences (…)*'.[22] The material (Article 6 of the Civil Code) and procedural (Article 232 k.p.c.) aspect of the burden of proof make a reference to the legal consequences of the (un)proven facts. The similarity of the above definitions (material and procedural) means that a clear distinction between the material and procedural aspects of the burden of proof is difficult to make.

28. There is uncertainty over whether Article 232 k.p.c. provides a right of evidence or an obligation of a party to supply evidence. The Polish Supreme Court stated that questioning authenticity of particular statements or facts and providing evidence stating otherwise constitutes a party's right of evidence.[23] The critics of this decision observed that assuming one's right of evidence requires a determination of the scope of this right and its counterpart obligation.[24] With regard to this procedural task (proving authenticity of a statement or document) the counter obligation is difficult to determine. Another view is that adducing

19 Dolecki 1998, p. 58.
20 Morawski 1982, p. 196.
21 SN 20.12.1933, C III 67/33.
22 Art. 232 k.p.c.: '*Strony są obowiązane wskazywać dowody dla stwierdzenia faktów, z których wywodzą skutki prawne. Sąd może dopuścić dowód nie wskazany przez stronę*'.
23 SN 24.10.2000, V CKN 132/00.
24 Piasecki 2010, p. 60.

evidence is merely conduct undertaken in the interests of a party to the proceedings, which is not based on the so-called right of evidence.[25]

There are also arguments stating that Article 232 k.p.c. imposes a peculiar type of obligation. It cannot be regarded as a procedural, neither as a legal obligation.[26] No legal sanctions are practically available for remaining passive in the course of proceedings. Some commentators therefore state that the duty formulated in Article 232 k.p.c. is 'merely' a civil duty arising from the principles of social coexistence[27] and from the intention to discover material truth.[28]

29. During the proceedings there are other burdens related to invoking facts and providing evidence. According to Articles 126 and 187 k.p.c., a claimant who starts an action is required to provide facts justifying and supporting his claim. If, according to the court, he did not meet this duty, the claim will lack a formal requirement. Pursuant to Article 130 k.p.c. the court will then ask a claimant to cure this formal lack within one week. In case of a party's inactivity, the court will return the claim to the claimant without any further legal consequences. Consequently, the burden to provide facts, sometimes referred to as the burden of argumentation, in the context of justifying the claim, is regarded as a purely procedural issue connected to the content of the burden of proof.[29]

30. The judge, while trying to discover the material true, should encourage the parties to demonstrate the necessary facts and evidence. Moreover, he is allowed, and in certain situations expected to act of his own motion to adduce evidence. The latter duty results from the second part of Article 232 k.p.c. which provides that the court may admit evidence of its own motion, not adduced by the parties to the proceedings. Pursuant to the above provision the judge has a discretional power to present facts and adduce evidence. This in fact might be regarded as a way of inducing the parties to present evidence and stimulating the activity of the parties. In this sense that if a party does not act in accordance with the court instructions, the court may of its own motion adduce evidence, which is not necessarily favourable for the party.

Interestingly, the court's right to adduce evidence of its own motion has been said to be incompatible with the general rule on the burden of proof set out in Article 6 of the Civil Code.[30] As already stated, the relationship between these two provisions is not entirely

25 Stefaniak 1973, p. 18.

26 Dolecki 1998, p. 54.

27 SN 3.10.2000, I CK 308/00. According to the Polish Supreme Court, the principles of social coexistence are defined as '*objective rules of conduct taken as a criterion for assessing what is worthy or not of endorsement from the perspective of society view*'.

28 Stefaniak 1973, p. 14.

29 Dolecki 1998, p. 120.

30 Dolecki 1998, p. 78 *et seq.*

clear and in some circumstances the characteristics of legal norms of Article 6 of the Civil Code and Article 232 k.p.c. may be regarded as inconsistent. Unfortunately, further analysis of this issue falls outside the scope of this book.

31. Summing up the topics on the material and procedural aspects of the burden of proof, it may be concluded that the rules regulating the burden of proof as such are of a material character. The substantive law provides legal protection and the consequences of the infringements of particular rights. It also determines legal consequences of certain factual occurrences. If any of these factual occurrences must be proven by the party to the proceedings, the substantive law indicates which party that would be. Consequently, an infringement of the rules of burden of proof constitutes an infringement of substantive law.

The procedural law regulates matters such as means of evidence, the process of taking and hearing evidence and the assessment of evidence. Consequently, the procedural rules allow for the discovery and determination of the existence of individual rights.

Despite the differences between both aspects of the burden of proof, they are closely connected and interdependent. Ultimately, the court's decision as to whether the facts are to be regarded as proven and whether the legal provision describing these facts may apply is based on information that has been obtained from various means of evidence in the frame of the legal proceedings.[31]

2.2.3 *Allocation of the burden of proof*

2.2.3.1 General rule of Article 6 of the Civil Code

32. The general rule on the burden of proof is located in Article 6 of the Civil Code. According to this provision, a person who relies on the legal consequences of certain facts bears the burden of proving these facts. Article 6 of the Civil Code is of a universal character and it applies to all legal relationships within Polish private law, unless provided otherwise. It means that there are special rules of substantive law, which distribute burden of proof and the risk of not proving differently from Article 6 of the Civil Code.

33. The allocation of the burden of proof does not depend on the position taken by the party in the proceedings.[32] Both claimant and defendant will have to bear the burden of proving the facts they rely on.[33] For example, in the situation of the rescission of a consumer sale contract due to the non-conformity of goods, the general rule of Article 6 of the Civil Code stipulates that a consumer bears the burden of proving that the circumstances con-

31 Dolecki 1998, p. 76.
32 SN 3.10.1969, II PR 313/69.
33 SN 20.12.2006, IV CSK 299/06.

stituting non-conformity have occurred. This is regardless of whether the consumer is a claimant (asking for remedy), or a defendant in the proceedings initiated by the seller for a payment (objecting to the duty to pay due to the rescission based on non-conformity).[34] The consequence of not satisfying the burden in the sense of Article 6 of the Civil Code is that the argument made by the party fails and the opponent wins the dispute regarding that particular issue.[35] This is also the case when facts cannot be discovered at all where, for example, the object of sale has been stolen and the assessment of the existence of non-conformity is impossible. In this situation a consumer claiming non-conformity will lose, because he is the one who bears the risks of not proving essential facts.

34. Another topic on the allocation of the burden of proof regards the order in which the parties are obliged to adduce evidence, which is regulated by procedural law. Article 210 (1) k.p.c. provides that a claimant firstly presents his claim, invokes facts and supporting evidence. The provision of Article 210 (1) k.p.c. is of an auxiliary character and it can be separated from the circumstances of particular dispute as required. The court is free to decide on a different sequence in order to ease the procedure of hearing evidence or to balance other inconveniences of the procedure. In general, the rules on the burden of proof do not contain any fixed order of adducing evidence. There is however, an exception in Polish summary proceedings.[36] The parties are obliged to provide the facts they rely on and the supporting evidence in fixed order and at a fixed time. First, a claimant provides all the necessary facts and proof in his claim. Subsequently, a defendant does the same in response to the claim. There is no further possibility for the parties to assume new facts or proof at a later stage of the proceedings in the same instance or in the appeal proceedings. There is an exception when the necessity of new facts or proof has arisen at the later stage, or the parties could not have known about these facts at the time of submitting the claim or the response. Finally, the facts and evidence not adduced and supplied in a fixed manner cannot constitute grounds for appeal.

2.2.3.2 Presumptions

35. As stated in the general rule of Article 6 of the Civil Code, the main rule of the burden of proof applies to all situations, unless the legislator provides for special regulations. These

---

34 Additionally to be able to invoke rescission of the contract, the previous repairs or replacement must have been unsuccessful, the burden of proof of these facts lies with the consumer - Article 8 (4) of the Consumer Sale Act.

35 There may be more than one issue in one case.

36 Polish summary proceedings regulated in 505^1–505^{14} k.p.c. are obligatory when the value under litigation does not exceed 10.000 *pln* in disputes arising from a warranty, guarantee, non-conformity of goods to the contract of consumer sale and when the value of the contract does not exceed the 10.000 *pln*, in disputes arising out of apartment rental contracts, regardless of the value. If during the proceedings the judge decides that the case should be adjudicated in the ordinary track he can move the case respectively.

special rules on the burden of proof may be located in the Civil Code or in separate statutes. The special provision may explicitly provide for a different allocation of the burden of proof. The burden of proof lying with a person claiming the existence of essential facts may also be eased through the operation of presumptions.[37]

The literature distinguishes between two main types of presumptions: material and factual.[38] Some also distinguish 'legal' presumptions, which reverse the risks of not proving.[39] It is however doubtful whether there are presumptions under Polish law which in fact can reverse the material burden of proof. Not many scholars share the above opinion.[40] Nevertheless, there is some uncertainty over how exactly the presumptions influence the allocation of the burden of proof. The majority agree that material presumption can facilitate merely the burden of proof in the procedural aspect.[41] Pursuant to Article 234 k.p.c. presumptions established by the legal provision are binding upon the court. These presumptions are governed by substantive law. The particular statutory provision states that the existence of an essential for a decision fact is to be regarded as proven, if other described in this provision fact(s) has/have been successfully shown. The construction of these presumptions is based on the idea that some facts are difficult to prove, and when a party to the proceedings deserves protection in litigation – the substantive law offers simplifications in supplying evidence.[42]

36. The statutory presumption can only be rebutted if a rule establishing the presumption so provides. In order to rebut the presumption it is necessary to state that, although the facts described in the legal provision and proven by the opponent are correct, the presumed fact did not occur. Those wishing to rebut the presumption are free to use all means of evidence, including factual presumptions.[43]

37. According to Article 231 k.p.c. when facts important for the dispute can be derived from other facts already proven during the proceedings, the court may apply factual presumptions. The judge has complete freedom in applying factual presumptions. The construction of factual presumptions facilitates the process of the discovery of material truth. The content of these presumptions is regarded as being a logical consequence of successful evidence of the existence of certain facts. The factual presumptions constitute rather evidence rules or means of evidence. They are not the instruments shifting burden of proof

37 SN 10.07.1980, II UZP 10/80; SN 20.04.1994, I CRN 44/94.
38 Piasecki 2010, p. 89-97; Dolecki 199, p. 150 *et seq.*
39 Dolecki 1998, p. 135 *et seq.*
40 Dolecki 1998, p. 159, 160.
41 Sokołowski 2012, Art. 6; Dolecki 1998, p. 150-153.
42 Piasecki 2010, p. 90.
43 Piasecki 2010, p. 90.

per se, but still may facilitate the burden of proof of the party in need for protection during the proceedings.[44] The judge has a duty to justify the application of factual presumptions.

Another instrument having influence on the allocation of burden of proof is *prima facie* evidence. This instrument does not have its source in the Polish legal system. It has been imported, especially by legal scholars, from foreign jurisprudence. *Prima facie* evidence is a measure very rarely used in Polish proceedings.[45]

38. In a situation where one party to the proceedings prevents or seriously impedes the other party's possibility of supplying evidence, and when latter bears the burden of proof, the court may decide that the burden of proof of essential facts will shift to the party who prevents or impedes the evidence hearing process.[46]

2.2.4 *Standard of proof*

39. Pursuant to Article 233 (1) k.p.c. the judge has discretion in his assessment of evidence. The freedom of assessment of evidence regards the choice of evidence means, its admission, and the evaluation of evidence in its importance for the final decision. The starting point is to take into consideration all presented during the proceedings facts and proofs. Based on the (life) experience and knowledge, the judge is free to choose which fact to regard as proven and which evidence to regard as satisfactory. The requirement of the evaluation of evidence is that it is to be done consistently, in accordance with logic, reasoning, and judicial awareness.[47] There are no further rules (external or internal) determining the degree of certainty the judge must have after the evaluation of evidence. After delivering a decision, the court must thoroughly explain which evidence has been satisfactory, and which facts the court regarded as proven. The duty to justify the decision and explain the process of reasoning constitutes a verification of the correctness of hearing of evidence and its evaluation.[48]

2.2.5 *Conclusions*

40. The notion of the burden of proof in Polish civil law is of a dual nature. The general rule of Article 6 of the Civil Code regulates the issue of who has the obligation to provide facts significant for the resolution of a dispute. This question is traditionally classified as

44 Piasecki 2010, p. 94.
45 Piasecki 2010, p. 97-99.
46 Piasecki 2010, p. 62.
47 Piasecki 2010, p. 66-67; Demendecki 2012, § 233.
48 Demendecki 2012, § 233.

a question of substantive law. The person bearing the burden of proof bears the risk of non-discovery of facts essential for the resolution of a dispute. It activates the principle of *non liquet.*

The legislator recognises that particular facts may be difficult to prove and provides for statutory presumptions facilitating the supply of evidence regarding such facts. The opposing party can use all means of evidence to rebut the presumed fact. The operation of the presumption is a way to protect a weaker party in litigation.

The procedural aspect is regulated by the civil procedural code (k.p.c.). Its function is almost as important for resolving the dispute. It organises the order of process of taking evidence and determines by whom and how a particular fact must be proven in the process. The substantive aspect of the burden of proof (risk of not proving) remains with one party during the whole time of legal proceedings, while the procedural aspect can shift between the parties, depending on the circumstances of the case.

After the process of hearing evidence, the judge will evaluate its weight and importance for the dispute. The judge has the freedom to choose whether or not to regard a particular fact as proven and a particular piece of evidence as satisfactory. The boundaries of this wide discretion regarding the assessment of evidence are experience, knowledge, logic and judicial awareness. The judge has an obligation to provide a detailed justification of the decision, explaining a line of reasoning and stating which evidence proves the occurrence of the facts that have been taken into account in order to come to the final decision.

2.3 Burden of proof in German law

2.3.1 *Introduction*

41. This section describes rules on the burden of proof in German civil proceedings. It begins with a brief explanation of the main definitions (2.3.2). It continues with the rules on the allocation of the burden of proof, including the role of presumptions (2.3.3). Finally, the rules on the standard of proof will be presented (2.3.4). In German literature the issues of the burden of proof are broadly researched and analysed.[49] For the purpose of this book a brief overview of the most important topics will be presented.

49 Rosenberg 1965; Rosenberg, Schwab and Gottwald 2010; Prütting 1983; Musielak 1975; Baumgärtel, Laumen and Prütting/Grundlagen 2009.

2.3.2 Definitions

42. Under the German system the term burden of proof has several meanings. Predominantly the concept is used in two senses: *objektive Beweislast* – objective burden of proof and *subjektive Beweislast* – subjective burden of proof. Unlike the concept of objective burden of proof, the subjective burden of proof is applicable only in civil proceedings and in some disputes before employment courts. Only in these types of cases does the lack of action regarding the burden of proof result in the procedural loss.[50]

As already mentioned, there is a great deal of German literature regarding the concept of the burden of proof and its theoretical and practical applicability. Yet, the relationship between *objektive Beweislast* and *subjektive Beweislast* is not entirely clear. In the following paragraphs the meaning and function of these terms will be further explained.

2.3.2.1 *Objektive Beweislast*

43. The first meaning of the burden of proof is *objektive Beweislast* (objective burden of proof). This type of burden of proof is also called *Feststellungslast*. Other terms used to describe *objektive Beweislast* are: *materielle Beweislast* (material burden of proof) *Beweisgefahr* (risk of proof) or *Beweislast im engeren Sinne* (burden of proof in the strict sense). Regardless of the term used, within the scope of *objektive Beweislast* there is no party's obligation to prove facts or provide evidence. The rules determining the objective burden of proof are directed to the court.[51]

The objective burden of proof enables the determination of which party bears the risk of losing the case when the legal provision on which a particular claim is based cannot be applied. The premises of the application of legal provision have not been met when the facts are being concluded as unproven. Likewise, the party to the proceedings will suffer negative consequences, when a disadvantageous legal provision is applicable because the requirements of that provision are regarded as fulfilled despite the non discovery of facts.[52]

44. The objective burden of proof refers to the question of who suffers the disadvantages of the situation when the presence or absence of the material conditions for the application of particular substantive right remains unidentified.[53] The concept of the objective burden of proof relates also to negative consequences or other inconveniences for the interested party. It does not include any particular imposition or requirement on the parties to the proceedings to provide evidence. The concept and regulation of the objective burden of

50 Musielak 2013, § 286 Rn. 33.

51 Baumgärtel, Laumen and Prütting/Grundlagen 2009, § 3 Rn. 10, 11; Musielak 2013, § 286 Rn. 32.

52 Heinrich 1996, p. 20.

53 Baumgärtel, Laumen and Prütting/Grundlagen 2009, § 5 Rn. 1; Rosenberg, Schwab and Gottwald 2010, § 115 Rn. 3.

proof concerns the court solely. The ultimate consequence of the objective burden of proof is the application of the *non liquet* principle. *Non liquet* provides for the consequences of a situation where, despite all efforts undertaken by the court and the parties, the factual assertions and statements cannot be proven. It may be seen as a default rule on how the court must act when all admissible evidence has been exhausted and the essential facts remain unproven. In such cases, the application of the principle *non liquet* is obligatory and it does not depend on the court's discretion. It takes place once the parties have presented their statements and supporting evidence – at the end of the court's hearing of evidence. The principle of *non liquet* applies regardless of any action or lack of action on the part of the parties. It is simply a legal consequence of the failure to discover the truth. It cans the avoidance of the decision-making despite the non-discovery of the essential facts of the case.[54] It confirms the court's duty to rule on the case. It also guarantees the legal certainty and the proper administration of justice. It should be considered by the court as a last resort.[55]

Summing up, the distribution of the objective burden of proof is recognised as a determining instrument for indicating which party bears the risk of provability due to the exhaustion of means of evidence of the facts required to sustain the claim or a defence.

2.3.2.2 *Subjektive Beweislast*

45. The second aspect of the burden of proof used in German civil proceedings regards the question of which party must prove certain facts. It is regarded as a *subjektive Beweislast* (subjective burden of proof).

The German procedural rules oblige parties to the proceedings to indicate, in their pleadings or oral representations directed to the court, all significant facts and evidence of these facts. Additionally, a party should indicate the means of evidence to be used in the proceedings, should the factual assertions be objected to. In other words, the *subjektive Beweislast* requires the parties to the proceedings to behave actively (for instance by requests for evidence) in order to win the case.[56] The burden of proof in this sense is often called the burden of the production of proof – *Beweisführungslast*, procedural or formal burden of proof.

Where a party fails to prove any assertion or fact, the court will usually disregard that assertion or fact. According to Murray and Stürner, the failure to provide the source of proof if needed, becomes apparent at a relatively early stage of the proceedings and potentially has little significance as to the final decision in the case.[57] That opinion may seem questionable especially when looking at regulations, practice and literature of other

54 Rosenberg, Schwab and Gottwald 2010, § 115 Rn. 3.
55 Baumgärtel, Laumen and Prütting/Grundlagen 2009, § 5 Rn. 2, 3.
56 Baumgärtel, Laumen and Prütting/Grundlagen 2009, § 3 Rn. 32; Musielak 2013, § 286 Rn. 33.
57 Murray and Stürner 2004, p. 267.

national systems which indicate that the procedural aspect of burden of proof also has a very significant role in the outcome of the case. On the other hand, from the procedural point of view the character of the rules on the burden of proof, their function and consequences at a particular stage of proceedings may differ among the various legal systems.

46. The issues regarding the *subjektive Beweislast* are regulated in the ZPO. There are a considerable number of provisions regarding the law of evidence. Some of these provisions are very detailed while others are more general. Articles concerning the law of evidence are basically spread out through the entire ZPO.[58] The German civil procedural code includes obligations to provide evidence while dealing with different stages of the procedure. For example, following from § 130 (3) and (5) ZPO, the parties, in their preliminary submissions, are required to establish the necessary factual grounds supporting their claim and to identify the appropriate means of evidence to prove or refute the allegations of facts. This means that the parties are expected to undertake action in order to satisfy their *subjektive Beweislast.*

Based on § 139 (1) ZPO the court has discretion to help parties to fulfil the *subjektive Beweislast.* The above-mentioned provision states that the court can make suggestions as to the usefulness of a particular piece of evidence to support a party's allegation of fact. The court can also discuss with parties the issues of evidence and the burden of proof to make sure that the parties are sufficiently informed of these matters.[59]

I Abstract (subjective) burden of proof

47. The subjective burden of proof is divided into abstract and relative (subjective) burden of proof.[60] The abstract (subjective) burden of proof relates to the question of which party bears the subjective burden of proof before and at the beginning of litigation. It is possible to determine when the allegations of fact made by the claimant and respondent are opposite. The abstract (subjective) burden of proof is the decisive factor for determining which party has the obligation for proving the facts alleged. In such a case where the party remains passive, the principle of *non liquet* regarding the particular allegation of fact applies. As a

58 For example: § 130 content of written pleadings, § 138 obligation to make declarations as to the facts, obligation to tell the truth, § 144 visual evidence taken on site, experts, § 281 referral in the event the court does not have jurisdiction, § 286 evaluation of evidence at the court's discretion and conviction, § 291 common knowledge, § 292 legal presumptions, § 308 binding effect of the parties' petitions, § 440 evidence of the authenticity of private records and documents.

59 Baumgärtel, Laumen and Prütting/Grundlagen 2009, § 3 Rn. 44.

60 Rosenberg, Schwab and Gottwald 2010, § 115 Rn. 40; Baumgärtel, Laumen and Prütting/Grundlagen 2009, Rn. 66.

result, the effects on the distribution of abstract (subjective) burden of proof seem to be similar to those concerning the objective burden of proof.[61]

The concept of the abstract (subjective) burden of proof has been criticised by some scholars for being too theoretical and having little practical importance.[62] It has been stated that regardless of the factual situation of a given set of proceedings, it is not entirely clear what is the importance of deliberation of which evidence should be provided by which party. In this context, the abstract (subjective) burden of proof is more about the judge's viewpoint with regard to the first stage of litigation. On the other hand, the burden of proof in presented context can be understood as a separate instrument, complementary to the relative (subjective) burden of proof, which alters in the course of proceedings, depending on the progress in an individual dispute, and which must be assessed respectively at each stage of the proceedings.[63]

II Relative (subjective) burden of proof

48. In addition to the abstract (subjective) burden of proof there is a concept of a relative (subjective) burden of proof.[64] This concept and its importance for the legal science and legal practice have been developed by Prütting.[65] In general, relative (subjective) burden of proof determines which party has to call evidence on a particular issue, based on the evaluation of evidence already received, in order to win the dispute.[66]

At the beginning of the proceedings the abstract and relative (subjective) burden of proof overlap and there is no clear line distinguishing them. In the course of proceedings, the relative (subjective) burden of proof develops independently and in the competition between alleged facts it is the judge who decides.[67] The legal and evidential position of the parties defined by the abstract (subjective) burden of proof remains unchanged in the course of proceedings, while the relative (subjective) burden of proof develops during the proceedings according to the assessment of the evidence already presented. With respect to the above characteristics of the relative (subjective) burden of proof, it has been stated that this concept does not belong to the doctrine of the burden of proof in the strict sense and it is not related to the allocation of risk. Nevertheless, the relative (subjective) burden

61 Baumgärtel, Laumen and Prütting/Grundlagen 2009, § 3 Rn. 38; Rosenberg, Schwab and Gottwald 2010, § 115 Rn. 40.
62 Heinrich 1996, p. 28; Baumgärtel, Laumen and Prütting/Grundlagen 2009, § 3 Rn. 38.
63 Baumgärtel, Laumen and Prütting/Grundlagen 2009, § 3 Rn. 38.
64 Rosenberg, Schwab and Gottwald 2010, § 115 Rn. 41; Baumgärtel, Laumen and Prütting/Grundlagen 2009, § 3 Rn. 40, 41.
65 Prütting 1983.
66 Bruder 2007, p. 210.
67 Baumgärtel, Laumen and Prütting/Grundlagen 2009, § 3 Rn. 41.

of proof does influence the final decision in the sense that the perception on which the decision is based has a factual legal basis.[68]

2.3.3 *Allocation of the burden of proof*

49. This sub-section provides information on the rules on the allocation of the burden of proof in German civil proceedings. The objectives of legal certainty and the equal application of the law require that the distribution of the objective burden of proof is established before the beginning of the proceedings. Nonetheless, the lack of general and abstract rule regarding the allocation of the objective burden of proof in German civil law and the number of various theories regarding the burden of proof may contribute to legal uncertainty. According to German scholars, the general burden of proof is regulated by the BGB, even though it is not explicitly incorporated.[69]

2.3.3.1 *Normentheorie*

50. The detailed approach to the general rule of burden of proof is based on the *Normentheorie* developed by Rosenberg in his dissertation in 1900.[70] According to Rosenberg's theory, each party must prove facts underlying and supporting the rule in favour of their position. Substantive law determines the classification of the legal rules creating or denying a right and the facts comprising that right. Therefore, the allocation of the burden of proof depends strongly on the wording and understanding of a particular legal provision – legal norm.[71] To identify which party bears the burden of proof, the legal norm describing a particular right and underlying a particular claim must first be interpreted. This theory (with some possible modifications) is principal when it comes to the distribution of the burden of proof.

The theory developed by Rosenberg has been adopted (often in a modified form) in many European countries and serves as a foundation for the objective theories of the burden of proof, as opposed to the procedural theories of the burden of proof. There is however also criticism regarding the *Normentheorie.* It states that this theory is not sufficient to determine the burden of proof in all situations. For this reason, some scholars try to find other complementary theories or exceptionally permit application of the procedural theories on the burden of proof.[72]

68 Baumgärtel, Laumen and Prütting/Grundlagen 2009, § 3 Rn. 41.
69 Baumgärtel, Laumen and Prütting/Grundlagen 2009, § 5 Rn. 20-22; Rosenberg, Schwab and Gottwald 2010, § 115 Rn. 7.
70 Rosenberg 1965.
71 Rosenberg 1965, p. 98.
72 This criticism explained in Giesen/*diss.* 2001, p. 83-87.

51. The general rule on the allocation of the burden of proof provides that the party asserting particular facts, on which the claim or defence is founded, bears the burden of proving these facts. In other words, a party who asserts a legal consequence has to prove facts, which allow the application of the legal rule from which these consequences are derived.[73] Accordingly, a party who asserts objections to the legal consequence has to prove the facts which hinder the right to come into the existence, prevent the holder from enforcing it, or extinguish the right.[74] The underlying principle has been defined by the BGH as being that justice demands a distribution of the burden so that the exercise of one's rights is not made excessively difficult.[75]

2.3.3.2 Presumptions

52. In some cases the subjective as well as the objective burden of proof may be specifically allocated or varied by both the procedural or substantive law. Often these specific rules on the allocation of the burden of proof are constructed as presumptions. These presumptions are divided into rebuttable versus non-rebuttable presumptions.[76] § 292 ZPO states that if the presumption applies on the ground of legal provision, the other party can provide evidence to the contrary, unless provided otherwise. The opponent can rebut the legal presumption by providing comprehensive evidence to the contrary. Merely undermining the grounds for a presumption is insufficient.[77]

The BGH also confirmed the possibility of reversing the burden of proof under particular circumstances. For instance, in cases concerning medical malpractice, the burden of proof that the patient's injuries were not caused by actions or negligence may be shifted to the involved practitioner.[78] In such cases the judge decides whether the circumstances require the reversal of the burden of proof of essential facts.[79] The special allocation of the burden of proof results from the accessibility and practicability of proof as well as the principle of public policy.[80] Similarly, the burden of proof may be shifted where the party acted to intentionally frustrate the opposing party's ability to fulfil the burden of proof and provide evidence.[81] This matter is also left at the judge's discretion.

---

73 Baumgärtel, Laumen and Prütting/Grundlagen 2009, § 5 Rn. 20-22; Rosenberg, Schwab and Gottwald 2010, § 115 Rn. 7.

74 Bruder 2007, p. 210.

75 BGH 17.02.1970, III ZR 139/67, BGHZ 53, 245; BGH 13.12.1984, III ZR 20/83, NJW 1985, 1774.

76 Musielak 2013, § 292 Rn. 1-5.

77 Musielak 2013, § 292 Rn. 5.

78 BGH 24.11.1976, VIII ZR 137/75, BGHZ 67, 359; BGH 30.04.1991, VI ZR 178/90, BGHZ 114, 284.

79 Murray and Stürner 2004, p. 268.

80 Murray and Stürner 2004, p. 268.

81 BGH 21.09.1982, VI ZR 302/80, BGHZ 85, 212; BGH 27.09.2001, IX ZR 281/00, NJW 2002, 825; OLG Naumburg 11.10.2012, 1 U 2/12, Beck RS 2013, 05532.

53. The issue of activity of the parties in the process is closely connected to the question of the distribution of the burden of proof. The court's role in the allocation of the burden of proof is similar in this regard. German courts have discretional power and sometimes a duty to demand from the parties to specify relevant facts. In certain situations there is a duty on the court to adduce evidence of its own motion. Moreover, to offer support in adducing evidence the court may state what facts the parties should rely on and explain the questions of law relevant to the dispute.[82] This means that the court not only decides on issues of facts, but can also offer evidence of its own initiative regarding the facts considered as essential for the dispute. These facts however, must have been already stated and alleged by one of the parties. The German courts do not *ex officio* search for new facts. Accordingly, the party can be relieved of the *subjektive Beweislast* to prove certain facts, while the *objektive Beweislast* and risk of the non-discovery of essential facts remains unchanged during litigation.[83]

The judge has discretion over whether to refuse the hearing of evidence when he decides that a particular fact is not relevant for the legal characterisation of rights and does not contribute to the party's situation, when it does not support alleged facts or is used only to postpone the proceedings. According to German civil procedure, the court's discretion is intended to ensure fairness, to discover the truth as well as being a safeguard of public interests.[84] The role of the court in navigating the procedure regarding evidence seems to be somewhat broader than in other systems.

2.3.4 Standard of proof

54. In order to identify whether evidence has been successfully provided and the burden of proof fulfilled it is necessary to assess whether the particular standard of proof has been reached. The standard of proof indicates the given level of certainty that the judge must reach. The issues of the standard of proof are broadly researched in Germany and some scholars regard them as one of the most important aspects of the law of evidence.[85]

To ensure legal certainty and predictability of judicial decisions, there are general and abstract provisions regarding the standard of proof. The ZPO sets out the general procedural principle regarding the assessment of evidence. § 286 ZPO provides the fundamental procedural principle of the free assessment of evidence. The court has discretion to decide, in light of the entire content of the proceedings and the conclusions reached following any evidence provided, whether a particular fact has occurred or not and whether an actual

82 § 139 ZPO.
83 Bruder 2007, p. 215.
84 Musielak 2013, § 139 Rn. 17-24.
85 Baumgärtel, Laumen and Prütting/Grundlagen 2009, § 4 Rn. 55, 56.

statement is true or false. It seems that in many cases an overwhelming or a very high probability of the occurrence of the alleged fact may not suffice.[86] On the other hand, reaching a decision does not require the complete absence of any doubt over the relevant facts. The judge has sole discretion to decide whether the conditions for the application of a particular legal norm have been met. This shows that the standard of proof is relative, since in each individual case, the judge must take into consideration the whole procedural material to decide whether he is convinced of the parties' statement. Furthermore, § 286 ZPO obliges the judges to provide the reasoning behind their decision and state which evidence was conclusive for this particular decision. It constitutes a control measure over the final decision given ensuring it is correct.

55. In order to fulfil the burden of proof the court must be sufficiently convinced that the party's assertions are true. The judge must content himself with a degree of certainty that is appropriate for practical life.[87] This degree of certainty must silence doubts without excluding them. Nevertheless, some authors state that the standard of proof is close to the one in criminal law.[88] The standard of proof which amounts to 'beyond reasonable doubt' applies to all civil cases, unless the statute specifically provides otherwise. This takes place only in exceptional circumstances.

The standard of proof in German law has also been defined by the BGH as reaching the degree of certainty which is useful for practical purposes and which will reduce the possibility of any doubts, as opposed to completely eliminating them.[89] The standard of proof in the majority of cases could be assessed as 'probability approaching certainty.'[90]

2.3.5 Conclusions

56. The issues of the burden of proof play a significant role in German litigation. They have been extensively researched and there is rich literature regarding the subject. Despite this, there is still uncertainty regarding the exact classification of the issues of the burden of proof.

The rules on the burden of proof in German civil proceedings are mainly used in two senses, the objective burden of proof and subjective burden of proof. The objective burden is related to the legal norms and the facts which are necessary for the rules to apply. The burden of proving these facts lies with the person who relies on the legal consequences. Where the facts cannot be discovered, the principle of *non liquet* applies. The person who

86 Musielak 2013, § 286 Rn. 18, 19.
87 Murray and Strüner 2004, p. 310.
88 Clermont and Sherwin 2002, p. 243.
89 BGH 17.02.1970, III ZR 139/67, BGHZ 53, 245.
90 Murray and Stürner 2004, p. 310-312.

bears the burden of proof bears negative consequences and risks when the essential facts remain unproven.

The exceptions to the above rule of the allocation of the burden of proof can be found in legal provisions, specific provisions or statutory presumptions. Presumptions facilitate the supply of proof. They can be rebutted, unless provided otherwise. To rebut the presumption the opponent must provide proof to the contrary. Undermining the grounds for a presumption is insufficient.

The subjective burden determines who has to provide evidence in the proceedings regarding particular facts and which means of evidence should be used to do so. The subjective burden of proof is divided into abstract and relative (subjective) burden of proof, and is governed by the ZPO. In German civil proceedings the court has a considerable role in taking and hearing evidence. There are measures that the judge can undertake to discover relevant facts. In general, the judge has a very active role in the proceedings. It seems that the role a judge has in the proceeding contribute to a high standard of proof that is required in Germany. The degree of conviction the judge must have in order to make a decision is often regarded as the same degree applicable to criminal cases – beyond reasonable doubt. The judge has a great deal of freedom in the evaluation of evidence.

2.4 Burden of proof in English and Welsh law

2.4.1 Introduction

57. This section describes the rules on the burden of proof in English civil proceedings. It starts with the explanation of the definitions of the burden of proof (2.4.2). Subsequently, it describes the rules regarding the allocation of the burden of proof and the possible exceptions (2.4.3). Finally, the topics regarding the standard of proof are discussed (2.4.4).

As with other jurisdictions, the notion of burden of proof is complex and multidimensional in the English system. There are two principal elements to the burden of proof that are used in English law, the persuasive burden of proof (legal burden) and evidential burden of proof. The characteristics of the above burdens will be briefly described. Finally, some information regarding the differences in relation to the burden of proof and the law of evidence that apply in English proceedings, in contrast to the continental civil proceedings, will be presented.

2.4.2 *Definitions*

58. As stated above, the notion of the burden of proof is used in two main ways. The persuasive burden is used to determine the outcome of the case if the court is unable to come to the conclusion as to what the relevant facts are. The evidential burden is applied to determine which party to the proceedings must show that there is sufficient evidence to support a particular statement or to deny the occurrence of a particular fact.

2.4.2.1 Persuasive burden

59. The first sense in which the burden of proof exists in English law is referred to as a persuasive burden of proof or legal burden of proof. In the literature these two terms are used interchangeably.

According to Cross and Tapper, the persuasive burden regards '*the obligation of a party to meet the requirement of the rule of law that a fact in issue must be proven (or disproven) either by the preponderance of evidence or beyond reasonable doubt*'.[91] The persuasive burden is therefore closely related to the standard of proof, since the case may only be decided on the persuasive burden of proof if the evidence upon the relevant fact in issue is found to be balanced to determine the matter. The fact in issue must be determined by the incidence of the burden.[92]

Further expression linked to the persuasive burden of proof is a risk of non-persuasion. It is used to show that a party bearing the burden of proving particular facts will lose on that issue if he or she fails to sufficiently persuade the court.[93]

60. Zuckerman, in *Civil Procedure, Principles of Justice*, uses another term for the persuasive burden of proof – the probative burden. He defines it as requiring a party who bears the burden to prove his case to the appropriate standard of proof.[94] In other words, the party who carries the persuasive burden also carries the risk of not showing the evidence supporting his claim with the required certainty.[95] Therefore, if the party is not able to provide sufficient proof, regardless of the true facts, the court must dismiss a claim based on these facts.

The persuasive burden regards an individual issue, so failing to provide evidence in case of a particular statement does not necessarily lead to losing the case as a whole. Although both parties may have to bear the persuasive burden regarding different facts,

91 Cross and Tapper 2010, p. 121; Phipson on Evidence 2010, nr. 6-02; Zuckerman 2013, nr. 22.39.
92 Bruder 2007, p. 208.
93 Keane and McKeown 2014, p. 83.
94 Zuckerman 2013, nr. 22.39.
95 Zuckerman 2013, nr. 22.39.

sometimes it is the claimant who bears the persuasive burden of proof on all the facts in issue.

61. The burden of proof is a determining factor for the outcome of the dispute. A problem may arise when the court is ultimately unable to come to a definite conclusion on the evidence, or some part of it. In such an event, the question of who should suffer the negative consequences of that situation arises. The decision in the *Pickford v Imperial Chemical Industries (ICI)*[96] provides an answer to this question. Ms Pickford was employed by the ICI as a secretary. In 1989 she complained of pain in her hands and consulted several doctors. A couple of months later she was unable to perform her duties and her employment contract was terminated. She claimed that the cramps in her hands were caused by the typing assignments imposed on her without breaks to rest. She pleaded that the negligence of the ICI caused her to sustain prescribed disease. To establish the moment her problems begun, Ms Pickford provided the court with her diary, medical records and expertise as to the cause of her condition. The ICI also provided a medical report regarding the cause of the condition and was contrary to the medical report submitted by the claimant. The court was not convinced by either of the expert reports submitted. Consequently, it was impossible to decide on the case according to the presented evidence material. As a result, the court of first instance decided that Ms Pickford did not satisfy the duty to provide sufficient evidence supporting her claim. The Appeal Court reversed the decision stating that the judge's findings were contrary to the weight of the medical evidence provided by the claimant. The case eventually came before the House of Lords. The main issue was how the court should rule in a situation where a party provided medical records or other evidence supporting the case, and whether the burden of proof was satisfied in a case where the opposing party provided contrary evidence of the same sort (medical report). Lord Hope of Craighead stated that in most cases the question of the burden of proof loses its importance as soon as all evidence is before the court and the court can rule as to the facts.[97] It is hard to deny that the question of the burden of proof as a determining factor does not arise except situations where the court is unable to deliver a final decision based on the evidence presented. Accordingly, the question arises as to who bears the risk in the above situation.

Based on the general rules regarding the burden of proof the burden lies with Ms Pickford to provide the court with evidence of a certain standard, which would be sufficient to convince the court that the facts stated by Ms Pickford were correct. After presenting her evidence the opposing party showed evidence presenting the opposite. Additionally, Ms Pickford failed to convince the court also on other matters, namely on negligence of

96 *Pickford v Imperial Chemical Industries* (1998) 1 WLR 1189.
97 *Pickford v Imperial Chemical Industries* (1998) 1 WLR 1200.

the ICI and the causal relationship. Finally, the court stated that it was the claimant's burden to show that her condition had a specific cause. The employer's failure to convince the court about the contrary was irrelevant for the decision as to whether Ms Pickford had established probable cause.

62. The approach taken in this case and the reasoning behind the decision are analogical to the approach taken by the other jurisdictions discussed, where in case of the non-discovery of facts the principle of *non liquet* applies. Under English law, when the judge finds it impossible to make a finding on a fact, he will decide by reference to which party bears the persuasive burden of proof.[98]

2.4.2.2 Evidential burden

63. The evidential burden or the burden of adducing evidence is the second principal type of burden of proof in English civil proceedings. It can be described as an obligation upon the party to adduce sufficient evidence of a certain standard to raise an issue as to the existence or non-existence of a fact.[99] According to Zuckerman, the evidential burden of proof is different from the persuasive burden as it involves different factors regarding the allocation of risks.[100]

Whether a party satisfied the evidential burden of proof can only be answered after the parties have given their evidence. The parties are obliged to discharge the evidential burden only if called upon to do so by the judge. Whether a party has discharged the burden is decided only once during the proceedings.[101]

Regarding the evidential burden, as with the case of the persuasive burden, the failure to meet the requisite standard of proof can determine the outcome of the case. When it comes to the burden of proof in general many aspects of it may fail for example, a party does not allege relevant facts and therefore does not show sufficient evidence, a party does not raise the legal issue or does not make reference to the correct provision. Regarding the evidential burden, if the party bearing that burden does not discharge it and fails to adduce evidence supporting the existence or non-existence of the relevant facts, the court proceeds as if the issue had not been raised.[102]

64. The evidential burden developed in the courts where there was a need for the possibility of omitting some facts from consideration. There was a need to filter the issues under consideration by the court that brought the evidential burden. Taking the above into

98 *Stephens v Cannon* (2005) EWCA Civ. 222.
99 Cross and Tapper 2010, p. 122; Zuckerman 2013, nr. 22.41; Keane and McKeown 2014, p. 85.
100 Zuckerman 2013, nr. 22.41.
101 Keane and McKeown 2014, p. 85.
102 Zuckerman 2013, nr. 22.44.

account, some commentators believe that the evidential burden is not a burden of proof. Rather it is an obligation that a party has to adduce evidence. It relates to the parties' duty to make a matter worthy of a judge's consideration.[103]

2.4.3 Allocation of the burden of proof

65. In civil cases the principle of '*who asserts must prove*' means that the burden may shift depending on who is trying to establish a relevant fact.[104] It does not mean that the burden of proof does not lay with the party who makes negative allegations. The burden of proof does not depend on the use of language or the structure of grammar and in certain circumstances it may be placed on the party who denies the occurrence of certain facts.[105]

The allocation of the risk of failing to discharge the burden is not simply a matter of the proceedings. In English law the burden of proof can be allocated as a matter of common law (including common law presumptions). It can also be prescribed by the statutory law both general and specific (including presumptions applicable by virtue of statutory provisions). Consequently, the allocation of the burden of proof can be a matter for substantive law and in practice the legislator often decides whether to lay the particular burden and the particular consequences of not satisfying it with the one party or another.[106] Finally, the burden of proof can be determined by the parties' agreement.[107]

66. In principle, in English civil proceedings, the allocation of the burden of proof is evident from the pre-trial pleadings.[108] This counts for both types of burdens mentioned above, the persuasive and evidential burden. An important characterisation is that the burden of persuasion and evidential burden does not shift in the course of proceedings. Once established they are constant in relation to the particular issue.[109] A party who bears the burden of proof must discharge it or face the negative consequences of not doing so.[110] The allocation of the burden of proof contributes to the determination of which party should begin calling evidence. The burden of proof therefore helps to organise the course of proceedings.

103 Cho 2012, p. 29; Munday 2013, p. 61.

104 Zuckerman 2013, nr. 22.47; Phipson on Evidence 2010, nr. 6-04; Joseph *Constantine Steamship Line Ltd v Imperial Smelting Corp Ltd* (1942) AC 154, HL; *Levison v Patent Steam Carpet Cleaning Co Ltd* (1978) QB 69, AC.

105 Phipson on Evidende 2010, nr. 6-06.

106 Keane and McKeown 2014, p. 86; Cho 2012, p. 44.

107 Cross and Tapper 2010, p. 128.

108 Spencer and Spencer 2007, p. 6.

109 Keane and McKeown 2014, p. 86; Cho 2012, p. 44; Spencer and Spencer 2007, p. 6.

110 Zuckerman 2013, nr. 22.45.

2.4.3.1 Allocation of the burden of persuasion

67. There are no general rules when it comes to the allocation of the persuasive burden of proof. As a matter of common sense, the burden of persuasion as to all essential facts of the claim lies with the claimant.[111] The general rule in civil cases is that '*who asserts must prove*'.[112] The essential facts, which a party must prove in order to gain remedies, must be presented by that party. Often, during proceedings both parties bear the persuasive burden as to the different facts. For example, the claimant suing based on the contract is obliged to firstly prove that the contract was concluded, then that it has been breached and finally that damages of a particular value have been suffered. The other party to the proceedings has a burden of frustrating the contract, if he invokes it to release himself from the contractual obligation. The claimant does not need to disprove the frustration. If the defendant wishes to make use of the advantages of frustration he needs to adduce sufficient evidence and he also bears the burden of persuasion on this particular issue. Both parties are entitled to equal protection in the proceedings. Therefore, while one party bears a higher risk on one issue, the opponent should bear the risk on another issue that he relies on.

Summing up, the allocation of the burden depends on the nature of the particular rights and it is determined by the statute or common law. Sometimes the court may need to adjust the distribution of the burdens as a matter of public policy.

2.4.3.2 Allocation of the evidential burden

68. In principle, a party bearing the persuasive burden of proof on a particular issue also bears the evidential burden.[113] In civil litigation, as a general rule, a claimant is obliged to provide evidence of the existence of facts that he bases his claim on. Regarding these facts he has the persuasive burden of proof and the evidential burden. There may however, be exceptions when one party bears the persuasive burden of proof but the evidential burden lies on the opponent.

To satisfy the evidential burden, a party needs to show that there is a sufficient amount of evidence of a certain standard supporting the statement. To satisfy the persuasive burden, a party needs to provide evidence confirming his factual statements. If the party does not discharge both of the above duties, he will (most often) lose the case. There could be two main reasons for losing the case. The party did not persuade the judge whereas the other party did provide sufficient proof. Consequently, the facts that have been established lead to negative consequences for the party bearing the burden of proof. The second possibility is that neither party successfully persuaded the court, or did not present evidence at all.

111 Cross and Tapper 2010, p. 130; Keane and McKeown 2014, p. 86.

112 Zuckerman 2013, nr. 22.47; Phipson on Evidence 2010, nr. 6-04; Keane and McKeown 2014, p. 86; Cho 2012, p. 44.

113 Cross and Tapper 2010, p. 128; Keane and McKeown 2014, p. 103, 104.

In the second situation, the person who bore the (persuasive) burden of proof loses the case, as a result of the negative consequences of the persuasive burden of proof.

2.4.3.3 Presumptions

69. The allocation of the burden of proof may also depend upon the proof of certain facts by means of presumptions. Basically, the successful proof of certain facts affects the burden related to other fact.[114] According to Zuckerman, different presumptions can have two different effects, they can conditionally shift the burden of persuasion or they can merely allocate the burden of adducing evidence.[115] When the presumption operates, the court may or must draw certain conclusions.[116] There are three main types of presumptions: presumptions of fact, rebuttable presumptions of law and non-rebuttable presumptions of law.[117] Below, the short characterisations of the first two types will be provided.

Legal presumption is established by the rule of law, which provides that based on the proof of a particular fact provided by one of the parties, the court is bound to find the existence of other facts, unless the opponent successfully provides evidence to the contrary.[118] The rules establishing presumptions contain the requirements of the application of the presumption indicating what the basic fact is and what the consequences of its application are. The consequences always regard the facts that must be considered as proven, when the basic fact has been shown. The rule establishing presumption will also indicate whether and how the presumption can be rebutted.

The second type of presumption that can be distinguished is a presumption of fact, which a judge develops in the course of proceedings based on common sense and logic. All factual presumptions are rebuttable. When it comes to presumptions of law, in the case of a lack of evidence to the contrary, the presumed facts will be regarded as proven. Regarding the factual presumptions, the court has discretion to decide what the consequences for the outcome of a case are. The court may well disregard the factual presumption.[119]

2.4.4 *Standard of proof*

70. In comparison to other systems discussed throughout this book the English approach to the role of the judge, when examining the burden of proof and adducing evidence in

114 Cross and Tapper 2010, p. 131.
115 Zuckerman 2013, nr. 22.62-22.65.
116 Phipson on Evidence 2010, nr. 6-16.
117 Zuckerman 2013, nr. 22.67; Phipson on Evidence 2010, nr. 6-17.
118 Zuckerman 2013, nr. 22.62.
119 Phipson 2010, nr. 6-17, 6-18.

the civil procedure, is visibly different. English civil proceedings have an adversarial character, where the role of a judge in the proceeding is passive.

The parties to the proceedings must persuade the court of the facts and other legal matters. Previous relevant decisions and essays from legal scholars, which were not brought and argued before the court cannot be taken into account in delivering the decision.[120] The role of the court is only to decide whether the facts stated by the parties are established and whether the legal provisions referred to justify the right or remedy that is sought.[121]

71. In order to satisfy the burden of proof, a party needs to persuade the court of the truth of his statements. The persuasive burden of proof in civil cases must be reached on the balance of probabilities, in other words preponderance of probabilities or preponderance of evidence. In essence this means that if one party can prove something is more likely to be true that not, he/she will usually be successful in asserting that what he/she seeks to prove.[122] Therefore, in proving any facts the burden will be discharged as long as the conclusion of facts suggest that it is more probable than not. If the probabilities are equal then the burden cannot be regarded as discharged.[123]

The standard of proof regards the question of the amount of evidence that is required to convince the judge. There is a tendency to apply the techniques of mathematics to its assessment. If the probabilities are equal, the standard of proof cannot be regarded as equal.[124] In theory, a probability of 51% is sufficient to satisfy the standard of proof. However, in practical terms a claimant must do much more to establish a case on the balance of probabilities. When the opposing party also provides the court with evidence, then it is not simply about the pure probability of stated facts. It must be proven that the claimant's version is more likely to have occurred than that of his opponent. In some cases, the claimant may also have to persuade the court of his credibility as well as the stated facts. If, at the end of a trial, the opposing statements are equally probable then the court has failed to be persuaded on the balance of probabilities. Consequently, the judge must rule against the person bearing the burden of persuasion.

Summing up, to satisfy the standard of proof on the balance of probabilities the claimant must establish that his allegation of facts is more probable than his opponent's, that it is sufficiently probable to be credible, and not merely a little more probable than an opposing highly improbable allegation.

120 Whittaker 2005, p. 205.
121 Whittaker 2005, p. 206.
122 Zuckerman 2013, nr. 22.53.
123 Zuckerman 2013, nr. 22.53.
124 Phipson on Evidence 2010, p. 6-54; Cross and Tapper 2010, p. 151 *et seq.*

2.4.5 Conclusions

72. In English civil proceedings the notion of burden of proof exists mainly in two senses, the persuasive burden of proof and the evidential burden of proof. A party bearing the persuasive burden of proof must provide the facts from which he derives his rights. The persuasive burden identifies who is going to lose the case when no facts could be discovered. Accordingly, when the essential facts remain unidentified, the person who bears the persuasive burden of proof loses the dispute. There is also evidential burden of proof, regarded as an obligation on the party to adduce sufficient evidence of certain standard to raise an issue as to the existence or non-existence of a fact. There is a direct link between both types of burden of proof and the standard of proof.

The burden of proof, persuasive and evidential, always applies to the individual issue and not to the case as a whole. Moreover, regarding one issue there can be one evidential and one persuasive burden, and each of them can be borne by only one person at a time. Usually, the persuasive and evidential burden lies with the same party. However, depending on the circumstances of an individual case, the burdens may be divided between the parties to the proceedings.

There is no general rule regulating the allocation of the burden of proof. There are several sources of rules determining the allocation. The allocation of the burden of proof is normally regulated by the statutory provision invoked by a person seeking protection. Similarly, the presumptions constituting conditional ways of the allocation of the burden of proof are usually located in the statutory law. There are also rules of the common law regulating allocation of the burden of proof, including the common law presumptions. There are three types of presumptions: factual presumptions, rebuttable legal presumptions and non-rebuttable legal presumptions. The presumptions, based on the proof of a particular fact, provide that the existence of other alleged facts has been proven. They mostly regard the allocation of the evidential burden. Finally, the parties may decide on the allocation of burden of proof in their agreement. The validity of an agreement on evidence is determined by contract law.

To meet the burden of proof, the parties must prove the essential facts up to a certain standard. The standard of proof applicable in England is the balance of probabilities. In general, a person must establish that his allegation of facts is more probable than his opponent's and that it is sufficiently probable to be credible. The English adversarial procedural system means that the judge's responsibility to ascertain facts is generally limited to reaching a decision on the basis of the evidence presented by the parties.

The rules on the burden of proof have two very important characteristics. First, they are a determining factor for the outcome of the case. Second, the rules on the burden of proof influence the proceedings and the order in which evidence is submitted.

2.5 Burden of proof in Dutch law

2.5.1 Introduction

73. This section describes the general issues of the burden of proof in Dutch civil proceedings. It includes an explanation of the main terms and definitions related to the burden of proof (2.5.2). It discusses the rules on the allocation of the burden of proof, including the role of legal and factual presumptions (2.5.3). It also discusses the standard of proof required (2.5.4).

74. The question of who bears the burden of proof is of great practical importance. It affects the individual dispute and determines legal consequences of satisfied or failed burden of proof. The party to the proceedings bearing the burden of proving relevant facts must satisfy this burden to be able to receive legal protection. If the burden has not been met, the chances for succeeding in litigation are very small.[125] Furthermore, the clear regulations regarding the burden of proof allow the assessment of what the final decision may be. They also enable an assessment of the courts' decisions as such. Finally, the clear rules on evidence and the burden of proof assure legal certainty in the material and procedural context.[126]

The issues of the burden of proof are (very) often difficult to define and to determine, given their position and function in the legal system. There are several theories underlying different principles surrounding the burden of proof, which at times may generate conflicting results.[127]

2.5.2 Definitions

75. According to Article 149 Rv, the judge must take all the facts and rights into consideration that were established in the process of taking of evidence governed by Articles 149-207 Rv. The general scope of the law of evidence and burden of proof in Dutch civil proceedings are determined by the general provisions of Articles 149-156 Rv.[128] There is however, no clear definition of the notion of the burden of proof found in the Dutch civil procedural code.

125 Rutgers and Krans 2014, nr. 28.

126 Asser/Procesrecht/Asser 3 2013, nr. 276.

127 *De billijkheidstheorie* (the procedural theory), *de objectiefrechtelijke theorie* (the objective theory); Rutgers and Krans 2014, p. 33-36.

128 Rutgers and Krans 2014, nr. 23.

76. The understanding and functions of the burden of proof are based on two main theories. The procedural theory (*de billijkheidstheorie*) and the objective theory (*de objectiefrechtelijke theorie*). Below, the most important characteristics of both theories are discussed. It should be observed that the procedural theory does not apply as such in Dutch civil law and that the below provided characterisation is regarded as a remnant of history.

The procedural theory was based on the principle of the equality of parties to the proceedings. This equality is based on the concept that each party has the same chance of winning the case.[129] Based on this principle, the judge is obliged to fairly allocate the burden of proving relevant facts between both parties. According to this theory, there are no material rules governing the burden of proof. In each case the judge must decide who bears the burden of proof on the grounds of equity (*billijkheid*).[130] In general, the claimant is required to prove all facts constituting the rights he relies on, and the defendant has to prove the extinction (non-existence) of these right or their temporary ineffectiveness.[131] The precise division of the facts that must be proven will depend on the individual case.

The objective theory, developed originally in Germany as *Normentheorie*, is based on the principle that the judge's task is to apply substantive law to the concrete factual situation.[132] Consequently, in determining the burden of proof, substantive law plays a significant role.[133] According to this theory, each party bears the burden of proving the facts on which the application of substantive law, that the party invokes, depends. There are negative consequences linked to the failure to prove these relevant facts. Namely, the legal consequences of substantive law, which a party relies on, will not be applied.

77. After a great deal of discussion in the Netherlands regarding the foundations of the burden of proof and its consequences for substantive and procedural law, it is the objective theory that finally prevailed.[134] The legal consequences of the facts and rights relied on by the parties took a central role in the formulation of the general rule on the burden of proof. The role of the court in applying substantive law was also emphasised.

Article 150 Rv states that a person who relies on the legal consequences of substantive law must prove all facts necessary for the legal rule to apply.[135] For example, if the buyer seeks remedies for the delivery of non-conforming goods, one of his obligations is to prove

129 Asser/Procesrecht/Asser 3 2013, nr. 278.
130 Rutgers and Krans 2014, nr. 29.
131 Asser/Procesrecht/Asser 3 2013, nr. 278.
132 Rosenberg 1965; Chapter 2, para 50, 51.
133 Rutgers and Krans 2014, nr. 30.
134 Rutgers and Krans 2014, nr. 31; Asser/Procesrecht/Asser 3 2013, nr. 9-13.
135 Article 150 Rv: '*De partij die zich beroept op rechtsgevolgen van door haar gestelde feiten of rechten, draagt de bewijslast van die feiten of rechten, tenzij uit enige bijzondere regel of uit de eisen van redelijkheid en billijkheid een andere verdeling van de bewijslast voortvloeit.*'

the facts and circumstances constituting the existence of non-conformity. If he cannot succeed in providing these facts, his request for remedies will be denied.

The element of equity (*billijkheid*) has not been entirely abandoned. Pursuant to the second part of Article 150 Rv, the reversal of the burden of proof can be applied when the principles of reasonableness and equity (*redelijkheid en billijkheid*) require so.[136] The Dutch approach to the burden of proof recognises the advantages of the procedural approach in exceptional circumstances. The introduction of *redelijkheid en billijkheid* is supported by the belief that the strict application of the objective theory does not always provide the best results.[137]

78. If a party who bears the burden of proof does not convince the judge of the existence of the required facts and rights, he will lose this particular argument, which in turn, could mean losing the case. Consequently, there are negative consequences connected to the burden of proof in the sense of Article 150 Rv. It does not necessarily mean that the other party provided satisfactory evidence, proving the opposite. These negative consequences of the burden of proof do not depend on the discovery of material truth. They are linked to the application of principle of *non liquet.* This principle compels the judge to deliver a decision even when no material truth has been discovered, or when uncertainty over whether the relevant facts took place or not remains, even after hearing all the evidence. In other words, the judge cannot avoid the delivery of a decision because the truth has not been discovered.[138] The risk of losing the case (the negative consequences) is attributed to the party who bears the burden of proof on the ground of Article 150 Rv. The burden of proof in the above-mentioned sense is also regarded as *bewijsrisico.*[139]

79. During the process, the parties bear the burden of proving the facts they invoke. The claimant has to show that the facts that substantiate the claim occurred. When a party to the proceedings does not oppose the facts and circumstances invoked by his opponent, but raises other facts or circumstances, which challenge the claim as a whole, the facts which substantiate the opposing argument must be proven by the defendant. An example would be a defence in the sense of an independent defence, having separate legal ground requiring proof of specific new facts.[140] For example, the buyer claims non-performance and the seller raises *force majeure.* Where this occurs the seller is not objecting to facts established by the buyer, but invokes other facts (relying on the legal consequences of these facts) justifying his actions and fighting the claim based on circumstances separate from

136 It regards the reversal of objective burden, shift of the *bewijsrisico.*
137 Asser/Procesrecht/Asser 3 2013, nr. 287, Rutgers and Krans 2014, nr. 31.
138 Asser/Procesrecht/Asser 3 2013, nr. 274.
139 Giesen/*diss.* 2001, p. 4, 5.
140 HR 15.12.2006, ECLI:NL:HR:2006:AZ1083 (NNEK/Mourik).

the first set of facts initially established by a claimant. Pursuant to Article 150 Rv, the duty to invoke the necessary facts for the defence, the burden of proving these facts and consequently the risk of not proving them, lie with the seller/defendant.[141]

80. The burden of proof exists also in a purely procedural sense. It should be understood as a duty to adduce evidence, which is governed by the Dutch procedural code. It is said the duty to supply evidence as such belongs exclusively to the affairs of parties to the proceedings.[142] In case of doubt regarding the probability of the occurrence of particular facts, the judge has a duty to distribute the burden of particular facts between the parties and to deliver a decision on the grounds of the submissions made by the parties.[143] This incidental distribution of proof flows from the question of which party in particular circumstances is required to prove certain facts. This duty to provide evidence does not constitute a legal obligation since there is no legal sanction for not complying. The only consequence thereof is of a procedural character, however it may also have an influence on the final decision, as the procedural change may affect the application of substantive law.

81. Within Dutch civil procedure, there are other notions of purely procedural character, hence closely connected to the burden of proof. *Stelplicht* entails the duty to invoke (to claim) facts and rights.[144] It designates a party who bears the burden of proof as having a duty to recognise, invoke and plead the facts and rights necessary for the application of legal consequences of substantive law, on which this party relies. If the party does not invoke all necessary facts and circumstances, the burden of proof and duty to supply evidence in relation to these facts will also not arise.[145] The scope of *stelplicht* depends on the individual case and consequences of the particular legal rule. It can be determined in particular case by the application of Article 150 Rv. The evidence can be provided only in relation to the facts that a party has successfully recognised, invoked and sufficiently justified.[146] The *stelplicht* lies with the claimant, and with the defendant so far as he challenges the original claim and relies on the legal consequences of an independent legal norm.[147] Consequently, shortcomings in the *stelplicht* may result in a party losing the case.[148]

141 Rutgers and Krans 2014, nr. 35.

142 Thoe Schwartzenberg 2013, p. 15.

143 Rutgers and Krans 2014, nr. 32.

144 Can be referred to as burden of argumentation.

145 HR 31.01.1992, ECLI:NL:HR:1992:ZC0491, NJ 1992/319 (Dijks/Delta Lloyd); HR 4.12.1998, ECLI:NL:HR:1998:ZC2796.

146 Rutgers and Krans 2014, nr. 33.

147 Asser/Procesrecht/Asser 3 2013, nr. 282.

148 In the situations when a person does not recognise and invoke all necessary facts, for example, in case of sale of goods, the buyer states that the goods are defective but does not state and prove that they were defective already at the time of delivery.

2.5.3 *Allocation of the burden of proof*

82. In the Dutch civil procedure the law provides for certain opportunities for gathering evidence ahead of the trial. Nevertheless, in most cases the parties will first argue their case in court (provide facts and statements), whereupon the court decides which issues need to be further backed up by evidence.[149] Once the claimant presents sufficient evidence, the defendant is allowed to provide counter-evidence.

According to Article 21 Rv the parties are obliged to provide every important fact for the case in question before the delivery of a decision. Pursuant to Article 22 Rv, the judge may demand that a party explain and prove specific facts and statements before delivering the decision.

2.5.3.1 General rule of Article 150 Rv

83. In the Dutch civil procedural code, there is a general rule on the burden of proof. Article 150 Rv states that a party which relies on the legal consequences of invoked facts or rights bears the burden of proving these facts or rights, unless a specific provision or the principle of reasonableness and equity (*redelijkheid en billijkheid*) require a different distribution of the burden of proof. The first part of this provision contains the main rule for the burden of proof in Dutch civil law. It illustrates the dominance of the objective theory. A person who invokes a particular legal provision must prove all the facts that are necessary for this provision to apply.[150]

The general rule determines a risk of being unable to prove necessary facts (*bewijsrisico*). These are negative consequences where the occurrence or non-occurrence of particular facts cannot be established, for example, due to a lack of evidence. A person who bears the burden of proof bears also the risk of the non-discovery of the material truth. When the above occurs the judge must decide against the person who bears *bewijsrisico*.[151]

84. There are situations where the burden of proof and the risks resulting from not satisfying the burden will differ from the general rule. According to Article 150 Rv (second part), the allocation of the burden of proof can be also determined by the specific rule of law (written or not), diverging from the general rule. An example of such a rule can be found in Article 6:99 BW, regarding a situation where the damage is caused by two or more events for which a different person is liable. Another example regards the allocation of the burden of proof in cases regarding accidents caused in the course of employment.[152] Both examples are exceptional and in practice they are applied rarely.

149 Van Hooijdonk and Eijsvoogel 2012, p. 3.
150 HR 23.10.1992, ECLI:NL:HR:1992:ZC0727 (Van der Pasch/Van der Velden).
151 Asser/Procesrecht/Asser 3 2013, nr. 287.
152 Rutgers and Krans 2014, nr. 37.

85. As already stated, the distribution of the burden of proof may also differ from the general rule found in Article 150 Rv, where the principles of reasonableness and equity (*redelijkheid en billijkheid*) require so. To employ this extraordinary allocation of the burden of proof, the individual circumstances of the case must lead to the necessity for an exceptional reversal of the burden of proof.[153] The allocation of the burden of proof based on the ground of reasonableness and equity (*redelijkheid en billijkheid*) occurs very rarely.[154] The question that arises regarding this allocation is whether the reasonableness and equity can be a ground for diverging from the allocation of burden of proof determined by the special legal provision, different from Article 150 Rv. The Hoge Raad has confirmed that it is indeed possible.[155]

2.5.3.2 Presumptions

86. The allocation of the burden of proof, the duty to supply evidence and assessment of evidence can be determined by the presumptions. Presumptions can be divided into legal (material) presumptions and factual (judicial) presumptions. Subsequently, legal presumptions can be divided into rebuttable and non-rebuttable (conclusive) presumptions. Below, the attention will only be given to the rebuttable presumptions.

The rebuttable presumptions are mainly formulated in substantive law. They constitute an exception to the allocation of the burden of proof based on a specific legal provision. The legal presumptions are usually explicitly formulated. The respective provisions contain the phrase 'it is presumed' (*wordt/worden vermoed*).[156] In this respect the legislator is relatively consistent. The provisions containing presumptions are comprised of rules specifying the allocation of the burden and supply of evidence. The operation of the presumption is linked to the right of the opponent to supply evidence to the contrary, which will be explained in para 89. The example of a legal presumption is provided in Article 7:18 (2) BW – the presumption of non-conformity. Article 7:18 (2) BW states that if the non-conformity becomes apparent within six months from the time of delivery, it is presumed to have existed at that time. The operation of the presumption does not change the allocation of the risk of not being able to prove facts on which legal consequences of the substantive law depend. The legal presumptions merely facilitate the supply of proof of particular facts. They create a fiction that if certain facts had been successfully proven, other fact must have occurred.

153 HR 9.09.2005, ECLI:NL:HR:2005:AT8238.

154 Rutgers and Krans 2014, nr. 38.

155 HR 29.06.2001, ECLI:NL:HR:2001:AB2432 (Industromontaza); HR 31.10.1997, ECLI:NL:HR:1997:ZC2476, NJ 1998/85.

156 Asser/Procesrecht/Asser 3 2013, nr. 300.

87. The factual presumptions are constructed by a judge in the course of court proceedings. The judge may presume the existence of particular facts based on other facts whose occurrence has been proven. Consequently, the duty to disprove presumed fact lies with the opponent of the party for whose advantage the presumption has been constructed. The situation is also regarded as the shift of the burden of proof/reversal of burden of proof.[157] It takes place mainly in cases of non-contractual liability, typically in cases regarding traffic accidents and infringements of health and safety rules, when there is a causal relationship between the loss and the conduct or an event.[158] Usually an injured party bears the burden of proving such relationship, but the court can apply the reversal of burden of proof. As with the legal presumption, the factual presumption does not shift the negative consequences of not satisfying the 'original' burden of proof.

88. The construction of the presumptions and the exceptions to the general rule of the burden of proof simplify the position of a party who bears the burden of proof and the negative consequences of being unable to prove the facts. *Vis-á-vis* this simplification with regard to evidence there is an aggravation of duty to invoke the facts and to supply evidence lying with the other party to the proceedings.[159] If the party does not meet all requirements regarding the facts and supply of evidence, the consequences will be determined by the court, unless there are statutory provisions regulating the matter.[160] There are no general sanctions regarding the above failures. The 'original' burden of proof and the risk of not proving remain by the party whose supply of evidence has been facilitated by the presumption.[161]

89. Regarding any proof, providing counter-evidence (*tegenbewijs*) in order to undermine the original proof is allowed, unless it is excluded by a legal provision, as provided in Article 151 (2) Rv. The term counter-evidence (*tegenbewijs*) covers (any form of) statements challenging evidence provided by the other party. It includes statements and evidence casting doubt and undermining grounds for evidence or the credentials of a person supplying evidence. The parties are always free to provide the counter-evidence.[162]

The counter-evidence must not be mistaken with the evidence to the contrary (*bewijs van het tegendeel*). The latter entails positive facts disproving the evidence supplied by the other party evidence, or disproving the presumed fact. For example, pursuant to Article 7:18 (2) BW it is presumed that the goods did not conform to the contract at the time of

157 HR 29.11.2002, ECLI:NL:HR:2002:AE7345 (TFS c.s/NS c.s.); HR 29.11.2002, ECLI:NL:HR:2002:AE7351 (Kastelijn/Gemeente Achtkarspelen).

158 Rutgers and Krans 2014, nr. 44; Giesen/*diss.* 2001, p. 152 *et seq.*

159 Rutgers and Krans 2014, nr. 45.

160 HR 15.12.2006, ECLI:NL:HR:2006:AZ1083 (NNEK/Mourik).

161 Asser/Procesrecht/Asser 3 2013, nr. 290.

162 Article 151 (1) Rv.

delivery. The evidence to the contrary entails the proof that at the time of delivery the goods conformed to the contract or, alternatively that the non-conformity was caused after the time of delivery.[163] Successfully providing evidence to the contrary entails more than simply undermining the presumed facts or the credentials of the supplier of evidence. The evidence to the contrary requires full positive proof that the presumed fact is incorrect.

2.5.4 *Standard of proof*

90. Pursuant to Article 151 Rv, the question of whether particular facts or rights have been successfully proven is left for the judge to decide, unless the legal provision expressly regulates this matter.[164] On the ground of stated facts and supplied evidence the judge can formulate a specific duty to provide facts supporting opposite statements.

According to Article 152 Rv, the facts and circumstances essential for the dispute can be proven by using all means of evidence, unless provided otherwise. Furthermore, as long as the law does not provide otherwise, the judge has complete discretion over his assessment of the evidence supplied.[165] The limitation of his freedom is to be found in the *dwingend bewijs* (the compulsory weight of evidence) and other provisions, for example legal presumptions. The definition of *dwingend bewijs* is provided in Article 151 (1) Rv. It states that the judge is obliged to assess the content of certain evidence as prescribed by a particular legal provision. The assessment of counter-evidence, including the counter-evidence in respect of facts assessed in accordance of *dwingend bewijs*, is always allowed without limitations, as provided in Article 151 (2) Rv.

Finally, the freedom to assess the evidence material is also restricted by the relatively passive role the judge occupies in Dutch civil proceedings. In civil cases the judge is required to search for material truth only as far as the parties ask for it. This means that in fact, unlike in criminal cases, the civil judges look for a formal truth.[166] In the discovery of this formal truth the Dutch judges remain passive.[167]

91. The standard the judge will apply in finding the truth based on the evidence provided during the proceedings must meet the reasonable degree of certainty. It is required that this degree of certainty reaches a preponderance of evidence.[168] The judge must be convinced

163 Hof Arnhem 2.05.2006, ECLI:NL:GHARN:2006:AX6541.

164 Rutgers and Krans 2014, nr. 43.

165 Art. 152 Rv: '*1. Bewijs kan worden geleverd door alle middelen, tenzij de wet anders bepaalt.*
2. De waardering van het bewijs is aan het oordeel van de rechter overgelaten, tenzij de wet anders bepaalt.'

166 Rutgers and Krans 2014, nr. 2.

167 Ancery 2012, p. 141-163.

168 Rutgers and Krans 2014, nr. 55.

that the alleged facts are true.[169] Furthermore, the judge has a duty to clearly justify his decisions with respect to which evidence he regarded as convincing and which pieces of evidence were unsuccessful.

According to Article 149 Rv, the facts and rights stated by one party and not or insufficiently contested by the other party must be treated as established. The most serious form of not objecting to the facts or rights is the acknowledgement/recognition described in Article 154 Rv. Once the facts or rights have been acknowledged and accepted by one of the parties, both the parties and the court are bound to it.

2.5.5 Conclusions

92. As with other jurisdictions investigated in this book, in the Dutch civil law term burden of proof can be considered from different perspectives. First, the burden of proof can be explained by the objective theory (*de objectiefrechtelijke theorie*) and second by the procedural theory (*de billijkheidstheorie*). In order to determine who bears the burden of proving essential facts, the objective theory refers to the substantive law and legal consequences of facts that the party to the proceedings relies upon. The procedural theory states that the burden of proof should be determined by the judge based on the principles of reasonableness and equity (*redelijkheid and billijkheid*). The objective theory prevails in the Dutch system, however the procedural theory is not altogether eliminated and it could still be exceptionally applied, when extraordinary circumstances call for it.

The general rule of burden of proof is contained in Article 150 Rv. It states that a party relying on the legal consequences of the alleged facts or rights bears the burden of proving these facts or rights, unless the specific provision or the principle of reasonableness and equity require otherwise. The most important function of Article 150 Rv is to identify the winning/losing party when no facts have been successfully provided. Based on Article 150 Rv and the principle of *non liquet* it is the party who bears the burden of proof who will lose the case.

There is also a procedural aspect to the burden of proof imposing the duty to provide evidence. The term *stelplicht* is also closely related to the issues of the burden of proof, both material and procedural. It requires a party to invoke and state all facts necessary for the legal consequences to apply. A satisfied *stelplicht* constitutes a condition to be allowed to provide evidence. A party who does not invoke, state and plead sufficient facts may lose the case as a result of shortcomings in *stelplicht*.

Additionally, there are instruments that may have an influence on the allocation of the burden of proof, such as presumptions. Dutch law distinguishes between legal presumptions and factual presumptions. The legal presumptions are constructed by the legislator. In

169 Asser/Procesrecht/Asser 3 2013, nr. 264.

general, they provide that if a particular fact has been proven, the existence of other fact(s) must also be regarded as proven. Regarding the factual presumptions, the court has discretion to deduce new facts from the facts already proven during the proceedings. The presumptions can be rebutted by the other party to the proceedings by providing counter-evidence or evidence to the contrary. Both types of presumptions simplify the evidential position of a party for whose benefit they apply.

Finally, at the end of a trial, after the evidence were heard, the judge will decide on the dispute based on the facts and evidence collected during the proceedings. In general, Dutch judges have a passive role in the proceedings. In their pursuit to discover the truth they are limited by the parties' requests. The judges have the freedom to evaluate evidence and must justify their decisions. The final decision must meet a reasonable degree of certainty and should be taken on the preponderance of evidence.

2.6 Conclusions

93. After comparing the general features of national systems on the burden of proof, it must be stated that there are many similarities among the countries. The general approach to the rules of burden of proof and other rules determining the allocation of the burden of proof are comparable.

In all national legal systems, the analysis of respective burdens of proof and assessing evidence on each proposition are part of the process of the evaluation of evidence and reaching a judgment in a logical and orderly manner. Therefore, it may be stated that the rules on the burden of proof in general have an influence on the structure of the proceedings and the final outcome of the case.

The notion of the burden of proof has several implications. It exists in the legal framework of the analysed systems mainly in two senses. The first sense of the burden of proof relates to the material aspect, which determines the essential facts and the person who has the burden of proving them, and which eventually identifies who bears the risk (burden) of not proving these facts. The second sense of the burden of proof is related to the procedural aspect, which describes the burden of proof as a duty to adduce evidence of alleged facts.

94. Although the systems are very similar in explaining the role of the burden of proof in its material and procedural aspect, there are differences when it comes to the existence and role of the general rule on the allocation of the burden of proof. In Polish law, the general rule is located in Article 6 of the Civil Code. It states that a person who relies on the legal consequences of certain facts bears the burden of proving that these facts occurred, unless provided otherwise.

In Germany, there is no general rule on the allocation of the burden of proof to be found in BGB or ZPO. It is agreed that a particular substantive provision that a party relies on determines the allocation of the burden of proof. It is also stated that the allocation of burden of proof is determined by the BGB, even though no general rule has been incorporated.

Similarly, there is no general rule on the allocation of the burden of proof in English law. It depends on the individual right a party invokes. The rules on the allocation of the burden of proof are determined by statutory law, common law (precedence), and the agreements made by parties.

In the Dutch system there is a general rule incorporated into the civil procedural code in Article 150 Rv. It states that a person who relies on the legal consequences of the invoked facts or rights bears the burden of proving these facts or rights, unless a specific provision or principles of reasonableness and equity require otherwise.

95. In all the jurisdictions analysed there are additional measures determining the allocation of the burden of proof. Apart from the general rules, other provisions may indicate who bears the burden of proof regarding a particular issue. Such a rule can be found in separate legal provisions regulating a particular legal relationship. Furthermore, there are presumptions which can simplify a party's duty to adduce evidence. Finally, there are factual presumptions and *prima facie* evidence that can be admitted at the judge's discretion. The construction and division of the presumptions may be different among national systems. The frequency of the application of the presumptions, in particular factual presumptions and *prima facie* evidence, can also differ considerably. The above-mentioned measures also require different evidence means to be rebutted by the opposing party. What they have in common is that they have an important role in the distribution of the burden of proof in all jurisdictions analysed throughout this book.

In general, in a situation where the specific rule of the burden of proof diverges from that found in a general statutory provision (by presumption, or the judge's discretion), it will most often mean that one of the parties to the proceedings deserves better protection, and the legal system provides for such additional protection, or the factual equality of parties must be reached through the application of the reversal of the burden of proof. The alternative allocation of the burden of proof is an instrument for providing legal (judicial) protection.

96. The systems analysed differ considerably when it comes to the role of the court in the proceedings. The German judge is the most active of all countries compared during proceedings. Also in Poland, the judge has considerable influence on the process of hearing evidence. The involvement of the judge is illustrated by their active role in adducing evi-

dence and looking for the essential facts to resolve the dispute. Their active role is explained by the duty of the court to discover material truth.

The Dutch judge has a much more passive role in the proceedings. He may however, have some influence on the hearing of evidence. In particular, he can formulate the facts that a person must prove and determine the means of evidence that should be used in doing so.

English civil proceedings are of an adversarial character, which excludes the possibility for the court to become involved in the gathering of evidence. It is in the parties' interests solely to provide all necessary facts and evidence and convince the judge about their rights.

97. Finally, all the systems differ somewhat when it comes to the assessment of evidence. In all systems the judges have the freedom to assess and evaluate evidence however, the scope of this freedom varies between the countries.

A Polish judge's freedom to assess evidence is restricted only by the rules of logic, reasonableness and judicial awareness. There is no set standard of conviction the judge has to reach. He is obliged to justify his line of reasoning and explain which facts he considers as proven and which evidence is satisfactory.

In Germany, the judges are also free in their assessment of evidence but there is a high standard of proof that must be reached. The judge must be content with a degree of certainty that is appropriate for practical life purposes and which will reduce the possibility of any doubts, but not necessary eliminating them. This standard is referred to as probability approaching certainty.

The English standard of proof requires a judge to reach a decision on the balance of probabilities. In general this means that a party should prove that the invoked fact is more likely to be true than not. There is a certain degree of conviction required. It is not sufficient that one unlikely theory is a little more probable than another implausible theory. Nevertheless, the degree of certainty to be achieved under English law appears to be lower than in other countries examined.

The Dutch judge has to reach its decision on the preponderance of probabilities. There are some provisions in the Dutch civil procedural code that clearly state what weight must be given to certain evidence. Notwithstanding, the Dutch judge has a freedom to evaluate evidence submitted and has an obligation to justify his decisions.

Summing up, it seems that there are some differences when it comes to the standard of proof. Together with the role of the judge in the proceedings, they may lead to a particular issue in one jurisdiction being regarded as proven (with court discretion to adduce evidence or because of a lower degree of certainty needed) while in other jurisdictions the same issue could be regarded as unproven. This means that even when the general rules distributing the burden of proof are similar, the practice in dealing with the issues of the burden of proof and issues of the law of evidence may render different results.

98. In all the systems investigated, the importance of the rules on the burden of proof for the resolution of a dispute is remarkable. Another characteristic of all the systems is that the burden of proof is difficult to grasp and define, in particular when one tries to define the burden of proof in abstract terms, independently of a particular dispute or litigation. Furthermore, the issues of the burden of proof are abstract and some of their aspects lie in a grey area between substantive and procedural law. Factors such as facts and circumstances of individual cases, the procedural interests of the parties, and the public policy may play an important role in determining the burden of proof.

3 Consumer Sales Directive and its national implementations

3.1 Introduction

99. This chapter presents several aspects of the Consumer Sales Directive. It describes its objectives and functions, and presents the implementation process in Poland (3.3), Germany (3.4), England and Wales (3.5), and the Netherlands (3.6). Several questions will receive special attention. First of all, does the Directive fit into the national systems of sales law? How it influences the domestic sales law? What are current developments regarding the application of consumer sales law. These issues are presented in light of the Directive's main objective – the protection of consumer interests. Finally, the recent matters regarding the application of national consumer sales law, including general issues related to the litigation in consumer cases, will be discussed.

3.2 Information about the Consumer Sales Directive

3.2.1 *Legislative process*

100. The process that has led to enactment of the Consumer Sales Directive began four decades ago. In 1975, the Council of the EEC adopted the first Consumer Programme.[1] The second ground-breaking moment was the Maastricht Treaty of 1992 which provided in Article 3 (s) that consumer protection was to be included into the activities of the Community.[2] The following year, the Green Paper concerning the necessity of harmonisation in the area of consumer sales was published.[3] In 1996, a draft of the Directive was announced and finally on 25 May 1999 the European Parliament enacted the Consumer Sales Directive. The Directive is a minimum harmonisation measure.[4] The Member States were obliged to implement the Directive by 1 January 2002.[5] Only Germany and Austria succeeded in implementing the Directive on time.[6]

1 Council Resolution of 14 April 1975 on a preliminary programme of the European Economic Community for a consumer protection and information policy OJ C 92, 25.4.1975, p. 1.
2 Treaty on European Union (92/C 191/01), Article 3 (s), Maastricht 7.02.1992.
3 Commission 1993.
4 Article 1 (1) of the Consumer Sales Directive.
5 Article 11 (1) of the Consumer Sales Directive.
6 Smits 2003, p. 3.

In 2008 the Commission adopted the proposal for the Directive on Consumer Rights in order to replace several consumer directives, including the Consumer Sales Directive. The proposed character of the harmonisation, maximum harmonisation, received criticism. In particular, the Member States that ensured higher degree of protection than proposed opposed to the Directive on Consumer Rights. On 25 October 2011 the Directive on Consumer Rights was adopted, however in much reduced form than initially proposed.[7] The Directive on Consumer Rights did not alter the scope and the main notions of the Consumer Sales Directive. The Consumer Sales Directive retained its minimum harmonisation character, which leaves the national legislators a considerable room to determine the scope and functioning of consumer protection in the context of consumer sales law.[8]

3.2.2 Objectives

101. The purpose of the Consumer Sales Directive is the approximation of the laws, regulations and administrative provisions of Member States on certain aspects of the sale of consumer goods and associated guarantees in order to ensure a uniform minimum level of consumer protection in the context of the internal market.[9] The Directive provides a minimum uniform standard of consumer protection by providing a coherent notion of conformity of consumer goods and common rules on the seller's liability in case of the non-conformity of goods. The protection of consumer interests as such is not a primary objective of the Directive, rather it is a measure to strengthen the functioning of the internal market.

The obligation of a seller to deliver conforming goods is mandatory and cannot be waived or restricted.[10] In this manner, the European legislator aims to equip consumers with the ability to purchase goods anywhere within the European Union with the confidence that should the products not conform to the contract, there will be a common standard of legal protection.[11] The Directive seeks to enhance the market integration through the harmonisation of rules related to conformity of goods.[12]

Article 2 (2) (a)-(d) of the Directive defines non-conformity of consumer goods, Article 5 (3) provides for the presumption of non-conformity facilitating the burden of proof that must be satisfied by the consumer. In Article 3, the Directive offers a set of remedies available to consumers in case of delivery of non-conforming goods. In the following chapters, the issues regarding the first two matters, the notion of non-conformity and the

7 Reich, Micklitz, Rott and Tonner 2014, p. 395, 396.
8 Reich, Micklitz, Rott and Tonner 2014, p. 170.
9 Article 1 of the Consumer Sales Directive.
10 Staudenmayer 2000, p. 551 *et seq.*
11 Miller 2007, p. 6.
12 Willett, Morgan-Taylor and Naidoo 2004, p. 95.

presumption of non-conformity, will be analysed. I believe that the above mentioned issues are the most crucial for consumer protection under the Consumer Sales Directive.

3.2.3 Implementation methods

102. Below, a brief explanation of the implementation methods used by national legislators when transposing the instruments of consumer protection will be presented. It should be noted that the full spectrum of topics regarding the entering into force of the European legal acts cannot be covered. At this point, it should be sufficient to mention that based on the case law of the ECJ, it is required that '*in order to ensure that directives are fully applied in fact as well as in law, Member States must provide a precise legal framework in the field in question*' which allows '*individuals to know their rights and rely on them before the national courts*'.[13] This means that the Member States have to provide for the national provisions of a binding nature so that the consumers can rely on the rights granted to them in the directives.

The location of an implemented provision may be of importance when it comes to the application and execution of a particular legal norm. In some instances, the fact that a certain rule is located in the secondary legislative act or in the codification may influence the frequency and accuracy of its application. The method of implementation may also effect whether the rule and its interpretation is (commonly) known and applied. In order to establish whether the above counts for the consumer sale provisions, the detailed analysis of national implementations of the Consumer Sales Directive is required.

103. There are several types of methods for implementation: legislative, non-legislative and follow-up measures. Regarding the legislative methods, several measures can be distinguished. The legislator may introduce minor amendments to the existing legislation or modernise the law in line with the European requirements. It can either adopt several separate acts transposing the European directives or enact one independent document covering the majority of the topics. Another possibility is to undertake the complete reorganisation of one area of law in accordance with European law. The European directives can also be implemented by the secondary legislation.

Regarding non-legislative methods, most often they are undertaken by the NGOs pursuing a policy of consumer protection for example *Federacja Konsumentow* (Consumer Federation) in Poland, or the organizations operating under *Verbraucherzentrale Bun-*

13 See among others: ECJ 18.01.2001, C-162/99, *Commission v Italy*, ECR (2001) I-00541; ECJ 15.06.1995, C-220/94, *Commission v Luxembourg*, ECR (1995) I-1589; ECJ 30.05.1991, C-361/88, *Commission v Germany*, ECR (1991) I-2567.

desverband e. V. (Federation of German Consumer Organizations) in Germany.[14] Generally, it can be said that ensuring the interested parties are thoroughly informed of the legal amendments and its interpretation can be regarded as a non-legislative method of implementation. It should be noted that non-legislative methods are very much indirect and difficult to evaluate. For the sake of legal certainty they are intended to play only a supplementary role in the implementation of European directives into the domestic legal systems.

Finally, there are certain measures that are to be undertaken after the actual implementation has taken place. The follow-up measures ensure the directives have been correctly transposed and are being properly applied and executed. They can be taken up by government bodies as well as by NGOs. They are often required by the Directives themselves which may set a date for an evaluation.[15]

3.3 Consumer sale in Polish law

3.3.1 *General information*

104. This sub-section presents general information about the consumer sale in the Polish legal system. It contains a summary of main issues and provisions implementing the Consumer Sales Directive. It also contains information about the reform of Polish consumer sales law that was enacted by the Polish Parliament on 9 May 2014 and will enter into force on 25 December 2014.[16] The sub-section begins with a brief presentation of the implementation process and its results. It also provides general information on the Polish system of liability for the delivery of defective goods. Subsequently, current problems related to the transposition, application and execution of consumer sales law will be presented. The information contained in this section is important to understand how the consumer law was being received in Poland and what problems occur in relation to this area of law. The comparison between the application and interpretation of previous and present provisions will help to understand whether the objectives of the Consumer Sales Directive have been achieved.

14 More information about consumer organizations on http://ec.europa.eu/consumers/archive/empowerment/cons_networks_en.htm (15.06.2014).

15 Article 12 of the Consumer Sales Directive.

16 Ustawa z dnia 30 maja 2014 r. o prawach konsumenta, Dz.U. 2014, poz. 827, referred to as the Consumer Rights Act.

3.3.1.1 Method of implementation

105. The Polish legislator initially opted for a 'mixed' model of implementation of the European law on consumer protection.[17] Some directives such as the Product Liability Directive and the Directive on Unfair Terms have been transposed into the Civil Code, while others such as the Timeshare Directive and the Consumer Sales Directive have been adopted in separate statutes.[18] Recently, the focus has moved towards including the most important directives in the Civil Code (or at least the necessity to do so has been recognised).[19]

106. The Codification Commission justified its initial decision to implement the Consumer Directive outside of the Civil Code in the Consumer Sale Act by arguing that the principle of stability of the Civil Code advocates for implementation of directives in separate statutes. The Consumer Sale Act had been regarded as an innovative instrument. It introduced a new system of seller's liability (liability for non-conforming goods).[20] For that reason, the Codification Commission was convinced that before transposing these provisions into the Civil Code, some observations and experiences concerning its application should be collected.[21] Furthermore, implementation of the Consumer Sales Directive coincided with Poland's accession to the EU. It was suggested that the European Commission had put the Polish Government under pressure to complete the implementation. Had the Polish Parliament been slow in implementing the Directive, among other legal acts, the accession to the European Union could have been delayed as a result.[22] Adoption of the Directive in a separate statute is considered in Poland to be a faster route of adoption than the transposition into the Civil Code. The latter usually requires a longer amendment process and often attracts political disputes, which at the time were particularly unwelcome due to the tight time-schedule.[23] Although the motives of the Codification Commission were understandable, they did not prevent criticism of the chosen implementation method.[24] The strongest argument was that the implementation of the Consumer Sales Directive outside the Civil Code might threaten the consistency of the civil law system.[25] An implementation outside the Civil Code does not require direct confrontation of the legal rules contained

17 Radwański 2006, p. 105.

18 New Act on Timesharing 16.10.2011 (Dz. U. Nr 230 poz. 1370), Consumer Sale Act 27.07.2002 r. (Dz.U. 2002 nr 141 poz. 1176).

19 Pecyna 2012, p. 145, 146.

20 To be distinguished from the liability for defects under the Civil Code, Articles 556-576.

21 Sejm RP 2014, Status justification, p. 12.

22 Radwański 2006, p. 105, 110; Kołodziej 2010, p. 62; Łętowska, Jagielska, Lis, Miklaszewicz and Wiewiórowska-Domagalska 2007, p. 875; Włodarska-Dziurzyńska 2009, p. 476.

23 Habryn 2003, p. 3.

24 Radwański 2006, p. 110; Łętowska, Jagielska, Miklaszewicz and Wiewiórowska-Domagalska 2007, p. 879, 880; Włodarska-Dziurzyńska 2009, p. 476.

25 Katner 2006, p. 1028.

in separate statutes (Civil Code and Consumer Sale Act). Consequently, the lack of systematic, methodological and terminological cohesion may cause an increasing discrepancy between the classical (codified) civil law and consumer law, creating difficulties (for the judges) in interpreting and applying civil law.[26]

107. In my opinion, whether the Consumer Sales Directive is implemented through the Civil Code or a separate statute is irrelevant as long as the European instrument is correctly introduced into the national legal tradition and the domestic legal system. The method of implementation is only a technical matter.[27] However, closer inspection of the Polish Consumer Sale Act, gives the impression that the time pressure on transposing the Directive may have affected not only this technical aspect of legislation but also the quality of legislation and substantive matters leaving the Polish system of liability for defective goods in certain aspects inconsistent.

3.3.1.2 Characterisation of the implementing act

108. As stated above, the Consumer Sales Directive was initially transposed outside of the Civil Code, in the Act of 27 July 2002 on the specific terms and conditions of consumer sale.[28] It entered into force on 1 January 2003. The scope of application of the Consumer Sale Act is determined by Article 1 (1). It states that the Act shall apply in the relationships between professional sellers and buyers – natural persons acting for the purposes not related to their businesses or professions. The provisions are of mandatory character and cannot be departed from to the disadvantage of a consumer.[29] The term buyer was used instead of the consumer in the Consumer Sale Act. The scope of buyer from Article 1 (1) is narrower than the notion of a consumer from Article 22^1 of the Civil Code which stated that a consumer is a natural person who concludes a legal act not related directly to the business or profession of that person. According to recently enacted Consumer Rights Act, provisions on consumer sale will be incorporated into the Civil Code. The new statute unifies several notions, for example the notion of defects[30] and the notion of consumer.

109. The proposal of statute amending consumer sales law was presented to the Parliament in January 2014. On 9 May 2014 the Polish Parliament passed the statute amending Polish sales law. On 22 May 2014 minor amendments were presented by Senate and on 30 May

26 Radwański 2006, p. 110.

27 Haas 1998, p. 33.

28 Translation from http://www.eu-consumer-law.org/legdetails_en.cfm (10.10.2014), original title: Ustawa o szczególnych warunkach sprzedaży konsumenckiej oraz o zmianie Kodeksu cywilnego z dnia 27 lipca 2002 r. (Dz. U. 141 poz. 1176), further referred to as the Consumer Sale Act.

29 SO Warszawa 27.01.2011, XVII AmC 452/10, decision regards standard terms infringing mandatory provisions found in the Consumer Sale Act.

30 Chapter 4, para 244-246.

2014 President signed the new Consumer Rights Act. The new law entered into force on 25 December 2014. First of all, the statute implements the Directive on Consumer Rights. Second of all, it contains provisions on consumer sales which have been (re)incorporated into the Civil Code. The act repeals the existing Consumer Sale Act. The changes have been partially triggered by the obligation to implement the Directive on Consumer Rights,[31] however, the general need to amend the consumer sale provisions was recognised almost from the very beginning following the initial implementation of the Consumer Sales Directive. The Codification Commission admitted that the level of legislation and protection offered was not satisfactory and therefore had to be amended.[32]

110. With the new reform of consumer sale entering into force on 25 December 2014 the criticism regarding the method of implementation of the Consumer Sales Directive became unfounded. The amendments provide for the incorporation of the consumer sales law into the Civil Code and they ensure (re)unification of the provisions regarding defects and seller's liability for the delivery of defective goods.[33]

3.3.1.3 Systematics of sales law

111. Before the amendments introduced in 2014, there were multiple systems of seller's liability for defective goods that exist under Polish law.[34] There was a traditional seller's liability as according to the Civil Code for physical and legal defects.[35] It applied in the contracts between two consumers (C2C) or between two businesses residing in Poland (B2B). The Consumer Sale Act introduced a new system of liability[36] applicable only to contracts between consumers and businesses (B2C).[37] Article 1 (4) of the Consumer Sale Act expressly excluded application of the traditional model of liability set out in Articles 556-581 of the Civil Code. The Polish legislator has decided to introduce liability for non-conformity, which was not necessarily required by the European legislator. The reason for this decision was questionable because from the very beginning the Civil Code-based liability had been perceived as more favourable to consumers than the Consumer Sale Act-based liability. Another system of liability which operates within Polish law is a system of protection set out in the CISG applicable to contracts of sale between Polish professionals

31 Pecyna 2012, p. 145, 146.
32 Sejm RP 2014, Statute justification, p. 2.
33 Sejm RP 2014, Statute justification, p. 3.
34 Radwański 2006, p. 113.
35 Articles 556-581 Civil Code, Rękojmia (often translated as warranty).
36 Liability for non-conforming goods.
37 Pecyna 2003, p. 4.

and professionals residing in the foreign country – a signatory to the CISG, when the rules of private international law lead to the application of law of the contracting state.[38]

112. For a better understanding of the Polish system of sales law a short summary of the seller's liability is presented. The following systems of seller's liability existed before changes introduced in 2014.

1. A system of liability provided by the Civil Code, which applied to contracts between Polish professionals acting for the purpose of their businesses, between the non-professionals not being natural persons, and anyone who purchases for the purpose of his business or trade. Furthermore, it applied to contracts concluded between two natural persons acting for their personal purposes.[39]
2. A system of liability governed by the Consumer Sale Act, which applied to contracts of sale of consumer goods concluded between the natural persons acting for personal purposes and the professionals. The consumer contracts regarded the purchase of movables, excluding the sale of electricity, water and gas for which the payment is determined by the 'meter reading'.[40]
3. A system of liability regulated by the CISG which applies to contracts of sale of movables concluded between Polish professionals and the professionals residing in the one of the countries – signatories of the CISG, when the rules of private international law lead to the application of law of the contracting state.[41]

This division was reduced when the new statute of the Consumer Rights Act entered into force and the Consumer Sale Act was repealed. Consequently, there are two systems of liability, one based on the Civil Code, applying to domestic contracts regardless of the character of the parties (B2B, B2C, and C2C). The second system is based on the CISG – applying to international contracts of sale.

3.3.2 *Legislative changes as a result of the implementation of the Consumer Sales Directive*

113. This sub-section briefly presents the characteristics of the system of liability for defective goods as it stood before the implementation of the Directive and the changes that the Consumer Sale Act introduced. It will also explore recently enacted amendments to the consumer sale – incorporating the respective provisions into the Civil Code. The

38 Article 1 (1) (a) (b) of the United Nations Convention on Contracts for the International Sale of Goods (1980), further referred to as the CISG.

39 Articles 556-581 of the Civil Code.

40 Articles 4 *et seq.* of the Consumer Sale Act.

41 Articles 25-52 of the CISG.

short comparison of these three sets of rules is important for the assessment of the level of protection available before and after implementation of the Consumer Sales Directive and for the evaluation of the level of protection emerging from the new Consumer Rights Act. This comparison will allow drafting conclusions on whether the expectations of the implementation of the Consumer Sales Directive have been met.

114. The implementation of the Consumer Sales Directive in the Consumer Sale Act excluded the application of the Polish Civil Code to contracts of sale concluded between consumers and professional sellers. The provisions of the Civil Code remained valid for contracts of sale between two professionals and between two consumers. This was an important and rather disadvantageous change introduced by the Consumer Sale Act especially in respect of the allocation of the burden of proof regarding the existence of a defect. The wording of Article 559 of the Civil Code (regarding the liability for defects)[42] in conjunction with Article 6 of the Civil Code (general rule on the burden of proof, as explained in chapter 2) was interpreted by the Supreme Court in the resolution of joint chambers of 30 November 1988, establishing an advantageous (for buyers) allocation of the burden of proof in case of a seller's liability for defects.[43] The buyer has an initial burden of proof that the purchased product was defective. In order to counter the buyer's proof, the seller has to show that the defects proved by the buyer have occurred only after the risk has passed. Subsequently, in order for the buyer to swing the balance in his favour he has to prove that defects originate in the purchased product or in unsuitable materials used to manufacture the goods. Consequently, to win the case, the buyer has to prove that the product was defective. Only after the seller has successfully shown that the defects occurred after the passing of risk, is the buyer required to provide further evidence.

115. In relation to the above, Article 559 of the Civil Code and its interpretation approved by the Supreme Court facilitated the consumer's position by operation of a factual presumption regarding existence of defects, unrestricted by the time period.[44] Article 4 (1) of the Consumer Sale Act introduced a legal presumption providing that if non-conformity

42 Article 559 Sprzedawca nie jest odpowiedzialny z tytułu rękojmi za wady fizyczne, które powstały po przejściu niebezpieczeństwa na kupującego, chyba że wady wynikły z przyczyny tkwiącej już poprzednio w rzeczy sprzedanej (*The seller is not liable for the material defects, which occurred after the passing of risk, unless the defects resulted from causes already existing in the product*).

43 SN 30.12.1988, III CZP 48/88 (Resolution of the joint chambers of the Supreme Court – Civil and Administrative chamber). According to Article 61 (6) of the Supreme Court Act, resolutions of joint chambers of the Supreme Court are binding upon this court. They can be departed by another resolution of joint chambers or resolution of full composition of the Supreme Court. Although the resolutions are binding upon on the Supreme Court, the lower courts often follow the line of interpretation in order to prevent the appeal to Supreme Court in case of contradictory to resolution decisions.

44 SN 30.12.1988, III CZP 48/88.

becomes apparent within six months from the time of delivery, it existed at that time.[45] The replacement of the factual presumption with the legal presumption should, in theory, improve consumer protection and secure legal certainty. However, in the case of the Consumer Sale Act it seems the opposite is true. Due to the fact that the presumption is time-restricted, there is tendency among the professionals not to accept complaints after the expiry of six months.[46] This problem had been observed by the Consumer Authority and described in the Daily Legal Newspaper *Gazeta Prawna* to warn consumers about these dubious practices.[47] Regarding the reason for this practice, it is most probably due to businesses pursuit of profit, and the lack of knowledge about the rights and obligations related to consumer sale among both, businesses and consumers. Consequently, the buyer's position under the previous regulation had been more favourable than according to the provisions of the Consumer Sales Act.

116. After the implementation of the Directive, Article 10 (1) of the Consumer Sale Act provided for a longer limitation period than the limitation period under the Civil Code.[48] Regardless of this fact, claiming remedies for non-conforming goods was considered easier before implementation of the Directive.[49] The literature and jurisprudence share the view of the Supreme Court that Article 559 of the Civil Code in conjunction with Article 6 of the Civil Code provides for a factual presumption, whose application is not subjected to any time limits (except the limitation for claiming remedies), unlike the presumption of non-conformity from Article 4 (1) of the Consumer Sale Act which is restricted to a six-month period. According to Żuławska, due to the special socio-economic function of traditional liability for hidden defects, the burden of proof that the defects were caused by the external factors should lie with the seller (as according to the previous provisions),[50] and not on the consumer (as according to the current provisions), even when the new legislation provides for temporary simplification of that burden.[51]

The new regulation on the allocation of the burden of proof in the context of the existence of defects seems to combine both of the above mentioned approaches. The newly enacted Article 556^2 of the Civil Code states that if the defect became apparent within one year from the time of the passing of risk, it is presumed that this defect or its cause existed

45 Article 4 (1) of the Consumer Sale Act.

46 Polubowny Sąd Konsumencki przy Zachodniopomorskim Wojewódzkim Inspektorze Inspekcji Handlowej w Szczecinie, 22.03.2006, sygn. akt 26/2006. (Consumer Arbitration Court by the Regional Trade Inspectorate).

47 Usowicz 2005.

48 One year under Article 568 of the Civil Code, two years under Article 10 (1) of the Consumer Sale Act.

49 Pecyna 2003, p. 5.

50 Żuławska 2005, p. 53.

51 In some cases the consumer bears burden of proving that the defect has not been caused by the external factors.

at the time of delivery.[52] It expands the period of application of presumption to one year, what in some cases will be equal to the limitation period.[53] Therefore, comparing current provisions of the Consumer Sale Act with the new reform, the level of consumer protection is to be increased.

117. Further criticisms of the Consumer Sale Act regarded remedies.[54] Since the topic falls outside the main research questions the matter will be dealt with very briefly. Under Article 560 (1) of the Civil Code, before the transposition of the Directive into the Consumer Sale Act, the consumer could claim rescission of the contract or a reduction in the price, unless the seller has immediately repaired or replaced the goods. The Consumer Sales Directive in Article 3 states that in case of non-conformity the consumer is entitled to claim repair or replacement, unless it is impossible or disproportionate. The remedy is deemed disproportionate if it imposes unreasonable costs on the seller taking into consideration the value of the conforming goods, significance of the lack of conformity and whether the alternative remedy could be completed without significant inconvenience to the consumer. If the consumer is not entitled to claim repair or replacement, he may claim price reduction or have the contract rescinded. In comparison to the freedom of remedies available under the Civil Code, the Consumer Sales Directive introduces a hierarchy of the remedies and restricts the consumer's choice.[55] Such situation favours keeping the contract which often might be more advantageous for the seller.[56]

To a great extent the new reform returns to the original regulations that date from before the implementation of the Directive. Introduced changes to Article 560 of the Civil Code provide that in case of defects, the buyer can ask to reduce the price or terminate the contract, unless the seller immediately and without undue inconvenience repairs or replaces defective goods. The above reservation does not apply if the goods have been already replaced or repaired. Instead of offered by the seller replacement, the consumer may ask for repair and otherwise, unless the remedy chosen by the consumer is impossible or requires excessive costs in comparison to the remedy offered by the seller. While assessing the costs, the value of the defect-free goods and inconvenience of other available remedy must be taken into account.[57]

118. Although the criticism of the Consumer Sale Act was widespread, there were also some positive opinions. Some stated that replacement of the traditional construction of

52 Chapter 5, para 398.
53 Article 568 (1) of the Civil Code allows to restrict the limitation period in cases of sale of the second-hand goods to one year from the time of delivery.
54 Stefanicki 2006, p. 246.
55 Stefanicki 2006, p. 247 *et seq.*
56 Kołodziej 2010, p. 224; Włodarska-Dziurzyńska 2009, p. 467.
57 Article 44 (14) of the Consumer Rights Act, an Act amending the Civil Code.

liability with the liability for non-conforming goods in general provides for a more complete protection.[58] In particular, a factor of including the content of commercial adverts or public statements about the product as a criterion of conformity is said to constitute a positive development. Another opinion is that from the practical point of view the regulations implementing the Directive introduced by the Consumer Sale Act were flexible. In particular, the notion of non-conformity leaves sufficient room for interpretation.[59]

119. Summing up, the statute implementing the Consumer Sales Directive has received severe criticism. The advantages of minimum character of the Consumer Sales Directive have not been used properly. The Polish legislator has not taken the chance to provide for a higher level of consumer protection and regarding several aspects has decreased the existing degree of protection. Finally, the consistency of system of liability for defective goods substantially deteriorated.

Not long after initial implementation of the Directive in the Consumer Sale Act it has become clear that the statute in question was a temporary solution and another more coherent solution would be necessary. On 30 May 2014 President signed the Consumer Rights Act amending Polish sales law. The objectives of the new statute are integration and harmonisation of the Polish rules on liability for delivery of defective goods. The existing consumer sale provisions will be amended and transposed to the Civil Code and the Consumer Sale Act will be repealed. The recent modernisation and harmonisation of consumer sales law (and Polish sales law in general) has also been referred to as a re-implementation of the Consumer Sales Directive.[60]

Although it is too early for a comprehensive assessment of the amendments to the consumer sales it can be observed that the majority of provisions attracting criticism are amended and the provisions of the Consumer Sale Act which have been received positively are incorporated in the Civil Code.

3.3.3 *Current issues regarding the law of consumer sale*

120. The implementation of the Consumer Sales Directive caused difficulties not only among the national legislators, but also among judges.[61] After presenting information regarding the legislative issues, it is now time for the questions regarding application and execution of the consumer sales law, mostly of a procedural nature. It is important to underline that in comparison to Germany and the Netherlands there have been, for a long

58 Stefanicki 2004, p. 10; Maliszewska-Nienartowicz 2002, p. 14; Koszowski 2013, p. 17.
59 Koszowski 2013, p. 12.
60 Sejm RP 2014, Statute justification, p. 8.
61 Stefanicki 2004, p. 10.

time, relatively few decisions regarding application and interpretation of the consumer sales law. However, starting from 2012 the number of decisions slowly increased allowing provisional analysis of the application of consumer sales rules.[62] Below, the sketch of the situation regarding litigation in consumer sale cases will be presented. It will be followed by the brief assessment of the current state of affairs for the level of consumer protection.

3.3.3.1 Implementation of the Directive on Consumer Rights

121. The process of the implementation of the Directive on Consumer Rights was used for the 're-implementation' of the Consumer Sales Directive and harmonisation of other consumer law provisions contained in the subject-matter directive.[63] On 8 May 2014, the Polish Parliament enacted the Consumer Rights Act (signed by President on 30 May 2014), implementing the Directive on Consumer Rights and modernising the existing consumer sales law.[64] The new act incorporates the majority of the consumer sales provisions into the Civil Code and repeals the Consumer Sale Act. Other implemented provisions are to be mainly found in the Consumer Rights Act. The act entered into force on 25 December 2014. It brings many important changes to the Polish consumer sales law. The amended provisions having importance for this thesis, in particular, regarding the definition of defects and the presumption of non-conformity are discussed throughout chapter 4 and 5.[65]

3.3.3.2 Existence of the case law

122. It has been suggested, that one of the reasons for the consumer cases being so troublesome to resolve is that Polish judges lacked the '*pro-consumer*' approach, and experience in adjudicating the disputes regarding legislation where interests of one particular group have to be generally protected.[66]

The basic type of the judicial proceedings envisaged for the consumer litigation is summary proceedings.[67] It is mainly characterised by the formality and strict requirements regarding the hearing of evidence. That does not encourage consumers to benefit from it.[68] Furthermore, the decisions adjudicated in the summary proceedings are excluded from the appeal to the Supreme Court. Article 398^2 k.p.c. states that in cases adjudicated

62 SO Białystok 17.01.2013, II Ca 996/12, SR Wroclaw-Fabryczna 23.01.2013, XI C 695/12; SO Słupsk 20.12.2013, IV Ca 608/13; SO Świdnica 12.03.2013, II Ca 44/13; SO Białystok 29.08.2013, II Ca 567/13, SO Elbląg 08.04.2013, I Ca 55/13, SO Słupsk 07.06.2013, IV Ca 262/13.

63 Sejm RP 2014, Statute justification, p. 8.

64 Ustawa z dnia 30 maja 2014 r. o prawach konsumenta, Dz.U. 2014, poz. 827, referred to as the Consumer Rights Act.

65 See para: 226, 244-247, 250, 261, 267, 397, 398, 422.

66 Stefanicki 2004, p. 10.

67 Gajda-Roszczynialska 2012, p. 300.

68 Łętowska, Jagielska, Lis, Miklaszewicz, Wiewiórowska-Domagalska 2007, p. 885.

in the summary proceedings and when the value under litigation amounts to 50,000 *pln* (approx. € 12,000) the cassation is inadmissible. Therefore, even when the consumer disputes are adjudicated in the ordinary proceedings, most of the time the value under litigation is too low for the case to be admitted for the appeal to the Supreme Court.[69] Consequently, in the field of consumer sales there are few chances to obtain the interpretation provided by the Supreme Court.

123. It is said that alongside the lack of judges' sensitivity for the weaker party's interests, consumers have a general lack of trust in the justice system what also contributes to the small number of court decisions. This lack of trust may be caused by the courts inefficiency or by the consumers' conviction thereof, as well as the consumers' insecurity and lack of knowledge about their own rights.[70] In particular, consumers who have no professional legal support often feel helpless and do not commence proceedings. Other significant factors might be the lengthiness of the proceedings as well as their costs. Including the costs of the expertise and advocates' fees, they are often highly disproportionate to the value under litigation.[71] A combination of these factors leads to consumers being unwilling to pursue their rights. In addition, businesses tend to take advantage of the above facts, hoping in cases where they infringe consumers' rights, that those consumers will be reluctant to take court action.[72]

3.3.3.3 ADR

124. In recent years, there have been a growing number of calls within the European Union for consumer claims to be sent to arbitration instead of ordinary courts. The European Parliament has enacted new instruments simplifying dispute resolution between consumers and businesses.[73] Also in Poland the role that arbitration plays has increased over recent years. However, it is clear that so far the arbitration has not provided sufficient assistance to Polish consumers. Currently, there are 16 permanent consumer arbitration courts attached to the regional trade inspectorates and 15 field centres, which settle disputes when

69 Based on Article 390 § 1 k.p.c., a court of the second instance may refer legal questions to the Supreme Court, regarding interpretation of law, necessary for solving the dispute. The institution of legal question is an exceptional measure available also in consumer cases.

70 Jezioro 2010, p. 63.

71 Jezioro 2010, p. 63.

72 Łętowska, Jagielska, Lis, Miklaszewicz, Wiewiórowska-Domagalska 2007, p. 884.

73 Directive 2013/11/EU of the European Parliament and of the Council of 21 May 2013 on alternative dispute resolution for consumer disputes and amending Regulation (EC) No 2006/2004 and Directive 2009/22/EC (Directive on consumer ADR); Regulation No 524/2013 of the European Parliament and of the Council of 21 May 2013 on online dispute resolution for consumer disputes and amending Regulation (EC) No 2006/2004 and Directive 2009/22/EC (Regulation on consumer ODR).

the value under litigation is up to 10,000 *pln* (*approx.* € 2,200).[74] According to the report of the Permanent Consumer Arbitration Court in Warsaw, between 2007-2012 the annual average number of cases adjudicated by this arbitration court amounted to 70.[75] Given that this is the biggest permanent arbitration court in Poland, it is without doubt too low number to effectively substitute ordinary proceedings, indicating that rights are not pursued.

125. The ADR proceedings should attract parties for the same reasons the ordinary proceedings discourage them from litigating. The insecurity of being a 'weaker party', lack of knowledge and information and finally length and costs of the ordinary proceedings create obstacles for consumers discouraging them from pursuing their own rights. The arbitration proceedings are cheaper, faster and less formal than ordinary court proceedings.[76] It is claimed that the inequality between the consumers and businesses may be balanced only by the positive intervention of an external body.[77] This role could be taken up by the arbitration courts.

126. The jurisdiction of an arbitration court to consider a particular dispute must be contingent upon mutual agreement.[78] The capacity and scope of the arbitration is set out by national legislation. Since amendment of the Civil Procedure Rules in 2005, parties, their representatives or guardians can sign the arbitration agreement.[79] Previously only parties themselves could sign such agreement. According to Article 87 (5) k.p.c., the consumer can be represented before the arbiters by an employee of the organisation whose *statutair* activity is to protect consumer interests.[80]

The arbitration court has an obligation to encourage parties to try to reach an amicable settlement.[81] During the trial, both parties have an opportunity to present their views, and furthermore the expert's opinions may be presented. If no settlement is reached, the arbi-

74 Interestingly, that the majority of cases under arbitration concerns complaints regarding defective shoes. Also many of ordinary proceeding concern these types of goods: SR Wrocław-Fabryczna 23.01.2013, XI C 695/12; SR Złotoryja 28.12.2012, I C 413/12; SO Szczecin 13.02.2013, II Ca 1268/12; SR Wrocław-Środmiescie 29.10.2013, VIII 1030/13; SR Wrocław Środmiescie 23.10.2013, VIII C 797/13; SR Lubań 07.11.2012, I C 388/12.

75 http://spsk.wiih.org.pl/pliki/20111217_spsk_statystyka_ogolna.pdf and http://spsk.wiih.org.pl/pliki/20111217_spsk_statystyka_szczegolowa.pdf (23.10.2014).

76 Tulibacka 2012, p. 181.

77 Stefanicki 2009, p. 70.

78 The Permanent Consumer Arbitration Court confirms that very often the sellers do not agree to the arbitration clause. Available online: http://www.bip.wiih.lodz.pl/index.php?podstrona_id=24 (23.10.2014).

79 Stefanicki 2009, p. 65, 66.

80 For example: Federacja Konsumentów (*Consumer Federation*), Stowarzyszenie Konsumentów Polskich (*Association of Polish Consumers*), Polskie Towarzystwo Ekonomiki Gospodarstwa Domowego (*Household Economics Association*).

81 Gajda-Roszczynialska 2012, p. 418.

tration court issues an award.[82] Both the parties' settlement and the award of arbitration court are binding upon the parties. When an enforcement order is issued by an ordinary court, the award has the same force as the decision of that court.

127. Some authors suggest that the lack of professionalism and independence of arbiters is one of the shortcomings of arbitration procedure in Poland.[83] It has been reported that there have been some cases when the same person was an expert in the complaint procedure[84] and subsequently was appointed by the arbiters as an expert witness in the arbitration proceedings.[85] Although such situations are exceptional, to win consumer trust they must be altogether eliminated. To ensure the ADR entities will become reliable and effective institution administrating justice, the organisation and the operation of the arbitration courts should be further reformed. Issues regarding arbiters' training and their remuneration should in particular be reconsidered.[86]

Another issue with regard to the arbitration is a low level of awareness among both professionals and consumers. There is a lot to do to provide consumers with sufficient information and to promote use of alternative dispute resolution among the market users to enhance the success of ADR. At the same time, the speed and efficiency of the ordinary proceedings must be improved. Until that time it seems that the consumers are left uncertain as to whether their rights will be observed and enforced.

3.3.3.4 Consequences for consumer protection

128. The consequences of present situation regarding the consumer litigation affect not only the consumers but also sellers. Without case law and judicial interpretation of the statutory provisions it is difficult to objectively assess the standard of consumer legislation and the level of consumer protection. It would be naïve to think that the initial shortage of court proceedings and respective judgments was a result of flawless operation of Polish consumer protection law. On the contrary, one might suspect that the shortage of case law regarding the application of the Consumer Sale Act indicated that the real standard of protection was much lower in comparison with the standard that emerged from the legislation.[87] The bystander may be left with an idea that the statutory provisions were just black letter laws that did not reflect a real protection of consumer interests. Furthermore, taking into account regulations of the Civil Code applicable to the consumer sale before the implementation of the Consumer Sales Directive, together with the settled practice

82 Tulibacka 2012, p. 181.

83 Stefanicki 2009, p. 67, 68; Torbus 2009, p. 93.

84 A complaint about the non-conformity presented to the seller, who may hire an expert to assess when and why the non-conformity has occurred.

85 Stefanicki 2009, p. 67.

86 Stefanicki 2009, p. 67, 68.

87 Stefanicki 2004, p. 2.

and line of interpretation, one may conclude that the level of protection emerging from the Consumer Sale Act is lower than the standards applying under the Civil Code provisions. Taking into account the new reform and partial return to the system applicable before the implementation of the Directive, the prognoses are that the level of consumer protection will significantly increase.[88]

3.3.4 Conclusions

129. The Consumer Sales Directive was reportedly implemented under time pressure, thanks to the tight schedule drafted before Polish accession to the European Union. It introduced new notions into Polish law. Some of them seemed to not have been entirely considered and failed to fit into the traditional system of Polish sales law. One may think the initial exclusion of the Civil Code would require the new legislation to cover the same legal problems (as under excluded provisions). In this sense, the Polish legislator has somewhat failed, in particular in case of legal defects as explained in chapter 4, para 230-232. The implementation of the Consumer Sales Directive created a plurality of systems of liability without cohesive criteria for distinguishing them.[89]

130. From the introductory information about the implementation of Consumer Sales Directive and the structure of the Polish system of seller's liability for defective goods several observations can be made. The comparison of particular types of sale contracts and the sources of seller's liability shows that from the beginning there was a general need to review the system of domestic sales law. Issues such as consistency within the Polish system of sales law should have been taken into account from the start of the implementation process.

In 2011, a new Codification Commission started its term and as stated in the reports for the years 2011 and 2012 the objective of the Commission was recodification of Polish civil law. In 2012 the Commission worked mainly on the new draft of the Polish Civil Code.[90] It also worked on the implementation of the Directive on Consumer Rights.[91] The research and analysis necessary for the implementation of this Directive and integration

88 Sejm RP 2014, Statute Justification, p. 8, 9.

89 Radwański 2006, p. 108.

90 Reports of the Codification Commissions: 1. Report for year 2011, http://bip.ms.gov.pl/Data/Files/_public/bip/kkpc/sprawozdanie-z-dzialalnosci-kkpc-2011.pdf (10.10.2014);
2. Report for year 2012, http://bip.ms.gov.pl/Data/Files/_public/bip/kkpc/sprawozdanie-z-dzialalnosci-kkpc-2012.pdf (10.10.2014).

91 Directive 2011/83/EU of the European Parliament and of the Council of 25 October 2011 on consumer rights, amending Council Directive 93/13/EEC and Directive 1999/44/EC of the European Parliament and of the Council and repealing Council Directive 85/577/EEC and Directive 97/7/EC of the European Parliament and of the Council.

of the consumer sale into the current Civil Code will be used later while working on the new draft of Polish Civil Code.[92] The new statute – the Consumer Rights Act implements the Directive on Consumer Rights and amends the consumer sales. It was presented to the Parliament in January 2014 and enacted in May 2014. It entered into force on 25 December 2014. The statute takes into consideration the great majority of criticism of existing consumer sales law and presents cohesive amendments, integrating and harmonising Polish sales law, which in the future will have a positive effect on the level of consumer protection.

131. The level of protection which has been achieved in other Member States through judicial interpretation, in Poland had to be achieved through legislation.[93] Regardless of how good that legislation would be it will not prevent future legal problems and uncertainties, and cannot replace judicial interpretation. The observation of the disputes resolution in consumer cases must lead to the conclusion that the correct application of Community law depends on the work of national judges. As presented in para 122-128, the standard of effectiveness of both ordinary and alternative dispute resolution systems is far from satisfactory.

Summing up, the original implementation of the Consumer Sales Directive did not entirely guarantee the fulfilment of the objectives set out by the European legislator.[94] To achieve this, the Directive must be successfully and effectively implemented into domestic legal systems. The Consumer Rights Act incorporating consumer sale into the Polish Civil Code ensures better implementation of the Consumer Sales Directive and secures improvement of the consumer protection in the area of sales law.

3.4 Consumer sale in German law

3.4.1 General information

132. In this section several aspects of German consumer sales law will be presented. The focus will be given mainly to the topics regarding the implementation of the Consumer Sales Directive and its consequences for German private law in general and for German consumer sales law in particular. Subsequently, current problems related to the application of consumer sales law, including issues related to litigation and arbitration, will be discussed.

92 Report Codification Commission 2012, http://bip.ms.gov.pl/Data/Files/_public/bip/kkpc/sprawozdanie-z-dzialalnosci-kkpc-2012.pdf (10.10.2014).

93 Łętowska, Jagielska, Lis, Miklaszewicz and Wiewiórowska-Domagalska 2007, p. 888.

94 Radwański 2006, p. 108; Stefanicki 2006, p. 64 *et seq.*

133. The implementation of the Directive has inspired a broad discussion about the place and character of the consumer provisions in German private law. The pre-implementation debate focused mainly on whether there should be major changes to the law of obligations, incorporating consumer law into the BGB, or whether the consumer sale provisions should be regulated in a special piece of legislation outside the BGB.[95] Both approaches had their advocates but in the end it was decided to modernise a large part of German contract law. This resulted in a great deal of work for German scholars, legislators, practitioners and judges, since the existing line of judicial decision-making in the field of contract law was no longer legitimate.[96]

3.4.1.1 Method of implementation

134. Before the implementation of the EC Directives, there were no special consumer protection provisions in the BGB.[97] The German legislator had always been very cautious about transposing consumer provisions into domestic law. The authors of EC Consumer Law Compendium distinguish three stages in the implementation of consumer law, which involved different implementation methods:

1. Consumer directives implemented by making minor modifications to existing legislation, such as the Unfair Contract Terms Act.
2. Consumer directives implemented by enacting separate acts, such as the Timeshare Act or the Distance Selling Act.
3. Consumer directives implemented by transposing them into the BGB. This resulted in a great modernisation of the German law of obligations. The previous acts on doorstep selling, distance selling, unfair contract terms, timesharing and consumer credit have been incorporated into the BGB.[98]

3.4.1.2 Characterisation of the implementing act

135. The need to modernise German sales law was recognised long before the promulgation of the Consumer Sales Directive. The debate had been continuing for over twenty years.[99] The amendment process developed in three phases. It started in the 1970s when the then Minister of Justice asked for academic opinions on several topics such as limitation periods, general rules on breach of contract, and topics regarding tort law and family law. In the mid-1980s an Expert Group was established and entrusted with the task of elaborating BGB draft provisions on the above-mentioned topics regarding general parts of the law of obligations and contract law. Issues surrounding tort law and family law were left aside.

95 Rott 2004, p. 239, 240; Grundmann 2005, p. 130; Honsell 2001, p. 280.
96 Rott 2004, p. 240.
97 Schulte-Nölke, Twigg-Flesner and Ebers 2008, p. 82.
98 Schulte-Nölke, Twigg-Flesner and Ebers 2008, p. 82 *et seq.*
99 Zimmermann 2005, p. 31, 33; Schlechtriem 2002, p. 2.

A draft for the renewed BGB was published in 1992. Opinions on this document varied but the reluctance to introduce it prevailed. In the end, the project was rejected by politicians as too risky to carry out.[100] It was put aside until the Consumer Sales Directive was enacted in 1999 and had to be implemented by 1 January 2002.

136. The debate was reignited with the question of how the Consumer Sales Directive should be transposed into the German legal system. There were two viable options, the Directive could be adopted as a separate document or it could be incorporated into the BGB, leading to a general modernisation of contract law. Another issue was whether the new provisions should apply only to consumer sales or to all types of sale contracts, laying the foundation for a uniform and cohesive system of sales law. On 9 May 2001, after a long nation-wide debate, the official draft of the *Act on the Modernisation of the Law of Obligations* was completed. On 10 November of the same year, after deliberations on the proposal, the *Bundesrat* finally accepted the draft and the *Act on the Modernisation of the Law of Obligations* entered into force on 1 January 2002.[101] In the end, more than 300 paragraphs were changed, replaced or introduced. The amended provisions of the BGB were more than 100 years old.[102] The incorporation of the consumer sale contracts into the BGB resulted in the creation of a single system of sellers' liability for defective goods. This prevented many competence and interpretation uncertainties with regard to the applicability of the rules on sales law. In addition to the provisions introducing the Consumer Sales Directive, other consumer provisions were incorporated into the BGB, such as those on doorstep selling, distance selling, and unfair contract terms. Furthermore, the general law of obligations was also amended. Among others, rules on limitation periods, rules regarding consequences for breach of contract, but also law on services, consumer credit and other fields of consumer law were reviewed and improved.[103]

3.4.1.3 Systematics of sales law

137. The sales law is regulated in Book 2, Division 8 of the BGB in § 433 to § 479. The first sub-section, § 433 to § 454, contains general provisions regarding rights and obligations of the parties in case of delivery of defective goods. The second sub-section, § 454 to § 473, contains special types of sale, for example purchase on approval, repurchase and pre-emption. The third sub-section, § 474 to § 479, provides rules applicable exclusively for the consumer sale implemented in accordance with the Consumer Sales Directive.[104]

100 Schlechtriem 2002, p. 2.
101 Schuldrechtsmodernisierungsgesetz, Bundesgesetzblatt 2001 I 3138.
102 Löwisch 2003, p. 142.
103 Grundmann 2005, p. 131, 132.
104 Hoeren and Martinek 2002, p. 2; Schermaier 2003, p. 196.

138. The modernisation of the BGB created a coherent system of German sales law, where all domestic types of sale contracts are governed by the BGB. There are several specific provisions applicable only to consumer sales: § 474, § 475, § 476, § 477 and § 478.[105] The respective provisions will be explained later in this sub-section.[106]

Germany is also a signatory of the CISG which regulates contracts between domestic and foreign professionals – signatories to the CISG, when the rules of private international law lead to the application of the law of the contracting state.[107] Consequently, the BGB applies to almost all domestic sale contracts while the international sale contracts are governed by CISG, if chosen as the applicable law. This means the provisions applicable to sale contracts are relatively predictable which contributes to a high level of legal certainty.

3.4.2 *Legislative changes as a result of the implementation of the Consumer Sales Directive*

139. As already mentioned, until the adoption of the Consumer Sales Directive, some parts of German contract law had not been modernised in over a century. The previous regime was outdated and overly complex. It had little in common with modern legal developments and market practice.[108] Below I present some of the most problematic features of the law of obligations under the 'old' BGB:

1. Replacement was available only when the goods were described in a general manner.
2. No distinction was drawn between factual impossibility and practical impossibility.
3. Repair was not a statutory remedy. It was not provided by the BGB, although often available in practice thanks to parties' agreement.
4. German law provided for various limitation periods of different lengths.
5. The buyer could claim damages only when the seller had guaranteed specific characteristics of the goods or if he acted fraudulently.[109]

Apart from the changes regarding the topics above, the general focus was moved from the sale of specific goods to the sale of generic goods. This was confirmed in 2002 and 2003 by the first court decisions adjudicated under the modernised BGB.[110]

105 Zerres 2007, p. 87; Möllers 2002, p. 782, 786-797.

106 Chapter 3, para 141.

107 Hoeren and Martinek 2002, p. 22.

108 Zimmermann 1996, p. 783, 806; Rott 2004, p. 240.

109 Zimmermann 2005, p. 48; Rott 2004, p. 240.

110 See: LG Ellwangen 13.12.2002, 3 O 219/02, NJW 2003, 517; OLG Braunschweig 04.02.2003, 8 W 83/02, NJW 2003, 1053.

140. Under the old provisions, limitation periods ranged from six months to thirty years. Different limitation rules applied depending on whether there were defects in quality or legal defects. The limitation period was six months for defects in quality, while it was thirty years for legal defects. Such a huge difference led to many uncertainties in practice. Even more confusing was that the short period did not apply to defects caused by the breach of ancillary duties and when the goods had been manufactured for a particular purpose.[111]

According to new § 195 BGB, the general limitation period amounts to three years. The Consumer Sales Directive introduced a fixed limitation period of two years with exception of second-hand goods to which a one year period may apply.[112] This regulation has been followed in § 438 (3) and § 634a (1) BGB. The amendment of limitation periods meant that the number of cases which were treated differently radically decreased, which clearly improved and simplified the rules applicable to sales law.[113]

141. The new provisions on sales apply to all types of sale contracts, irrespective of the capacity of the contracting party, and irrespective of the type of goods: immovable, movables, new goods, second-hand goods.[114] It means that the German legislator managed to create a system that overall was consistent.[115] Although the provisions of the Directive have been implemented for all types of sales, there are several paragraphs applicable exclusively to consumer sales:

1. § 474 BGB provides a definition of sale of consumer goods.
2. § 475 (1) BGB states that a professional seller may not rely on agreements which derogate from his warranty obligations to the detriment of a consumer. For example: it is prohibited to include in a contract that a consumer may not claim reparation in case of defects, while any other remedies remain available. The reduction of limitation periods is explicitly excluded by § 475 (2) BGB.[116]
3. § 476 BGB introduces the presumption of non-conformity, meaning that if defects become apparent within six months from the time of passing of risk, it is presumed that the goods were defective at that time.
4. § 477 BGB provides for special provisions on guarantees in the consumer sale contracts.
5. § 478 (1) BGB strengthens the seller's position with respect to the original supplier or producer.

111 Grundmann 2001, p. 255.
112 Article 5 (1) and 7 (1) parts 2 and 3 of the Consumer Sales Directive.
113 Grundmann 2005, p. 143, 144; Zimmermann 2005, p. 157, 158.
114 Grundmann and Ochmann 2007, p. 456.
115 Grundmann 2001, p. 244 *et seq.*; Grundmann and Uhlig 2011, p. 79.
116 Regarding new goods the period amounts to two years. There is an exception in case of sale of second-hand goods, parties may reduce the limitation period, which must amount to not less than one year.

142. Another significant change following the modernisation of the law of obligation concerns the construction of parties' obligations set out in § 433 BGB. It shows that the approach taken by the BGB has altered from the traditional warranty theory to the performance theory.[117] Before the modernisation of the BGB and the implementation of the Directive, the delivery of defective goods was considered as performing an obligation which had to be remedied. According to the new approach, the seller is regarded as performing his obligation only if he delivers goods free from defects, possessing agreed quality. This means that delivery of non-conforming goods constitutes a non-performance of the obligation and not a defective performance.[118]

143. Thanks to implementation of the Consumer Sales Directive, as well as introducing new concepts, others had to be re-interpreted, for example the moment of occurrence of a defect which is essential for the seller's liability. The Consumer Sales Directive defines this moment as the time of delivery. In German law, for the seller to be liable for delivery of defective goods, the moment when the defects must have existed is the moment of the passing of risk. To be effective for the purpose of consumer sale contracts this term has been altered. In the German system a new concept has been created, that is 'the time of the passing of risk in the consumer sale contracts'. The scope of this notion is narrower in comparison to the time of passing of risk in ordinary sales.[119] More details regarding this topic will be provided in chapter 5 when presenting the second condition for the application of the presumption of non-conformity, existence of defects within six months from the time of the passing of risk.[120]

144. Summing up, the implementation of the Consumer Sales Directive has received huge attention and led to a general modernisation of the BGB. There are views that the German legislator failed to go beyond the requirements of EU law. It could have gone much further, especially in the area of manufacturers' guarantees and their liability towards consumers.[121] However, the overall evaluation of the modernised BGB should definitely be positive. After a long process, a solid and cohesive system of seller's liability for defective goods has been successfully created.[122]

117 *Entwurf eines Gesetzes zur Modernisierung des Schuldrechts*, Deutscher Bundestag 14/6040 (Draft statute amending law of obligations).
118 Rott 2004, p. 239; Löwisch 2003, 148.
119 Doehner/*diss.* 2004, p. 154.
120 Chapter 5, para 451-455.
121 Micklitz 2002, p. 387.
122 Möllers 2002, p. 785 *et seq.*; Grundmann 2005, p. 148; Rott 2004, p. 256.

3.4.3 *Current issues regarding the law of consumer sale*

145. The German law transposing the Consumer Sales Directive, regarding the majority of topics, is said to be in accordance with the requirements of the Directive.[123] The legislator changed the wording of most of the relevant provisions and ensured that the provisions were compatible with the Consumer Sales Directive while attempting to fit the style of the BGB. It also brought German law in line with the generally challenging environment of European contract law.[124] There was however some uncertainty, in particular regarding the application of § 437 and § 439 BGB, which is discussed in para 147-153.

3.4.3.1 Implementation of the Directive on Consumer Rights

146. The process of implementation of the Directive on Consumer Rights in Germany has not affected the provisions on consumer sale as it did in England and Poland.[125] On 14 June 2013 the *Bundestag* passed the law ensuring the requirements of the Directive on Consumer Rights are fulfilled. The new amendments entered into force on 13 June 2014.[126] Regarding the provisions related to consumer sales, similarly to the Dutch implementation of the Directive on Consumer Rights the definitions of consumer and consumer sale have been further specified. For the purpose of this thesis, the most interesting amendments concern the definition of consumer sale and the moment of passing of risk. The amended § 474 (1) BGB provides that the contract of sale of consumer goods covers agreements where in addition to the sale of a good a service is rendered by an entrepreneur to the consumer. Furthermore, § 474 (3) BGB inserts the provision on the time of performance in consumer contracts. It states that if it is not agreed otherwise, the seller shall deliver the goods to the consumer within thirty days of the conclusion of the contract. Finally, § 474 (4) BGB specifies the rules regarding the passing of risk when the goods are delivered by a third person, originally regulated in § 447 BGB. Before the amendment, § 447 (1) BGB which provides that in case of a shipment or carriage of goods the risk passes as soon as the seller has handed the goods over to the carrier, did not apply to consumer contracts. Currently, the moment of passing of risk depends on whether the consumer has chosen a third person, a carrier. If not, the risk passes at the time the goods are handed to the consumer or a person designated by the consumer to receive the delivery (actual delivery). When the

123 Schulte-Nölke, Twigg-Flesner and Ebers 2008, p. 693, 694; Rott 2004, p. 256.

124 Micklitz 2002, p. 398.

125 Polish and English legislators have used the implementation process to amend the existing consumer sales law. In both countries the project of new statute implementing the Directive on Consumer Rights and amending the consumer sales law had its 1st reading in the respective parliaments on 23 January 2014.

126 The statute implementing the Directive on Consumer Rights (*Gesetz zur Umsetzung der Verbraucherrechterichtlinie und zur Änderung des Gesetzes zur Regelung der Wohnungsvermittlung*) BGBl. Teil I Nr. 58/3642, http://www.bundesgerichtshof.de/SharedDocs/Downloads/DE/Bibliothek/Gesetzesmaterialien/17_wp/VerbraucherrechteRL/bgbl.pdf;jsessionid=63E97C323BF73C2C6411B187BA613BDC.2_cid344?__blob=publicationFile (23.10.2014).

consumer did choose the carrier which has not been made available by the seller, the risk passes at the time of handing over the goods to the carrier. Except § 474 (4) BGB which may affect commencement of the six-month period for the application of the presumption of non-conformity, the changes introduced by the implementation of the Directive on Consumer Rights do not affect the application of the presumption of non-conformity.

3.4.3.2 Interpretation of German provisions on consumer sales in conformity with the Directive

147. After implementation of the Consumer Sales Directive the case law on issues of defectiveness was to large extent no longer legitimate.[127] From the first years following the implementation of the Directive and modernisation of the law of obligations to the present, judges and scholars have struggled to break with the previous line of reasoning. However, from the beginning they demonstrated their willingness to engage with the conceptual changes to German sales law.[128]

148. Some provisions of the new sales law, such as § 476 BGB, are especially important for consumer protection. Their application and interpretation regularly cause uncertainties. The BGH has been called upon numerous times to determine the final interpretation of the rules on the application of the presumption of non-conformity. The issues under consideration concern in particular the requirements and consequences of the application of the presumption of non-conformity and the conditions for its exclusion.

There are also numerous references in German literature to the role and the place of § 476 BGB in the domestic legal system.[129] It proves that the presumption of non-conformity is crucial to the consumer's position in litigation and his chances to successfully rely on remedies provided by the Consumer Sales Directive. In general it should be stated that German scholars pay particular attention to the issues of the burden of proof, which are for instance presented in the extended volumes of the *Handbuch der Beweislast*, analysing the BGB from the perspective of the burden of proof.[130]

149. One of the most important judgments on the implementation of the Consumer Sales Directive in German law was the ECJ's decision in *Quelle* case.[131] The case considered the interpretation of German domestic law in light of the Directive.[132] The case concerned a

127 Rott 2004, p. 240.

128 Rott 2004, p. 254.

129 For example: Pfeiffer 2002; Massimo Bianca and Grundmann 2002; Grundmann 2001; Grundmann 2005; Maultzsch 2006.

130 Baumgärtel, Laumen and Prütting 2009.

131 ECJ 17.04.2008, C-404/06, *Quelle AG v Bundesverband der Verbraucherzentralen und Verbraucherverbände*, ECR I-2713.

132 OLG Nürnberg 23.08.2005, 3 U 991/05, NJW 2005, 3000.

purchase of consumer goods (a stove oven) from the German retailer, *Quelle AG*. After a year and a half, within the legal guarantee period of two years, the oven appeared to be defective and beyond repair. The consumer requested a replacement of the defective oven, and *Quelle* did not object to this claim. However, relying on § 439 (4) BGB, *Quelle* claimed compensation for the use of defective goods, amounting to € 69,97. The question arose whether the obligation to pay such compensation was in accordance with the Consumer Sales Directive.

The ECJ decided that the German legislator misinterpreted Recital 15 of the Directive.[133] The ECJ did not approve of an equivalent construction between the costs of repair and compensation for the use of goods. The ECJ stated that a consumer who receives new goods in place of defective goods is merely receiving what he was entitled to from the start and is therefore not unjustly enriched. Consequently, the compensation for use of goods is unlawful.[134]

150. Although the above outcome was predictable, the consequences of the decision were quite extensive. They concerned the question whether the German courts have power to comply with the judgment by interpreting § 439 (4) BGB in light of the Consumer Sales Directive as interpreted by the ECJ, or whether they should follow the express wording of § 439 (4) BGB.[135] As established in previous ECJ case law, when applying the rules of domestic law adopted for the purpose of transposing obligations laid down by the directives, the national court is required to consider the whole body of rules of national law and to interpret them as far as possible in light of the directive.[136] Taking that into account, the *Quelle* judgment initiates an obligation on the BGH to interpret § 439 (4) BGB in accordance with the Consumer Sales Directive. Nevertheless, the ECJ does not require the interpretation of domestic law *contra legem*. The issue was that the wording of § 439 (4) BGB seemed to be clear and was supported by jurisprudence.[137] Furthermore, Article 20 (3) of the German Basic Law states that the courts are bound by the law, and they have to follow the clear and explicit will of the legislator. The counter-argument, ultimately approved by doctrine and jurisprudence was that the principal reason for the reform of the German sales law

133 Recital 15 '*Whereas Member States may provide that any reimbursement to the consumer may be reduced to take account of the use the consumer has had of the goods since they were delivered to him; whereas the detailed arrangements whereby rescission of the contract is effected may be laid down in national law.*'

134 ECJ 17.04.2008, C-404/06, *Quelle AG v Bundesverband der Verbraucherzentralen und Verbraucherverbände*, ECR I-2713, para 41.

135 Rott 2008, p. 1123.

136 ECJ 25.10.2005, C-350/03, *Elisabeth Schulte v Deutsche Bausparkasse Badenia AG*, (2005) ECR I-9215; ECJ 4.07.2006, C-212/04, *Konstantinos Adeneler and Others v Ellinikos Organismos Galaktos* (ELOG), (2006) ECR I-6057; ECJ 10.04.1983, C-14/83, *Sabine von Colson and Elisabeth Kamann v Land Nordrhein-Westfalen* (1983) ECR I-1891; ECJ 5.10.2004, Joined Cases C-397/01 - C-401/01, *Bernhard Pfeiffer and Others v Deutsches Rotes Kreuz, Kreisverband Waldschut eV*, (2004) ECR I-8835.

137 Lorenz 2006, p. 3201, 3202.

was the correct implementation of the Consumer Sales Directive.[138] Consequently, § 439 (4) BGB must have been interpreted according to the Directive, even if that was contrary to the express wording of the paragraph. Consequently, the BGH has followed the ECJ in the judgment of 26 November 2008[139] and cured a defective implementation of the Consumer Sales Directive into German Law. The BGH held that the interpretation in light of the Directive was justified by a fact that the national legislator had clearly expressed his intention to create a national rule in conformity with the Directive. Ultimately, in case of consumer sale § 439 (4) BGB has a restrictive application.[140]

In 2008, § 474 BGB has been amended and the provision § 474 (2) BGB was introduced stating that § 439 (4) BGB applies to the contracts of sale of consumer goods under the condition that the seller cannot claim the restitution of the benefits for the use of the defective goods that he was obliged to replace or repair.[141]

151. Another two cases referred to the ECJ by the BGH and Amtsgericht Schorndorf also concerned replacement of goods provided in § 439 BGB. The ECJ decided to join the cases for adjudication due to their similarity. The first decision, *Gebr. Weber GmbH v J. Wittmer*[142] concerned delivery of defective tiles. Mr Witter ordered tiles for a sum of € 1,382.27. After having two thirds of them laid, he noticed marks which according to the expert witness were impossible to remove. The only available remedy was to replace the tiles. The cost estimated by the expert witness amounted to € 5,830.57. The price included the costs of new tiles and the costs of removal of old ones. The procedure took to the BGH which referred two questions to be answered by the ECJ. The first question concerned the interpretation of Article 3 (3) of the Consumer Sales Directive, and whether it precludes national provisions under which, in the event of a lack of conformity, the seller may refuse a remedy required by a consumer, if this remedy incurs costs, which compared to the value of the goods in conformity, would be unreasonable. The second question was whether Article 3 (2) and (3) of the Consumer Sales Directive is to be interpreted that if the non-conforming goods are replaced by the seller, he must also bear the cost of removing defective goods and installing conforming ones.[143]

152. The second case referred to the ECJ, *I. Putz v Medianess Electronics GmbH*[144] concerned the purchase of a dishwasher which following its delivery and installation appeared to be

138 Grundmann and Ochmann 2007, p. 450, 460.

139 BGH 26.11.2008, VIII ZR 200/05, BGHZ 179, 27.

140 Gebauer 2008, p. 83, 84, 86

141 Gebauer 2009, p. 84.

142 BGH 14.01.2009, VIII ZR 70/08, NJW 2009, 1660.

143 ECJ 16.06.2011, C-65/09, *Gebr. Weber GmbH v J. Wittmer and I. Putz v Medianess Electronics GmbH*, 3 C.M.L.R. 27, para 16-23.

144 AG Schorndorf 25.02.2009, 2 C 818/08, Beck RS 2009, 88603.

defective and beyond repair. The parties agreed on the replacement of the dishwasher. Ms Putz demanded that *Medianess Electronics* not only deliver a new dishwasher, but also remove the defective machine and install a new one, or pay the costs of removal and subsequent installation. The *Medianess Electronics* failed to respond to the notice sent by Ms Putz, and consequently she rescinded the contract of sale.[145] Amtsgericht Schorndorf stayed the proceedings and referred the case to the ECJ formulating very similar questions to those of the BGH in *Gebr. Weber GmbH v J. Wittmer* case.

First, the ECJ in its decision considered the seller's obligation to bear the costs of removing non-conforming goods and installing replacement goods, notwithstanding the fact that under the contract the seller was not obliged to install the goods. The court stated that if the consumer, in the event that non-conforming goods would be replaced, could not require the seller to bear the cost of removing and installing the conforming goods, the replacement would impose an additional financial burden on him that he would not have had to bear if the seller had correctly performed the original obligation. In such case, contrary to Article 3 (2) and (3) of the Consumer Sales Directive, the goods would not be replaced free of charge.[146]

The second issue considered by the ECJ regarded the possibility to refuse to bear costs of removing defective goods and installing conforming goods if the costs are disproportionate in relation to the value of the conforming goods.[147] Article 3 (3) of the Consumer Sales Directive states that '*a remedy shall be deemed disproportionate if it imposes costs on the seller, which in comparison to other available remedy are disproportionate (...)*'. In the present case there was no alternative remedy suitable to protect consumer's interests. Consequently, Article 3 (3) of the Directive must be interpreted in principle as precluding national legislation which allows the refusal to replace goods if the cost would be disproportionate to the value of conforming goods and no alternative remedy was available to protect the consumers' interests.[148]

153. From the perspective of consumer protection, the ECJ's decision must undoubtedly be welcomed. It clarified the meaning to be given to § 437 and § 439 BGB, and it emphasised that the new German law has to be read and applied in light of the Consumer Sales Directive.[149] Before the clarification given by the ECJ, it seemed that the BGB provisions

145 ECJ 16.06.2011, C-87/09, *Gebr. Weber GmbH v J. Wittmer and I. Putz v Medianess Electronics GmbH*, 3 C.M.L.R. 27, para 25, 26.

146 ECJ 16.06.2011, C-87/09, *Gebr. Weber GmbH v J. Wittmer and I. Putz v Medianess Electronics GmbH*, (2011) 3 C.M.L.R. 27, para 47-49.

147 In *Gebr. Weber GmbH v J. Wittmer* the costs of removing defective goods and delivery of new conforming goods amounted to 150% of the original price.

148 ECJ 16.06.2011, C-87/09, *Gebr. Weber GmbH v J. Wittmer and I. Putz v Medianess Electronics GmbH*, 3 C.M.L.R. 27, para 67, 73-78.

149 Rott 2004, p. 242.

could have been interpreted as allowing the seller to refuse the only remedy (in this case replacement) because of the disproportionality of costs in comparison to the value of the conforming goods. Additionally, the BGB provisions seemed to allow the seller to escape the costs of removing the defective goods and installing the replacement. The explanation provided by the ECJ confirmed that such an interpretation would be contrary to aims and objectives of the Consumer Sales Directive. The BGH revised the application of § 439 BGB and ensured its conforming to the Directive interpretation in consumer sale cases.[150] It should be noted that BGH decided differently in a C2C cases well as in B2B case.[151] Concluding, there is a split interpretation of § 439 BGB, depending whether the case in question arises from a consumer sale contract or from an ordinary contract of sale.

3.4.3.3 ADR

154. With more than 200 public and private ADR bodies it can safely be said that Germany has more ADR bodies than any other Member State.[152] They are run by professional organisations and guilds. Some ADR schemes operate at a local level, others offer national coverage.[153] Despite the numerous arbitration bodies, this type of dispute resolution is not particularly popular with individuals. Furthermore, a large number of ADR bodies focus mainly on mediation cases.[154]

Regardless of the large number of ADR bodies, their role in adjudicating consumer disputes is fairly insignificant, with exceptions in a few fields such as insurance, online travel, transport and energy.[155] One reason for ADR's slow development in consumer sale cases may be that in Germany ordinary court procedures for seeking remedies are relatively quick, efficient, predictable and cheap. As a result the German justice system produces considerably higher level decisions concerning small claims than most other European jurisdictions.[156] Interestingly, Germany is also one of a few Member States where it is said that the costs of arbitration, especially in contracts of sale of goods or services may actually be higher than the costs of an ordinary court.[157] On the other hand, arbitration has its advantages in comparison to the ordinary courts, especially when parties require confidentiality, when the special expertise of the arbitrator is required, or when it comes to international contracts.[158]

150 BGH 16.04.2013, VIII ZR 375/11, Beck RS 2013, 15325.
151 BGH 17.10.2012, VIII ZR 226/11 NJW 2013, 220.
152 Hodges, Benöhr and Creutzfeld-Banda 2012, p. 73.
153 http://ec.europa.eu/consumers/redress_cons/docs/MS_fiches_Germany.pdf (10.10.2014).
154 Hodges, Benöhr and Creutzfeld-Banda 2012, p. 74.
155 Hodges, Benöhr and Creutzfeld-Banda 2012, p. 96, 99, 100.
156 Hodges, Benöhr and Creutzfeld-Banda 2012, p. 73-75, 115.
157 In Poland and England it has been underlined that the costs of arbitration are much lower than the cost of ordinary proceedings.
158 Hodges, Benöhr and Creutzfeld-Banda 2012, p. 74.

3.4.4 Conclusions

155. In 2002 the German legislator, discharging its duty to implement the Consumer Sales Directive, enacted a new sales law. The implementation resulted in the general modernisation of the German law of obligations. A large part of the historic BGB has been changed and despite a general tendency to consider amendments with reluctance, the changes have been assessed positively.[159] It is widely acknowledged that the Consumer Sales Directive led to the most important law reform in German contract law since the entering into force of the BGB in 1900.[160] It created a solid, cohesive system of the seller's liability for defective goods and explained many existing uncertainties. It was also a huge step towards the modernisation and simplification of the German system of private law.

156. Regarding the implementation of the Consumer Sales Directive, there were several areas plagued by uncertainties. Especially issues regarding the application of remedies, specifically the interpretation of § 439 BGB needed to be clarified by the ECJ. First of all, the obligation to pay compensation for the use of goods provided in § 439 (4) BGB had to be resolved by the ECJ. It came as a shock to German jurisprudence that German law would have to be interpreted contrary to its express wording. Eventually, the BGH followed the ECJ's decisions regarding this issue.

Another two cases adjudicated by the ECJ also concerned § 439 BGB (and § 437), specifically whether the seller must bear the costs of removing non-conforming goods and installing the replacement. The ECJ has confirmed such obligation. Furthermore the question arose whether the seller can refuse replacement as the only available remedy, because of the disproportionality of costs of replacement and the value of conforming goods, to which the ECJ gave a negative reply. Once the issues of remuneration for the use and the costs of installing the replacement have been clarified, the last topic on consumer sales which causes a great deal of uncertainty regards the issues of the burden of proof concerning the existence of defects. These issues are mainly discussed in chapter 5 of this book.[161]

157. The most important characteristic of the modernised German law of obligations is that it followed the international trend not only for sales law but also for general contract law.[162] It has been said that the approach in German law has undergone a complete change from the years of de-codification to re-codification.[163] On the other hand, it has also been

159 Möllers 2002, p. 785 *et seq.*; Grundmann 2005, p. 148; Rott 2004, p. 256.
160 Schulte-Nölke 2002, p. 1.
161 Chapter 5, section 5.4.
162 Grundmann 2001, p. 244 *et seq.*; Grundmann and Uhlig 2011, p. 78.
163 Möllers 2002, p. 781.

claimed that the new sales law has been hastily drafted and that it lacks the technical precision for which the BGB was once renowned. Consequently, some of the provisions are unclear and difficult to understand.[164] Regardless of the above-mentioned criticism, it must be stated that the modernisation of the BGB has been a very important development for German private law and the Consumer Sales Directive continues to prove to be one of the most important pieces of European legislation.

3.5 CONSUMER SALE IN ENGLISH AND WELSH LAW

3.5.1 *General information*

158. This section describes several aspects of English consumer sales law. The focus will be given to topics regarding implementation of the Consumer Sales Directive. Specifically, how the implemented provisions fit into the English system of sales law and what implementation of the Directive meant for English consumers will be discussed. Furthermore, current developments and uncertainties related to the implementation and application of the Consumer Sales Directive (and implementation of the Directive on Consumer Rights) will be presented, including substantive and procedural issues of consumer protection in the area of consumer sales.

159. English law concerning the sale of goods has several main sources. The first and still the most important is the Sale of Goods Act 1979, which consolidates with additional amendments the original Sale of Goods Act of 1893.[165] The protection of consumer rights was a subject of English legislation long before any of the European initiatives.[166] It has evolved over many years, through different pieces of legislation, having its origins in domestic and EU law.[167]

The English legislator introduced the notion of consumer contracts in the context of exclusion clauses. Since 1977 there has been a concept of 'dealing as a consumer', indicating the inequality of contracting parties and requiring protection of weaker party's interests.[168] Despite a long tradition of consumer protection, the English legislator did not implement the Consumer Sales Directive on time. This might have resulted in the legal action for not fulfilling harmonisation duties. Only days before the Commission launched an action, the

164 Zimmerman 2004, p. 48, 49; Zimmermann 2005, p. 120, 121.

165 Sale of Goods Act (Amendment) 1994; Sale and Supply of Goods (Amendment) Act 1994.

166 For example: Part III of the Fair Trading Act 1973, The Unfair Contract Terms Act 1977, Timeshare Act 1992.

167 Benjamin's sale of goods 2010, nr. 1-001; Atiyah/Adams and Macqueen 2010, p. 3.

168 Macleod 2007, nr. 1.01; Brown 1999, p. 384, 385.

Consumer Sales Directive got finally implemented. As a result, the Commission's action has been withdrawn.[169]

160. At present, twelve pieces of legislation cover key consumer rights. The obligation to implement the Directive on Consumer Rights triggered so far the biggest and the most cohesive amendment process regarding consumer rights. The new project of the Consumer Rights Bill was put before Parliament on 23 January 2014.[170] The Law Commissions suggested that there was a high degree of confusion among consumers about what rights they had under consumer law.[171] Therefore, the objectives of new legislation are to clarify and simplify consumer sale and supply contracts. Until the Consumer Rights Bill is enacted, the issues of the consumer sale are mainly contained in the following legislative acts:

1. Supply of Goods (Implied Terms) Act 1973.
2. Sale of Goods Act 1979.
3. Supply of Goods and Services Act 1982.
4. Sale and Supply of Goods Act 1994.
5. Supply of Goods to Consumers Regulations 2002.
6. Unfair Contract Terms Act 1977.
7. Unfair Terms in Consumer Contracts Regulations 1999.
8. Unfair Terms in Consumer Contracts (Amendment) Regulations 2001.
9. Competition Act 1998.
10. Enterprise Act 2002.[172]

The objective of a new statute, amending the majority of above-mentioned acts and implementing the Directive on Consumer Rights, is to bring together the most important rights from all the enactments provided above, and to clarify, modernise and enhance measures to protect consumers.[173] The provisions which regulated the relationship between consumer and professional seller will be repealed. The new statute's goal is to harmonise existing legislation and provide for a single approach where appropriate.[174]

161. Finally, it should be stated that before the implementation of the Consumer Sales Directive there was no distinction between implied obligations regarding the quality of

169 Schulte-Nölke, Twigg-Flesner and Ebers 2008, p. 162.

170 The legislative process can be followed at http://services.parliament.uk/bills/2013-14/consumerrights.html (10.10.2014).

171 Law Commissions 2009.

172 BIS 2014, Consumer Rights Bill – Explanatory Notes, p. 2, 3.

173 Consumer Rights Bill: Statement on Policy Reform and Responses to Pre-Legislative Scrutiny, Presented to Parliament by the Secretary of State for Business, Innovation and Skills by Command of Her Majesty, January 2014, p. 6, 9, 10.

174 BIS 2014, Consumer Rights Bill – Explanatory Notes, p. 2, 3, 9.

the goods in consumer sales and commercial sales. The same terms have always applied for all contracts.[175] The transposition of the Directive introduced the above distinction. It is said that the distinction itself causes uncertainty and incoherence not experienced in English law before the implementation of the Consumer Sales Directive.

3.5.1.1 Method of implementation

162. There are two main ways in which a directive can be transposed into English law. The first, when there are no statutory provisions upon which to base it, is to implement the directive literally, leaving it to the court to interpret it appropriately and make sense of it.[176] The second method is to transpose and integrate a directive into an existing statutory framework, however difficult and time-consuming it might be.[177] Because there is no Civil Code, the English legislator did not have to address difficult issues such as where the implementation of Consumer Sales Directive should take place.[178] This question was very important, for example, for German and Polish legislators.

163. The Consumer Sales Directive was implemented by the Sale and Supply of Goods to Consumers Regulations 2002,[179] amending the Sale of Goods Act 1979 and the Supply of Goods and Services Act 1982. The implementation process ended when the Sale and Supply of Goods to Consumers Regulations 2002 entered into force on 31 March 2003. Other important pieces of legislation determining the content of sale contracts are contained in UCTA 1977 and UTCCR 1999. The implemented provisions apply exclusively to the consumer sale. They have no retroactive force and apply only to contracts concluded after it entered into force.[180]

The transposition of the Consumer Sales Directive was carried out by means of secondary legislation, in parallel with the existing provisions. There are several advantages of implementing directives by means of secondary legislation. First of all, they can be implemented much faster, avoiding excessive political debates and discussions, often present when European law is being transposed by acts of primary legislation. Furthermore, staying close to the wording and construction of the directive, the government minimises the risk of being accused of not properly implementing it. Having said that, this method of implementation may compromise the coherency and uniformity of the domestic legal

175 The ability to exclude or modify them has been controlled in consumer sales, e.g. Unfair Contract Terms Act 1977.

176 The problem with the interpretation of EU law is that there can be contradicting interpretations depending on the general approach of an individual judge towards EU law.

177 Bridge 2003, p. 173; Whittaker 2007, p. 402.

178 Whittaker 2007, p. 383.

179 Secondary legislative act, SI 2002/3045.

180 Woodroffe and Lowe 2013, p. 108, 109.

system.[181] It might also cause confusion since consumers receive two substantially overlapping sets of rules, yet they are not exactly the same. A similar problem was encountered for example in case of unfair terms.[182] Finally, the language of the directives is often too vague and not suitable for literal implementation and it may interfere with the wording and construction of the domestic provisions.[183] Summing up, the above presented approach to harmonisation of legislation is often a lost opportunity for real unification of legal provisions.

164. The English approach to the European legislation is of a *copy and paste* character.[184] Such approach rarely guarantees accuracy with regard to the domestic provisions. The most natural method of implementation would be modification of the Sale of Goods Act 1979 and the Supply of Goods and Services Act 1982 in light of the Directive. This would also be consistent with the government's adopted policy of legislative consolidation.[185] In recent transposition guidance it was expressly stated that '*when transposing EU law the Government will (...) whenever possible, seek to implement EU policy and legal obligations through the use of alternatives to regulations*'.[186] On the other hand, such consolidation requires a sufficient amount of time, which at that point was not available.[187]

The proposal for new Consumer Rights Bill seems to finally deal with the above-mentioned issues of implementation method. It will, to a large extent, solve the problem of overlapping provisions in the areas of both consumer sales law and unfair terms. The Consumer Rights Bill contains most of the provisions regarding the aforementioned areas of law and with minor exceptions it excludes the application of the Sale of Goods Act 1979 to the contract of sale of consumer goods.[188]

3.5.1.2 Characterisation of the implementing act

165. The Sale and Supply of Goods to Consumer Regulations 2002 implementing the Consumer Sales Directive entered into force on 31 March 2003. One year and three months later than the time allowed by the Directive and when the majority of European implementations had already entered into force. One may speculate that the English legislator was slightly reluctant to implement the Consumer Sales Directive. One of the reasons could

181 Naidoo 2011, p. 804-815; Whittaker 2007, p. 394.

182 Watterson 2001, p. 221.

183 Twigg-Flesner and Bradgate 2000, p. 3.

184 Schulte-Nölke, Twigg-Flesner and Ebers 2008, p. 163 *et seq*.

185 DTI 1999.

186 Transposition Guidance: How to implement European Directives effectively, HM Government, http://www.bis.gov.uk/assets/BISCore/better-regulation/docs/T/11-775-transposition-guidance.pdf (23.10.2014).

187 Twigg-Flesner and Bradgate 2000, p. 3.

188 BIS 2014, Consumer Rights Bill – Explanatory Notes, p. 9 (10.10.2014).

be that there was a concern that if the Directive's regime were adopted with all its limitations, the overall result could be a reduction in consumer protection.[189] The Directive has not added much to the already existing English protective provisions and well established practice.

3.5.1.3 Systematics of sales law

166. English sales law is mainly governed by the Sale of Goods Act 1979. It came into force in 1980 and it consolidates the law related to the sale of goods. It replaces the Sale of Goods Act 1893 and parts of other statutes, and applies to the whole of the United Kingdom. The Sale of Goods Act 1979 has retroactive effect, it applies to all contracts of sale made after 1 January 1894, when the Sale of Goods Act 1893 came into force.[190]

The Sale of Goods Act 1979 has been repeatedly amended,[191] also through the implementation of European consumer protection measures. It is said that implementing directives applicable throughout the European Union has had huge impact on traditional English domestic law. It can be stated that consumer sales became an independent branch of law.[192] The Sale of Goods Act 1979 applies to contracts for the sale of all types of goods,[193] unless special rules governing particular categories of goods exist, of which the sale of consumer goods is an example.

Regarding the international sale of goods, the UK has not signed the CISG unlike Germany, Poland, and the Netherlands. Therefore, it is impossible to explain particular implemented notions by their origins and existence in the CISG. For this reason, there will be no further references between the CISG and English consumer sales law.

167. The Unfair Contract Terms Act (UCTA) 1977 is indispensable for determining the content of consumer sale contracts. It provides that where the buyer is a consumer, any term restricting or excluding the scope of the obligations created by the implied terms as to description, satisfactory quality and fitness for particular purpose, or restricting or excluding the remedies available for breach of implied terms shall be ineffective.[194] The Directive requires that neither the criteria of non-conformity nor the remedies contained in the Directive should be able to be excluded or restricted directly or indirectly. This is achieved by Section 6 of the UCTA to the extent that the implied terms and the remedies for their breach reflect the conformity standard and remedies from the Directive.[195]

189 Watterson 2001, p. 197.
190 Benjamin's sale of goods 2010, nr. 1-001.
191 Sale of Goods Act (Amendment) 1994; Sale and Supply of Goods (Amendment) Act 1994.
192 Benjamin's sale of goods 2010, nr. 1-001.
193 There is an uncertainty regarding the sale of the computer software.
194 Watterson 2001, p. 208; Oughton and Willett 2002, p. 311.
195 Willet, Morgan-Taylor and Naidoo 2004, p. 116.

3.5.2 *Legislative changes as a result of the implementation of the Consumer Sales Directive*

168. Before the implementation of the Consumer Sales Directive, the law relating to the sale of goods to consumers was covered by the Sale of Goods Act 1979. Currently, as already stated, the Sale of Goods Act 1979 regulates all types of sale contracts with all types of buyers, it is just that the consumer is sometimes treated differently. Below, information relating to several topics important for the scope of the seller's liability for the delivery of non-conforming goods will be provided.

3.5.2.1 Remedies

169. Historically, in England, a buyer in case of delivery of defective goods had two options for remedies, right to reject and damages. These two options emerged from English case law and were included in the Sale of Goods Act 1893. These remedies are still applicable with a few changes in accordance with the Sale of Goods Act 1979.[196] Currently, in case of delivery of defective goods a consumer has more options. He can rely on traditional remedies as well as additional remedies introduced by the Sale and Supply of Goods to Consumer Regulations 2002 implementing the Consumer Sales Directive. The traditional (based on Sale of Goods Act 1979) remedies include:

1. Right to reject.[197]
2. Damages.[198]
3. Specific performance.[199]
4. Termination.[200]

I will focus mainly on the first remedy as it is most likely to cause practical uncertainties.

170. For the valid rejection of goods there must be a clear notice that they are not being accepted and remain at the risk of the seller.[201] Section 35 (1) of the Sale of Goods Act 1979 provides an explanation of when the buyer is deemed to have accepted the goods rendering rejection no longer possible. There are three circumstances where there will be acceptance of goods:

196 Benjamin's sale of goods 2010, nr. 1-013.
197 Section 35 (1) and 35A of the Sale of Goods Act 1979.
198 Section 51 of the Sale of Goods Act 1979.
199 Section 52 of the Sale of Goods Act 1979.
200 In case of a breach of condition, where implied terms of sections 13-15 of the Sale of Goods Act are regarded to be conditions; See: Willet, Morgan-Taylor and Naidoo 2004, p. 108; Bradgate 2004, p. 558; Apps 1994, p. 525.
201 *Graanhandel T Vink BV v European Grain & Shipping*, Ltd (1989) 2 Lloyd's Rep. 531 at 533; *Lee v York Coach* (1977) RTR 35; *Macdonald v Pollock* (2012) CSIH 12.

1. The buyer intimates acceptance.
2. The buyer performs an act inconsistent with the ownership of the seller.
3. The buyer retains the goods after the lapse of reasonable time.[202]

The right to reject is not lost when the consumer has asked or agreed to an attempted repair.[203] The interpretation of reasonable time is very important for the scope of buyer's protection. Below, several cases illustrating what constitutes reasonable time are presented.

171. Interpretation of the term reasonable time, on which validity of the right to reject depends, has often led to uncertainty. Initially, English courts tended to require the buyer to investigate goods immediately. Over the years, as goods have become more complex, the courts began to allow the buyers more time to inspect the goods.

In the case *Bernstein v Pamson Motors (Golders Green) Limited*, it was held that a reasonable time for rejecting a new car had lapsed after three weeks.[204] This decision has been criticised for too strict interpretation of reasonable time to reject the car.[205] Taking current developments in the protection of consumer interests into account, it can be stated that it is unlikely that today this case would have had a similar outcome. In another case *Clegg v Andersson T/A Nordic Marine* – expressly rejecting the approach taken in *Bernstein v Pamson Motors*, the buyer was entitled to reject a yacht six months after the time of delivery. The court has justified this relatively long period by the fact that the buyer did not receive information in relation to the problems he encountered with the goods, which he had requested continuously for around six months.[206] In *Fiat Auto Financial Services v Conelly*, the buyer was entitled to reject a car nine months after the time of delivery. There were numerous problems with the purchased vehicle, some of them occurred just after delivery and others at later stages. The seller had carried out some repairs but not all of them were successful. The court decided that the buyer did not have opportunity to assess the repairs and the state of his goods, therefore he could not have accepted them.[207]

Based on the above case law, it can be concluded that a reasonable time for rejection of goods is difficult to determine or predict. It depends on the character of goods and facts of the individual case. English law has been in the past criticised for its uncertainty regarding reasonable time.[208] It can be observed that the period permitted for a rejection

202 Willet, Morgan-Taylor and Naidoo 2004, p. 108, 109.
203 Benjamin's sale of goods 2010, nr. 14-027.
204 *Bernstein v Pamson Motors (Golders Green) Limited* (1987) 2 All ER 220.
205 Goode/McKendrick 2010, p. 355; Reynolds 2003, p. 544.
206 *Clegg v Andersson T/A Nordic Marine* (2003) EWCA Civ 320.
207 *Fiat Auto Financial Services v Conelly* (2007) SLT (Sh ct) 111; See also: *Jones v Gallagher* (2004) EVCA 10; *Truk (UK) Ltd v Tokmakidis GmbH*, (2000) 1 LL Rep 543.
208 Watterson 2001, p. 215.

has gradually been extended depending on the character of defects and steps taken by the seller to remedy the defects.

172. The Sale and Supply of Goods to Consumer Regulations 2002 introduced new remedies in cases when the goods do not conform to a contract. Generally speaking, the remedies from the Consumer Sales Directive were introduced into the Sale of Goods Act 1979 (SSGCR 2002) to serve as additional measures available to the consumers alongside traditional remedies.[209] The new remedies are located in Sections 48B and 48C of the Sales of Goods Acts 1979:

1. Repair and replacement of goods.[210]
2. Reduction of purchase price and rescission of contract.

These statutory remedies are split into two tiers. The first tier allows for a repair or replacement of goods. The buyer cannot claim any of these remedies if they are impossible or disproportionate in comparison to other statutory remedies. The remedy is disproportionate if it imposes costs on the seller which, in comparison to those imposed on him by another remedy, are unreasonable. Relevant circumstances can be taken into account such as the value which the goods would have if they conformed to the contract of sale, the significance of the lack of conformity, and whether the other remedy could be effected without significant inconvenience to the buyer.[211]

If repair and replacement are not applicable or the seller failed to perform any of them there is a second tier – rescission of contract or reduction of price.[212] In theory, the choice between the repair and replacement and between rescission and reduction of price is left to the consumer. However in practice, the choice often remains with the seller. As already explained he may refuse to carry out repair or to replace the goods on the ground that it is impossible, disproportionate or causes significant inconvenience.

173. The proposed reform provides some clarification in respect to the available remedies. In Section 20 of the proposed Consumer Rights Bill, the English legislator states that there are three types of right to reject:

1. The short-term right to reject.[213]
2. The final right to reject (rescission of contract).[214]

---

209 Bridge 2003, p. 175.

210 Section 48B of the Sale of Goods Act 1979; The repair and replacement although not regulated before the implementation of the Consumer Sales Directive might have been provided by the seller under the contract; See: Willet, Morgan-Taylor and Naidoo 2004, p. 112.

211 Section 48B (4) of the Sale of Goods Act 1979.

212 Watterson 2001, p. 210 *et seq.*

213 Section 20 of the Consumer Rights Bill.

214 Section 24 of the Consumer Rights Bill.

3. The right to reject when the seller has no right to transfer possession or no right to sell.[215]

Each of these rights entitles the consumer to reject the goods and end the contract. In order to exercise any of the above rights to reject, a consumer must clearly communicate to the seller that he is rejecting the goods and will treat the contract as at an end. The seller is obliged to give a consumer refund and the consumer must make the goods available for collection or return the goods as agreed.[216] The short-term right to reject expires after thirty days from the time of passing of ownership, delivery or the moment of installation, unless the goods are perishable and are reasonably expected to perish within a shorter period than the statutory thirty days.[217]

Apart from the above rights to reject, the consumer may also resort to the remedies having its origin in the Consumer Sales Directive: repair or replacement[218] and price reduction.[219]

174. In light of the provisions at hand, there are a number of uncertainties regarding the application of remedies for non-conforming goods. First of all there is an uncertainty regarding the interaction between traditional remedies and remedies implemented after the Consumer Sales Directive. Section 48D of the Sale of Goods Act 1979 provides only that the consumer cannot reject the goods and terminate the contract until the reasonable time allowed for a repair or replacement has passed. On the other hand, as already stated the acceptance of repair does not exclude the short-term right of rejection.

Second, there are problems with the interpretation of several terms affecting the application of available remedies. There is uncertainty as to what exactly significant inconvenience means in cases where the seller can refuse remedies chosen by the consumer. Furthermore, there are uncertainties regarding the reasonable time that must be given to the seller to carry out the repair or replacement. And finally there is reasonable time whose expiry constitutes the acceptance of goods and makes the rejection of goods no longer possible. A different question arises regarding the notion of acceptance, what role will it play when the new right of rejection from the Consumer Rights Bill enters into force.

Summing up, at this moment there are two regimes of remedies available for the consumer in case of delivery of non-conforming goods. Application of both of them depends on the determination of vague terms which may lead to the reduction of legal certainty and decrease of consumer confidence as to which remedy should be applicable in particular

215 Section 19 (4) of the Consumer Rights Bill.
216 Section 20 (7) of the Consumer Rights Bill.
217 Section 22 (4) of the Consumer Rights Bill.
218 Section 23 of the Consumer Rights Bill.
219 Section 24 of the Consumer Rights Bill.

circumstances. The amendments proposed in the Consumer Rights Bill may clarify some of the issues however, they will not solve all the problems regarding remedies.

3.5.2.2 Non-conformity

175. Another important provision introduced by the SSGCR 2002 concerns the definition of non-conformity. Section 48F states that for the purpose of the provisions introduced by the SSGCR 2002 '*goods do not conform to a contract of sale if there is, in relation to the goods, a breach of an express term of the contract or a term implied by Section 13, 14 or 15.*' The notion of non-conformity as such was not present under the Sale of Goods Act 1979. The Sale of Goods Act 1979, from 1994 onwards, uses the term satisfactory quality and fitness for purpose, while the Sale of Goods Act 1893 used term merchantable quality. The SSGCR 2002 introduced important amendments to the concept of satisfactory quality in relation to consumer contracts. The definition of non-conformity applied only when the consumer claims one of the remedies provided by sections 48B and 48C of the Sale of Goods Act 1979 that is repair, replacement, price reduction and rescission of contract.[220]

The new Consumer Rights Bills provide comprehensive provisions[221] concerning the requirements that the goods must meet to be regarded as in conformity with the contract.[222] Similarly, as under the Sale of Goods Act 1979 the notion of non-conformity with the contract seems to be used only in the context of consumer remedies: short-term rejection, repair, replacement, price reduction and final right to reject (rescission of the contract).

3.5.2.3 Limitation and the burden of proof

176. The Consumer Sales Directive contains in Article 5 (1) a two-year limitation period, which can be extended by the national legislator.[223] Regarding the claims founded on to the Sale of Goods Act 1979 a much longer period of limitation applies. Pursuant to Section 5 of the Limitation Act 1980, a consumer is entitled to claim remedies for up to six years after a breach of contract. This period applies to traditional remedies as well as new remedies. The policy was to not allow the levels of existing protection to decrease. Attention must be drawn to the fact that the accepting goods excludes the possibility of rejecting of goods, one of the remedies available to the consumer. It can therefore be stated that the traditional right to reject is available only within reasonable time and not within a six year period. The Consumer Rights Bill provides for a new remedy. A short-time rejection is available only for thirty days from the time of delivery, transfer of possession or installation.

220 Relationship between satisfactory quality and non-conformity to be found in chapter 4, para 298.

221 Sections 9-17 of the Consumer Rights Bill.

222 Section 19 (3) of the Consumer Rights Bill.

223 According to Article 5 (1) of the Consumer Sales Directive, the limitation period amounts to two years. It can be limited to one year in case of second-hand goods.

Concluding, the limitation period of six years seems to apply to all available remedies with the exception of the (short-term) right to reject.

It should be noted that in English sales law it is quite common for different general rules to apply to different remedies. For example, a provision of Article 5 (3) from the Consumer Sales Directive regarding the presumption of non-conformity applies exclusively when one relies on the statutory remedies. When a consumer wishes to make use of traditional remedies, the traditional rule on the allocation of burden of proof applies.[224] This means the consumer needs to prove that the purchased goods were not of satisfactory quality at the time of delivery.

3.5.2.4 Conclusions

177. Following the implementation of the Consumer Sales Directive there are two parallel regimes of remedies, common law traditional remedies and new statutory remedies. Both regimes use different notions and concepts and they impose a different burden of proof. To both sets of remedies the same six-year limitation period applies. Such situation may pose a risk of confusion for consumers.[225] Taking the above into account, the provisions of the Sale of Goods Act 1979 applicable to consumer sales contracts have received some criticism for being disjointed and incoherent.[226] The new statute – the Consumer Rights Bill will bring some clarity regarding the system of remedies. Under the Consumer Rights Bill the remedies are more transparent however, it seems that the issue of two systems of remedies available to the consumer will remain. The reform offers only limited solutions and in the future the application of remedies may still cause practical uncertainties.

3.5.3 Current issues regarding the law of consumer sale

178. The implementation of the Consumer Sales Directive proved to be challenging for the English legislator. After more than ten years there are still questions regarding the application of European consumer sale provisions in England and Wales. The latest developments and uncertainty regarding provisions of consumer sales law will be discussed below. The issues will be categorised into three groups. The first group concerns the issues of substantive law, second, procedural issues and the last group considers issues of arbitration in consumer cases. These developments will be presented in the context of the provisions of the Sale of Goods Act 1979 (including changes introduced by the implementation of the Consumer Sales Directive), and the proposed Consumer Rights Bill.

224 Chapter 2, para 59, 67.
225 Benjamin's sale of goods 2010, nr. 12-071.
226 Miller 2007, p. 378.

3.5.3.1 Implementation of the Directive on Consumer Rights

179. As with the Polish implementation of the Directive on Consumer Rights, the process of the implementation of the Directive in England has been used for the extensive modernisation of sales law applicable to consumer contracts.[227] On 21 January 2014, the proposal of the Consumer Rights Bill has been presented to English Parliament.[228] It included new rules on consumer sales law and the provisions of the Directive on Consumer Rights on other topics. It seems that the legislative process takes longer than expected and it appears that the English implementation will not be ready within the required time. At this moment there are consultations taking place in the House of Lords (committee stage). The next event of the legislative process is scheduled for 27 October 2014. The proposed amendments regarding the implied terms on satisfactory quality and fitness for purpose, the presumption of non-conformity, and the amendments of the consumer remedies are discussed throughout chapter 3, 4 and 5.[229]

3.5.3.2 Substantive law

180. As already stated, there are two regimes of remedies applicable in the case of the delivery of defective goods that co-exist in the English legal system.[230] This situation creates several issues for market users and practitioners. The exact interpretation of terms, such as significant inconvenience when it comes to repair and replacement, reasonable time for repair and replacement, and reasonable time for exercising right to reject, is unclear. There are different burdens of proof imposed depending on whether a consumer is claiming traditional remedies or new statutory remedies. Finally, the remedies applicable to the contracts for supply of goods and ordinary sale of goods differ, what may also cause uncertainly among the consumers.[231]

181. Both systems of remedies, traditional and statutory, from which the consumer can choose aim to equip him with proper protection in case of the delivery of defective goods. However, one of the most unclear aspects of the state of current consumer sales law is the interaction between available systems of remedies. What might cause difficulties is the fact that some general rules, such as rules on limitation apply to both regimes, while other rules, such as presumption of non-conformity apply only to new remedies. This situation may, in particular, influence the consumer's knowledge and confidence in claiming remedies.

227 BIS 2014, Consumer Rights Bill – Explanatory Notes, p. 2, 3.

228 http://www.publications.parliament.uk/pa/bills/cbill/2013-2014/0161/14161.pdf (22.10.2014).

229 See para: 160, 173, 183, 191, 302, 305, 331, 505, 508, 509, 517.

230 Law Commissions 2009, p. viii, ix, 1.

231 Twigg-Flesner and Bradgate 2000, p. 18.

Another issue concerns the question of what the buyer has to prove to obtain a particular set of remedies. Due to the applicability of the presumption of non-conformity, the consumer's burden of proof may differ depending on which remedy is being claimed. In case of traditional remedies, the consumer must prove that the goods were not of satisfactory quality or lacked fitness for a particular purpose at the time of delivery. In case of statutory remedies, the consumer must prove the existence of defects within six months from the time of delivery and the burden of proof that the goods possessed satisfactory quality at that time shifts to the seller. The above facts demonstrate how the interaction between traditional and statutory remedies proves to be challenging.

182. Furthermore, it seems that the provisions of the Consumer Sales Directive do not apply to supply contracts, those that are not ordinary sale contracts. The language and construction of the Directive throughout refers to 'seller' and 'contract of sale' which may suggest that agreements such as hire-purchase and barter are excluded from its scope of application.[232] The remedies for supplying non-conforming goods in consumer contracts other than sale are regulated in Part 1B of the Supply of Goods and Services Act 1982. Moreover the Sale of Goods Act 1979 and the Supply of Goods and Services Act 1982 are mutually exclusive.[233] This is a poor development for English law, where for more than thirty years there has been a gradual merging of sale and non-sale supply contracts.[234] The implementation of the Consumer Sales Directive introduced diversity regarding applicable remedies, which causes legal uncertainty and insecurity in relation to which remedy is applicable in particular circumstances.[235] The problem of differing remedies depending on the type of the contract will most probably be solved by the new amendments. Section 3 of the proposed Consumer Rights Bill provides that in the context of quality and remedies available to the consumers Chapter 2 of the Consumer Rights Bill applies to a sales contract, a contract for the hire of goods, a hire-purchase contract and a contract for the transfer of goods.[236]

183. Summing up legislative issues, there have been some questions regarding future consumer legislation in England, specifically what it should look like.[237] Some ideas consider whether there should be one single code for all types of sales or a separate consumer sales

232 Twigg-Flesner and Bradgate 2000, p. 6.
233 Bradgate 2004, p. 561.
234 Interestingly in case *Jones v Gallagher* (2004) EVCA 10 the court extensively considered the possibility to reject the unsatisfactorily fitted kitchen, regardless of the fact that the contract did not constitute contract of sale. It may raise confusion in respect of the law governing non-sale supply contract; See: Bradgate 2004, p. 562; Lawson 2004, p. 1134.
235 Twigg-Flesner and Bradgate 2000, p. 25.
236 Section 3 (2) of the Consumer Rights Bill.
237 Bridge 2003, p. 176.

code should be created. The second uncertainty concerns the question of how the new statutory provisions should be kept up to date.[238] Taking into account the shape of the Consumer Rights Bill it seems that the middle route has been chosen. The new statute provides for unified law in case of sales of goods, services, computer software and unfair terms. The reform is seen as a huge step forward collecting almost all provisions regarding above topics in one piece of legislation. The prognoses of success of the Consumer Rights Bill, or at least of major improvements of the consumer legislation are optimistic.

3.5.3.3 Court proceedings

184. If the consumer rejects the goods or claims other remedies for non-conforming goods and the seller refuses to refund the purchase price or refuses another remedy, the consumer is entitled to initiate court proceedings. In England, the consumer will normally start a claim in the county court by filling in a claim form.[239] Claims, where the value under litigation is lower than £ 10,000 will be allocated to the small claims track. In the majority of cases the costs of proceedings will not be awarded against the losing party.[240] Claims worth over £ 10,000 are allocated to the normal track. Unlike in the small claims track, the normal track awards costs, but sometimes the maximum amount can be limited. In particular, the winning party can claim only a fixed amount for the trial costs.[241] In case where the value of dispute is higher than £ 15,000 the winning party may be awarded a higher amount of costs, since the trial costs are not fixed and parties may claim the expenses that they have incurred respectively.

185. There is an opinion that taking court action is not what the consumer does in day-to-day practice, even stating that this is a rare event.[242] Especially when the value of a claim is low and pursuing legal right would be uneconomic.[243] In the majority of cases, the consumer together with seller is able to reach a satisfactory solution without court intervention. Furthermore, the parties may choose alternative dispute resolution procedures or trade associations, which means cutting costs of the dispute resolution and usually saving time.

3.5.3.4 ADR

186. In England, the consumer alternative dispute resolutions are relatively well developed. They operate on a sectoral basis without general unification, but come in many different

238 Brownsword and Howells 1999, p. 287.

239 Andrews 2003, p. 236; http://www.moneyclaim.gov.uk (10.10.2014).

240 Macleod 2007, p. 105.

241 The Civil Procedure Rules 1998, (1998) No. 3132 (L. 17), Part 45, amended in January 2013, entered into force in April 2014.

242 National Consumer Council 2004, p. 69.

243 Willett and Morgan-Taylor 2013, p. 388.

models and types.[244] The consumer ADR has grown in particular since the 1990s. In England, court proceedings have been expensive for any of the claim tracks for years, and the legal aid once quite extensive has been drastically reduced.[245] For some, the court proceedings in consumer cases are regarded as a last resort.[246] Furthermore, the arbitration in general has similar advantages in England as in other Member States. The main advantages are: relative speed of procedures, flexibility, low costs and privacy. On the other hand, in some situations a court of law is still more suitable to adjudicate the consumer case, for example in case of establishing precedents or interpreting legal rules.[247]

187. There are a large number of public regulatory authorities, working vertically and horizontally, whose activities might have specific assistance in helping consumers to obtain remedies.[248] For many years consumer protection has been the primary responsibility of the OFT at the national level, which was shared with sectoral regulators, whereas at the local level the responsibility for consumer protection was shared with the Trading Standards Services operated by local councils. The OFT closed on 31 March 2014 and its work and responsibilities have been passed to a number of different bodies. Regarding the duties surrounding the sale of goods and distance selling they will be taken over by the Trading Standards Institute.

The policy of encouraging the resolution of disputes can be identified in many sectors, however it emerges in a rather uncoordinated manner.[249] In May 2010 the OFT published a summary guide to consumer disputes resolution systems, which identified 95 district schemes across 35 sectors.[250] More schemes are related to consumer services than to consumer goods.[251] The distribution of ADR mechanisms shows that more than half of the schemes offer mediation.[252] The overall arbitration system in consumer cases is somewhat confusing. The bodies of alternative dispute resolution are widespread, but they are still unpopular among market users. It has been said that it would only take small steps for consumer ADR to be far more widely known and thereby offer greater benefits.[253] Taking the duty to implement the Directive on consumer ADR and Regulation on consumer ODR into account, the system of alternative dispute resolution will most likely be reformed to ensure better protection of consumer interests.[254]

244 Hodges, Benöhr and Creutzfeldt-Banda 2012, p. 253.
245 Hodges, Benöhr and Creutzfeldt-Banda 2012, p. 253.
246 OFT 2010, p. 9.
247 Macleod 2007, nr. 3.23.
248 Hodges, Benöhr and Creutzfeldt-Banda 2012, p. 258.
249 Hodges, Benöhr and Creutzfeldt-Banda 2012, p. 257, 261.
250 OFT 2010, p. 3.
251 Hodges, Benöhr and Creutzfeldt-Banda 2012, p. 258.
252 OFT 2010, p. 2.
253 Hodges, Benöhr and Creutzfeldt-Banda 2012, p. 338.
254 BIS 2014, p. 16 *et seq.*

3.5.4 *Conclusions*

188. Like other national legislators, the English legislator encountered difficulties in implementing the Consumer Sales Directive. The English legislator was late with the implementation process, but at the very last moment escaped a penalty for late transposition. Late implementation was caused by reluctance to introduce the provisions which could limit level of consumer protection which was already well established in England and Wales long before the Consumer Sales Directive was drafted.[255]

189. The Consumer Sales Directive has been implemented in a secondary legislation unlike in Poland, Germany and the Netherlands. The SSGCR 2002 to the great extent copied the provisions from the Consumer Sales Directive. There were doubts whether the new provisions would fit within the English legal system. The implementation of the Directive caused several specific problems. It was clear that England and Wales already had protective rules and if the Consumer Sales Directive would be fully transposed, the level of protection could be diminished. For this reason the legislator did not carry out a thorough analysis of the English sales system and has implemented the Directive using a *copy and paste* technique, hoping that any further issues regarding the implementation can be solved internally. The national legislator has been criticised for not trying to create a uniform system.[256] It can be concluded that the English legislation regarding the consumer sale is somewhat patchwork.[257]

190. As a result of above described approach towards implementation, the English consumers were left with two regimes of applicable remedies. To make things more complicated, some rules, such as rules on the presumption of non-conformity only apply to new statutory remedies, while other general provisions for example regarding limitation periods apply to both regimes. Taking that into consideration, one may conclude that the English system regulating consumer sales has been incoherent, or at least unclear, especially for inexperienced market users. Moreover, the costs of ordinary proceedings and legal assistance in addition to the alternative dispute resolution measures, which are far from popular among the consumers, may further impede the protection of consumers' interests.

191. The initial criticism of the state of consumer legislation has been taken seriously. On 23 January 2014 the new reform was announced and presented to Parliament. The project of new Consumer Rights Bill is set to amend majority of consumer law provisions included *inter alia* in the Sale of Goods Act 1979, the Supply of Goods and Services Act 1982, and

255 Watterson 2001, p. 197; Schulte-Nölke, Twigg-Flesner and Ebers 2008, p. 162.
256 Watterson 2001, p. 220; Twigg-Flesner and Bradgate 2000, p. 3.
257 Atiyah/Adams and Macqueen 2010, p. 3.

the Unfair Contract Terms Act 1977. Its objective is also to implement the Directive on Consumer Rights, and to bring together the most important rights from all the enactments regarding the consumer protection. The existing provisions regulating the relationship between consumer and professional seller will be repealed. The new statute's goal is to harmonise existing legislation and provide a single approach where appropriate.[258]

3.6 CONSUMER SALE IN DUTCH LAW

3.6.1 *General information*

192. This section describes several aspects of Dutch consumer sales law. The main focus will be on the implementation of the Consumer Sales Directive and its consequences for Dutch private law in general, and for consumer sales law in particular. Subsequently, current problems related to the application of consumer sales law and development of Dutch consumer sales law, including issues regarding litigation and alternative dispute resolution will be presented.

193. The Consumer Sales Directive was transposed into the Dutch Civil Code (Burgerlijk Wetboek – BW) and entered into force on 1 May 2003.[259] The provisions of the Directive are incorporated into Book 7, Title 1 of the BW[260] amending the previous provisions on sales law introduced in 1992. The Dutch legislator did not rush to implement the Consumer Sales Directive. There are more than two years between the date of enactment of the Directive (25 May 1999) and the date of the statute proposal (1 June 2001), and two years until its actual implementation (1 May 2003).[261] The criticism that the original proposal received is partly to blame for the further delays.[262] The legislator's reluctance to implement the Directive has been also caused by the conviction that the Dutch consumer sales law already provided proper rules on consumer protection. This view was shared by many scholars and practitioners.[263] For example, there have already been detailed provisions regarding the definition of a consumer sale and the notion of non-conformity. Due to the fact that the Dutch legislation already contained extensive provisions protecting consumer interests, the Consumer Sales Directive did not have such importance for Dutch law as it did for example for German law.[264] Nevertheless, it appeared that there were several

258 BIS 2014, Consumer Rights Bill – Explanatory Notes, p. 2, 3, 9.
259 Stb. 2003, 110 and Stb. 2003, 151.
260 Book 7 Bijzondere overeenkomsten, Titel 1 Koop en ruil.
261 Smits 2003, p. 3.
262 Smits 2001, p. 1047.
263 Asser/Hijma 7-I* 2013, nr. 73a; Hondius and Schelhaas, 2001, p. 327; Loos 2003, p. 161.
264 Sirks 2003, p. 275.

shortcomings in the previous Dutch sales law. Eventually, in order to meet the implementation duty, the transposition of the Consumer Sales Directive became an inevitability.[265] Starting on the 1 January 2002 up until May 2003 the Netherlands was breaching its duty to implement the Consumer Sales Directive.

3.6.1.1 Method of implementation

194. The Dutch legislator decided to implement the Directive in the Dutch Civil Code (BW) and to transpose the provisions within the already existing system of sales law. A similar approach was taken by the German legislator.[266] Taking into account that the Dutch Civil Code already contained modern protective provisions in relation to consumer sales, very few amendments were required to meet the implementation duties. From a technical point of view, the implementation did not seem to be a particularly challenging task, since as already stated only minor changes of a few provisions were needed to ensure the level of consumer protection required by the Consumer Sales Directive.[267]

3.6.1.2 Characterisation of the implementing act

195. According to Article 7:5 BW the consumer sale is defined as a contract of sale concluded between a seller acting for the purposes of his business or profession and a buyer acting for purposes not related to his business or profession. The consumer sales regard sale of movables, regardless of whether they are new or second-hand. The wording of Article 7:5 (1) BW already contained a very similar definition before implementation. The exception being that it excluded application of the consumer sales provisions to the sale of registered goods, such as planes and bigger boats bought for private use. The Consumer Sales Directive does not provide for such an exclusion. Consequently, Article 7:5 BW has been amended and from May 2003 the sale of planes and bigger boats concluded by a professional seller and person acting for the purposes not related to his business or profession is regarded as a sale of consumer goods.[268]

According to Article 1 (2) (b) of the Consumer Sales Directive sale of gas and water has been excluded from the application of consumer sales law. The Dutch legislator originally followed the European provision, however on 14 June 2004[269] it decided that the sale of electricity should be treated as a consumer sale if the remaining constituents of consumer sale are met. Article 7:5 (1) BW has been amended, stating that '*the consumer sale is meant by sale of movables (including electricity) concluded by (...)*'. Pursuant to 7:5 (3) BW, the

265 Especially taking into consideration the previous situation with the implementation of the Directive on Unfair Terms, the Dutch legislator did not want to risk penalties for non-implementation.

266 Smits 2003, p. 3; Micklitz 1999, p. 485.

267 Asser/Hijma 7-I* 2013, nr. 73a; Hondius and Schelhaas 2001, p. 327.

268 MvT *Kamerstukken* 2000-2001, 27 809 nr. 3, p. 3.

269 *Wet van 1 juli 2004 tot wijziging van de Elektriciteitswet 1998 en de Gaswet in verband met implementatie en aanscherping toezicht netbeheer*, Stb. 2004, 328-330.

sale of water delivered by pipelines is still excluded from the application of consumer sales law.

196. The provisions of the Consumer Sales Directive implemented into the BW are mandatory. Articles 7:1-38 BW cannot be excluded or diverged from to the disadvantage of consumer interests. Although the majority of the provisions protect the interests of the consumer, some of these mandatory rules are also meant to protect the interests of the seller.[270] Article 7:21 (4) and (5) BW provide that in case of delivery of defective goods no repair or replacement can be required if they are impossible or if their costs are disproportionate in comparison to any other available remedy, taking into account the value of the defect-free goods, seriousness of the defects, and whether any other remedy can be exercised without serious inconvenience to the buyer.[271] Other examples of Articles protecting seller's interests are: Article 7:24 BW – limiting general contractual liability, and 7:25 BW – providing the right to redress.

197. The first questions regarding application of the Consumer Sales Directive arose before the implementation of the Directive took place. There was uncertainty regarding the applicable law to disputes between 1 January 2002 – when the implementation should have taken place, and 1 May 2003 – when the provisions implementing the Directive actually entered into force. Bearing in mind that directives have no direct horizontal application and natural persons cannot rely on the provisions of the directive in litigation, they nonetheless have an indirect effect before the transposition into domestic law. The judges are obliged to interpret the national law in light of the directive.[272] The interpretation conforming to the directive is limited by the principle of legal certainty.[273]

In the decision of Gerechtshof Amsterdam mentioned above questions of applicable law were considered.[274] The Gerechtshof confirmed that pursuant to Article 196 (2) OBW (*Overgangswet Nieuw Burgerlijk Wetboek*) provisions on consumer sales which entered into force on 1 May 2003 do not apply to contracts concluded before that date. In this case, the parties concluded a contract of sale of a horse in September 2002. Sometime after the delivery (within six months) it became apparent that the animal did not conform to the

270 Loos 2004, p. 7, 8.

271 Other examples of Articles protecting seller's interests are Article 7:24 and 7:25 BW.

272 ECJ 27.06.2000, C-240-244/98, *Oceano v Murciano Quintero c.a.*, (2000) ECR I-04941; ECJ 28.92005, C-350/03, *Elisabeth Schulte v Deutsche Bausparkasse Badenia AG*, (2005) ECR I-9215; ECJ 4.07.2006, C-212/04, *Konstantinos Adeneler and Others v Ellinikos Organismos Galaktos* ELOG, (2006) ECR I-6057; ECJ 10.04.1983, C-14/83, *Sabine von Colson and Elisabeth Kamann v Land Nordrhein-Westfalen*, (1983) ECR I-1891; ECJ 5.10.2004, Joined Cases C-397/01 - C-401/01, *Bernhard Pfeiffer and Others v Deutsches Rotes Kreuz, Kreisverband Waldschut eV*, ECR I-8835.

273 Wissink/*diss.* 2001, p. 175 *et seq.*, 183 *et seq.*

274 Hof Amsterdam 21.12.2010, RCR 2011/36.

contract. It turned out that contrary to what the parties discussed, the horse was unfit to be insured as a dressage horse. Based on Article 196 (2) OBW, the court decided that the consumer was not entitled to benefit from the presumption of non-conformity of Article 7:18 (2) BW. It was explained that the provisions implementing the Directive apply only to the contracts concluded after 1 May 2003. Consequently, the consumer was required to prove that the purchased horse did not conform to the contract at the time of delivery.

3.6.1.3 Systematics of sales law

198. Sale is a special type of contract regulated in Book 7, title 1 of the BW.[275] The title 1 of Book 7 is comprised of 13 sections. The first three sections: general provisions, obligations of the seller and remedies for non-performance are of special importance for the purpose of this study. The remaining provisions will rarely be referred to.

Regarding the consumer sale, there are several specific regulations having its origins partially in the BW from 1992 and partially in the Consumer Sales Directive. The majority of these provisions rely on the assumption that the consumer requires additional protection because of his weaker position relative to a professional seller. Pursuant to Article 7:6 BW the consumer sales provisions are mandatory. Article 3:40 BW states that any conflicting contractual term is null and void.[276]

Some of the provisions of Book 7 apply exclusively to consumer sales contracts. For the purpose of this study, special attention will be drawn to Article 7:5 BW containing the definition of consumer sales, Article 7:6 BW providing for mandatory character of the provisions, Article 7:11 BW stating the moment of the passing of risk in case of delivery of goods by a third party and Article 7:18 BW introducing, *inter alia*, the presumption of non-conformity. Article 7:17 BW provides for the definition of non-conformity and applies to consumer sale contracts as well as to ordinary sale contracts. Finally, Article 7:23 BW provides for a duty to inform the seller about the existence of defect within reasonable time (at least two months). In cases of infringement of this Article the buyer loses the right to claim remedies.

199. On 1 January 1991 the Netherlands acceded to the CISG. It applies to international contracts of sale of movables if both parties reside in the countries – signatories to the CISG, and the rules on international private law denote law of the contracting state as the applicable law to a particular contract. The CISG applies only to the contracts concluded between professional parties and it does not apply to the consumer contracts.[277] Regardless of the above exclusion, it must be underlined that the Consumer Sales Directive was initially

275 Wessels 2010, p. 1.

276 Bijzondere overeenkomsten (Schelhaas) 2013, nr. 48.

277 Asser/Hijma 7-I* 2013, nr. 47-53.

inspired by the CISG and some of the provisions of the Directive have their origins in the Convention.[278]

3.6.2 *Legislative changes as a result of the implementation of the Consumer Sales Directive*

200. The 'old' sales law from 1838 has regulated rights and obligations regardless of the characteristics of the involved parties. There was one set of rules applicable to all contracts of sale.[279] Over the last few decades of the 20th century the focus of the development of sales law has been centred on protection of the weaker party. From the perspective of protection of the weaker party, three groups of developments having particular influence on the creation of consumer sales law can be distinguished:

1. Decision of the Hoge Raad of 13 March 1981.[280]
2. Application of the principle of reasonableness and equity (*redelijkheid en billijkheid*).
3. Duty to inform and to investigate.

For the purpose of this book the third point is the most interesting and has had the most importance for the development of consumer sales law and therefore will be briefly explained.

In all types of sale the seller's main obligation is to deliver conforming goods. According to Article 7:17 (2) BW (also before the implementation of the Directive), the goods do not conform to the contract, if taking into consideration their nature and information provided by the seller, they do not possess characteristics that the buyer was reasonably entitled to expect.[281] The question of what the buyer is entitled to expect depends on various factors.[282] To assess the extent of these expectations one must establish what an average ('medium' informed) consumer could expect from the purchased goods.[283] Any special expectations, lower or higher, can be based only on specific statements about the goods made by the seller (or the statements that he should have made). Therefore, the statements about the goods and information provided by the time of the conclusion of the contract may lead to a reasonably higher expectation of the goods than if that information had been withheld, or if certain flaws or drawbacks of the goods would have been revealed.

278 Massimo and Grundmaan 2002, p. 17 *et seq.*
279 Asser/Hijma 7-I* 2013, nr. 71.
280 HR 13.03.1981, ECLI:NL:HR:1981:AG4158, NJ 1981, 635 m.nt. CJHB (Haviltex).
281 Loos 2004, p. 45, 46.
282 Factors regarding nature of the goods, e.g. new goods, second-hand, bought on sale, luxurious goods.
283 ECJ 16.07.1998, C-210/96, *Gut Springenheide GmbH v Oberkreisdirektor des Kreises Steinfurt*, I-4657; Asser/Hijma 7-I* 2013, nr. 334.

The provisions amended in accordance with the Directive have further specified the expectations of the buyer. For example according to Article 7:17 (3) and (4) BW the consumer can expect the delivered goods to correspond to a model and that the goods match the description of the ones agreed under the contract. Furthermore, alongside any information directly provided by the seller about the product, any public statements about the characteristics of the goods made by the seller, producer or his representative, are to be taken into consideration in establishing what the consumer was entitled to expect under the contract (Article 7:18 (1) BW).[284]

On the other hand, the consumer may have certain obligations concerning the investigation of the delivered goods. First of all, according to Article 7:17 (2) BW the buyer is (to a certain extent) obliged to investigate whether the goods possess the characteristics needed for normal use. This duty emerges from the first sentence of paragraph two providing that '*the goods are not in conformity if they do not possess the characteristics which existence under the contract should/could not have been doubted by the buyer*'. If the goods do not possess the characteristics which under the contract the buyer should/could have had doubt, the lack of such characteristics does not amount to the non-conformity.[285] These duties are to be carried out at the time of sale. According to Article 7:23 BW, the buyer has a duty to inform a seller about the non-conformity within reasonable time of having discovered the defect. In consumer sale contracts two months' time is always regarded as a reasonable time, and depending on the characteristics of goods it can be longer. The duty to inform is to be carried out within a reasonable time from the time of delivery. If the buyer fails to carry out above duties he loses the right to claim remedies.[286]

The balance between the information duties lying with the seller and the duty of investigation lying with the buyer depends on the character of the parties, whether they act for the purposes related to their business and trade or whether they act in a personal capacity. The accurate interpretation of these duties ensured the protective approach to the consumer sales law even before the implementation of the Consumer Sales Directive. It was an important development in ensuring the required level of protection of the interests of the weaker party under Dutch civil law.

201. Comparing the consumer provisions introduced in 1992 with the Consumer Sales Directive, it can be observed that there are some differences related to the scope of application of the consumer sales law. The Directive applies also to the contracts for manufacture

284 Both Article 7:17 and 7:18 (1) BW further discussed in chapter 4, para 335 *et seq*.

285 Castermans and Krans 2013 (T&C Vermogensrecht), art. 7:17 BW, aant. 3; Bijzondere overeenkomsten (Schelhaas) 2013, nr. 30.

286 Castermans and Krans 2013 (T&C Vermogensrecht), art. 7:23 BW, aant. 2; Asser/Hijma 7-I* 2013, nr. 541, 542.

of consumer goods and the installation contracts.[287] Before the implementation, pursuant to Article 7:400 BW the above mentioned contracts were considered as hire for work and services contracts and fell outside the scope of protective provisions.[288] The Dutch consumer law of 1992 applied only to *stricte* sale contracts. Considering the types of contracts, the scope of application under the Directive is broader than under the Dutch consumer sales law from 1992. From the point of view of the consumer it is a positive change.

202. Generally speaking, before the implementation of the Consumer Sales Directive the state of Dutch legislation with respect to consumer protection, although quite comprehensive, was still considered insufficient. After the detailed debate it became clear that the protection provided by the Directive is wider than the protection provided under the national provisions. Consequently, the Dutch legislator could not escape the duty to implement the Directive. However, the final result of implementation and the number of amendments made in comparison to the previous system cannot be regarded as overwhelming. Some scholars were of the opinion that the Dutch provisions did provide a level of protection comparable with the Directive.[289] For example, the Dutch definition of the consumer sale introduced in 1992, set out in Article 7:5 BW was to a great extent compatible with the definition from Article 1 (2) of the Consumer Sales Directive. The exclusion provided in Article 1 (2) (b) of the Consumer Sales Directive had already been introduced in the Netherlands through Article 7:5 (3) BW.[290] Furthermore, the 'old' Article 7:17 BW contained similar aspects of non-conformity equivalent to the criteria of non-conformity of Article 2 (2) (a)-(d) of the Consumer Sales Directive. However, several criteria of non-conformity of Article 2 (2) of the Directive were missing or they were not as detailed as required by the European legislator. For this area the Dutch legislator amended the notion of non-conformity accordingly.[291] Furthermore, Article 7:18 (2) BW – introducing the presumption of non-conformity, as well as several other regulations previously not existing, have been transposed to the Dutch legal system.

3.6.3 *Current issues regarding the law of consumer sale*

203. In this sub-section current issues, developments and observations regarding the consumer sale will be presented. First, the attention will be given to the recent implementation of the Directive on Consumer Rights. The new provisions do not provide substantial changes in the field of consumer sales as such, however several topics deserve a closer look.

287 Rb Rotterdam 28.01.2009, ECLI:NL:RBROT:2009:BH3367.
288 Hondius and Schelhaas 2001, p. 329.
289 Asser/Hijma 7-I* 2013, nr. 72; Hondius and Schelhaas 2001, p. 327; Loos 2003, p. 161.
290 Smits 2003, p. 7.
291 Chapter 4, para 335-352.

Subsequently, two very important current matters will be discussed: an *ex officio* assessment of the capacity of the buyer acting as a consumer and the question of who has the burden of proof as to the existence of non-conformity. Finally, some procedural issues will be briefly presented, including the role of the *Geschillencommissie* in consumer dispute resolution.

3.6.3.1 Implementation of the Directive on Consumer Rights

204. The statute implementing the Directive on Consumer Rights[292] which entered into force on 13 June 2014 changed several elements of consumer sales law. For the purpose of this thesis, the most interesting amendments concern the definition of consumer sale and the moment of passing of risk. Amended Article 7:5 (1) BW provides for more specific regulation stating that consumer sale relates to a contract of sale of moveable concluded by the seller acting for purposes within his business, craft or profession (regardless whether through intermediary or not) and the seller, natural person, acting for the purposes not related to his business or profession.[293] Pursuant to Article 7:5 (5) BW rules on consumer sales also apply to the sale of electricity and gas as well as to the sale of heating services. Furthermore it applies to the sale of digital content not incorporated in physical form.[294] The rules regarding the passing of risk and delivery (Articles 7:9, 7:11 and 7:19a BW) are excluded from application in relation to the above-mentioned contracts.

Article 7:11 BW specifies the rules regarding the passing of risk when the goods are delivered by a third person. The moment of passing of risk will depend on whether the consumer has chosen a third person, a carrier. If not, the risk passes at the time the goods are handed to the consumer or a person designated by the consumer to receive the delivery. When the consumer did choose the carrier which has not been made available by the seller, the risk passes at the time of handing over the goods to the carrier.[295]

The new statute introduces Article 7:19a BW which contains a fixed period of time when the seller must deliver the goods to the consumer. It states that if it is not agreed otherwise, the seller shall deliver the goods to the consumer within thirty days of the conclusion of the contract. The remaining changes to Article 7:6 and 7:7 BW do not affect the topics of this research.

292 Eerste Kamer, vergaderjaar 2013-2014, 33 529 A, http://www.eerstekamer.nl/9370000/1/j9vvhwtbnzpbzzc/vjimc6ms48yi/f=y.pdf (23.10.2014).

293 Previous definition: '*consumer sale means the sale of movables, including electricity, entered into by a seller acting in the conduct of a profession or business with the buyer, natural person not acting in the conduct of profession or business.*'

294 Eerste Kamer, vergaderjaar 2013-2014, 33 529 A, p. 15.

295 Eerste Kamer, vergaderjaar 2013-2014, 33 529 A, p. 16.

3.6.3.2 Preliminary questions for the ECJ: *ex officio* application of consumer sales law and specificity of the burden of proof

205. One of the current questions on the application of consumer sales law provisions concerns the *ex officio* evaluation of whether the buyer acts in the capacity of a consumer in the sense of Article 7:5 (1) BW. In other words, whether the contract concluded between the parties amounts to a consumer sales contract, enabling the application of protective provisions. The issue is significant for the purpose of applying of Article 7:18 (2) BW altering the general rule of the burden of proof regarding the existence and moment that the non-conformity appears. In the interim ruling of 9 April 2013 the Gerechtshof Arnhem-Leeuwarden formulated and referred several questions to the ECJ regarding the *ex officio* application of Article 7 (5) BW and the specificity of proof of the existence of non-conformity.[296] In its final decision of 10 September 2013, the court provided further arguments to support the request for a preliminary ruling.[297] The court stated that the questions regard topics which have not yet been addressed by the ECJ and a uniform interpretation cannot be determined based on earlier ECJ decisions.

The case concerns the sale of a second-hand car concluded on 27 May 2008. On 26 September 2008 the car caught fire and was written off. The police decided not to start an investigation regarding the origins of the fire. Shortly after that, in May 2009, the written off car was crushed. Several days later, the owner claimed the repayment of costs of the car based on the non-conformity in the sense of Article 7:17 BW and the loss resulting from the fire. Because the car had been crushed it was no longer possible to establish the cause of the fire. The seller objected to the claim stating that the initial complaint of non-conformity had not been sent in time in the sense of Article 7:23 (1) BW. The court of first instance decided in favour of the seller, and the buyer lodged an appeal. The appeal court stated that in order to decide on this dispute, issues regarding the interpretation of the Consumer Sales Directive and the scope of the *ex officio* application of consumer law needed to be clarified.[298] The first uncertainty regards the status of a buyer. At no stage of the proceedings was it pleaded or established whether the buyer acted in the capacity of a consumer or in a professional capacity.[299] This fact determines the scope of several Articles which must be applied to resolve the dispute: 7:17 BW, 7:18:2 BW, and 7:23 (1) BW. The question of whether the buyer acted as a consumer affects the allocation of the burden of proof which has enormous significance for the outcome of this dispute, especially because

296 Hof Arnhem-Leeuwarden 09.04.2013, ECLI:NL:GHARL:2013:BZ6346.

297 Hof Arnhem-Leeuwarden 10.09.2013, ECLI:NL:GHARL:2013:6635.

298 Hof Arnhem-Leeuwarden 10.09.2013, ECLI:NL:GHARL:2013:6635, para 6.

299 Title of the written contract '*particulaire koop*' indicates the consumer sale, on the other hand when the accident occurred the buyer was going to the business meeting.

the object whose non-conformity must be established no longer existed.[300] The court also observed that there is serious uncertainty regarding the question of when the burden of proof of the existence of non-conformity can be regarded as satisfied. The first question was whether the national judge is obliged to *ex officio* investigate whether the buyer acts in the capacity of a consumer in the sense of Article 1 (2) (a) of the Consumer Sales Directive, and whether such obligation can be assumed if the proceedings file does not contain (sufficient) facts regarding the status of the buyer? Furthermore, the court asked whether the *ex officio* application should also take place in the procedure before the appeal court, where the consumer did not object to the lower court's decision regarding his status. In connection to the possible obligation of the *ex officio* investigation into the buyer's capacity, the *ex officio* application of consumer sales provisions and the legitimate grounds for such an investigation, the court asked whether Article 5 of the Consumer Sales Directive should be regarded as equal to the national provisions having the status of provisions of public order. Other uncertainties the court raised concerned the burden of proof. Namely, are the Dutch rules on the duty to inform of defects and the burden of proof regarding this duty (*stelplicht en bewijslast*) in conformity with the principle of effectiveness and the high level of consumer protection of the Consumer Sales Directive, or other provisions of the EU law? Additionally, the court referred a question of how specific the consumer's proof regarding the facts and circumstances of the origins of non-conformity must be. Is it sufficient to prove non-conformity by showing that the goods did not work properly, or is the consumer required to specifically provide which defect caused the goods to not function as sold? With regard to all these questions the court asked whether the fact that the consumer was represented before both instances of the proceedings by a professional legal counsel was significant for assessing the above circumstances.

206. On 27 November 2014 Advocate General (AG) Sharpston issued an opinion on the above case.[301] AG Sharpston shortly presents the facts, legal grounds of the case, and some procedural rules and practices, in particular regarding the passive role of the Dutch judge in the appeal proceedings.[302] Written observations were submitted by the Austrian, Belgian and Dutch Governments. The Commission presented oral submission at the hearing on 11 September 2014.[303] Interestingly, although the case may be of a considerable relevance

300 The party which is obliged to prove non-conformity (at the time of delivery) practically already lost the case, as there is no object which could be investigated. The means of evidence that are available are probably previous reports, approvals to traffic (APK), previous repairs, and witnesses.

301 Opinion of Advocate General Sharpston, 27.11.2014, *F. Faber v Autobedrijf Hazet Ochten BV*, C-497/13, to be referred to as Opinion AG Sharpston.

302 In the Dutch appeal proceedings, the judge may decide based strictly on the parties' submissions. The judge may also apply rules *ex officio*, only when they are of public order character, Opinion AG Sharpston para 25-27.

303 Opinion AG Sharpston, para 42.

for the German approach[304] to consumer sales cases, no observations have been submitted by the German Government.

As presented in paragraph 205, for the purpose of this thesis the preliminary questions that will be discussed regard the *ex officio* investigation into whether the buyer acted in the capacity of a consumer, and the scope and standard of the burden of proof of the existence of non-conformity. It should be observed that under Dutch law, most aspects of consumer protection law are not considered to be rules of public policy.[305]

Regarding the first topic, the *ex officio* investigation of the status of the buyer, AG Sharpston correctly suggested that the status of the buyer as such did not arise at first instance. The Rechtbank Arnhem took the position that in any event the buyer's duty to inform the seller of the existence of non-conformity pursuant to Article 7:23 (1) BW has not been performed on time, and consequently the buyer lost her right to remedies.[306] Furthermore, the buyer did not at any point of the proceedings state that she had contracted as a consumer. As already stated, the Gerechtshof Arhnem-Leeuwarden was prevented from establishing this fact of its own motion because the appeal court is bound by the submissions of the parties. The court may examine the particular issue *ex officio* only where the relevant laws are of public order character, which according to the court was not the case.

The Consumer Sales Directive does not contain any provisions regarding the duty of national judges at any stage to *ex officio* investigate whether the Consumer Sales Directive and protection which it offers apply to disputes before them.[307] The *ex officio* application is available when the applicable provisions are of a public order character. This evaluation is made by national legislators and judges. After the short discussion comparing the Directive on Unfair Terms and the Consumer Sales Directive in terms of the necessity of *ex officio* application in order to provide the high level of consumer protection, AG Sharpston states that this sort of assessment may have been necessary when it comes to the provisions related to the seller's non-performance. However, as confirmed by the AG Sharpston the questions of *ex officio* assessment in the present case do not arise in relation to the provisions on the performance of the contract or remedies. The question of *ex officio* application is related to the preliminary issue of the scope of the application of the Consumer Sales Directive. Consequently, according to AG Sharpston the question of the *ex officio* application cannot be answered because it arises at the general and abstract level.[308] Nevertheless, on the ground that the legislator has chosen to guarantee consumers a high degree of protection, AG Sharpston has concluded that where a buyer initiates the proceed-

304 Chapter 5, para 448.
305 Opinion AG Sharpston, para 24.
306 Opinion AG Sharpston, para 38.
307 Opinion AG Sharpston, para 55.
308 Opinion AG Sharpston, para 68.

ings for remedies based on provisions of national law applicable to (*inter alia*) consumer contracts a rule of national law cannot preclude the national court from examining whether a person is indeed a consumer within the meaning of the Consumer Sales Directive and consequently applying the national consumer protection law as interpreted in conformity with the Consumer Sales Directive.[309] This however does not mean that a national judge must, of its own motion, examine every provision of the Consumer Sales Directive, that requirement must be determined by the ECJ on a case-by-case basis.[310] Finally, AG Sharpston argues that the above answer cannot depend on whether or not the consumer has legal assistance.

Another issue of uncertainty was whether in a situation where the court established *ex officio* that the buyer was acting in a capacity of a consumer, the court must also *ex officio* apply Article 7:18 (2) BW offering the reversed burden of proof of the existence of non-conformity.[311] AG Sharpston suggests that this issue of evidence should be solved based on national procedural law, for example by remitting the case to the first instance for a further factual examination. As a result she states that the *ex officio* examination of the rule of Article 5 (3) of the Directive (and consequently Article 7:18 (2) BW) is not relevant to treat the plaintiff's appeal.[312] On the other hand, AG Sharpston underlines the importance of Article of 5 (3) of the Consumer Sales Directive for consumer protection and its mandatory character. She states that without at least partial reversal of the burden of proof, the effective execution of consumer rights in an area that is the main source of disputes with sellers would be considerably undermined.[313] For this reason, AG Sharpston suggests that the principle of effectiveness seems to require the *ex officio* application of Article 5 (3) of the Directive, provided the national court has the necessary legal and factual elements available and does not change the ambit of the dispute as defined by the parties. In so far as Article 5 (3) has the feature of rules of public order under national law, the principle of equivalence may require its *ex officio* application.

The last important issue for this book, specificity of proof (standard of proof) of the existence of non-conformity, also affects the application of Article 5 (3) of the Consumer Sales Directive. In order to benefit from it the consumer must assert that the goods delivered to him do not match the standards of quality, performance and fitness for purpose which

309 Opinion AG Sharpston, para 69, 70; Another question to the ECJ that could be formulated is whether the EU law require a national court to *ex officio* assess the status of a buyer in a circumstances when the national law appears to preclude such an examination.

310 Opinion AG Sharpston, para 71.

311 Interestingly Commission was of the view that the questions referred to the ECJ by Gerechtshof Arnhem-Leeuwarden are inadmissible, because they are purely hypothetical, as according to the Commission during the national proceedings none of the parties to the main dispute appeared to had doubts that the buyer acted in the capacity of a consumer, para 52.

312 Opinion AG Sharpston, para 78.

313 Opinion AG Sharpston, para 79.

the consumer was entitled to expect based on the contract and information provided in public statements. It is the lack of the above that the consumer must prove rather than its cause. In the present case it is insufficient for a consumer to prove only that the fire occurred. Rather, the consumer must prove why this happened and why as a result of the fire a buyer considers the delivered car defective. The consumer is not required to show that the fire was attributable to the seller. AG Sharpston suggests that in the present circumstances it may be sufficient to prove that the goods (a car) can no longer perform the function for which it was purchased without being required to identify the cause. The question of how the consumer must prove the above must be answered by applying national laws of evidence.

207. The opinion of AG Sharpston will most probably start a broader discussion on the presented topics. The questions referred to the ECJ are of crucial importance for the consumer sale cases and will without doubt influence how these cases will be resolved. The issues touching upon the *ex officio* investigation of whether the buyer acts in its capacity as a consumer, considerably affect the allocation of the burden of proof with respect to non-conformity and the application of Article 7:18 (2) BW (Article 5 (3) of the Consumer Sales Directive). The opinion of AG Sharpston underlines the importance of rules on the burden of proof for the resolution of consumer disputes, in particular in the situation where the goods sold to the consumer are no longer existent for inspection.

The affirmative answer on the referred questions would greatly increase the level of consumer protection. The question of whether such level would not be too excessive may still yet arise. Finally, the question regarding the specificity of the proof of the existence of non-conformity is very interesting from the perspective of German law and German practice dealing with the proof of the existence of defects.[314]

3.6.3.3 ADR (*de Geschillencommissie*)

208. The Netherlands is considered an arbitration-friendly jurisdiction.[315] The popularity of alternative dispute resolution in the Netherlands has its origins in the general conflict-avoiding approach to disputes.[316] A primary principle of Dutch legal doctrine is that although people should have access to justice, litigation should only be available as an *ultimum remedium*, once all alternative options have been exhausted.[317] The litigation costs are said to serve as incentives to refrain from litigation as long as there are other ways to resolve the dispute. Regarding the policy on consumer ADR in the Netherlands, the main consideration that is put forward is to provide fast, simple and cheap procedures.

314 Chapter 5, para 441-449, 460.
315 Van Hooijdonk and Eijsvoogel 2012, p. 127.
316 Tuil 2010, p. 402, 403.
317 Snijders, Klaassen and Meijer 2011, nr. 400 *et seq.*

The consumer is encouraged to use ADR instead of the court,[318] and it seems that in most of the sectors where ADR exists, it has grown to the extent that overshadowed the courts in the number of claims in consumer-business disputes.[319]

209. The alternative disputes resolution in the Netherlands is based on a well-established structure and functioning of the Consumer Complaint Commissions (the *Geschillencommissie*).[320] The *Geschillencommissie* procedure is based on the binding advice, introduced to the Dutch Civil Code in Articles 7:900-906. The binding advice is a settlement agreement where a third party rules on a dispute between parties. The parties will have agreed on this particular form of dispute resolution beforehand, either by a specific agreement or by means of general terms and conditions applicable to the contract.[321]

The ADR model is standardised nationally for almost all sectors except the financial sector.[322] There are 54 sectoral consumer commissions within the structure of the *Geschillencommissie.*[323] The approach to processing claims is sequenced, and the first stage entails the duty of the consumer to contact the professional party and to try to resolve the matters amicably, such possibility is often available throughout the process. If the negotiations fail, the consumer or the professional may initiate the complaint. In many cases the expert report is required while in other cases the document evidence is sufficient to make a decision. Initiating a complaint and obtaining binding advice precludes access to ordinary court, except for limited appeal possibilities.[324]

210. The costs of procedure are very 'consumer friendly', which is also a factor contributing to the popularity of the *Geschillencommissie.* The majority of fees range between € 25 and € 125 depending on the sector. The fee in the procedure before the commission of newly built private houses (*Garantiewoningen*) is an exception and amounts to € 320. The wining party receives the reimbursement of the registration fee, however, in general no additional costs such as advocate fees, traveling expenses, etc., can be recovered.[325]

211. In 2012 there were 5,073 complaints procedures initiated, with 51% lodged digitally. The decrease in number of cases (7,826 in 2010) were said to be a result of the economic

318 De Geschillencommissie, online http://www.wodc.nl/onderzoeksdatabase/evaluatieonderzoek-stichting-geschillencommissies-voor-consumentenzaken-sgc.aspx?cp=44&cs=6798#project-informatie (10.10.2014).
319 Hodges, Benöhr and Creutzfeld-Banda 2012, p. 133.
320 Hodges, Benöhr and Creutzfeld-Banda 2012, p. 129.
321 Asser/Hartkamp and Sieburgh 6-III* 2014, nr. 432.
322 Hodges, Benöhr and Creutzfeld-Banda 2012, p. 135.
323 De Geschillencommissie, online http://www.degeschillencommissie.nl/over-ons/over-de-organisatie (10.10.2014).
324 Hodges, Benöhr and Creutzfeld-Banda 2012, p. 141-143.
325 Hodges, Benöhr and Creutzfeld-Banda 2012, p. 143.

crises and the fact that fewer transactions have been concluded. The average duration of disputes was 3,6 months.[326] There are two main reasons for which the *Geschillencommissie* is regarded as a very successful mechanism. First of all, they settle the consumer disputes faster and cheaper than ordinary courts. Secondly, the *Geschillencommissie* provides a simple and familiar system of consumer protection. This system is supported by business and by the governmental and non-governmental consumer institutions, which encourage consumers to pursue the complaints within the structure of the *Geschillencommissie.* Furthermore, the *Geschillencommissie* has a well-established image of being an independent and fair body producing very satisfactory results. Moreover, it seems that this model of dispute resolution has developed in line with market demands, and aspires to be an even more popular body for producing legal decisions in consumer cases.[327] Summing up, the Dutch model of ADR in consumer cases could be regarded as the most successful and most effective form of alternative resolution models from the four systems discussed in this book.

One must remember that regardless of the popularity and effectiveness of ADR there is still a huge number of court decisions on the application of consumer sales. It shows that even with a very well-constructed and functioning ADR system, there are some issues[328] of such importance that the judge's intervention and judicial interpretation of legal rules are inevitable.

3.6.4 *Conclusions*

212. As with the English legislator, the Dutch legislator did not meet its implementation duties on time and also escaped a penalty for late transposition at the very last moment. The reluctance to implement the Consumer Sales Directive has been attributed to the belief that the Dutch Civil Code already contained consumer sale provisions ensuring a level of consumer protection corresponding to that required by the Directive.

From a technical point of view, the Consumer Sales Directive has not had a tremendous effect on Dutch private law. As presented, the Dutch Civil Code already provided consumer sales provisions, and the implementation required only minor changes to the existent Articles to ensure that Dutch law reflects (or in some cases exceeds) the level of protection provided in the Directive.[329] The protective provisions apply predominantly to all types of sale contracts. The emergence of a separate consumer sales law was thereby avoided.

---

326 http://www.degeschillencommissie.nl/userfiles/file/Jaarverslag%202012%20SGC.pdf (10.10.2014).
327 Hodges, Benöhr and Creutzfeld-Banda 2012, p. 164, 165.
328 For example: interpretation of non-conformity and application of the presumption of Article 7:18 BW.
329 Hondius and Schelhaas 2001, p. 336.

213. Regarding the application of the Consumer Sales Directive in the Netherlands, the issue of *ex officio* application of the provisions of the Directive has emerged. The Gerechtshof Arnhem-Leeuwarden formulated several questions which may change the role and impact of the consumer protective provisions when answered affirmatively. Furthermore, in the same case very important questions of how detailed must be the burden of proof regarding the existence of non-conformity have been raised. The ECJ's opinion on the matter is needed in order to see how consumer sales will evolve. Eventually, it will have an effect on the substantive provisions and procedural duties of the court as well as the issues of the burden of proof.

214. While one must wait until the ECJ deliver the final decision, the AG Sharpston has already presented her views on the case.[330] It must be underlined that this is the first case regarding the *ex officio* application of the buyer' capacity, *ex officio* application of the rules on the allocation of the burden of proof, and the specificity of proof regarding the existence of non-conformity. The opinion of AG Sharpston will most probably start a broader discussion on the above-mentioned complex issues. If the ECJ confirms the judges' obligation of the *ex officio* investigation as to the buyer's capacity and *ex officio* application of the presumption of non-conformity, the duty placed upon the courts regarding the activity in the process will considerably increase. The question arises how this will be received by national courts and whether the presented approach regarding the status of a consumer and the burden of proof will fit into national systems of consumer sales law, national systems of civil procedure, and systems of the burden of proof. Depending on the final decision of the ECJ the case may have a great importance for national systems of consumer sales law and the level of consumer protection.

215. Summing up, the Consumer Sales Directive hardly revolutionised Dutch private law, since the protective provisions ensuring high level of protection existed before the implementation. The number of concluded consumer sale contracts as well as amount of cases adjudicated before the *Geschillencommissie* and before ordinary courts indicate that consumer sales law has a great practical importance and that it is applied daily.

3.7 Conclusions

216. The broad attention that the Consumer Sales Directive receives is because it inserts principles into the law of Member States which concern the very core of their national

330 Opinion of AG Sharpston, 27.11.2014, *F. Faber v Autobedrijf Hazet Ochten BV*, C-497/13, presented above in para 206.

civil law systems.[331] After investigating the implementation of the Directive in four Member States, it must be underlined that the implementation acts, although in general in line with the Consumer Sales Directive, were often affected by time pressure, political interests, advisory and lobby groups and other Members States.

It can also be observed that all mentioned countries have initially used different methods of implementation. The Polish legislator adopted the Directive in a separate statute, mainly due to the time pressure related to the Polish accession to EU and reluctance of bringing before Parliament the issue of amending the Civil Code (which in Poland very often proves to be difficult and time-consuming). The new reform provides for the transposition of the consumer sale into the Civil Code and harmonisation of Polish sales law.

The German legislator has took a long time and decided to integrate the provisions on consumer sale into the BGB, leading to the overall modernisation of the law of obligations.

The English legislator has chosen a secondary act (the Regulations) to implement the Consumer Sales Directive, which in the near future will be replaced by the Consumer Rights Bill, presented to Parliament in January 2014.

Finally, the Dutch legislator reluctantly amended several provisions of the Dutch Civil Code ensuring the level of consumer protection corresponds to the one emerging from the Directive. Both Poland and England have been initially criticised for not taking the opportunity to make the system more cohesive, which arose when these two Member States implemented the Consumer Sales Directive.

217. As to the current developments and issues encountered with the application of the Consumer Sales Directive several points shall be made. In Poland there was an initial problem with exclusion of the application of the Civil Code and the consistency of sales law, which has been recently resolved by the new statute that transposes consumer sales into the Polish Civil Code and harmonises Polish sales law. Regarding the enforcement of the consumer sales law, there was, for a long time very little case law which prevented proper analysis of how consumer law is being applied in Poland. Recently there have been more decisions, however there is still uncertainty regarding the effectiveness of the Polish system of administrating justice including ordinary and alternative dispute resolution methods.

In Germany, most of the issues regarded the interpretation of § 439 BGB, which eventually required clarification from the ECJ. It triggered further questions on the scope of the interpretation of national law in order for it to conform to the Directive. Regarding the procedural developments, it seems that Germany has one of the most effective justice systems when it comes to resolving consumer cases in the ordinary proceedings. There might be however some room for improvement regarding the consumer ADR.

331 Schermaier 2003, p. 3.

In England, as in Poland there was initial criticism regarding the inconsistency of English sales law. A new statute, the Consumer Rights Bill, deals with the majority of problems of inconsistency. It clarifies and harmonises law of consumer sales. For consumers seeking justice, the ordinary proceedings are too expensive and usually not worth the time as the value under litigation is often lower than the costs. The position of the consumer in ADR is also not optimal, which in some cases might indicate that English consumers, when the negotiations with the professional seller regarding the defects fail, are left without appropriate means to challenge the seller.

The Netherlands only had to introduce several changes to ensure the required level of consumer protection in the area of consumer sales. The issues that have been encountered in the Netherlands regard the *ex officio* application of consumer sales law. Furthermore, there are uncertainties expressed in the questions referred to the ECJ regarding specificity of the proof that must be provided by the consumer to successfully show the existence of non-conformity. Finally, regarding the seeking of justice, the Netherlands has a very effective and popular system of consumer ADR.

4 Non-conformity

4.1 Introduction

218. This chapter presents information on non-conformity of the consumer goods according to the Consumer Sales Directive and its national implementations. The focus will be given to the differences between the Directive's meaning of non-conformity and its national counterparts. Furthermore, the issues of the burden of proof regarding non-conformity will be presented. Attention will be given to the questions such as who bears the burden of proof and what facts have to be proven in order to satisfy the burden of proof regarding the existence of non-conformity. Additionally, an effort will be made to explain the practical effect of the Directive's presumptions contained in Article 2 (2). Finally, how these presumptions have been implemented in the domestic systems and what their role in the allocation of the burden of proof is will also be analysed.

4.2 Non-conformity in the Consumer Sales Directive

219. Article 2 (1) of the Consumer Sales Directive provides that the seller is liable to the consumer for the delivery of non-conforming goods. It is important to precisely identify the scope of the Directive's notion of non-conformity as it determines whether the consumer is entitled to remedies set out in Article 3 of the Directive.

The notion of non-conformity is generally familiar to the legal systems of the Member States since it was primarily a product of the CISG.[1] However, not all Member States ratified the Convention.[2] According to the Directive, the goods are presumed to be in conformity if they meet the criteria set out in Article 2 (2) (a)-(d):

(a) the goods comply with the description given by the seller and possess the qualities of the goods which the seller has held out to the consumer as a sample or a model;
(b) the goods are fit for any particular purpose for which the consumer requires them, and which he made known to the seller at the time of the conclusion of contract, and which the seller has accepted;
(c) the goods are fit for the purposes for which goods of the same kind are normally used;
(d) the goods show the quality and performance which are normal for goods of the same kind and which the consumer can reasonably expect, given the nature of the goods and taking into account any public statement on the specific characteristics of goods

1 Article 35 CISG.
2 Twigg-Flesner and Bradgate 2000, p. 6.

made about them by the seller, producer or his representative, particularly in advertising or on labelling.

The compliance with the above criteria gives rise to a presumption of goods' conformity to the contract. The criteria should be regarded as cumulative.[3]

220. Due to the character of the Consumer Sales Directive and the national implementations which often do not follow the exact wording of Article 2 (2), omit some criteria of non-conformity, set others or formulate the criteria differently than in the Directive, the precise effect of Article 2 (2) remains unclear. It has been suggested that Article 2 (2) should be understood as stating that '*the goods are presumed not to be in conformity if any of the requirements from a-d are not satisfied.*'[4] The sections regarding the national implementations of the notion try to determine what the actual effect of Article 2 (2) of the Consumer Sales Directive is.

221. Recital 8 of the Consumer Sales Directive indicates that the list of criteria of conformity is not exhaustive. The goods which meet requirements of Article 2 (2) of the Directive are presumed to be in conformity with the contract and the presumption can be rebutted by the buyer. This means that the goods which do meet the requirements of Article 2 (2) may lack conformity if they do not comply with other express or implied terms of the contract. Therefore, Member States can require consumer goods to meet additional conditions in order to be regarded as conforming to the contract.[5]

222. Additionally, Article 2 (5) of the Consumer Sales Directive provides that any lack of conformity resulting from incorrect installation of the consumer goods shall be deemed to be equivalent of the lack of conformity of goods, if an installation forms part of the contract and the goods were installed by the seller or under his responsibility. This shall apply equally if a product was intended to be installed by the consumer and the incorrect installation was due to shortcomings in the instruction manual.

223. After a detailed analysis of how the above requirements have been implemented in the national laws it will be possible to deduce what is the scope of seller's liability towards the consumer. Below, the issues of non-conformity in Poland, Germany, England and Wales and the Netherlands, will be presented.

---

3 Recital 8 of the Consumer Sales Directive: '(...) *whereas the elements mentioned in the presumption are cumulative* (...).'; Reich, Micklitz, Rott and Tonner 2014, p. 174.

4 Willet, Morgan-Taylor and Naidoo 2004, p. 95.

5 Beale and Howells 1997, p. 28.

4.3 Non-conformity in Polish law

4.3.1 *Introduction*

224. This section describes the notion of non-conformity of consumer goods within the meaning of the Consumer Sales Directive and the Polish concept of non-conformity from Article 4 (2) and 4 (3) of the Consumer Sale Act and the concept of defects of Article 556 (1) of the Civil Code, with the recently enacted Article 556^1 of the Civil Code (4.3.2). Attention will be paid to the consumer's knowledge of the existence of defects and the consequences thereof (4.3.3). Finally, the character of Articles 4 (2) and (3) of the Consumer Sale Act and the issues of the burden of proof of the existence of defects will be discussed (4.3.4).

225. The notion of non-conformity has been implemented into Polish law through Article 4 (2) and 4 (3) of the Consumer Sale Act. For the purpose of consumer sales it replaced a notion of defects found in Article 556 of the Civil Code, applicable to consumer sale contracts before the implementation of the Directive.[6] The notion of non-conformity is not entirely unfamiliar to Polish law. It entered the Polish legal system after ratification of the CISG.[7] However, the implementation of the Consumer Sales Directive introduced the notion of non-conformity on a much larger scale. It applies to movables purchased for private use by a natural person from a seller acting for the purpose of his profession or business.[8] The new Consumer Rights Act repeals the notion of non-conformity and returns to traditional notion of defects.

226. Both notions, defects and non-conformity, trigger seller's liability independently of his knowledge or fault. Below, the scope of non-conformity found in Article 4 (2) and 4 (3) of the Consumer Sale Act and the definition of defects from Article 556 of the Civil Code, will be presented. It will be followed by a discussion of whether the scopes of defects and non-conformity cover the same range of occurrences. Finally, the wording of recently passed Article 556^1 of the Civil Code, amending the notion of defects, will be presented. As explained later, Article 556^1 of the Civil Code combines both, the previous and existing notion. It will apply to all contracts of sale regardless of the character of the parties.

---

6 Article 556 (1) – physical defects, Article 556 (2) – legal defects.

7 Product of the CISG which Poland is a signatory. See: Kołodziej 2006, p. 89 *et seq.*; Jezioro 2010, p. 135 *et seq.*

8 Article 1 of the Consumer Sale Act.

227. The meaning and the scope of the notion of non-conformity is very broad and not every aspect of it is relevant for this thesis. The main question is whether the scope of non-conformity covers defects within the meaning of the Civil Code applicable to ordinary contracts of sale concluded between two professionals or two consumers. In order to answer this question the comparison of the term non-conformity according to the Polish Consumer Sale Act with the one from the Consumer Sales Directive and with the amended definition of defects of Article 556^1 of the Civil Code will be made (4.3.2). The consumer's knowledge of the non-conformity and its influence on the seller's liability will be discussed (4.3.3). Subsequently, it will be investigated what effects the criteria of non-conformity have in Polish law, whether they create a presumption of (non)conformity or have a different effect. Also, general issues concerning the burden of proof of non-conformity will be discussed, for example, what facts are required to satisfy the burden of proof and who has to prove them? (4.3.4). After discussing the above presented issues and comparing the outcome with other jurisdictions, it will be possible to draw conclusions on whether the scope of non-conformity and facts necessary to prove are alike, and whether the requirements set out by the European legislator in the context of non-conformity have been met.

4.3.2 *Non-conformity: definitions*

228. One of the seller's main obligations towards consumer is to deliver conforming goods. Non-conformity of goods is a prerequisite for the seller's (obligatory) liability. This liability is characterised by an obligation to remove the reason for non-conformity and to satisfy the main obligation from Article 4 of the Consumer Sale Act.[9] In this sense, the defectiveness from the Civil Code and the non-conformity from the Consumer Sale Act are nearly identical.

4.3.2.1 Physical defects of Article 556 (1) of the Civil Code (before implementation of the Consumer Sales Directive)

229. Polish law traditionally distinguishes between two types of defects: legal and physical defects. The latter are divided into two categories: visible and hidden defects,[10] including defects whose causes originate in the product.[11] The existence of the defects raises liability

9 Żuławska/Bieniek 2007, p. 315.

10 Following Szczotka 2007, at p. 48, by visible defects I mean defects existing at the time of delivery about which a consumer could reasonably be aware if inspected the goods; by hidden defects I mean defects existing at the time of delivery about which a consumer could not reasonably be aware because its appearance at that time was impossible to reveal or it required professional inspection; the last instance is when the defects are not existent at the time of delivery, they appear at the later stage, however the internal factors causing the future defect do exist at the time of delivery.

11 Szczotka 2007, p. 48; Jezioro 2010, p. 141.

for quality of the performance.[12] According to Article 556 (1) of the Civil Code the seller is liable for a defect which decreased the market value of the goods or its suitability to use it for a purpose expressed in the contract, or implied by the circumstances in which the goods were sold.[13] Furthermore, the seller is liable if the goods do not possess the characteristics as assured by the seller or when the goods were delivered in an incomplete form.[14] The goods are incomplete when delivered without necessary (substitute) parts, required certificates, or safety warnings.[15] While the notion of non-conformity generally focusses on the buyer's expectations towards the goods, the notion of defects initially focuses on the correspondence of the quality of goods with the paid price.[16]

Generally, the defects have to be caused internally, meaning they cannot develop by simply exploiting the goods. For example, an earlier date of manufacture of a car than is stated in the documents and lower than provided level of tiles' endurance on abrasion.[17] The Polish Supreme Court stated that when the product is being used in a normal manner for this type of goods and the suitability of these goods for a common purpose decreases, it means that the product is defective.[18] Based on the presented information, supported in the following paragraphs, it can be stated that any physical defect according to the provisions of the Civil Code will be considered as non-conformity under the Consumer Sale Act. This view is broadly approved by the doctrine.[19]

4.3.2.2 Legal defects of Article 556 (2) of the Civil Code (before implementation of the Consumer Sales Directive)

230. According to Article 556 (2) of the Civil Code '*(...) the seller is liable to the buyer, if the sold goods remain property of a third party, or if a third party has other rights towards the goods against the buyer.*' The Consumer Sale Act is silent on the legal status of consumer goods. Bearing in mind that the application of Article 556 of the Civil Code is excluded in consumer sale contracts, it is unclear whether the notion of non-conformity also covers legal defects.

There are various opinions in the literature regarding this matter.[20] The first view supported by the literal interpretation of Article 2 of the Consumer Sales Directive and Article 4 of the Consumer Sale Act state that the legal defects are not covered by the non-

12 Łętowska 2004, p. 378.
13 Żuławska and Trzaskowski 2013/Kodeks Cywilny, art. 556 nr. 9, p. 64.
14 Łętowska 2004, p. 396; Żuławska/Bieniek 2005, t. 2, p. 44-46; Jezioro 2010, p. 153, 155, 156.
15 SN 28.6.1972, II CR 218/72, OSCN 1972, Nr. 12 poz. 228.
16 Żuławska and Trzaskowski/Kodeks Cywilny 2013, art. 556 nr. 9, p. 63.
17 Jezioro 2010, p. 153, 154.
18 SN 2.4.2003, I CKN 244/01.
19 Kołodziej 2006, p. 102 *et seq.*; Jezioro 2010, p. 153; Szczotka 2007, p. 50, 51; Pecyna 2003, p. 103, 104; Pisuliński 2004, p. 180.
20 Jezioro 2010, p. 160 *et seq.*; Stefanicki 2006, p. 163 *et seq.*; Habryn 2010, p. 55; Szczotka 2007, p. 50-51; Kołodziej 2006, p. 99.

conformity. Above provisions contain detailed criteria of non-conformity, and in none of these criteria is the legal status of goods mentioned.[21] However, the above argument is relatively easy to refute. There are many situations where the occurrence of legal defects directly leads to one of the criteria set out in Article 4 (2) and (3) of the Consumer Sale Act being met. For example, due to a legal defect a product is not suitable for the purpose for which it has been purchased.[22]

An argument, more difficult to refute, regards substantially different limitation periods applicable to liability for non-conformity and liability for legal defects, and a different moment when the period begins to run.[23] According to the Consumer Sale Act, the limitation period is two years from the time of the delivery of goods and is shorter than the three year period to acquire ownership (in good faith) of the stolen goods, pursuant to Article 169 of the Civil Code.[24] This may indicate that the liability for non-conformity and liability for legal defects should be regarded separately.

231. On the other hand, despite the lack of adequate provisions, it does not seem likely that the Polish legislator wanted to exclude the liability for legal defects. There are at least three reasons supporting the argument that the liability for legal defects fall within the scope of non-conformity:

1. The tradition of unity of physical and legal defects together with the correspondence between the terms: consumer goods and movables.
2. The exclusion of the application of Articles 556-581 of the Civil Code interpreted from the perspective of protection instruments, the relations between professionals and consumers are covered by new provisions to the same full extent as previously under the Civil Code therefore including legal defects.
3. The purpose and wording of the Consumer Sale Act supports the interpretation that the legal defects fall within the scope of non-conformity. Article 4 of the Consumer Sale Act contains non-exclusive criteria for conformity.[25]

In cases where the characteristics of goods were individually negotiated (paras 235-239), it is implied that the parties did not agree on the product charged by third parties' rights. Furthermore, regarding the specific purpose for which the product is being purchased, most often it would be impossible to achieve it, due to the existence of legal defects.[26] The above view has been confirmed by the Supreme Court. According to the decision of

21 Habryn 2010, p. 55; Szczotka 2007, p. 50-51; Kołodziej 2006, p. 99.

22 Szczotka 2007, p. 50, 51; Kołodziej 2006, p. 99.

23 SO Sieradz 09.10.2013, I Ca 369/13, the case regards the difference in rules regarding legal defects under the Civil Code and the Consumer Sale Act.

24 Grochowski 2013, p. 380.

25 Kołodziej 2006, p. 99-101.

26 Kołodziej 2006, p. 170 *et seq.*

3 December 2008,[27] the consumer product does not conform to the contract if the buyer may not freely use the purchased product (second-hand car) due to the existence of a legal defect (the car has been stolen and retained by the police). The legal defect may result for example, in the lack of power to dispose, which constitutes one of the criteria of non-conformity set out in Article 4 of the Consumer Sale Act. The view has been confirmed by a further decision of the Supreme Court of 14 October 2011.[28]

232. Summing up, the exclusion of the seller's liability for legal defects was being projected by the majority of scholars as against the consumer's justified expectations of the goods.[29] They regarded the lack of the seller's express liability for legal defects as a legislator's omission. Furthermore, the Supreme Court has confirmed that the legal defects in certain cases fall within the scope of non-conformity as mentioned in Article 4 (2) and (3) of the Consumer Sale Act. Taking the above into account it must be stated that under the Consumer Sales Directive the level of certainty in respect to consumer sale is lower than the level of certainty in regard to the contracts of sale governed by the Civil Code. To eliminate the uncertainties and provide complete protection, the argument *de lege ferenda* was to introduce the provision concerning the legal defects or to amend Article 1 (4) of the Act which excludes the application of the Civil Code (to allow the application of the provision regarding legal defects).[30]

The legislator has followed the concerns of the doctrine. The new reform of consumer sales provides an express liability for legal defects of consumer goods. The new statute reintroduces the application of the provision on legal defects to consumer contracts. Article 556^3 of the Civil Code states the following: '*the seller is liable towards the buyer if the sold goods belong to third party or they are charged by a third party's rights (...)*'.[31] The existing uncertainties regarding the legal defects will no longer be founded after the changes to the Civil Code enter into force.

4.3.2.3 Non-conformity of Article 4 (2) and 4 (3) of the Consumer Sale Act

233. Articles 4 (2) and 4 (3) of the Consumer Sale Act provide circumstances where the goods can be regarded as being in conformity. They are amended by the recently passed statute incorporating provisions on consumer sales into the Civil Code. Mentioned Articles will continue to determine when the goods are to be regarded to be in conformity until the Consumer Rights Act enters into force.[32] They remain applicable to the contracts

27 SN 3.12.2008, V CSK 293/08.
28 SN 14.10.2011, III CZP 50/2011.
29 Jezioro 2010, p. 160 *et seq.*; Szczotka 2007, p. 50, 51.; Stefanicki 2006, p. 163 *et seq.*; Habryn 2010, p. 55; Kołodziej 2006, p. 99.
30 SN 14.10.2011, III CZP 50/2011; Grochowski 2013, p. 381.
31 Chapter 4, para 228.
32 25 December 2014.

concluded before the entering into force of new rules. For the above reason and because the provisions in question drew a considerable amount of criticism, the detailed analysis will be presented.

Article 4 (2) of the Consumer Sale Act states that where the parties individually negotiated characteristics of goods, they are presumed to be in conformity if:
1. They match the description given by the seller.
2. They possess the characteristics of a sample or a model.
3. They are suitable for the purpose of purchase communicated by the buyer and not objected to by the seller.

Article 4 (3) of the Consumer Sale Act states that if the parties did not individually negotiate the characteristics of goods they are presumed to be in conformity provided:
1. They are suitable for normal purpose, or they possess characteristics that are normal for these types of goods.
2. They meet expectations based on any public statement regarding specific characteristics of the goods made by the seller, producer or his representative.

234. The Polish legislator did not follow the European legislator exactly. The Consumer Sale Act makes the application of particular criteria depending on whether characteristics of goods have been individually negotiated by the parties.[33] This distinction made by the Polish legislator is nowhere to be found in the Consumer Sales Directive or in any of the jurisdictions examined in this study.

Regarding the incorrect installation, the Consumer Sale Act follows the Directive and provides in Article 6 that an incorrect installation carried out by the seller or a person for whom the seller is responsible, or a buyer based on faulty instructions, constitutes non-conformity. Consequently, under the Consumer Sale Act there are three situations where consumer goods can be considered to be non-conforming:
1. In cases where the goods have been individually negotiated.
2. In cases where the goods have not been individually negotiated.
3. In cases of incorrect installation.

Below, more information on each of the above three situations will be presented. Furthermore, what facts have to be proven when establishing whether a certain type of non-conformity has occurred will be determined. The precise determination of the scope of non-conformity and analysis of the burden of proof regarding non-conformity is of particular importance for the application of the presumption of non-conformity from Article 4 (1) of the Consumer Sale Act, presented in chapter 5.

33 Schulte-Nölke, Twigg-Flesner and Ebers 2008, p. 669; Stefanicki 2006, p. 159, 160; Jezioro 2010, p. 126, 127.

I Goods individually negotiated

235. The application of a particular criterion of conformity depends on whether the characteristics of the goods have been individually negotiated or not.[34] Therefore, to identify whether delivered goods are in conformity one must first establish what exactly individual negotiations mean. For the purposes of Article 4 (2) and 4 (3) of the Consumer Sale Act it is suggested that if the buyer accepts the characteristics of the goods as given by the seller, regardless of the form of this information, the characteristics of goods were individually negotiated. Accepting standard terms may fall within the scope of meaning 'individually negotiated'.[35] The individually negotiated characteristics of goods should not be mistaken with the specification of object of contract. The specification of sale contract belongs to the *essentialia negotii* without which the legal relationship (sale contract) could not have been created. The individually negotiated characteristics in the sense of Article 4 of the Consumer Sale Act regard rather additional elements of sale contract which are not essentially important for the creation of legal relationship – *accidentalia negotii.*[36] For example, the colour of a purchased car. The individually negotiated characteristics can also be formulated as a set of features which the goods are not to possess.

Based on presented information, Article 4 of the Consumer Sale Act understands individual negotiations as the situation there is a sort of communication regarding the characteristics of the goods between the consumer and professional. Nevertheless, it seems unreasonable to assume that the consumer has individually negotiated the characteristics of goods in the situations when:

1. He had no influence of any sort over the content of the description of goods.
2. The characteristics of the goods have been determined long before the conclusion of contract, for example at the time of manufacturing the sample.[37]

236. There are several remarks regarding the particular criteria set out in Article 4 (2) of the Consumer Sale Act. It should be observed that the description, sample or model concerns the activity of the seller (or the producer). They are presented to consumer, who usually has no influence on any of them. The Consumer Sale Act does not provide the definitions of a sample or model, neither does it indicate how detailed the description of the consumer goods should be. It has been suggested that the description may concern the product as a whole or its specific characteristics. Therefore, all characteristics of the product resulting from the seller's description are binding upon the parties.[38]

34 Schulte-Nölke, Twigg-Flesner and Ebers 2008, p. 669; Stefanicki 2006, p. 159, 160; Jezioro 2010, p. 126, 127.
35 Habryn 2010, p. 51; Pecyna 2003, p. 121; Jezioro, p. 165.
36 Pecyna 2003, p. 121; Habryn 2010, p. 51.
37 Jezioro 2010, p. 166.
38 Jezioro 2010, p. 165, 166; Habryn 2010, p. 53; Pecyna 2003, p. 123.

237. A sample is generally defined as a '*part of a particular product or product as a whole which is being the object of research or comparison to the sold product taking into consideration the existence of the characteristics or functions that are expected to be present in a purchased product and which are certainly present in a sample*'.[39] In other words, it is defined as a minimum amount of the product which provides the possibility for a buyer to become familiar with the quality of product.[40] Generally, it is required that the sample is representative and authentic.[41] There are opinions that the seller is obliged to deliver the goods having the same characteristics as the demonstrated sample.[42]

When it comes to the model, it is argued that it is used purely to present some of the product's characteristics.[43] The goods must possess characteristics for which the model has been shown. The question of the remaining characteristics of the product, for which the model has not been presented but which existence at the moment of concluding the contract was definite, may arise. It seems that in such situation the seller will not be liable for a lack of these additional characteristics. The burden of proof of these circumstances will lie with the seller.[44]

Summing up, the purchased goods must possess the characteristics that a model has been shown for to the buyer. With regard to the sample, the goods must possess all of its characteristics.[45]

238. The last criterion set out in Article 4 (2) of the Consumer Sale Act considers the purpose for which the goods are being purchased. The purpose must be communicated to the seller by the consumer at the time of the conclusion of the contract. There are no doubts that in this case a consumer has real involvement in determining/negotiating characteristics of goods. It has been stated that the purpose of the goods must be established in the process of determining the content of contract. The amount of discussion and the nature of the determination of characteristics of goods may decide whether the contract has actually been concluded in the manner of an offer and acceptance or it has been concluded in the process of negotiations.[46] There is no formal requirement regarding the purpose for which the goods are being purchased however, the fact that the burden of proof of the above facts lies with the consumer may indicate the necessity of using written form, taking into account consumer interests.[47]

39 Jezioro 2010, p. 166.
40 Stefanicki 2006, p. 167.
41 Stefanicki 2006, p. 167.
42 Habryn 2010, p. 54; Stefanicki 2006, p. 167, 168; Jezioro 2010, p. 166.
43 Jezioro 2010, p. 167; Stefanicki 2006, p. 170; Jagielska 2001, p. 394.
44 Jezioro 2010, p. 169.
45 Jezioro 2010, p. 168, 169; Habryn 2010, p. 54; Stefanicki 2006, p. 170, 171.
46 Pecyna 2003, p. 130.
47 Jezioro 2010, p. 171.

239. Summing up, within the group of contracts where the characteristics of goods have been individually negotiated it is possible to distinguish between various criteria. According to Article 4 (2) of the Consumer Sale Act, the individually negotiated characteristics of goods are presumed to be in conformity when they match the description, sample or model provided by the seller. Next to that, the goods are presumed to be in conformity if they are suitable for the purpose determined by the buyer at the time of the conclusion of contract.[48] It can be stated that in the first situation the activities discussed above are the responsibility of the seller, while the latter regards the consumer's activities. In both situations it is necessary that the buyer accepts the description, sample or model and that the seller does not object to the purpose for which the goods are being purchased. Taking the above into consideration, not all the criteria reflect the meaning of characteristics individually negotiated. Next to introduction of the presented distinction in the first place, this has been one of the biggest criticisms of Article 4 (2) of the Consumer Sale Act.[49]

II Goods not individually negotiated

240. Article 4 (3) of the Consumer Sale Act concerns the criteria of conformity in cases where the characteristics of the goods have not been individually negotiated. It states that such goods are presumed to be in conformity if:

1. They are suitable for the normal purpose for which these types of goods are normally used.
2. They possess the characteristics normal for these types of goods.
3. The characteristics of goods match the characteristics and expectations of these types of goods based on the public statements, advertisements or labelling provided by the seller, producer or his representative.

The listed criteria cover the majority of consumer sale contracts which usually regard the standardised manufactured products. In these contracts individual negotiations do not take place.[50] Consequently, 'the goods of this type' becomes reference point to determine whether the goods are in conformity with the contract. This reference point has a very broad scope. It certainly covers the identical products, but is not limited to them. Some commentators argue that there should be additional factors such as functionality, and other characteristics of products in order to narrow the scope.[51]

241. The first two criteria in Article 4 (3) of the Consumer Sale Act do not seem to cause much uncertainty provided there is a normal purpose for the goods and their normal

48 And not objected to by the seller.
49 Stefanicki 2006, p. 180 *et seq.*; Jezioro 2010, p. 171.
50 SR Wrocław-Fabryczna 23.01.2013, XI C 695/12.
51 Stefanicki 2006, p. 160 *et seq.*

characteristics are established. The application of this criterion is an assessment of whether the product is suitable for normal use for this type of goods. Normal use means all ways of use which can be expected from the point of view of a reasonable buyer.[52] It is an objective notion and personal opinion of the consumer is irrelevant. In establishing the normal use of a product the technical data may be taken into account.[53] To be suitable for normal purpose, the goods delivered to the consumer must be complete. Finally, in establishing the normal use of goods other circumstances such as aesthetic requirements[54] and durability[55] may be taken into account.

242. The third criterion of Article 4 (3) of the Consumer Sale Act regards public statements and buyer's reasonable expectations of the goods, based on these statements.[56] There is some uncertainty as to the precise meaning of public statements. It is agreed that such statements must be made specifically about characteristics of the goods. To be regarded as public they must be accessible to an indefinite number of recipients.[57] For example, TV/press advertisements, leaflets, information on the packages, including information about expiry date.[58] The statements about the product may target one particular group of recipients, for example, mothers of small children, or consumers residing in a particular geographical region.[59]

Article 5 of the Consumer Sale Act provides that the seller is not liable for the content of public statements on the characteristics of goods if he can prove that:

1. He was not aware of the content, or reasonably assessing he could not have been aware of it.
2. The public statements could not have influenced the consumer's decision to enter into the contract.
3. The public statements have been rectified before the contract has been concluded.

The first defence requires negative proof regarding the state of the sellers' knowledge at the time of the conclusion of the contract. The second regards rather general objective rules of the market and not an individual consumer decision. The last one depends on whether the public statement has been rectified before the conclusion of contract. Such

52 Jagielska 2001, p. 388.
53 The technical data may also be regarded as a description of the product.
54 Łętowska 2004, p. 395.
55 Habryn 2010, p. 71, 72.
56 Pecyna 2003, p. 132; Koszowski 2013 (SIT), p. 115, 119.
57 Jezioro 2010, p. 179, 179; Pecyna 2003, p. 138; Stefanicki 2006, p. 185.
58 Pecyna 2003, p. 138.
59 Stefanicki 2006, p. 185; Koszowski (SIT) 2013, p. 116, 117.

rectification should correspond to an original statement and should correct it in part or in whole.[60] It is sufficient to invoke one of above presented defences.

III *Incorrect installation*

243. The seller is liable for installation and starting up the product as well as for its further proper functioning. Incorrect installation is understood as a lack of a final result. In other words, the lack of the ability to use the product caused by the incorrect installation, which deprives consumers of using the purchased goods in a way he expected or in the way it is normally used, constitutes a non-conformity.[61]

Article 6 of the Consumer Sale Act provides further regulation regarding non-conformity of consumer goods, and complements the rules of Article 4 (2) and (3). It states that the incorrect installation amounts to non-conformity if it has been performed within a sale contract:

1. By the seller or other person for which the seller is responsible.
2. By the consumer when using incorrect manuals provided by the seller or the producer.

Article 6 of the Consumer Sale Act states that the manuals should be handed to the consumer at the time of sale. However, this should be understood as the time of delivery, since between the moment of the conclusion of contract of sale and the moment of the delivery of goods the seller can replace incorrect or missing instructions.[62]

4.3.2.4 Defects of Article 556^1 of the Civil Code (amendments introduced in 2014)

244. Article 556^1 of the recently amended Polish Civil Code in the area of (consumer) sale provides a uniform definition of defects. Article 556^3 of the Civil Code provides a definition of legal defects applicable to all contracts of sale. They formally repeal the notion of non-conformity. In practice, the new definition of defects includes the current notion of non-conformity and clarifies the criteria establishing defective goods. As already stated, the notion of defects had already been in use in Polish civil law and it had a well-established application and settled interpretation which had evolved in accordance with market requirements and trade developments. The provision of Article 556^1 is therefore not new as such, but rather returns to the pre-implementation reality.

Article 556^1 (1) of the Civil Code states that (physical) defects occur when the delivered goods do not conform to the contract. In particular the goods do not conform when:

60 Pecyna 2003, p. 148 *et seq.*

61 Stefanicki 2006, p. 222 *et seq.*

62 Jezioro 2010, p. 190.

1. They do not possess characteristics which they should have possessed based on the purpose agreed under the contract or flowing from the circumstances and use of the goods.
2. They do not possess characteristics whose existence the seller assured the buyer of, including characteristics of a sample and model shown to the buyer.
3. They are not suitable for the purpose of which the buyer informed the seller, and which was not objected to.
4. They are incomplete.[63]

The new definition eliminates the division on the characteristics individually negotiated and characteristics not individually negotiated introduced by the Consumer Sale Act which simplifies and clarifies the determination of the state of the goods.[64] It harmonises the notion of defects for all types of sales contracts, what increases legal certainty and improves the cohesiveness of the legal system.

245. Article 556^1 (2) provides that '*in the consumer contracts, the public assertions of the producer or his representative or any other person who puts the product into circulation within his/her profession must be treated equally with the assertions of the seller.*' The legislator refers to assertions of the seller mentioned in Article 556^1 (1) (nr. 2). The purpose of this provision is to regulate the liability of a seller for public statements made by the producer or his representative. The wording however, does not clearly indicate this purpose. Furthermore, amended provisions do not precisely describe which assertions (statements) of what content are meant by Article 556^1 (1) and 556^1 (2) and what their consequences are for the determination of defects.

The new Article 557 (3) of the Civil Code includes the seller's defences in a situation where the goods do not possess the characteristics ensured by public statements: the seller was not aware of them and could not have reasonably been aware of them, the statements could not have influenced the consumer's decision to purchase the goods or they were corrected before the conclusion of the contract. Consequently, the matter of public statements is regulated in three articles of the Civil Code: 556^1 (1) (nr. 2), 556^1 (2), and 557 (3). In comparison to Article 4 (3) of the Consumer Sale Act,[65] the enacted provisions on public statements are less clear and may raise uncertainty over the substance and purpose of these articles.

63 New Article 556^1 of the Civil Code.

64 Under the Consumer Sale Act a particular criterion of non-conformity depended on whether the characteristics were individually negotiated or not.

65 In respect to the public statements.

246. Article 556^1 (3) of the Civil Code provides that the goods are defective if they are incorrectly installed and the installation has been carried out by the seller, a third person for whom the seller is responsible, or a buyer who installed the goods in accordance with the instructions provided to him by the seller (or producer). It seems that the new provision on incorrect installation may broaden the scope of protection as it does not state that the instructions provided to the buyer must be incorrect. However, in the statute's justification it has not been explained whether that was in fact the objective of the legislator.

247. As already stated, the new statute clarifies the issue of seller's liability for legal defects. Article 556^3 states that '*the seller is liable towards the buyer if the sold goods belong to the third party or they are charged by a third party's rights, also when the limitations and restrictions in using or disposing the goods stem from the decision of an appropriate public authority.*' The proposed provision expressly prescribes seller's liability for legal defects. When the statute enters into force (25 December 2014) the current uncertainty regarding the scope of liability in this respect will disappear.

4.3.2.5 Conclusions

248. Based on what has been presented, with respect to the notion of non-conformity the Polish legislator did not follow the structure of the Consumer Sales Directive and has chosen a different method for regulating the matter of non-conformity. Article 4 of the Consumer Sale Act provides a division of the consumer contracts on the contracts where characteristics of the goods were individually negotiated and the contracts where these characteristics were not individually negotiated. The introduced division proved to be inconsistent, especially in relation to the first group regarding the goods individually negotiated.[66] The Consumer Sale Act as with the Consumer Sales Directive has given priority to the individually agreed terms before the general criteria.[67] When it comes to the incorrect installation, Article 6 of the Consumer Sale Act states that it shall be considered as non-conformity regardless of whether the characteristics have been negotiated individually or not.

249. The Consumer Sale Act makes a reference to second-hand goods in relation to the limitation period. Including such goods into the scope of protection is in line with the principle that every product must be fit for the purpose for which it has been purchased.[68] The purchase of second-hand goods often comes with a risk that the goods will not meet

66 As explained in chapter 4, para 235-239; See also Koszowski 2013, p. 15.
67 Jezioro 2010, p. 135 *et seq.*
68 Stefanicki 2006, p. 180, 181.

the buyer's expectations, which should therefore remain moderate taking into account the character of these goods.

250. The new reform of the consumer sale provides a new definition of defects which replaces the definition of non-conformity and applies to all contracts of sale. The new definition of defects incorporates the notion of non-conformity and uses criteria such as unsuitability for the agreed or common purpose or lack of characteristics that are normal for the goods in question in order to explain the existence of defects. It harmonises the rules regarding contract of sale regardless of the character of the contracting parties. One may observe that creating a uniform definition for commercial, consumer and private sale contracts improves the level of legal certainty. There are also minor drawbacks of the introduced definition. In particular provisions on liability for the content of public statements are formulated less clearly than it was done under the Consumer Sale Act or as it appears in Article 2 (2) (d) of the Consumer Sales Directive. Nevertheless, the new changes must be assessed positively.

4.3.3 *Buyer's knowledge of the non-conformity*

251. The seller's liability under the Consumer Sale Act is independent from his fault or the fault of the undertakings hired to perform his obligation.[69] The liability may be excluded only in the situations provided in the statute. According to Article 7 of the Consumer Sale Act the seller is not liable for non-conformity of goods when:

1. The consumer knew or reasonably must have known of the non-conformity.
2. Non-conformity results from the defective materials supplied by the consumer.

The consumer's knowledge of the non-conformity, or unjustified lack of knowledge thereof, plays an important role in limiting seller's liability. Below, the most important issues regarding the consequences of knowledge or unjustified lack of knowledge regarding the non-conformity of goods will be presented. Similarly, the question of defective materials delivered by the buyer to manufacture the goods will be discussed.

252. Article 7 of the Consumer Sale Act implements Article 2 (3) of the Consumer Sales Directive[70] which is founded on the assumption that the characteristics and quality standards of goods are determined by the parties. The shortcomings of goods of which the

69 Kołodziej 2010, p. 195.

70 Article 2 (3) Consumer Sales Directive '*There shall be deemed not to be a lack of conformity if, at the time the contract was concluded, the consumer was aware, or could not have reasonably been unaware of the lack of conformity, or if the lack of conformity had its origins in materials supplied by the consumer.*'

consumer was aware at the time of the conclusion of the contract must be considered as being in conformity.[71]

253. Comparing Article 2 (3) of the Directive and Article 7 of the Consumer Sale Act, it can be observed that the consequences of the consumer's knowledge about the non-conformity are formulated slightly differently. Where under the Directive, there shall be deemed a lack of non-conformity in case of the consumer's knowledge, Article 7 of the Consumer Sale Act provides that the consumer's knowledge of the non-conformity excludes the seller's liability. Article 7 of the Consumer Sale Act is founded on the assumption that if at the time of the conclusion of the contract the consumer knows about the non-conformity and decides to enter the contract regardless, then he consents to these particular characteristics of the goods. The price he pays for those goods is therefore an equivalent of goods in this particular state.[72] Comparing the foundations of Article 2 (3) of the Consumer Sales Directive and Article 7 of the Consumer Sale Act it is clear that they are similar. Therefore, different wording of the consequences does not have any further significance.

The same applies to the defectiveness of materials delivered by the consumer to manufacture the goods. The Consumer Sales Directive in Article 2 (3) provides that if the lack of conformity of goods had its origins in the materials supplied by the consumer then there is deemed to be no lack of conformity. The Consumer Sale Act in Article 7 states that the liability of the seller for non-conformity caused by the defectiveness of the materials supplied by the consumer is excluded.

254. It seems that there is one situation where the consumer's knowledge about the non-conformity will not result in the exclusion of liability. Namely, when the consumer, at the time of the conclusion of the contract, knows about non-conformity and states that he does not accept the goods. Even though he accepts the delivery, he immediately informs the seller that he will make use of his rights regarding non-conforming goods. In such a situation the seller's liability will not be excluded.[73]

255. In the recent reform of the Polish consumer sales law and redrafting of the Civil Code, the matter of the exclusion of the seller's liability as a result of the consumer's knowledge of the defects at the time of the contract's conclusion has been regulated in Article 557 (1) without any major changes. Although it omits the part regarding defective materials, it seems that a proper interpretation of new provisions implementing the Consumer Sales

71 Massimo Bianca and Grundmann 2002, p. 144.
72 Żuławska/Bieniek 2007, p. 55.
73 Jezioro 2010, p. 196.

Directive will ensure that the seller's liability will also be excluded in the above-mentioned circumstances.

4.3.4 *Burden of proof of the non-conformity*

256. This section presents the topics regarding burden of proof of the existence of non-conformity. The attention will be given to the issue of who has the burden of proof regarding the facts constituting non-conformity, stated in Article 4 (2) and (3) of the Consumer Sale Act, and the facts constituting defects found in Article 556^1 of the Civil Code.[74] The matter is important because whether the buyer will be able to make use of the presumption of conformity of Article 4 (1) of the Consumer Sale Act (Article 556^2 of the Civil Code) depends on the non-conformity being proven. More importantly from the successful proof of the existence of non-conformity depends whether the consumer will be able to receive remedies for the delivery of defective goods.

257. Article 2 (2) of the Consumer Sales Directive states that the consumer goods are presumed to be in conformity with the contract if they meet criteria listed under the letters (a)-(d). The question arises how the wording of Article 2 (2) (a)-(d) must be understood and what is its actual influence on the position of the parties. According to the Consumer Sale Act, two sets of presumptions can be formulated:

1. Under Article 4 (2) the presumption of conformity of goods individually negotiated.
2. Under Article 4 (3) the presumption of conformity of goods not individually negotiated.

Article 4 (2) and (3) of the Consumer Sale Act *verbatim* introduced a presumption of conformity of consumer goods. In theory, to rebut the presumption, the consumer has to prove the lack of at least one criterion provided in Article 4 (2) or 4 (3). Accordingly, when the purchased product is not suitable for the agreed purpose, but at the same time it matches the description and sample, the presumption of conformity of Article 4 (3) should be considered as rebutted. The seller bears the burden of proof of the existence of all criteria, or following above example, suitability for the purpose expressed by the buyer.[75] That means the criteria of conformity must be considered as cumulative.

In the Polish literature, there is a debate whether Article 4 (2) and (3) of the Consumer Sale Act factually provides for presumptions[76] or rather Article 4 (2) and (3) simply contains

74 After the reformed provisions enter into force these facts are stated in Article 556^1 of the Civil Code.

75 Jezioro 2010, p. 164.

76 Radwański 2006, p. 116; Habryn 2010, p. 42-44; Pisuliński 2004, p. 176-178; Koszowski 2012, p. 36 *et seq.*

definition of non-conformity.[77] Below, I will briefly present the most important arguments regarding this matter.

258. Koszowski claims that the criteria of Article 4 (2) and (3) constitute rebuttable presumptions of conformity.[78] He states that the initial burden of proof regarding the (non)existence of (non)conformity lies with the seller, who may make use of the presumptions provided in Article 4 (2) and 4 (3) of the Consumer Sale Act. According to Koszowski, the buyer can rebut the presumption by providing the proof to the contrary (defeating the criteria by showing that one of them does not exist). The exception would apply to situations of incorrect installation, legal defects and lack of fitness for agreed purpose. Koszowski states that above presented view is supported by procedural factors, legislative principles and characteristics of the Consumer Sales Directive and Polish Consumer Sale Act.[79] The above interpretation of Article 4 (2) and (3) is not shared by many scholars.

Pisuliński argues that Article 4 (2) and (3) of the Consumer Sale Act provide the definition of conformity. Based on criteria of this conformity, serving as a basis for the presumption, it can be deduced when the goods are not in conformity.[80]

259. Radwański in the Green Paper on the Polish Civil Code denied the possibility of presumptions of Article 4 (2) and (3) of the Consumer Sale Act.[81] He underlines the problematic nature of Article 2 (2) of the Consumer Sales Directive and points out contradictions between Article 2 (2) and Article 5 (3) of the Directive. According to Article 2 (2) (a), the seller has the burden of proving that the goods match those shown to the consumer as a sample. Having said that, according to Article 5 (3) of the Directive, after a period of six months, the consumer has to prove that the goods were not in conformity (also with regard to the sample). According to the author, this contradiction in the Directive excludes the possibility of considering Article 4 (2) and (3) as a containing presumption of conformity.[82]

Habryn agrees with the above view. She states that Article 4 (2) and 4 (3) of the Civil Code do not meet the requirements set out by Polish law of giving them the status of a presumption.[83] For the seller to be able to use the presumption he would have to show all criteria provided by the legislator. In practice, that would amount to supplying positive evidence that the goods are in conformity.[84] Furthermore, according to Gajek, introducing

77 Gajek 2003, p. 208; Pecyna 2003, p. 98.
78 Koszowski 2012, p. 36 *et seq*.
79 Koszowski 2012, p. 39, 45.
80 Pisuliński 2004, p. 176, 177.
81 Radwański 2006, p. 116.
82 Radwański 2006, p. 116.
83 Chapter 2, para 35, 36.
84 Habryn 2010, p. 42-44.

the presumption of conformity has in fact no significance for the legal position of the consumer in pursuing his rights before a court.[85]

It has been agreed about the character of Article 4 (2) and (3) that included there criteria constitute definition of non-conformity and not a presumption of conformity. This definition cannot be considered as statutory in character, primarily because of its incompleteness.[86] The parties can modify and add other criteria of non-conformity. In general the parties' agreements should be taken into account in the first place. For a complete definition of conformity the interpretation of the entire agreement is needed.

260. Based on what has been said, the opinion that, for the purpose of consumer-seller relations, Article 4 (2) and 4 (3) should be treated as a definition of non-conformity rather than providing a presumption is convincing. As stated above, the definition of non-conformity flowing from Article 4 (2) and (3) cannot be regarded as a statutory one. There have been attempts to create a complete definition of non-conformity. One of such attempts has been presented in the commentary to the Polish Consumer Sale Act.[87] On the ground of Article 4 (2) and (3) and Article 6, it can be concluded that the goods are not in conformity when they:

1. Do not match the description given by the seller and do not possess characteristics of the sample or model shown to the consumer.
2. Do not fit the purpose determined by the consumer and not objected to by the seller at the time of the conclusion of the contract.
3. Do not fit the purpose for which this type of goods is normally used or do not have the normal characteristics of this type of goods.
4. Do not match the expectations regarding the goods of this type, based on public statements made by the seller, producer or his representative, or the distributor.
5. Have not been correctly installed, if the installation has been carried out by the seller, or the third party for whom the seller is responsible, or by the consumer using the instructions handed to him at the time of sale (delivery).
6. Do not possess other characteristics agreed under the contract or based on practice, good faith and fair dealing.[88]

261. In light of the amended definition of defects which will replace the definition of non-conformity, there are no grounds for stating that there are any presumptions of (non)conformity. Article 556^1 expressly states that a physical defect occurs when the delivered goods do not conform to the contract. Several circumstances where goods do

85 Gajek 2003, p. 208 *et seq.*
86 Kołodziej 2006, p. 97, 137; Gajek 2003 p. 208; Habryn 2010, p. 42-44.
87 Jezioro 2010, p. 133, 134.
88 Jezioro 2010, p. 134.

not conform to the contract are given as an example. As with the definition of non-conformity of Article 4 (2) and (3) of the Consumer Sale Act, the proposed definition of defects of Article 556^1 of the Civil Code is incomplete, as the given circumstances are only exemplary. To assess the existence of defects other factors may be taken into account, including the content of the parties' agreement.

262. When analysing issues of the burden of proof one should always start with the general rule of Article 6 of the Civil Code.[89] In general, there might be possible alterations resulting from the application of particular presumptions set out by the legislator. Their existence in Polish law in the context of non-conformity was denied by legal scholars.[90] According to Article 6 of the Civil Code, the primary burden of proving non-conformity (defects) of goods lies with the buyer. The Supreme Court has however expressed that it is not possible to generally state that in accordance with Article 6 of the Civil Code, the burden of proving the existence of defects always lies with the buyer.[91] The issues of the burden of proof regarding the exclusion of liability for delivery of defective goods requires a flexible approach, where eventually the facts of particular case must be taken into account.

In an ordinary sale the buyer would have to prove that the goods were not in conformity at the time of delivery in order to be able to pursue and enforce his rights. In the area of consumer sales, the presumption introduced in Article 4 (1) of the Consumer Sale Act, amended by Article 556^2 of the Civil Code, extensively discussed in chapter 5, changes the allocation of burden in relation to the second fact. The consumer still has to prove the existence of non-conformity.

263. Summing up, in Article 4 (2) and (3) of the Consumer Sale Act the legislator *verbatim* provided for the presumptions of conformity, which might have resulted in a shift in the burden of proof. As explained above, neither in theory nor practice was Article 4 (2) and (3) considered as introducing presumptions of (non)conformity. The construction of Article 4 (2) and (3) does not constitute the presumption according to Polish law. It may however simplify the proof in a way that it shows in which direction the hearing of evidence should head and which criteria are relevant for successfully proving the existence of non-conformity.[92] The consumer has to prove a lack of one of the criterion to be successful in establishing that the goods are not conforming to the contract. An exceptional situation seems to occur regarding the proof that the goods match the sample shown to the consumer.

89 Chapter 2, para 32-34.

90 Chapter 4, para 258-260.

91 SN 26.10.2000, II CKN 305/00.

92 Sikorska (A.) 2005, p. 61.

In that case the burden of proof always seems to lie with the seller, as he is the keeper of the sample.[93]

264. Additionally, the legislator has caused uncertainty by introducing the initial division in contracts where the goods were individually negotiated and contracts where they were not. It is unclear whether it is first necessary to establish how the characteristics of goods have been determined. In particular circumstances this fact could serve as a seller's defence. For example, when the consumer claims that a product is not suitable for a specific purpose determined by him and therefore does not conform to the contract. The seller might claim that the characteristics of the goods have not been individually negotiated and that they are suitable for the purpose for which they are normally bought, therefore there is conformity. If we assume the division is valid, the burden of proof was to be allocated as follows:

1. According to Article 4 (2), the consumer has to present facts proving that the goods were individually negotiated, and then prove that one of the criteria set out in Article 4 (2) has not been met.
2. According to Article 4 (3), the consumer has to present facts proving that the goods were not individually negotiated, and then prove that one of the criteria set out in Article 4 (3) has not been met.

265. Regarding the burden of proof of the circumstances from Article 6 of the Consumer Sale Act regulating incorrect installation, the general rule of Article 6 of the Civil Code applies. The burden of proving the facts constituting incorrect installation lies with the consumer. The seller may try to escape the liability for incorrect installation by showing that the consumer did not use the instructions correctly. Given that in reality the instructions are very poorly written and often automatically translated from one language into another, the seller's defence may well be unsuccessful. Additionally, the seller is not liable for incorrect installation if the consumer, despite being aware of the faulty instructions, decided to continue with the installation. Finally, the seller is not liable for incorrect installation if the installation has been performed based on separate contract, or it has been entrusted with a third party on the ground of a separate contract.[94]

266. Regarding the burden of proof of circumstances mentioned in Article 7 of the Consumer Sale Act, describing the consumer's knowledge of the defects, pursuant to Article 6 of the Civil Code, the burden of proof lies with the seller.[95] The seller does not have to prove the absolute state of consumer's knowledge but rather he needs to show what it was

93 Radwański 2006, p. 116.
94 Jezioro 2010, p. 192.
95 Żuławska/Bieniek 2007, p. 57.

in the given circumstances that the average consumer should have reasonably known of the non-conformity.[96] The consumer's knowledge of the non-conformity may not be presumed, unless it results from the circumstances of a particular purchase, for example the purchase of second-hand goods.[97]

The seller may back up his proof by showing that he fulfilled the information duties of Article 3 of the Consumer Sale Act[98] and that he offered a consumer an opportunity to investigate the goods.[99] He cannot satisfy the burden only by stating that he offered the consumer the possibility of investigating the goods and the consumer refused to do so.[100] Unless this offer regarded particular characteristics of goods and at the same time it served as information about the state of goods.[101] The court should be assessing these types of matters taking into account the knowledge of the average consumer, his experience and his ability to make decisions based on the available information about the product.[102]

267. Article 556^1 of the Civil Code which will replace the articles of the Consumer Sale Act defines defects as existing when the goods do not conform to the contract, especially when particular circumstances occur. The provision does not contain the division found in Article 4 (2) and (3), what must be assessed positively. Nonetheless, the legislator defines the notion of defects by the existence of non-conformity, what may be misleading. Regarding the burden of proving the existence of defects, the consumer must prove that the goods do not conform to the contract, in particular, because they do not possess certain characteristics, are unfit for a common or special purpose or they are delivered incomplete.

---

96 Kołodziej 2010, p. 203.

97 Stefanicki 2006, p. 233, 234.

98 Article 3 of the Consumer Sale Act (similar information duties provided in recently amended Article 546 of the Civil Code):
1. *Seller is obliged to give the buyer clear, understandable and not misleading information, sufficient for the proper and full use of sold consumer goods. In particular, information should include: the name of the product, identification of the manufacturer or importer, the designation marks required by separate provisions, information on the authorisation for the product circulation at the territory of the Republic of Poland and, depending on the type of product, information on its energy consumption as well as other information specified in separate regulations.*
2. *The information referred to in paragraph 1, should be located on the consumer goods or be permanently attached to it, where the product is sold in packaging. In other cases the seller is obliged to provide information, which can be limited to the name of the product and its main features, and identification of the manufacturer or importer, where the sale of the product takes place.*
3. *The seller is obliged to provide appropriate conditions, in the place where the contract of sale is concluded, allowing the buyer to check the quality, completeness and functioning of the product and its basic components.*
4. *At the request of the buyer the seller is obliged to explain the meaning of particular provisions of the contract (...).*

99 Jezioro 2010, p. 213 *et seq.*

100 Pecyna 2003, p. 156; Olczyk 2006, p. 142 *et seq.*

101 SN 3.12.2008, V CSK 293/08.

102 Stefanicki 2006, p. 233.

268. Summing up, based on Article 6 of the Civil Code, the general burden of proof of non-conformity lies with the consumer. The exceptional situation seems to occur when it comes to proof that the goods do not match the sample. It might be practically impossible for the consumer to provide such evidence as long as the seller remains the keeper of the sample. He may have to make his case as probable as possible. As a consequence of the presented facts, the judge may apply a factual presumption regarding the non-correspondence of the goods with the sample and shift the burden onto the seller. Finally, it should be underlined that the consumer is a party whose interest is in proving the existence of non-conformity and should undertake initiative to secure and provide sufficient evidence. On the other hand, the wording of Article 4 (2) and (3) of the Consumer Sale Act (and 556^1 of the Civil Code) strongly indicates that the second receiver of the norm is a seller, who in particular circumstances might be obliged to present evidence. Nevertheless, pursuant to Article 6 of the Civil Code, the general burden of proof of facts constituting non-conformity lies with the consumer.[103]

4.3.5 *Conclusions*

269. The Polish legislator did not follow the exact provisions of the Directive when regulating issues of non-conformity. In the Consumer Sale Act the criteria regarding non-conformity have been divided into two groups depending on whether the goods have been individually negotiated or not. The new reform presented to Parliament in January 2014 and enacted in May 2014 repeals the above mentioned division.

270. The Consumer Sale Act regulates liability for non-conforming goods and was silent on seller's liability for the delivery of goods charged with the third parties rights. Following a lively debate shortly after the Consumer Sale Act entered into force, practitioners and the jurisprudence finally approved the line of interpretation stating that the liability for non-conformity must cover liability for legal defects. Otherwise, there would be a lacuna regarding seller's liability for legal defects and the provided level of the protection would have been unreasonably low.[104]

271. Based on articles of the Consumer Sales Directive, there is further uncertainty over the scope of the definition of non-conformity. For example, the repeatedly mentioned division on contracts with the characteristics of goods individually negotiated and contracts with the characteristics of goods not individually negotiated, or the issue of general

103 Jezioro 2010, p. 131.

104 Especially in comparison to the level that existed before the implementation, or level of protection under the Civil Code applicable to C2C and B2B.

exclusion of the Civil Code. The recent amendments incorporate provisions on consumer sales into the Civil Code, provide for a uniform notion of defects for all sale contracts, as well as regulate liability for legal defects. For these reasons the amendments must be assessed positively. Nevertheless, the new provisions contain several uncertainties, for example regarding the regulation of public statements. Regardless of these shortcomings, the overall result of the amendments is a simplification and harmonisation of rules governing Polish sales law.

272. The question of consumer's knowledge of the existence of defects at the time of the conclusion of the contract did not seem to cause major problems under the Consumer Sale Act. This matter has been very briefly regulated in the recently enacted Article 557 (3) of the Civil Code, which omits circumstances of the defective materials delivered by the buyer. Regardless of this, the exclusion of liability because of consumer's knowledge of defects and because of delivery of defective materials should not cause many practical problems in the future.

273. When it comes to the issues of burden of proof, the Consumer Sale Act seems to follow the Directive in terms of introducing a set of presumptions of conformity. However, contrary to the wording of Article 4 (2) and (3) the majority of scholars agreed that these provisions, contrary to its express wording, contain a definition rather than a presumption of non-conformity. In practice the burden of proof of the existence of non-conformity lies with the consumer, in accordance with Article 6 of the Civil Code.

The wording of new Article 556^1 of the Civil Code states that the defects occur when the goods do not conform to the contract and when one of the specific criteria listed in this Article occurs. Article 556^1 of the Civil Code does not provide any presumptions simplifying the facilitation of proof of the existence of defects. Similarly as it is under the Consumer Sale Act, pursuant to Article 6 of the Civil Code the burden of proof of the existence of defects lies with the consumer.

4.4 NON-CONFORMITY IN GERMAN LAW

4.4.1 *Introduction*

274. This section describes the notion of non-conformity of consumer goods within the meaning of the Consumer Sales Directive and the German concept of defects found in § 434 and § 435 BGB. The main focus will be given to the differences between the meaning of non-conformity and the meaning of defects (4.4.2). Furthermore, attention will be paid to the issues of the consumer's knowledge of the existence of defects (4.4.3). Finally, the

question of who bears the burden of proving the existence of defects will be discussed (4.4.4).

275. According to Article 2 (1) of the Consumer Sales Directive, the seller's main obligation is to deliver the goods in conformity with the contract. Similarly, according to § 433 BGB the sellers is obliged to deliver the goods which are free from material and legal defects. The seller is also obliged to deliver ownership.

When implementing the Consumer Sales Directive, the German legislator did not introduce the notion of non-conformity. It retained the traditional definitions of material and legal defects, amending them in line with the Directive. The 'old' definition of material defects was set out in § 459 BGB. Following the modernisation of the law of obligations it is located in § 434 BGB.[105] Regarding the sellers' obligations, § 433 BGB contains the same duties as Article 2 (1) of the Consumer Sales Directive. The one difference is that the BGB specifically requires the seller to transfer ownership of the goods. This is a consequence of the German system of transfer of property, which requires a separate act of transfer.[106] The definition of defects will be presented below and will be compared with the notion of non-conformity from the Consumer Sales Directive. This will lead to the discussion of whether the definition of defects is consistent with the meaning of non-conformity and whether the scope of the seller's liability according to the BGB and the Consumer Sales Directive are alike.

4.4.2 Defects: definitions

276. As stated above, the German legislator did not introduce the notion of non-conformity of consumer goods. It uses the traditional concept of defects applicable to all types of sale contracts. The BGB distinguishes between two categories of defects, the material defects, in other words defects in quality or quantity, are governed by § 434 BGB (*Sachmangel*). The legal defects, in other words defects in legal status of goods, are governed by § 435 BGB (*Rechtsmangel*).[107] Such division does not exist under the Consumer Sales Directive which has caused some uncertainty as to whether protective provisions shall also apply to legal defects of goods. Below, first the definitions of both types of defects will be presented

105 Looschelders 2003, p. 395.

106 Domestic rules on transfer of property are beyond the scope of the Consumer Sales Directive.

107 For the purpose of this section, I will refer to defects from § 434 BGB as defects or material defects and to defects from § 435 BGB as legal defects. The term non-conformity is used in the sense of Article 2 (2) of the Consumer Sales Directive, and § 434 BGB as implementing the notion of non-conformity, except when talking about 'presumption of non-conformity' which may mean both presumption of Article 5 (3) of the Directive or the presumption of § 476 BGB.

and subsequently how they relate to the notion of non-conformity of Article 2 (2) (a)-(d) of the Consumer Sales Directive will be analysed.

4.4.2.1 Material defects

277. According to § 434 BGB, the goods are free from material defects when they possess the quality that has been agreed upon by the parties. To the extent that the quality of goods has not been expressly agreed upon, the goods are free from material defects if:

1. They are suitable for use intended under the contract.
2. They are suitable for the customary use and their quality is of normal quality for this type of good and/or the buyer can expect this quality from this type of good.[108]

According to the wording of Article 2 (2) (d) of the Consumer Sales Directive, the quality stated under § 434 (1) nr. 2 includes characteristics which the buyer can expect based on public statements about the specific characteristics of goods made by the seller, the producer or his representative.[109] Public statements include, without being limited to, advertisements, leaflets and labelling of the product. As with the Directive, the seller is not liable for the content of a public statement if he was not aware of the statement and had no duty to be aware of it. Furthermore the seller's liability is excluded, if at the latest, at the time of the conclusion of the contract, the statement had been corrected or it did not influence the consumer's decision to purchase the product.

278. The German legislator introduced two reference points with respect to whether the goods are free from material defects. The first involves the parties' intention. § 434 (1) nr. 1 states that if there was an agreement between the parties on the quality of goods, the goods will be free from material defects as long as they match the quality agreed in the contract. This allows parties to conclude a contract for the sale of goods which objectively could have been regarded as defective, but in light of the parties' agreement must be considered as defect-free.[110] For example, the sale of second-hand goods requiring repair. If the parties' expectations regarding the quality of goods cannot be established based on the contract, the goods must be suitable for normal use and possess the quality usual for goods of the same kind (§ 434 (1) nr. 2).[111] From the wording of § 434 BGB it appears that the criteria for defects are constructed hierarchically. The parties' agreement must be taken into consideration at first. If quality characteristics have not been agreed upon, the customary use and the normal characteristics of the goods will be taken into account.[112] The above

108 Zimmermann 2005, p. 96; Löwisch 2003, p. 148.
109 Sections 4 (1) and (2) of the Product Liability Act (Produkthaftungsgesetz).
110 OLG München 06.09.2006, 20 U 1860/06.
111 Leible 2010, p. 429.
112 Looschelders 2003, p. 401.

construction of § 434 BGB differs from the Consumer Sales Directive, where the criteria of non-conformity have to be considered cumulatively, as provided in Recital 8 of the Directive.[113] Furthermore, the actual wording of the BGB does not seem to require the interpretation that goods conforming to the contract should also possess the normal characteristics of this type of good and be suitable for normal use. One could argue that the consumer should be able to assume without any further conditions that if the goods possess the agreed characteristics, they also possess characteristics that are normal for that type of good and that they are suitable for a normal use. It would appear that in order to allow the above assumption, one would need to construe the provision in light of the Directive.[114]

279. It has been observed that § 434 (1) BGB may conflict with the requirements of the Directive.[115] In particular, where parties expressly agree on a level of quality for a product that is lower than the market average, doubts exist as to its compliance with the Directive.[116] In such cases, although the goods meet the quality standards agreed by the parties, they do not meet the general criteria of fitness for normal use or possessing the normal quality of the same type of goods.[117]

Having said that, a question that arises in this context is to what extent the quality of goods can be lowered below usual standards. In general, the option to determine the quality of goods below the market average is understandable, as it is particularly important for maintaining parties' autonomy. On the other hand, there is undoubtedly a need to restrict a freedom to lower the quality standards.[118] It has been confirmed by the Amtsgericht Marsberg that the descriptions which clearly reflect the specific defects prohibited in automotive sales provisions must be rejected.[119] The unlimited freedom to lower quality standards could in reality mean the disguised waiver of rights and could significantly undermine the level of consumer protection.

113 Recital 8 of the Consumer Sales Directive: '*Whereas, in order to facilitate the application of the principle of conformity with the contract, it is useful to introduce a rebuttable presumption of conformity with the contract covering the most common situations; whereas that presumption does not restrict the principle of freedom of contract; whereas, furthermore, in the absence of specific contractual terms, as well as where the minimum protection clause is applied, the elements mentioned in this presumption may be used to determine the lack of conformity of the goods with the contract; whereas the quality and performance which consumers can reasonably expect will depend inter alia on whether the goods are new or second-hand;* whereas the elements mentioned in the presumption are cumulative; *whereas, if the circumstances of the case render any particular element manifestly inappropriate, the remaining elements of the presumption nevertheless still apply*'.

114 Leible 2010, p. 429.

115 Schulte-Nölke, Twigg-Flesner and Ebers 2008, p. 667; Grundmann and Ochmann 2007, p. 457.

116 Grundmann and Ochmann 2007, p. 457.

117 Grundmann and Ochmann 2007, p. 457.

118 Müller 2003, p. 1975, 1976.

119 AG Marsberg, 9.10.2002, 1 C 143/02, Beck RS 2002, 14584.

280. The wording of § 434 BGB does not expressly contain all the criteria for establishing defects provided by Article 2 (2) of the Consumer Sales Directive. § 434 BGB does not expressly cover situations where the characteristics of goods must correspond to a description provided to the consumer. Next to that it does not literally provide criteria requiring goods to possess the characteristics of a sample and/or a model shown to the consumer by the seller. For these reasons, the BGB is said to diverge from the Consumer Sales Directive.[120] When compared to the definition of non-conformity of Article 2 (2) (a)-(d) of the Directive, the definition of material defects of § 434 seems to be incomplete.[121]

However, the German courts can broaden the scope of material defects through the interpretation of the notion of non-conformity found in the Consumer Sales Directive.[122] For example the Landgericht Ellwangen held that the fact that a purchased car had been manufactured in a different country than the one initially stated constitutes a material defect within the meaning of § 434 BGB. In this particular case, the car had been made in South Africa but sold as manufactured in the European Union. The court stated that although place of origin is not included in the characteristics of defect and does not influence the physical state of a product, a consumer may particularly value the goods' place of manufacture. Therefore, delivery of a car manufactured in a different country to that stated is considered as a material defect within the meaning of § 434 BGB.[123] Moreover, under § 434 BGB, any of the characteristics of goods that the parties agree upon are important, including those that are not physically relevant. The parties may therefore agree that the goods must correspond to the sample or model shown at the time of the conclusion of contract. Interestingly, under the previous provisions on sales law, such an interpretation of material defects would have been unlikely.[124]

281. Following the Consumer Sales Directive, § 434 BGB contains the liability for public statements made by the seller, the producer or his representative. According to the current wording of § 434 (1) BGB, the product possesses a material defect if it does not possess characteristics which the buyer can expect based on the public statements made by the seller, the producer or his representative. The public statements include advertisements, merchandise descriptions and labelling. The defences available for the seller are also implemented in line with the Directive.[125] The seller is not liable if he was not aware and

120 Gsell 2001, p. 65, 66.

121 Gsell 2001, p. 65, 66; Schulte-Nölke, Twigg-Flesner and Ebers 2008, p. 667.

122 Binding only in individual disputes.

123 LG Ellwangen 13.12.2002, 3 O 219/02, NJW 2003, 517. See also: LG Düsseldorf 22.04.2003, 24 S 548/02, Beck RS 2003, 12280, the sale of the import car has been regarded as defective; LG Bonn 27.02.2004, 10 O 618/03, software which causes the hardware to work slower might constitute material defect in the sense of § 434 BGB.

124 Rott 2004, p. 255.

125 Grundmann and Ochmann 2007, p. 457.

had no duty to be aware of the content of statement. Furthermore, liability for public statements is excluded if at the time of the conclusion of contract, the statements had been corrected, and finally, if the statements did not influence the consumer's decision to purchase the goods. The burden of proving the above facts lies with the seller.[126]

282. The BGB contains provisions on the delivery of different goods and goods of different quantity. § 434 (3) BGB states that the delivery of the wrong quantity, less than agreed under the contract, constitutes a material defect.[127] It is unclear whether the delivery of a different quantity amounts to non-conformity under Article 2 (2) (a)-(d) of the Consumer Sales Directive. It is arguable that the delivery of goods of a quantity different to that agreed always prevents the consumer from using the goods for their customary or specific purpose. The above interpretation seems to apply to delivery of too little. Another question is whether the delivery of too much can also be considered as a material defect. The BGB expressly regulates a delivery of lesser amount of goods, but is silent as to a larger amount.[128] Taking into consideration a remark given above, the first reference point to assess the defectiveness is the parties' agreement. Consequently, the delivery of a larger amount can be sometimes regarded as a material defect.

4.4.2.2 Incorrect installation

283. Following Article 2 (5) of the Consumer Sales Directive, § 434 (2) BGB provides rules on incorrect installation. The installation should be understood in a broad sense. It includes all activities necessary to be performed to enable the buyer to use the goods, also an installation of software.[129] Two situations can be distinguished therein. First, when the material defects occur due to the incorrect installation carried out by the seller or persons he is responsible for. Second, when the purchased goods are intended for installation to be carried out by the buyer, the so-called IKEA clause.[130] The goods are deemed to be defective if instructions given to consumers are misleading, unless they are installed correctly despite the misleading instructions.[131]

The application of § 434 (2) BGB has been considered by the BGH in connection with the application of the presumption of non-conformity of § 476 BGB. The question was whether the application of the presumption can be excluded if the goods have been installed by a third party who was acting in the course of a profession, for which the seller was not responsible. The case concerned a third party who did not acknowledge a legal obligation

126 Becker 2009, p. 19, 20.
127 Leible 2010, p. 439; Rott 2004, p. 245.
128 Beckmann 2013, § 434 Rn. 138.
129 Faust 2011, § 434 Rn. 89.
130 Löwisch 2003, p. 148.
131 Faust 2011, § 434 BGB Rn. 99; Westermann 2012, § 434 BGB Rn. 39.

to deliver the goods free of defects, but who was hired by the consumer to perform the installation of a garden pond.[132] The BGH stated that the application of the presumption of non-conformity of § 476 BGB is not affected by the fact that the consumer had a pond installed by a third party. In this respect German law seems to go further than the Directive and the legislation of other Member States.[133]

4.4.2.3 Legal defects

284. According to § 435 BGB goods are free from legal defects if no one can assert their rights against the buyer. This concerns property rights, for example, co-ownership, servitudes, IP rights as well as obligatory rights such as rent. In cases of the sale of immovable, when a particular right does not exist but is nonetheless registered, it is treated as an equivalent to a legal defect.[134]

There are several points to note with respect to the seller's liability for legal defects. The Directive does not contain any reference to the legal status of goods. Due to the explicit definition of legal defects under the BGB, the seller is liable for both material and legal defects. The question remains whether the liability for legal defects is connected to the liability for non-conformity.[135]

One view might be that adding liability for the legal status shows that the BGB makes positive use of the minimum harmonisation of the Directive and provides an additional protective provision applicable to consumer sales.[136] On the other hand, it seems that the liability for legal defects under the German law constitutes a separate obligation resulting *inter alia* from the system of transfer of property applicable in Germany. This means that in every case of sale of consumer goods charged with a legal defect the seller will be held liable on the grounds of § 435 BGB.[137]

4.4.2.4 Conclusions

285. § 434 (1) BGB implements Article 2 (2), (4) and (5) of the Consumer Sales Directive and defines material defects for the purpose of German sales law. The German legislator revised the BGB's traditional concept of defects in light of the Consumer Sales Directive. The definition of defects applies for all types of contracts of sale. There is some uncertainty regarding the scope of defects as the wording of § 434 BGB does not contain all the criteria of non-conformity set out in Article 2 (2) (a)-(d) of the Consumer Sales Directive.

132 BGH 22.11.2004, VIII ZR 21/04, NJW 2005, 283.
133 Chapter 5, para 475.
134 Becker 2009, p. 24.
135 Faust 2011, § 435 BGB Rn. 4; Massimo Bianca and Grundmann 2002, p. 128, 129.
136 Leible 2010, p. 445.
137 Faust 2011, § 435 BGB Rn. 4; Westermann 2012, § 435 BGB Rn. 6.

286. Based on the information presented in this sub-section it can be concluded that similarly to the Polish provisions, the German legislator places emphasis first and foremost on the parties' individually negotiated characteristics of the goods and expressly agreed terms as to quality. Only when there are no individual determinations as to the quality will the general criteria apply. Summing up, based on § 434 the goods are defective if:

1. They do not possess quality agreed by the parties.
2. They are not suitable for the purpose stated in the contract.
3. They are not suitable for normal use.
4. They do not possess qualities that the buyer can expect from this type of goods based *inter alia* on public statements regarding the quality of the goods.
5. The seller delivers fewer goods or different goods from those agreed.
6. The agreed installation is carried out incorrectly or the installation is carried out by the consumer in accordance with unclear or misleading manuals.

Analysing the list presented above, it should once again be underlined that in determining the defectiveness of goods the parties' agreement takes the most important role. The remaining criteria are also important and are often to be looked at when establishing and assessing the existence of defects. Additionally, above criteria from § 434 BGB appear to apply hierarchically, while the ones set out in Article 2 (2) (a)-(d) of the Consumer Sales Directive have been constructed cumulatively. Additionally, the wording of § 434 BGB does not contain the criteria of correspondence to the sample and model shown to consumer at the time of the conclusion of the contract. It may cause uncertainty as to whether § 434 BGB can be considered as correctly implementing Article 2 (2) (a)-(d) of the Consumer Sales Directive.

Finally, § 435 BGB provides the definition of legal defects. The Consumer Sales Directive does not mention legal defects when describing the criteria of non-conformity. Under German law, liability for legal defects constitutes a separate liability not being interconnected with liability for non-conformity. The above stems from the general obligations on the seller set out in § 433 (1) BGB) where one of them is the obligation to deliver ownership of the purchased goods.[138]

4.4.3 *Buyer's knowledge of the defects*

287. The consumer's knowledge of defects is relevant for the scope of the seller's liability. Article 2 (3) of the Consumer Sales Directive provides that there is a deemed lack of non-conformity if the consumer was aware or could not have been reasonably unaware of the non-conformity at the time of the conclusion of the contract. § 442 BGB follows the Con-

138 Westermann 2012, § 435 BGB Rn. 4; Faust 2011, § 435 BGB Rn. 15.

sumer Sales Directive and prescribes the consequences of consumer's knowledge of the defects. According to § 442 BGB, the seller's liability for delivery of defective goods is excluded if at the time of the conclusion of contract, the consumer knew about the defects. If the consumer lacks the knowledge about the defects due to his gross negligence, the seller can be held liable only if he fraudulently concealed the defect or specifically assured the consumer about the quality of goods.[139]

The German legislator formulates the consequences of consumer knowledge of defects in a slightly different way from that of the European legislator. § 442 BGB includes more details regarding consumer knowledge than Article 2 (3) of the Consumer Sales Directive. First of all, gross negligence is easier to determine than the circumstances when a consumer 'could not have been reasonably unaware'. Furthermore, § 442 BGB provides that even in the case of an inexcusable lack of knowledge, the seller can still be held liable if he acted fraudulently or gave guarantees that the goods were defect-free.[140] This provision applies by analogy to cases of legal defects.[141] Comparing the regulation with the Consumer Sales Directive, the BGB seems to put the consumer in a better position, mainly by clarifying the circumstances of applicability of the above presented rule and by broadening its scope.[142]

4.4.4 *Burden of proof of the defects*

288. The construction and effect of Article 2 (2) of the Consumer Sales Directive cause uncertainties regarding the implementation and application of this Article in various domestic legal systems. As already mentioned, Article 2 (2) (a)-(d) of the Directive provides a set of presumptions of conformity, which theoretically should result in the simplification of the burden of proof of non-conformity. The criteria (set of presumptions) of Article 2 (2) are to be interpreted cumulatively, meaning that if a consumer is able to challenge one of these presumptions, he will be successful in proving non-conformity and/or shifting the burden of proof regarding the existence of conformity to the seller.

The BGB does not implement the notion of conformity. As already stated, it uses the traditional notion of defects instead, modernised in light of the Directive. Furthermore, § 434 BGB defining material defects does not indicate that the criteria thereof constitute legal or factual presumptions in order to simplify the proof of the existence or absence of expected quality of goods. As already explained, § 434 and § 435 of the BGB contain the definitions of a material and legal defect. To be more specific, these provisions define the absence of material and legal defects. Unlike the Directive, they do not create any presump-

139 Becker 2009, p. 42; Leible 2010, p. 445.
140 Rott 2004, p. 247.
141 Westermann 2012, § 442 BGB Rn. 2.
142 Faust 2011, § 442 BGB Rn. 4; Westermann 2012, § 442 BGB Rn. 2.

tions. Therefore, following the general rules on the burden of proof,[143] in order for a consumer to be successful in his claim he must prove the circumstances described in § 434 or § 435.

289. There is no explicit general rule on the allocation of the burden of proof to be found in the BGB.[144] There is however a rule of § 363 BGB regulating the burden of proof in case of non-performance of the obligation. It requires the consumer to prove specific facts regarding the content of contract and facts constituting the defects.[145] Regarding the existence of defects, German law does not provide much simplification regarding the proof of the existence of defects.

290. § 433 BGB describes a typical duty of the seller to deliver defect-free goods. Knowing, from § 434 BGB the facts which constitute defects, it is possible to conclude that for the consumer to be successful in his claim he has to prove that the quality agreed in a contract was not present. This can sometimes require detailed information and evidence regarding the content of a contract. Moreover, where the parties had not agreed on the specific quality of goods, the consumer has the burden of proving other facts constituting the material defect. If the consumer is able to show that the defects existed at the time of passing of risk, it will be concluded that the seller did not perform his obligation and that the consumer has a right to remedies. If the consumer is able to show that the defects became apparent within six months from the time of passing of risk, the requirements for the application of the presumption of non-conformity of § 476 BGB apply, shifting the burden to prove the contrary to the seller.[146]

291. Regarding the circumstances mentioned in § 442 BGB, regulating the buyer's knowledge of the defects, the burden of proof that the buyer knew about the defects, or did not know by virtue of gross negligence lies with the seller.[147] This results from the general concept of the burden of proof which requires the person who benefits from the existence of a certain legal fact to prove it.[148] On the other hand, the consumer bears the burden of proving that the seller acted fraudulently in concealing the defects, or that he assured the consumer about the quality of goods.

143 Chapter 2, para 43, 44, 50, 51.
144 Chapter 2, para 49, 94.
145 Beckmann 2013, § 434 Rn. 229.
146 The conditions and consequences of the application of § 476 BGB are discussed in chapter 5, para 440-463.
147 Becker 2009, p. 41, 42; Gsell 2011, p. 86, 87.
148 Chapter 2, para 43, 44, 50, 51.

292. Summing up, taking the construction of § 433 and § 434 BGB into account, there are not much simplifications regarding the proof of the existence of defects available to the consumer. § 363 BGB determines the allocation of burden of proof in cases of non-performance of the obligation. It may require the consumer to prove specific facts regarding the content of a contract and facts constituting the defects.[149]

When considering the Directive's provisions, it would appear to be sufficient to prove the lack of one of the criteria from Article 2 (2) (a)-(d) to shift the burden of proving that the goods were in non-conformity. On the other hand, the effect given to Article 2 (2) depends strictly on the national legislation.[150] Under German law, the consumer often has to prove the content of a contract, the existence of defects and in some cases the facts that the contract concluded between the parties is a consumer contract, or that he acts in the capacity of a consumer in the sense of § 13 BGB.[151] Only if there was no agreement on a specific quality may the consumer use the additional elements of § 434 BGB.

4.4.5 Conclusions

293. It is apparent from the wording of § 434 and § 435 BGB that the German legislator diverges from the general construction of Article 2 (2) (a)-(d) of the Consumer Sales Directive. According to German law, the starting point for establishing the existence of defects is the parties' express agreement as to the quality of goods. It prioritises parties' agreement when establishing whether the goods delivered are free from material defects. Only in the absence of an explicit agreement as to the quality, do the criteria stating that the product must be suitable for the purpose stated in the contract apply. If the contract does not state the purpose for which the purchased goods are to be used, the objective criteria from § 434 (1) point 2 BGB apply. They contain general characteristics, such as the customary use of the type of goods or the normal quality of the type of goods.

294. Furthermore, the wording of § 434 BGB does not provide all criteria contained in Article 2 (2) (a)-(d) of the Consumer Sales Directive. Consequently, the opinion has been put forward that in order to provide a complete protection the BGB has to be interpreted in light of the Directive with regard to the 'missing' criteria of non-conformity. Furthermore, the BGB provides for the additional (separate) seller's liability in case of legal defects. According to § 435 BGB, goods must be free of legal defects regardless of whether the quality of goods has been expressly agreed or not.

149 Beckmann 2013, § 434 Rn. 229.
150 Massimo Bianca and Grundmann 2002, p. 129, 130; Beale and Howells 1997, p. 28.
151 BGH 11.07.2007, VIII ZR 110/06, NJW 2007, 2619.

The seller's liability is excluded in case of the buyer's knowledge about the defects at the time of the conclusion of the contract. § 442 BGB provides that if the buyer's lack of knowledge resulted from his gross negligence the seller can be held liable for material defects only when he fraudulently concealed the defects or gave a guarantee of quality.

295. Finally, the BGB does not implement presumptions of conformity of Article 2 (2) of the Directive. The construction of § 433, § 434 and § 435 BGB require the consumer to provide specific evidence of the contract's content, the absence of the agreed quality or other facts to prove the existence of the defect and qualify for remedies. At this point there are very few measures available for a consumer which facilitate his proof of the existence of defects. Therefore, proving defects may appear burdensome at times.[152]

4.5 Non-conformity in English and Welsh law

4.5.1 Introduction

296. This section describes the notion of non-conformity of consumer goods within the meaning of the Consumer Sales Directive and the English concept of satisfactory quality and fitness for purpose.[153] It focuses on the differences between the meaning of non-conformity from the Consumer Sales Directive and the satisfactory quality with other aspects regarding the state of goods, including the notion of non-conformity adopted in English law (4.5.2). Furthermore, attention is paid to the consumer's knowledge about the non-conformity (4.5.3). Finally, the issues of burden of proof regarding the existence of non-conformity will be discussed (4.5.4). The description takes into account changes found in the proposed Consumer Rights Bill and possible consequences of the Bill in the context of the notion of non-conformity, knowledge of the non-conformity and the burden of proof thereof.

297. The implementation of the notion of non-conformity has not proven to be easy for several reasons. The English legislator was unfamiliar with this particular notion. Before the implementation of the Consumer Sales Directive the definition of non-conformity had no particular legal significance for the English law on the sale of goods. As already stated the notion was primarily a product of the CISG, which the UK did not ratify. Nonetheless,

152 Further discussion about the burdensomeness of proof regarding the existence of defects in chapter 5, para 440-450.

153 The reference made to English law should be understood as English and Welsh law.

the criteria of non-conformity found in the Consumer Sales Directive closely resemble implied terms as to the quality and fitness for purpose.

Article 2 (2) (a)-(d) of the Consumer Sales Directive provides for the requirements necessary to presume that the purchased goods are in conformity with the contract. Sections 12-15 of the Sale of Goods Act 1979 provide similar standards, which take effect as implied terms of the contracts of sale. The standards set out by Sections 12-15 apply to all types of contracts. As with the aspects of non-conformity from the Consumer Sales Directive, the implied terms are cumulative.[154]

The vast majority of case law regarding Sections 12-15 of the Sale of Goods Act 1979 is concerned with the law before the amendments made in 1994. There are even fewer decisions regarding the latest amendments on the satisfactory quality and fitness for purpose, and non-conformity which were made in 2003.[155] Therefore, in relation to particular issues the overview of legislation and the study of literature will be the main source of the problem analysis.

298. As already stated, the scope of non-conformity of Article 2 (2) of the Consumer Sales Directive has a lot in common with the English implied terms as to the quality and fitness for purpose. According to both documents, the Directive and the Sale of Goods 1979, the seller's duty to deliver the goods of satisfactory quality is obligatory. Consequently, the seller is not able to avoid liability by proving he neither knew nor should have known about the defects.[156] Nevertheless, the implementation still brings important amendments in contracts for the sale and supply of goods to the consumers. As will be explained later, not all aspects of non-conformity are to be found in the domestic law of England and Wales.

299. Section 48F of the Sale of Goods Act 1979 provides that the goods do not conform to the contract if one of the express or implied terms of the contract is breached. The English legislator refers to non-conformity in the context of Article 2 (2) (a)-(d) of the Consumer Sales Directive only with respect to the implemented remedies, that is repair, replacement, price reduction and rescission. In relation to the traditional remedies, such as right to reject and damages, the traditional notions of satisfactory quality and fitness for purpose apply.[157] The reference to the goods not conforming to the contract is also made in Section 48A (3) of the Sale of Goods Act 1979 that governs presumption of non-conformity. Consequently, there is a lack of a general notion of non-conformity applicable to the

154 Watterson 2001, p. 202.
155 Atiyah/Adams and Macqueen 2010, p. 3 *et seq.*
156 Woodroffe and Lowe 2013, p. 43.
157 Watterson 2001, p. 199.

consumer sale. As will be demonstrated later, this will not change once the new Consumer Rights Bill enters into force.

4.5.2 *Non-conformity: definitions*

4.5.2.1 Satisfactory quality

300. The notion of satisfactory quality means quality that a reasonable person would regard as satisfactory, taking into account any description of the goods, price, and all other relevant circumstances.[158] It includes their state and condition, and in particular cases, their fitness for all purposes for which goods of this kind are commonly supplied. Other aspects important for the evaluation of goods are: appearance, freedom from minor defects, safety and durability.[159] Satisfactory quality is to be tested against the standard of a reasonable person, where a reasonable person is not an expert.[160] In *Bramhill v Edwards* it was confirmed that a reasonable person must be the one who is in the position of a buyer, with his knowledge regarding the background of the transaction.[161] Therefore, a reasonable person must have full knowledge about all relevant matters which might be important in determining (un)satisfactory quality of goods with a hidden defect.[162]

301. Satisfactory quality set out in Section 14 (2) of the Sale of Goods Act 1979 is said to be the most important statutory weapon for consumers.[163] This Section as amended is virtually identical to the old wording of the provision, apart from 'satisfactory' being substituted for 'merchantable'. To determine the meaning of satisfactory quality, Section 14 (2A) provides non-exhaustive list of aspects of goods' quality to be taken into account:

1. Fitness for all purposes for which goods of the kind in question are commonly supplied.
2. Appearance and finish.
3. Freedom from minor defects.
4. Safety.
5. Durability.

Special attention will be given to the aspect of durability while establishing (un)satisfactory quality. In legal practice it has been agreed that the breakdown or malfunction of goods within an unusually short (for this specific type of good) period of time after the delivery at least raises a factual presumption that the goods were not of a proper quality and condi-

158 The Sale of Goods Act 1979, Section 14 (2a).
159 The Sale of Goods Act 1979, Section 14 (2b) (a)-(e).
160 Ervine 2004, p. 695.
161 *Bramhill v Edwards* (2004) EWCA Civ 403, para 39.
162 Atiyah/Adams and Macqueen 2010, p. 175.
163 Woodroffe and Lowe 2013, p. 43.

tion at the time of delivery.[164] In particular, it has been confirmed that where the perishable goods deteriorate shortly after delivery, they cannot be considered as having satisfactory quality at the time of delivery.[165] Regarding other types of goods, Goode gives an example that if a person buys a new car which, without an obvious cause, becomes defective after a week, this is strong evidence that it was faulty when delivered, and therefore the burden of proof will lie with the seller to show that the breakdown did not occur through faulty design or manufacture. He continues that premature breakdown raises the factual presumption that the goods were not of satisfactory quality at the time of delivery. This presumption can be rebutted by proving that the buyer's use was excessive or not in accordance with instructions accompanying the goods.[166] The understanding of durability and application of factual presumption is therefore similar to the presumption of non-conformity found in Section 43A (3). It is not limited to the scope of the consumer sale or the type of remedy the buyer relies on. It depends on the circumstances of the case and a judge's reasonable opinion of the average time particular goods should remain in an agreed state and possess the agreed quality.

302. Section 9 (1) of the Consumer Rights Bill provides that every contract to supply goods is to be treated as including a term that the quality of goods is satisfactory. The quality of goods is satisfactory if the goods meet the standard that a reasonable person would consider satisfactory, taking into account any description of the goods, the price or other consideration of the goods (if relevant) and all other circumstances identical to the circumstances from Section 14 (2A) of the Sale of Goods 1979 presented in the previous paragraph. Comparing Section 14 (2A) of the Sale of Goods Act 1979 and Section 9 of the Consumer Rights Bill it must be stated that they do not differ substantially, albeit that Section 9 of the Consumer Rights Bill is more detailed and more clearly formulated.

4.5.2.2 Correspondence with the description, sample or model

303. Section 13 (1) of the Sale of Goods Act 1979 provides that where there is a sale by description, there is an implied condition that the goods will correspond with it. The burden to prove otherwise lies with the buyer.[167] In case of breach of this implied condition, the buyer will be able to claim traditional remedies set out in Sections 35, 51 and 52 of the Sale of Goods Act 1979 and the remedies introduced in Sections 48B and 48C of the Sale of Goods Act 1979 by the implementation of the Consumer Sales Directive.

164 Benjamin's sale of goods 2010, nr. 11-040; *Whitecap v John H Rubdle Ltd*, (2008) 2 Loyd's Rep 216 at 45.
165 *Mash and Murrell v Joseph I Emmanuel Ltd*, (1962) 1 WLR 16.
166 Goode/McKendrick 2010, p. 336, 337.
167 Atiyah/Adams and Macqueen 2010, p. 154.

It has been stated that Section 13 (1) applies to the descriptions identifying goods as being of a certain type.[168] Another requirement is that the buyer must have relied on the seller's description. The latter condition is not prescribed by Article 2 (2) (a) of the Consumer Sales Directive. Finally, if the description is a part of a contract it constitutes an express term. The breach of express terms allows the consumer to claim available remedies, whether under the Sale of Goods Act 1979 or the Consumer Sales Directive.[169]

304. The description can be defined as a term of the contract that determines a substantial element of the identity or essence of the subject-matter.[170] It also covers other elements which do not directly identify the goods but determine whether the delivered goods are what the parties agreed upon.[171] Essentially, goods do not correspond with the contractual description if they are different in kind or constitute a different substance.[172]

In English law, the description of goods given by the seller may have several different consequences. First of all, it is possible that a statement has no legal effect at all. Second of all, the description can be a representation, giving rise to the liability for misrepresentation. Finally, it may also be incorporated in the contract terms. In the last situation, failure to deliver products conforming to the seller's description will constitute a breach of contract.[173] The extent of the seller's duty depends on the degree of precision in the description. If the description is vague, the duty can be minimal, the more precise the description, the more onerous the duty.[174]

The possible effect of description may be confusing and to the disadvantage of a consumer it seems that not every description will increase the seller's liability for delivery of non-conforming goods.[175] There is also an additional burden on the consumer wishing to invoke this term. He has to prove to a certain level of detail the content of the description, which is not always straightforward, in particular, when the description or contract was verbal. Consequently, the description as mentioned in Article 2 (2) (a) of the Consumer Sales Directive is not entirely recognised when it comes to the interpretation of Section 13 (1) of the Sale of Goods Act 1979. It seems that the obligation to deliver the goods matching the description is limited and does not always ensure actual satisfactory quality. Finally, very often goods may correspond with the description and still be of poor quality.[176]

---

168 Willett 2000, p. 63, 64.
169 Watterson 2001, p. 205 *et seq.*
170 *Ashington Piggeries Ltd v Christopher Hill Ltd* (1972) AC 441, HL.
171 Atiyah/Adams and Macqueen 2010, p. 153.
172 Goode/McKendrick 2010, p. 319.
173 Willett 2000, p. 203.
174 Macleod 2007, nr. 13.12.
175 Benjamin's sale of goods 2010, nr. 11-086.
176 Benjamin's sale of goods 2010, nr. 14-010; Atiyah/Adams and Macqueen 2010, p. 140, 152.

305. The new Consumer Rights Bill provides in Section 11 (1) that every contract to supply goods by description is to be treated as including a term that the goods will match the description. The new Bill clarifies in the latter sub-sections the meaning of description and supply by description. For example, it states that if the supply of goods is made by sample and description, it is not sufficient that the bulk of the goods match the sample if they do not also match the description. Furthermore, it is provided that supply is not prevented from being a supply by description just because the goods are demonstrated for supply and they are selected by the consumer.

306. According to Article 2 (2) (a) of the Consumer Sales Directive, the goods are presumed to be in conformity if they '*possess the qualities of goods which the seller has held out as a sample or model*'. Section 15 (2) of the Sale of Goods Act 1979 provides that if there is a contract by sample it is implied that '*the bulk will correspond with the sample in quality*'. It closely resembles Article 2 (2) (a) of the Consumer Sales Directive. The function of a sample has been described by Lord Macnaghten: '*The office of sample is to present to the eye the real meaning and intention of the parties with regard to the subject-matter of the contract which owing to the imperfections of language, it may be difficult or impossible to express in words. The sample speaks for itself.*'[177] In the same case it has been stated that there is normally a presumption that if the bulk corresponded with the sample it satisfied the contract. The buyer can rebut this presumption by proving that the goods possess a latent defect rendering their quality unsatisfactory.[178]

307. There is uncertainty over the difference between 'contract made by showing a sample' and 'holding out a sample'. In particular, the situations where the seller provides a sample and he is the sample's only keeper, can be misleading. This sample may be not intended to form a contractual basis for comparison with the delivered goods.[179] It has been observed that the mere fact that a sample is provided for the buyer's inspection does not constitute a sale by sample. There is only a sale by sample if there is evidence of intention that it should be such.[180] Furthermore, the Consumer Sales Directive does not indicate whether the delivery of goods must possess every characteristic of the sample or rather have its main characteristics. The Sale of Goods Act 1979 provides that the goods will be considered as free from any defect if it would not be apparent upon reasonable examination of the sample.

Section 13 of the Consumer Rights Bill states that the goods supplied by a reference to the sample of goods, which was seen or examined by the consumer before the conclusion

177 *Drummond v Van Ingen* (1887), 12 App Cas 284, HL at 297.
178 Benjamin's sale of goods 2010, nr. 11-078 – 11-080.
179 Watterson 2001, p. 205.
180 Atiyah/Adams and Macqueen 2010, p. 205.

of contract, will be treated as including a term that the goods will match the sample except to the extent that any differences between the sample and the goods are brought to the consumer's attention before the contract is concluded. Furthermore, the goods must be free from any defect that makes their quality unsatisfactory and that would not be apparent upon a reasonable examination of a sample.

308. Finally, the English provisions of the Sale of Goods 1979 are not clear on whether they are similar in the context of a requirement that the goods must correspond with a model shown to the consumer. This will change once the new Consumer Rights Bill is passed. It is provided in Section 14 of the Consumer Rights Bill that every contract to supply goods by a reference to the model of goods that are seen or examined by the consumer before the entering into the contract, is to be treated as including a term that the goods will match the model except to the extent that any differences between the model and the goods are brought to the consumer's attention before the contract is entered into. Comparing recent changes regarding the provision on a sample and a model, it must be stated that the English legislator provides matching regulations in respect of these two aspects. This change will clarify the rules in case of contracts of supply of goods made by showing the sample or model, which is undoubtedly a positive development in comparison with the provisions of the Sale of Goods Act 1979.

4.5.2.3 Fitness for purpose (ordinary and specific)

309. Section 14 (2B) (a) of the Sale of Goods Act 1979 states that one of the aspects of the quality of goods is that they must be fit for all the purposes for which goods of the kind in question are commonly supplied. Before the Sale of Goods Act of 1979, if the goods had several purposes, and were suitable for some of those purposes, there was no breach of merchantable quality. Under the Sale of Goods Act 1979, it was required that the goods are fit for 'the purpose of purposes'.[181] Under current legislation, for the goods to be regarded to be of satisfactory quality they are required to be fit for all their common purposes.[182] Section 9 (3) (a) of the Consumer Rights Bill seems to follow the interpretation developed under the Sale of Goods Act 1979, which is in accordance with the Directive. Furthermore, if the goods are unfit for their only proper purpose of use they cannot be regarded as being of satisfactory quality.[183] For example, if a mobile phone is unfit to make calls, while still fit to send messages, use internet, and play music etc., the seller still will be liable for the delivery of goods being unfit for their common purpose.

181 Woodroffe and Lowe 2013, p. 46.
182 *Aswan Engineering Co v Lupdine Ltd*, (1987) I W.R.L.I.
183 Woodroffe and Lowe 2013, p. 45.

310. Pursuant to Article 2 (2) (c) of the Consumer Sales Directive, the consumer goods are required to be fit for normal purpose, which covers goods commonly bought. English legislation does not make any reference to normal use. Some interpret the wording of Section 14 (2B) (a) of the Sale of Goods Act 1979 in this respect as not having reference to the normal purpose of use.[184] As already stated, the goods must be fit for all purposes for which the goods are commonly supplied, which is not the same as fit for normal purpose. It is argued that many products are normally used for the purposes for which they are not commonly supplied, for example, a chair used to stand on in order to change a light bulb.[185] The incorrect or misleading instructions supplied with the goods can determine whether the goods are unfit for their purpose.[186]

311. Section 14 (3) of the Sale of Goods Act 1979 provides that the goods must be reasonably fit for the purpose for which the buyer specifically purchases the product, if this purpose has been communicated expressly or by implication to the seller.[187] The Consumer Sales Directive requires that the goods must be (absolutely) fit for the specific purpose. The English provision will not apply when the buyer does not rely, or should not reasonably rely, on the seller's skill and judgment regarding the goods' fitness for a specific purpose.[188] The burden of proof lying with the buyer in the first instance is only to show that he has informed the seller of the purpose for which the goods are being bought. Reliance will be presumed unless the seller is able to positively disprove the above fact, or unless he can show it has been unreasonable for a consumer to rely upon his skills and judgment.[189] Furthermore, it seems that English law, unlike the Consumer Sales Directive, does not require the seller to accept a purpose for goods as described by the consumer. The provisions say only that the specific purpose must be communicated to the seller.[190] In this respect the scope of protection seems to be broader.

In the new Consumer Rights Bill, the fitness for a particular purpose is regulated in Section 10. If a consumer makes known to the seller before the contract is concluded, expressly or by implication, any particular purpose for which he purchases the goods, the contract is treated as including an implied term that the goods are reasonably fit for the purpose described, whether or not that is a purpose for which goods of that kind are reasonably supplied. The rules on fitness for purpose seem to be much clearer under the Consumer Rights Bill and they seem to provide a broader protection than the provisions of the Sale of Goods Act 1979.

184 Willett, Morgan-Taylor and Naidoo 2004, p. 98.
185 Willett, Morgan-Taylor and Naidoo 2004, p. 98.
186 Woodroffe and Lowe 2013, p. 55.
187 Benjamin's sale of goods 2010, nr. 11-055.
188 Watterson 2001, p. 206. See also: *Jewson Ltd v Boyhan* (2003) EWCA Civ 1030.
189 Atiyah/Adams and Macqueen 2010, p. 193; Woodroffe and Lowe 2013, p. 54.
190 It should be agreed that he can object to the purpose for which the goods are being purchased.

4.5.2.4 Correspondence with the characteristics based on the public statements

312. As already stated, the standard of satisfactory quality requires goods to meet the '*standard that a reasonable person would regard as satisfactory, taking into account of any description of the goods, price if relevant and all other relevant circumstances*'. Regarding consumer sale contracts, based on Section 14 (2D) of the Sale of Goods Act 1979, these relevant circumstances include any public statement on the specific characteristics of goods made by the seller, producer, or his representative, particularly in advertising or on labelling'.[191] Consequently, the characteristics of the goods, presented in catalogues, leaflets, brochures, posters, notices, labelling and advertisements create justified expectations that this specified product possesses the advertised characteristics.[192]

313. It is important to determine which types of statement will be relevant for the assessment of satisfactory quality. First of all, the statements must be made as to the specific characteristics of goods. This excludes the importance of other information which is intended to persuade the consumer to buy a product and which often cannot be objectively verified.[193] Examples of relevant information which should be taken into account while assessing the public statements are as follows:

1. Information regarding the basic identity of goods.
2. Information ensuring that particular inspections have been carried out.
3. Characteristics indicated by particular certificates.
4. Durability.
5. Fitness for other specific purposes.

The public statements can be made by the seller, producer, manufacturer or their representative.[194]

Before the implementation of the Consumer Sales Directive, the Sale of Goods Act 1979 did not contain the criterion of correspondence with the public statements within the circumstances determining satisfactory quality. In this respect, changes introduced by the Sale and Supply of Goods to Consumer Regulations 2002 broaden the notion of satisfactory quality of goods sold to the consumer.

314. There were some doubts over whether the criterion of public statements will be successful within English jurisdiction. Some commentators have noted that national courts have, in the past, been reluctant to impose direct contractual liability upon the manufac-

191 Introduced in Section 14 of the Sale of Goods Act 1979 by Regulation 3 of the SSGCR 2002.
192 Willet, Morgan-Taylor and Naidoo 2004, p. 96-98.
193 Willet, Morgan-Taylor and Naidoo 2004, p. 96.
194 Willet, Morgan-Taylor and Naidoo 2004, p. 96.

turers for their advertising statements.[195] Nonetheless, a manufacturer will be contractually bound every time he makes a promise to do something, such as paying a sum of money or provide a service in exchange for entering into a contract. The English courts are very cautious where general advertising statements are concerned. Most probably, the producer (or seller) could be held liable when he confirms the statement in response to an inquiry by a consumer planning to enter into a specific transaction.[196] However, in the absence of such confirmation the court will probably deny that there was an intention to undertake a contractual obligation.[197]

315. Following the Consumer Sales Directive, according to Section 14 (2E) of the Sale of Goods Act 1979, public statements shall not be taken into account while establishing the seller's liability if:

1. The seller could not have reasonably been aware of the statement at the time of the conclusion of contract.
2. Before the contract has been concluded the statements have been withdrawn or corrected. To be successful, such correction or withdrawal requires a reference to the original statement.
3. The decision of whether to buy the goods or not could not have been affected by the statement.

The defences available to the seller match those in the Directive. The burden of proving the above facts lies with the seller.

The new Consumer Rights Bill provides in Section 9 (5)-(7) an identical regulation regarding the public statements made by a seller, producer or his representative. The public statements are not regarded as a separate criterion of non-conformity but rather as relevant circumstances to be taken into account when determining satisfactory quality. Also the exceptions applying to public statements appear in a new statute in an unchanged manner.

4.5.2.5 Incorrect installation

316. Article 2 (5) of the Consumer Sales Directive states that '*any lack of conformity resulting from incorrect installation of the consumer goods shall be deemed to be equivalent to the lack of conformity of the goods if installation forms a part of the contract of sale of goods and the goods were installed by the seller or under his responsibility*'. This shall apply equally if the product was intended to be self-installed and it was installed by a consumer

195 Benjamin's sale of goods 2010, nr. 10-005; See: *Hummingbird Motors v Hobbs* (1986) R.T.R. 278.

196 Benjamin's sale of goods 2010, nr. 10-004, 11-034.

197 Willet, Morgan-Taylor and Naidoo 2004, p. 96; Benjamin's sale of goods 2010, nr. 10-005.

following poor instruction manuals. There is uncertainty over whether English law falls short when it comes to the incorrect installation as an aspect of satisfactory quality.[198]

317. When the incorrect installation is carried out by the seller or a third party for whom the seller is responsible, Section 14 of the Sale of Goods Act 1979 indicates that a buyer has a right to remedies.[199] The liability for incorrect installation requires consumer's reliance on the seller's reasonable care and skills. The Consumer Sales Directive does not provide such reservation. It offers the protection in cases where there has been an incorrect installation performed by the seller, producer, or his representatives. This also applies to the installation performed by the buyer, using (misleading) instructions provided by the seller or producer. It can be stated that Article 2 (5) of the Consumer Sales Directive imposes 'strict' liability for incorrect installation. On the other hand, the seller's liability for non-conforming goods is in principle 'strict', in the sense that it does not depend on the fault or negligence. Accordingly, it seems that Article 2 (5) of the Consumer Sales Directive has not been properly implemented into English Law, or at least the scope of the liability for incorrect installation is narrower under the Sale of Goods Act 1979 than under the Directive.[200]

318. The installation carried out by the consumer is deemed to amount to non-conformity under the Directive if it has been caused by the shortcomings of the instruction manual. The Sale of Goods Act 1979 does not contain similar provisions. At one point, there was an issue whether and to what extent the instructions are relevant in establishing whether or not goods are of satisfactory quality.[201] It was explained that the instructions are a part of what has been supplied and they affect the ability to use the goods.[202] Therefore, they are covered by the 'relevant circumstances' mentioned by Section 14 (2A) of the Sale of Goods Act 1979. However, an express provision or case law stating that incorrect installation by the consumer, due to the faulty instructions, amounts to a lack of satisfactory quality or fitness for purpose is lacking. This situation may create some uncertainty. The Consumer Sales Directive provides for incorrect installation regardless of who causes it. It constitutes a separate criterion of non-conformity and not general circumstances determining liability for non-conformity as under the Sale of Goods Act 1979. According to some opinions a

198 Schulte-Nölke, Twigg-Flesner and Ebers 2008, p. 670.

199 Department of Trade and Industry, Consumer and Competition Directorate, The Sale and Supply to Consumer Regulations, A brief Introduction, p. 18.

200 Woodroffe and Lowe 2013, p. 44.

201 Second Consultation on the Directive 1999/44 EC on Certain Aspects of the Sale of Consumer Goods and Associated Guarantees (DTI, London, 2002), p. 55.

202 Benjamine's Sale of Goods 2010, nr. 12-118.

lack of the distinct provision regulating this matter might amount to the non-implementation as far as incorrect installation is concerned.[203]

The uncertainty that exists under the Sale of Goods Act 1979 regarding installation will most probably disappear when the Consumer Rights Bill is enacted. Section 15 of the Consumer Rights Bill provides that the goods do not conform to the contract to supply goods if installation of goods forms part of a contract, the goods are installed by the seller or under his responsibility and the goods are installed incorrectly. Although Section 15 still does not list the situation when the buyer himself incorrectly installs the goods, it seems that applying a conforming interpretation in the above mentioned case, it will fall within the scope of the Section 15 of the Consumer Rights Bill.

4.5.2.6 Legal defects

319. In English law the notion of legal defects is not often used. Such a situation is described as (no) right to sell which results in the impossibility of transferring the title. The rules as to the passing of property and title are the same for consumers and commercial buyers.[204]

According to Section 12 (1) of the Sale of Goods Act there is an implied term that the seller has a right to sell the goods, and in the case of an agreement to sell he will have such a right at the time of the transfer of ownership. Furthermore, Section12 (2) provides that there is an implied term that the goods are free, and will remain free from any charge or legal encumbrance not disclosed or known to the buyer before the contract is concluded until the time of transfer of ownership; and that the buyer will enjoy quiet possession of the goods except so far as it may be disturbed by the owner or any other person entitled to the benefit of any charge or encumbrance disclosed or known.

If the goods supplied under the contract of sale do not belong to the seller, the buyer will acquire no title unless one of the exceptions to the rule *nemo dat* applies.[205] When the buyer does not acquire a title, the seller is in breach of the condition of the contract under Section 12 of the Sale of Goods Act 1979. This Section is applicable to all contracts of sale.

320. If the seller has no right to sell, the buyer can undertake two courses of action. He can rescind or affirm the agreement. If the consumer wants to rescind the contract and recover the price he has to take action in '*quasi*-contract' on the ground of total failure of consideration. If the buyer chooses to affirm the agreement, knowing of the breach, he will be able to claim damages.[206]

The question arises of whether the defects in conveying property are covered by the notion of non-conformity as adopted in English law. It seems that unlike in Poland, the

203 Willet, Morgan-Taylor and Naidoo 2004, p. 99.
204 Macleod 2007, nr. 12.04 A.
205 *Nemo dat quod non habet.*
206 Macleod 2007, nr. 12.04 A.

question of the lack of a right to sell is not associated with satisfactory quality (neither with non-conformity) as such. Similarly to German and Dutch law, it constitutes an independent legal concept.[207] Therefore, it can be concluded that the satisfactory quality (non-conformity – as adopted in English law) regards only the physical state of goods and their fitness for purpose. The new Consumer Rights Bill does not bring change in this respect

4.5.2.7 Conclusions

321. Summing up, Section 48F of the Sale of Goods Act contains a definition of the non-conformity which applies only in case when the consumer makes use of one of the statutory remedies. It states that the goods do not conform to the contract if one of the express or implied terms of the contract is breached. The non-conformity also exists in the context of the presumption of non-conformity, as provided in Section 48A (3) of the Sale of Goods Act 1979.

The criteria implemented into the Sale of Goods Act 1979 and proposed in the Consumer Rights Bill which are significant to determine whether the consumer goods lack satisfactory quality are as follows:

1. Goods do not breach any express term that the parties agreed to.
2. Goods should match any description given by the seller.
3. Goods should be of satisfactory quality i.e. they should meet the standard a reasonable person would regard as satisfactory, taking into account any description of the goods, price (if relevant) and all other relevant circumstances.
4. The quality of goods includes their state and condition and the following:
   a. fitness for all purposes for which goods of the kind in question are commonly supplied,
   b. appearance and finish,
   c. freedom from minor defects,
   d. safety,
   e. durability.
5. Goods should be reasonably fit for any particular purpose that was made known to the seller (unless the seller disputed their appropriateness for that purpose at the time).[208]
6. Goods should be correctly installed.

In case of the delivery of goods of non-satisfactory quality or that are unfit for purpose the consumer has a right to remedies, unless one of three exceptions applies. According to

207 In some situations it is possible that these two notions will overlap; See *Bramhill v Edwards* (2004) EWCA Civ 403.

208 Woodroffe and Lowe 2013, p. 43.

English law, the rights to remedies are excluded in cases of ordinary wear and tear, there has been misuse or accidental damage to the goods.[209]

322. Under the current law, the criteria mentioned above fall short in some aspects when compared to the criteria from Article 2 (2) (a)-(d) of the Consumer Sales Directive.[210] For example, incorrect installation, correspondence to sample, and fitness for ordinary purpose. Taking into account the proposed reform of consumer protection in the area of sales law, the existing uncertainty seems to be, to some extent, clarified. The Consumer Rights Bill contains detailed rights the consumer is entitled to, in case of delivery of goods of unsatisfactory quality, unfit for purpose or breaching any other term provided in Sections 9-18 of the Consumer Rights Bill. Furthermore, the new amendments will ensure that nearly all the criteria of non-conformity found in the Directive are implemented. This increases legal certainty regarding the characteristics that the purchased goods must possess.

323. Finally, there is a great deal of attention given to the consumers in English legal culture. Besides several aspects of non-conformity pointed out in this sub-section, there do not seem to be serious failures in implementing the provisions of the Consumer Sales Directive in the Sale of Goods Act 1979. Taking into account the long tradition of the consumer provisions in England, the impact of the Consumer Sales Directive should not be overstated, especially regarding the notion of non-conformity.[211]

4.5.3 *Buyer's knowledge of the non-conformity*

324. Article 2 (3) of the Consumer Sales Directive provides that '*there shall be deemed not to be a lack of conformity if at the time of conclusion of the contract, the consumer was aware, or could not reasonably be unaware of the lack of conformity*'. In English law there are similar exclusions when the goods may not be considered as being of unsatisfactory quality. One of such exclusions concerns the fact that consumers, after a reasonable inspection of goods, should have discovered the defects. Furthermore, the buyer will not be able to rely on the lack of satisfactory quality when particular characteristics have been specifically drawn to his attention before the contract was concluded.[212]

325. The implied condition that the quality of goods must be satisfactory is excluded in two situations. Section 14 (2C) of the Sale of Goods Act 1979 states that the implied term

209 Woodroffe and Lowe 2013, p. 43.
210 Schulte-Nölke, Twigg-Flesner and Ebers 2008, p. 670.
211 Bridge 2003, p. 176.
212 Benjamin's sale of goods 2010, nr. 14-014.

of satisfactory quality does not extend to any matter which would otherwise make the goods unsatisfactory, which is specifically drawn to the buyer's attention before the contract was concluded, or as confirmed by case law, at the time of the delivery.[213] Other situations are when the buyer examines the goods and this examination should reveal the defects, or when the goods are sold by a sample and the defects should have been apparent on a reasonable examination of a sample. Accordingly, under English law, in some situations a buyer seems to have a duty to examine the goods.[214] If he does not do so within reasonable time, he may lose the right to complain, also in situations where had he examined the goods he would have discovered the defect in question.[215] English law often makes references to the investigation and inspection of goods. It does not however project an investigation as a legal obligation. It indicates that a consumer's negligence in checking the state of goods may influence the scope of the seller's liability.[216]

Section 9 (4) of the Consumer Rights Bill, as with Section 14 (2C) of the Sale of Goods Act 1979, excludes the existence of unsatisfactory quality which is specifically drawn to the consumer's attention. A similar rule applies when the consumer examines the goods before the conclusion of contract and reasonable examination should have revealed the unsatisfactory quality. The same counts for the contracts concluded by showing a sample, when the lack of satisfactory quality and fitness for purpose should have been discovered upon the inspection of the purchased goods and the sample.

4.5.4 *Burden of proof of the non-conformity*

326. In general it must be stated that English law does not provide for presumptions of existence or lack of existence of (non)conformity, satisfactory quality or fitness for purpose.[217] The criteria constituting the satisfactory quality indicate what the buyer should focus on in order to satisfy the burden that the goods delivered to him are not of satisfactory quality or lack conformity. In practical terms, the criteria of non-conformity include all criteria of satisfactory quality, fitness for purpose and other aspects of the (physical) state of goods as stated in Section 48F of the Sale of Goods Act 1979. When collecting all criteria of satisfactory quality, one might construct a legal definition of this term, yet again without any consequences for the applicability of the presumptions contained in Article 2 (2) of the Consumer Sales Directive.

213 *Clegg v Olle Anderson T/A Nordic Marine*, (2003) EWCA Civ 320.
214 Benjamin's sale of goods 2010, nr. 11-042.
215 Twigg-Flesner and Bradgate 2000, p. 9.
216 Benjamin's sale of goods 2010, nr. 11-045.
217 Schulte-Nölke, Twigg-Flesner and Ebers 2008, p. 670.

327. In English law, the criteria demanding satisfactory quality and fitness for purpose are constructed as implied terms. One of the functions of implied terms is to give effect to the presumed intention of the parties.[218] They are important especially for buyers as they provide them with a number of rights against the seller. Before the implied terms from Sections 12-15 of the Sale of Goods Act 1979, the rule governing English sales law was described as *caveat emptor.*[219] Under this rule the burden of proving the specific undertaking from the seller regarding the standard of quality of goods was on the buyer. After the formulation of the implied terms the requirement to seek a specific undertaking from the seller has been significantly reduced.[220] Therefore, it can be concluded that the implied terms from Sections 12-15 of the Sale of Goods Act 1979, although not constructed as presumptions, may still simplify and facilitate the burden of proving the lack of satisfactory quality or unfitness for purpose. The regulations found in the new proposal for Consumer Rights Bill provide even more detailed implied terms that the contracts of sale include. The formulation of these terms in the new Bill is quite comprehensive and it seems to provide more clarity as to which terms are to be implied and which facts the consumer is required to provide to be successful in proving the defectiveness of purchased goods.

328. The burden of proof regarding the existence of non-conformity, unsatisfactory quality and unfitness for purpose will be allocated according to the general principle.[221] A person who claims the (non)existence of facts and relies on the legal consequences thereof is obliged to provide sufficient evidence. When it comes to the unsatisfactory quality, the buyer is the one who relies on it in order to receive remedies. Consequently, a buyer is the person who has the burden of proving the facts constituting non-conformity. The judge can ease the consumer's burden by applying factual presumptions, what has been observed in particular when the goods do not possess a sufficient degree of durability.[222]

4.5.5 Conclusions

329. The English legislator does not follow the wording of the Directive with respect to the notion of non-conformity. Some of the criteria from Article 2 (2) (a)-(d) of the Consumer Sales Directive have not been fully introduced into English law. On the other hand, the scope of other criteria extend beyond what has been required under the Directive. The

218 Goode/Mckendrick 2010, p. 342.

219 '*A common-law maxim warning a purchaser that he could not claim that his purchases were defective unless he protected himself by obtaining express guarantees from the vendor*'; See Law and Martin 2009, Oxford Dictionary of Law.

220 Mckendrick 2013, p. 342 *et seq.*; Willett and Morgan-Taylor 2013, p. 394.

221 Chapter 2, para 59-61, 67.

222 Chapter 4, para 301.

view that has been taken by the legislator is that all elements of non-conformity were covered by the existing criteria of standards of satisfactory quality and fitness for purpose and that English law already provided for a sufficient level of protection.

The standards set out in sections 12-15 of the Sale of Goods Act 1979 indeed correlate to those set out in Article 2 (2) (a)-(d) of the Consumer Sales Directive, nevertheless, they are not formulated identically and some of them differ in scope. In some instances it is difficult to state whether English provisions meet the Directive's requirements regarding the notion of non-conformity.[223] However, it seems that there are not many practical problems. It is possible that more time is needed to assess whether the above mentioned differences are relevant for the effective protection of consumers' interests.[224]

330. Similar conclusions must be drawn when it comes to the exclusion of seller's liability. According to the Consumer Sales Directive if the consumer was aware, or could not reasonably have been unaware of the lack of conformity at the time of the conclusion of the contract, the seller is not liable. The Sale of Goods Act 1979 already contained a very similar reservation however, requiring investigatory activities not included in the Directive.

Regarding the issues of burden of proof, the criteria of non-conformity (implied terms of satisfactory quality and fitness for purpose) existing in English law do not resemble the construction found in Article 2 (2) (a)-(d) of the Consumer Sales Directive. The provisions of the Sale of Goods Act 1979 contain the facts that must be provided by the consumer in order to convince the judge of the existence of defects and the existence of valid rights to remedies. On the other hand, the construction of implied terms facilitates the formulation of what was a presumed intention of the parties. Finally, as illustrated on the example of durability in paragraph 301 of this chapter, the factual presumption that the goods lacked satisfactory quality may be applied to facilitate the burden of proof.

331. The proposed Consumer Rights Bill has specific provisions regarding the state of goods clarifying some of the existing uncertainty. They clearly state which terms must be treated as included in the consumer sale contracts. The construction of the new Bill seems to be more approachable and understandable also for less experienced buyers/consumers, especially in comparison to the construction of the implied terms from the Sale of Goods 1979. It also deals with some of the criticism of the current consumer sales legislation. Overall, it seems that the Consumer Rights Bill carries an improvement and clarification for English consumers.

223 Bridge 2002, p. 79.
224 Watterson 2001, p. 202.

4.6 Non-conformity in Dutch law

4.6.1 *Introduction*

332. This section describes the notion of non-conformity of consumer goods within the meaning of the Consumer Sales Directive and the Dutch concept of non-conformity found in Articles 7:17 and 7:18 BW. The focus will be on the differences between the meaning of non-conformity under the Directive and under the Dutch Civil Code (4.6.2). Furthermore, attention will be paid to questions of the consumer's knowledge of the non-conformity (4.6.3). Finally, the issues of burden of proof regarding the existence of non-conformity will be discussed (4.6.4).

333. According to Article 7:1 and 7:9 BW the seller's main obligations are to transfer the ownership of goods and deliver them to the buyer. According to Article 7:17 (1) BW, the delivered goods must conform to the contract (*conformiteitvereiste*).[225] The obligations of the seller are formulated just as in German law, emphasising the obligation to transfer the ownership. The Consumer Sales Directive does not mention such obligation.[226]

The majority of disputes between the seller and the consumer regard the question of whether the goods delivered by the seller conformed to the contract.[227] The goods are to be assessed as to their conformity at the exact time of delivery.[228] The assessment regards the presence of the non-conformity. The fact that the seller was not aware of the defects is insufficient to exclude liability for non-conforming goods.[229]

334. Before the implementation of the Directive, Article 7:17 BW – originally based on Article 35 CISG was introduced into the Dutch Civil Code in 1992 and regulated the issues of non-conformity.[230] The definition of non-conformity introduced in 1992 to large extent reflected the criteria of non-conformity of Article 2 (2) of the Consumer Sales Directive. In particular, the provisions regarding requirements of conformity for the normal use of goods, normal quality and particular purpose of goods communicated to the seller were very similar to the ones found in the Directive. Nevertheless, some other aspects of Article 2 (2) of the Consumer Sales Directive were missing from Dutch regulation and had to be

225 Asser/Hijma 7-I* 2013, nr. 268; Klik 2011, p. 27; Loos 2004, p. 43; Castermans and Krans 2013 (T&C Vermogensrecht), art. 7:9 BW, aant. 1, 2.

226 It is related to the system of transfer of property which falls outsite of the scope of this research.

227 Klik 2011, p. 54.

228 Castermans and Krans 2013 (T&C Vermogensrecht), art. 7:17 BW, aant. 2.

229 Asser/Hijma 7-I* 2013, nr 332; Hijma 2013, p. 258.

230 Asser/Hijma 7-I* 2013, nr. 325.

implemented. In the end the implementation of Article 2 (2) of the Directive provided for more specific rules regarding non-conformity.

4.6.2 Non-conformity: definitions

335. The notion of non-conformity is defined in Articles 7:17 (2)-(6) and 18 (1) and (3) BW. Article 17 (2) BW states that the delivered goods are not in conformity with a contract if they do not possess the characteristics which the buyer was entitled to expect under the contract, taking into account the nature of the goods and the statements about the goods made by the seller.[231] The main reference point in establishing non-conformity are the buyer's reasonable expectations of the goods.[232]

The buyer may expect the goods to have characteristics necessary for normal use, whose existence should not have been doubted and the characteristics necessary for a specific use which were foreseen in the contract. Article 7:17 (3) BW provides that goods other than those agreed or of a different kind do not conform to the contract. The same applies if the goods vary in quantity, size or weight from the parties' agreement. In case of sale of goods by showing a sample or a model, Article 7:17 (4) BW provides that the goods must conform thereto, unless the sample or the model was shown to the consumer only for an indicative purpose.[233] According to Article 7:17 (5) BW, the buyer cannot rely on non-conformity if at the time of the conclusion of the contract he knew or reasonably should have known about the non-conformity. Similarly, the buyer cannot rely on the non-conformity if it results from the defective materials provided by him to manufacture the goods, unless the seller had a duty to warn the consumer about the defectiveness of these materials. Finally, Article 7:17 (6) BW provides that in the case of the sale of an immovable, the stated size/surface of this immovable is deemed to be merely a designation with which the immovable should correspond.[234]

In the consumer sale, pursuant to Article 7:18 (1) BW, the public statements made about the goods by the seller must be taken into account to determine whether the goods lack conformity, unless these statements have been rectified before the conclusion of the contract or did not influence the buyer's decision to enter into the contract. Moreover, in the contracts between consumer and professional, the incorrect installation carried out by the seller or by the buyer (based on misleading instructions) is regarded as non-conformity, pursuant to Article 7:18 (3) BW.

231 Hof Arnhem 17.07.2012, ECLI:GHARN:2012:BX2358, para 4.8.
232 Klik 2008, p. 49.
233 Description of Article based on the translation of the Dutch Civil Code: Warendorf, Thomas and Curry-Sumner 2009, p. 725, art. 17.
234 Outside the scope of consumer sale.

336. In general the non-conformity has been explained as any difference between the agreed goods and the goods that have been delivered.[235] The Dutch Civil Code provides the non-exhaustive enumeration of circumstances where the goods do not conform to the contract. The non-conformity may regard the quality of goods, their identity and quantity.[236] Besides, Article 7:18 (3) implements the non-conformity in case of incorrect installation. All aspects of non-conformity: quality, identity and quantity, and incorrect installations are discussed below.

4.6.2.1 Quality

I The characteristics that the buyer is entitled to expect

337. The quality aspect entails the seller's obligation to deliver goods which possess the characteristics that the parties agreed upon and which the buyer is entitled to expect under the contract. The characteristics of goods should also be understood as the sum of the difference in quality between the delivered goods and the parties' agreement. It includes the discrepancies decreasing the use of goods, as well as any other aspects not affecting the physical state of goods, for example colour, place of manufacture, or facts whether the goods do not possess all safety certificates.[237]

338. The question of which characteristics the buyer is entitled to expect from the goods at the time of the conclusion of the contract depends on all existing circumstances of the case.[238] Article 7:17 (2) BW provides for two specific circumstances: the nature of the goods and information and statements about the goods provided by the seller. Regarding the nature of the goods one may think of aspects such as whether the goods are new or second-hand, brand goods or of unknown origins, the price of the goods, place where the goods are purchased (outlet, boutique, flea market), and other circumstances surrounding the purchase (sale, clearance, new arrivals).[239]

Moreover, the question of whether the goods conform to the contract also depends on information and statements the seller makes about the goods. The quality that the buyer is entitled to expect is based on quality that an average (informed) buyer is entitled to expect. Special expectations, lower or higher, can be based on specific statements about the goods made by the seller, or statements that he should have made. Therefore, statements about the goods and information provided by the time of the conclusion of the contract may lead to higher expectations of the goods than if certain information had not been

235 T.M., Parl. gesch. NBW (Inv. Boeken 3, 5 en 6), Boek 7 (Reehuis and Slob 1991), p. 118.
236 Asser/Hijma 7-I* 2013, nr. 333.
237 Asser/Hijma 7-I* 2013, nr. 334; See also HR 23.11.2007, ECLI:NL:HR:2007:BB3733, NJ 2008/552.
238 HR 21.05.2010, ECLI:NL:HR:2010:BL8295, NJ 2010/275.
239 Asser/Hijma 7-I* 2013, nr. 335.

provided (or if certain flaws or drawbacks of the goods had been revealed).[240] In some situations, particular information regarding the goods provided by the seller or the producer will not be sufficient to claim non-conformity. For example, in a case regarding the sale of a new car the fact that the average fuel consumption was higher than in the technical specifications did not constitute non-conformity.[241]

Summing up, the balance between the information duty lying with the seller and buyer's duty to investigate, which indicate what the buyer is entitled to expect under the contract, depends on (*inter alia*) the following circumstances: the nature of the goods, information about the goods made by the seller and the character of the parties in terms of participating in the B2B, B2C or C2C contracts.[242]

II Normal use

339. According to Article 7:17 (2) BW, under the contract the buyer is entitled to expect that the goods possess characteristics that are necessary for the normal use of those goods. There is no definition of normal use of goods. Where there is a dispute it must be established individually, depending on the circumstances and facts of the case. It has been observed that the meaning of normal use should be approached objectively. Therefore, the general standards will determine the scope of normal usage in respect of the purchased goods and not the parties' own personal understanding.[243] The term normal use should be interpreted broadly.[244]

340. In the decision *Kousedghi/Westminster Rental* regarding a second-hand car, the Hoge Raad ruled against the narrow interpretation of normal use.[245] The statement that '*as long as the nine year old car is suitable (admitted) to the traffic, it is in conformity*' is insufficient for the purpose of Article 7:17 (2) BW. To assess the conformity of the second-hand car, not just road safety must be taken into account but other elements too. According to Article 7:17 (2) BW in the assessment of non-conformity of goods, the nature of goods and the statements about the product made by the seller play an important role. Summing up, factors such as the agreement itself, the normal use of goods, the nature of goods, durability, and the statements about them made by the seller, determine what the buyer reasonably is entitled to expect from the purchased goods.[246]

---

240 See: Rb Assen 16.10.2012, ECLI:NL:RBASS2012:BY1448; Topic discussed also in chapter 3, para 202.

241 Rb Utrecht 18.03.2009, ECLI:NL:RBUTR:2009:BH6552, Hof Amsterdam 17.04.2012, ECLI:NL:GHAMS: 2012:BW3101.

242 Castermans and Krans 2013 (T&C Vermogensrecht), art. 7:17 BW, aant. 3.

243 Asser/Hijma 7-I* 2013, nr. 345.

244 Asser/Hijma 7-I* 2013, nr. 345; Klik 2008, p. 72.

245 HR 8.07.2005, ECLI:NL:HR:2005:AT3097, NJ 2006/22 (Kousedghi/Westminster Rental).

246 Bijzondere overeenkomsten (Schelhaas) 2013, nr. 30.

341. As stated before, Article 7:17 (2) BW requires the buyer to carry out (some) sort of investigation in order to establish whether the goods possess the characteristics necessary for a normal use. It laid out in the first sentence of paragraph two stating that '*the goods are not in conformity if they do not possess the characteristics which existence under the contract should/could not have been doubted by the buyer.* Therefore, if the goods do not possess the characteristics which under the contract the buyer should/could have doubted, the lack of such characteristics do not amount to non-conformity.[247]

III Special use

342. Besides the normal use, in some circumstances the consumer may expect more from the purchased goods. Article 7:17 (2) BW states that the buyer is entitled to expect the goods to have characteristics necessary for special use, known by the seller and not objected to at the time of the conclusion of contract. For example, the watch that is water-resistant and suitable for a deep dive,[248] or shoes which are suitable for hiking.[249] The consumer can rely on the additional characteristics necessary for the specific use only when the intended purpose of use has been foreseen in the contract. A case decided by the Rechtbank Zutphen is an example.[250] It regarded the sale of a mare which, after the delivery, was no longer able to become pregnant. The buyer claimed rescission of the contract due to non-conformity, since according to the buyer a mare was purchased for breeding purposes. The court decided against the seller, stating that he did not prove that the purpose of purchase had not been sufficiently communicated. Although the decision was handed down before the implementation of the Directive, it is still valid for the purpose of interpretation of non-conformity due to the lack of suitability for a specific use.

When a buyer informs a seller of the special purpose, he can respond in four ways. First of all, he can inform the buyer that the goods will possess the special characteristics, second, he cannot assure the buyer that the goods are suitable for the given purpose, he can remain silent about the suitability of the goods for the given purpose, and finally, he can state that the goods' fitness for the special purpose is impossible.[251] Depending on the seller's reaction, the buyer's expectations may differ considerably affecting the scope of non-conformity in that particular case. It must be concluded that regarding the suitability of goods for special use, both the communication of a special purpose for which the goods are purchased and statements about the goods (its suitability) made by seller are of particular importance.

247 Castermans and Krans 2013 (T&C Vermogensrecht), art. 7:17 BW, aant. 3; Bijzondere overeenkomsten (Schelhaas) 2013, nr. 30.

248 Klik 2011, p. 43.

249 Asser/Hijma 7-I* 2013, nr. 347.

250 Rb Zutphen 18.07.2002, ECLI:NL:RBZUT:2002:AE6846.

251 Asser/Hijma 7-I* 2013, nr. 348.

4.6.2.2 Identity and quantity

343. Further aspects of non-conformity regard the identity and quantity of goods. Article 7:17 (3) BW explicitly states that the goods differing in identity or in what has been agreed as to in terms of size, type, weight or quantity, do not conform to the contract. For example, a consumer ordered wine from Bordeaux but received wine from Anjou.[252] This issue has been also recognised under German law, when the court decided that stating the place of a car's manufacture incorrectly constitutes a defect under § 434 BGB.[253] Furthermore, other aspects of identity which in principle might not affect usage or quality can be of significance. For example, an incorrect kilometre reading in a second-hand car.[254] Another example is whether a particular food product is organic or not. Additionally, Castermans argues that the scope of Article 7:17 BW also covers the ban of child labour in the process of manufacturing the goods and that the ban has not been infringed. Therefore, the opposite constitutes non-conformity.[255] Summing up, it must be stated that alongside the aspects of non-conformity affecting the quality of goods, there are aspects of non-conformity which do not diminish the quality and have nothing to do with the ability to use the goods. Nevertheless, the lack of these aspects entails the seller's liability for the delivery of non-conforming goods.[256]

344. When a contract has been concluded based on a sample or model demonstrated to the consumer, Article 7:17 (4) BW provides that the characteristics of goods must correspond to the characteristics of this sample or model, unless they have been presented only for indicative purposes. The burden of proving the latter lies with the seller.[257]

4.6.2.3 Incorrect installation

345. Article 2 (5) of the Consumer Sales Directive states that incorrect installation carried out by the seller, a third party for which the seller is responsible, or by a consumer based on instructions provided by the seller, amounts to non-conformity. Under Dutch law before the implementation of the Directive the installation was regarded as a separate contract, hire for work or services, subject to Article 7:400 BW – outside of the scope of consumer protection. The Dutch legislator has amended the rules regarding the installation and in Article 7:18 (3) BW provided proper protection in cases of incorrect installation.[258] The new provision follows Article 2 (5) of the Consumer Sales Directive and provides that '*where in a consumer sale the seller is responsible for installation of the thing, incorrect*

252 T.M., Parl. gesch. NBW (Inv. Boeken 3, 5 en 6), Boek 7 (Reehuis and Slob 1991), p. 118.
253 LG Ellwangen 13.12.2002, 3 O 219/02, NJW 2003, 517, mentioned in chapter 4, para 280.
254 Rb 's-Gravenhage 04.06.2008, ECLI:NL:RBSGR:2008:BE8794.
255 Castermans 2009, p. 157-160.
256 Asser/Hijma 7-I* 2013, nr. 349.
257 Asser/Hijma 7-I* 2013, nr. 351; Castermans and Krans 2013 (T&C Vermogensrecht), art. 7:17 BW, aant. 5.
258 Castermans and Krans 2013 (T&C Vermogensrecht), art. 7:18 BW, aant. 5.

installation shall be equated to a lack of conformity of the thing to the contract. This shall apply equally where the thing is incorrectly installed by the buyer and the incorrect installation is due to the installation instructions provided to the buyer on delivery of the thing'.[259] The incorrect installation applies to cases where the seller was responsible for assembling the goods. The same applies when the consumer incorrectly installed the goods, based on a misleading instructions provided by the seller or producer. Article 7:18 (3) BW does not cover situations where the buyer hires a professional third party to install the goods or when the incorrect installation results from the negligent acts of a third party.[260]

346. The right to claim remedies under the Dutch Civil Code also depends on whether the buyer has informed the seller of the existence of non-conformity (*klachtplicht*). Article 7:23 BW provides that the buyer must inform the seller of the non-conformity within a reasonable time from the point where he discovered it or – except in B2C cases – should have discovered it. Following the option given in the Consumer Sales Directive,[261] Article 7:23 BW states that in the relationship between consumers and professionals a period of two months is always reasonable.[262] The provision of Article 7:23 BW protects sellers from too late reported defects of goods that could make it too difficult to counter and disprove their existence. In cases of an infringement of the duty stemming from Article 7:23 BW the buyer loses the right to claim remedies. There was a period where the seller's argument regarding infringement of buyer's duty to notify of the existence of non-conformity became a very popular argument before the court.[263] Eventually, the Hoge Raad specified the scope of the reasonable time to inform of the defects, in a way that it is in principle favourable to the consumer.[264]

4.6.2.4 Legal defects

347. One of the main obligations of the seller under Article 7:9 BW is to transfer the ownership of the goods. Pursuant to Articles 7:15 and 7:16 BW, the goods should be free from any rights a third party may have towards the goods, with an exception to the existing rights a buyer is aware of.[265] Mentioned articles apply to all types of sales, including consumer sales. Accordingly, the obligation to deliver goods in conformity to the contract is purely of factual character and does not cover legal defects.[266] Consequently, the notion

259 Warendorf, Thomas and Curry-Sumner 2009, art. 7:18 (3) BW.
260 Asser/Hijma 7-I* 2013, nr. 355.
261 Recital 19 and Article 5 (2) of the Consumer Sales Directive.
262 Castermans and Krans 2013 (T&C Vermogensrecht), art. 7:23, aant. 2.
263 Asser/Hijma 7-I* 2013, nr. 543a.
264 HR 25.02.2005, ECLI:NL:HR:2005:AR5383 (Fabels/Meenderink); HR 29.06.2007, ECLI:NL:HR:2007:AZ7617, NJ 2008/606 (Pouw/Visser).
265 Asser/Hijma 7-I* 2013, nr. 274.
266 Asser/Hijma 7-I* 2013, nr. 326.

of non-conformity covers only material aspect of defectiveness, including aspects not affecting quality such as colour or place of manufacture, and as with German and English law does not affect the legal status of goods.[267] The transfer of ownership and legal aspects of defectiveness are regulated separately by Articles 7:15 and 7:16 BW.

4.6.2.5 Conclusions

348. Even before the implementation of the Directive, the Dutch Civil Code already contained a modern definition of non-conformity, originally inspired by the CISG. However, to meet the level of protection emerging from the Directive some minor amendments had to be made. These amendments concerned incorrect installation, public statements about the goods, and provisions regarding model or a sample. The definition of non-conformity under the Dutch law is formulated in a different way to that of the Consumer Sales Directive. It does not provide for presumptions of (non)conformity. Generally, under Article 7:17 (2) BW, the existence of non-conformity depends on whether the goods possess the characteristics that the buyer was entitled to expect under the contract, taking into consideration the nature of the goods and the statements made by the seller about the goods.

349. According to Articles 7:17 and 7:18 of the Dutch Civil Code, the interpretation provided by the Hoge Raad and legal scholars,[268] the consumer goods lack conformity in the situations where the goods do not possess characteristics which the buyer was entitled to under the contract, in particular:

1. The goods do not possess characteristics necessary for normal use.
2. The goods do not possess characteristics necessary for specific purpose, foreseen under the contract.
3. The goods do not possess the characteristics corresponding to the characteristics of the sample or model.
4. The goods differ in kind, size or quantity.
5. The goods were incorrectly installed.

350. Comparing the definition of non-conformity with the Directive, the Dutch Civil Code does not expressly mention the first criterion of non-conformity from Article 2 (2) (a) of the Consumer Sales Directive, that the consumer goods will be presumed to be in conform-

267 Asser/Hijma 7-I* 2013, nr. 336; Castermans and Krans 2013 (T&C Vermogensrecht), art. 7:17 BW, aant. 1, 2.

268 Asser/Hijma 7-I* 2013, nr. 334; Castermans and Krans 2013 (T&C Vermogensrecht), art. 7:17 BW, aant. 3; Klik 2011, p. 41; See also HR 23.11.2007, ECLI:NL:HR:2007:BB3733, NJ 2008/552; HR 21.05.2010, ECLI:NL:HR:2010:BL8295, NJ 2010/275.

ity if they comply with the description given by the seller.[269] It seems that the above-mentioned aspect of non-conformity is comparable with the question of what the consumer can expect from the goods based on the contract, which is found in Article 7:17 (2) s. 1 BW.[270] In fact, information about the goods and their descriptions may considerably affect what the consumer is entitled to expect. Additionally, the court, by using an interpretation consistent with the Directive, must conclude that the goods are not in conformity with the contract if they do not match the description given by the seller.[271]

4.6.3 *Buyer's knowledge of the non-conformity*

351. Following Article 2 (3) of the Consumer Sales Directive, the Dutch legislator introduced the exclusion of the liability for non-conformity in Article 7:17 (5) BW in cases where the buyer knew or should have reasonably known about the non-conformity at the time of the conclusion of the contract. Furthermore, the buyer cannot rely on the non-conformity when it resulted from the defectiveness and unsuitability of materials delivered by the buyer, from which the goods were manufactured, unless the seller had a duty to inform the buyer about this unsuitability. The provision relies on the assumption that if the buyer knows about the goods' non-conformity and decides to purchase them regardless, allowing the buyer at the later stage to execute his rights to remedies based on this non-conformity would be against the principle of reasonableness and equity (*redelijkheid en billijkheid*).[272]

352. The relationship between buyer's knowledge of the non-conformity from Article 7:17 (5) BW and the buyer's duty to investigate described in the second sentence of Article 7:17 (2) BW is not entirely clear. The latter provision requires, in certain situations, the buyer's investigation as to the existence of the characteristics which he is entitled to expect. This duty of investigation takes place at the time of sale and is linked to the scope of the expectations regarding normal use of goods. If these investigation duties have not been carried out, the buyer may not rely on the non-conformity.

The provision of Article 7:17 (5) BW directly refers to the knowledge, or unjustified lack of knowledge about the non-conformity, existing at the time of the conclusion of contract. Although Article 7:17 (5) BW is much more specific, the scopes of both regulations overlap. It seems that using an interpretation of Article 7:17 (2) BW in conformity with the Directive would be sufficient to ensure the objective of Article 2 (3) of the Consumer Sales Directive. However, to be sure that the Dutch law meets the level of protection

269 Hondius and Schelhaas 2001, p. 331.
270 MvT *Kamerstukken* 2000-2001, 27 809 nr. 3, p. 4.
271 Asser/Hijma 7-I* 2013, nr. 333, 334; Wissink/*diss*. 2001, p. 288, 289.
272 Asser/Hijma 7-I* 2013, nr. 356.

stemming from the Directive, the legislator decided to introduce Article 7:17 (5) BW. Due to the fact that these regulations have similar scopes and consequences, the delineation between these provisions is difficult and the relationship between them is somewhat unclear.

4.6.4 *Burden of proof of the non-conformity*

353. According to the general rule of the burden of proof found in 150 Rv, a person who relies on the legal consequences of certain facts bears the burden to prove them.[273] The burden of proving that delivered goods do not conform to the contract lies with the buyer.[274] Based on Article 7:18 (2) BW, a consumer-buyer benefits from the presumption of non-conformity if this non-conformity became apparent within six months from the time of delivery, unless the presumption is incompatible with the nature of the goods or the nature of the non-conformity.[275]

To satisfy the burden of proof, the consumer in particular, has to show that the goods do not possess the characteristics which he was entitled to expect under the contract taking into account the nature of the goods and the statements about the goods made by the seller. Furthermore, he can prove that the goods do not possess the characteristics necessary for normal use, or special use, if the special purpose has been foreseen at the time of the conclusion of the contract. Moreover, the buyer can prove that the goods do not correspond to the model or sample shown to the buyer. Finally, he can rely on the facts establishing incorrect installation.

354. Regarding the characteristics of goods which the buyer was entitled to expect the crucial moment for its evaluation is the time of conclusion of contract. The events that occurred after that time (not modifying the contract) for example, public statements about the goods made after the conclusion of contract have no influence on the content of the agreement and consequently on the consumer's reasonable expectations of the goods.[276]

Regarding public statements as a criterion for a non-conformity, the consumer bears the burden of proving the exact content of the description included in such statement and the fact that the goods do not comply therewith.

355. Finally, it must be observed that contrary to Article 2 (2) (a)-(d) of the Consumer Sales Directive, the Dutch Civil Code does not provide of any form of presumption of (non)conformity, simplifying the supply of proof of the existence of non-conformity.

---

273 Chapter 2, para 83.
274 See Rb Zwolle 21.05.2003, ECLI:NL:RBZWO:2003:AH8762.
275 Chapter 5, para 552 *et seq.*
276 Loos 2004, p. 51.

Exceptionally such simplification may be offered by the judge in the particular proceedings through the application of factual presumptions.[277]

The definition of non-conformity from Article 7:17 (2) BW is formulated in the negative manner: '*the goods do not conform to the contract if (...) they do not possess characteristics which the buyer was entitled to expect under the contract*'. As a result, Article 7:17 (2) BW requires buyer to first prove what he is entitled to expect under the contract and subsequently that the goods do not possess these reasonably expected characteristics.

4.6.5 Conclusions

356. The Dutch Civil Code contained modern criteria of non-conformity (*conformiteitvereiste*) long before the implementation of the Consumer Sales Directive. Generally, the criteria from Article 2 (2) (a)-(d) of the Directive did not provide new solutions. To ensure a level of consumer protection conforming to the Directive, the Dutch legislator introduced several minor amendments regarding the criteria of non-conformity.[278]

357. According to Dutch law, the non-conformity is defined as any difference between agreed goods and the goods that have been delivered. The focus of 7:17 (2) BW is placed on the characteristics that the buyer is entitled to expect under the contract, taking into account the nature of the goods and the seller's statements about the goods. Consequently, the goods must possess the characteristics agreed under the contract and the characteristics which the buyer is entitled to expect under the contract. Furthermore, to meet the conformity requirement the goods must possess characteristics corresponding with the sample and model. Finally, the Dutch Civil Code expressly states that the delivery of different goods or goods which differ in size or quantity amounts to non-conformity. In accordance with the Directive, the Dutch legislator provides that when the buyer was aware of or could not have been reasonably unaware of the existence of non-conformity at the time of the conclusion of the contract, he is not entitled to claim remedies.

Summing up, the Dutch law provides for the modern notion of non-conformity. The minor amendments introduced by the Dutch legislator ensured that the notion of non-conformity corresponds with the notion contained in the Consumer Sales Directive.

277 Asser/Hijma 7-1* 2013, nr. 332c.

278 Article 7:18 (1) public statements; Article 7:18 (3) incorrect installation; Article 7:17 (5) knowledge of the goods; Article 7:17 (4) model/sample.

4.7 Conclusions

358. Having presented information about the non-conformity in four legal systems it can be concluded that in the analysed countries the criteria of non-conformity of Article 2 (2) (a)-(d) of the Consumer Sales Directive have been, to a great extent, implemented in accordance with the Directive. Nevertheless, there is some uncertainty over whether there are shortcomings in national law regarding several specific aspects of non-conformity. Below, the most important features of national notions of non-conformity, including the questions of burden of proof, are briefly summarised.

359. The implementation of the Consumer Sales Directive in the Polish Consumer Sale Act introduced liability for non-conforming goods, excluding the application of the Civil Code regarding the defects. In general all criteria of non-conformity have been implemented. The Consumer Sale Act introduced a rather unfortunate division in contracts where the characteristics of goods have been individually negotiated and ones where they have not. Accordingly, the aspects of non-conformity applied depending on the type of contract. This division brought confusion in terms of what exactly the consumer must have proven to show the existence of non-conformity. A further question arises whether the above mentioned division has any practical relevance. The major uncertainty, besides the mentioned division, arose in relation to the liability for legal defects. This issue will be resolved by the new statute repealing the Consumer Sale Act.

The criteria of non-conformity contained in Article 4 (2) and 4 (3) of the Consumer Sale Act are said to constitute a definition. They do not form presumptions as occurs in the Directive. Nevertheless, the detailed character of these criteria may help illustrate which particular fact should be proven. The consumer has the burden of proving that one of the criteria of non-conformity has been met.

The new reform of consumer sale repealed the Consumer Sale Act and returns to the system of protection based on the Civil Code, amended in line with the Consumer Sales Directive. This must be assessed as a positive step. The new definition of defect is common for all types of sales. It is explained by the existence of non-conformity, which on the other hand may be misleading. The provisions on the consumer's knowledge of the defects remain intact, meaning that if the buyer knew about the defects at the time of the conclusion of the contract, the seller's liability is excluded. The new statute does not contain any form of presumptions therefore it lies with the consumer to prove the existence of defect. The new statute harmonises provisions of Polish sales law and provides a relatively cohesive system of liability for defective goods.

360. The German legislator did not introduce the notion of non-conformity. The BGB uses the traditional notion of defects amended in light of the Directive. The BGB does not

follow the general approach taken by the Directive. It provides a clear hierarchy in assessing the existence of defects, giving the priority to the parties' agreement. There are some questions on whether the definition of defect in § 434 BGB contains all the aspects of non-conformity found in the Directive. The wording of BGB does not refer explicitly to the normal characteristics of goods, and does not mention the description of goods provided to the consumer. It seems that these shortcomings could be easily overcome through a conforming interpretation of the German provisions to the Consumer Sales Directive.

The BGB contains specific provisions regarding the issues of the buyer's knowledge of the defects. The circumstances and the consequences of such a knowledge are detailed, which offers a higher level of legal certainty in comparison to the provisions of the Directive.

The definition of defects from the BGB does not provide presumptions. According to the German general principle of the burden of proof, the consumer bears the risk of proving circumstances constituting defects of § 434 BGB. In this respect, no simplifications are provided.

361. In English law, to all contracts of sale, a long-existing notion of satisfactory quality and fitness for purpose applies. It is constructed as implied terms, whose elements closely reflect the criteria of non-conformity of the Consumer Sales Directive. There is also a definition of non-conformity in Section 48A (3) of the Sale of Goods Act 1979. It is explained as a breach of one of express or implied terms. There are doubts as to whether the content of implied terms reflects all criteria from Article 2 (2) of the Consumer Sales Directive. In particular, English law seems to fall short in the area of incorrect installation and liability for public statements.

The proposed Consumer Rights Bill both modernises and harmonises provisions of English consumer sales. It provides more detailed criteria regarding the implied terms of satisfactory quality and fitness for purpose. The terms formulated in Sections 9-18 of the Consumer Rights Bill seem to bring clarity and more certainty to consumers in the context of the standard of quality of goods. The proposed statute still adopts the notion of non-conformity when describing the application of the presumption of non-conformity. Accordingly, the notion of non-conformity, implied terms of satisfactory quality and fitness for purpose function simultaneously within the English system. The provisions of the Sale of Goods Act 1979 and of the Consumer Rights Bill contain a provision, stating that when a buyer was aware or should have been aware of the state of goods the right to invoke the breach of implied terms may be excluded.

The burden of proving the breach of implied terms lies with the consumer. There are no simplifications offered in the form of the presumptions. However, the construction of implied terms itself may facilitate the evidential position of a consumer in the context of providing evidence. Additionally, in cases of durability of goods, the burden of proof can often be eased by the application of factual presumptions.

362. The Dutch Civil Code contained criteria comparable with the ones from the Consumer Sales Directive long before its promulgation. To ensure an equal level of protection, several minor amendments had to be made. The central question in cases of non-conformity is what the consumer is entitled to expect under the contract taking into consideration the nature of the goods and statements made by the seller about the goods. Article 7:23 BW imposes a duty to inform of the non-conformity. The buyer must inform the seller of the non-conformity within a reasonable time (at least two months). Infringement of this duty entails that the goods did not lack conformity what excludes the buyer's right to claim remedies. Furthermore, the Dutch Civil Code excludes the seller's liability when the consumer was aware or should have been aware of the existence of the non-conformity at the time of the conclusion of the contract.

Articles 7:17 and 7:18 BW relating to the notion of non-conformity do not contain the presumptions as provided in Article 2 (2) (a)-(d) of the Consumer Sales Directive. There are no simplifications in terms of providing evidence of the existence of non-conformity. Consequently based on the main rule of Article 150 Rv, the burden of proof of the existence of non-conformity lies with the consumer.

363. What all the systems have in common regarding non-conformity, defects and satisfactory quality is the supremacy of the parties' agreement and supplementary role of the general criteria. The exact content of the criteria among the examined countries differ, yet all of them seem to implement the Directive correctly. All systems provide for the exclusion of the seller's liability in case of the knowledge of the defects of goods at the time of the conclusion of the contract. In this regard, there are also some minor differences regarding the circumstances and content of the knowledge.

The different focus of national notions of defects may affect the scope of evidence the consumer must provide to successfully show the existence of non-conformity, which consequently, may influence the assessment of evidence. This could have importance for the scope and frequency of the application of the presumption of non-conformity and eventually on the application of remedies for the delivery of non-conforming goods, as will be discussed in chapter 5.

5 Presumption of non-conformity

5.1 Introduction

364. The burden of proof is an essential factor for resolving civil law disputes. The rules on the burden of proof are regulated by the substantive and procedural law of Member States. Chapter 2 of this book provides an overview of the general rules on the burden of proof in the jurisdictions investigated.

This chapter presents the presumption of non-conformity of Article 5 (3) of the Consumer Sales Directive, which determines a specific rule on the allocation of the burden of proof regarding the existence of non-conformity. To be more specific, the presumption of non-conformity was enacted to simplify certain burdens of evidence that the consumer must demonstrate to be awarded remedies for the delivery of non-conforming goods. There are several main questions this chapter will deal with. The first question concerns the conditions for the application of the presumption of non-conformity, the existence of non-conformity within a six-month period of delivery and the legal consequences of the application of the presumption. The second question concerns the rebuttal of the presumption of non-conformity. The third question concerns the criteria for the exclusion of the presumption, the incompatibility with the nature of the goods and the nature of the non-conformity.

The objective of this chapter is to analyse how the presumption of Article 5 (3) of the Consumer Sales Directive is constructed, and whether it has been correctly implemented in the national legal systems. Subsequently, the questions of whether the presumption achieves the aims for which it has been enacted and whether it is a suitable tool to achieve these aims, will be discussed.

At the time of the Directive's drafting, the mere introduction of such a rule into European law had been expected to ensure its proper application. It has not been predicted that simply introducing such rule into European law might be insufficient for its proper application within national framework. The national laws governing the rules on the allocation of the burden of proof, even when the protection of a consumer is involved, might require a different approach.[1] In this chapter the approach towards the presumption of non-conformity taken in Poland, Germany, England and Wales, and the Netherlands, will be analysed. It should be observed that when terms such as 'presumption', 'reversed burden of proof', or 'shift of the burden of proof' are used without further specification,

1 Storskrubb 2008, p. 14 *et seq.*

they should be understood that the general duty to provide evidence regarding particular facts has been altered.

5.2 The presumption of Article 5 (3) of the Consumer Sales Directive

5.2.1 *Introduction*

365. Article 5 (3) of the Consumer Sales Directive states that '*unless proved otherwise, any lack of conformity which becomes apparent within six months of delivery of the goods shall be presumed to have existed at the time of delivery unless this presumption is incompatible with the nature of the goods or the nature of the lack of conformity.*' This provision introduces the presumption of non-conformity altering the general allocation of the burden of proof regarding the time the non-conformity came into existence. According to the general rule on allocation of the burden of proof, the burden of proving that the goods were defective at the time of delivery lies with the buyer.[2] The European legislator suggested that above allocation would be too burdensome for consumers. Pointing out the seller's experience, knowledge and resources, the legislator decided that the professional seller rather than the consumer should provide evidence that at the time of delivery the goods conformed to the contract.[3] Consequently, the presumption of non-conformity has been enacted to simplify and to ease consumer's duty to supply evidence in order to be awarded remedies for the delivery of non-conforming goods.

5.2.2 *General information*

366. The presumption in Article 5 (3) of the Consumer Sales Directives concerns facts only related to the state of goods not conforming to the contract at the time of delivery. This means that the burden of proof regarding other facts necessary to support the claim, such as the existence of a contract, its content and its character remain unchanged. According to the general rules on the burden of proof the consumer must prove the above facts.[4] Furthermore, the presumption of non-conformity at the time of delivery applies only to the defects that become apparent within six months from the time of delivery. After the expiry of that period, the burden of proof regarding the existence of non-conformity

---

2 *Actori incumbit probatio.*

3 Guarantees for consumer goods and after-sales services (Green Paper), COM (93) 509 final, Official Journal C 338, 15.12.1993, p. 92.

4 Chapter 2 – National rules of the burden of proof.

at the time of delivery will be allocated according to the national rules, meaning that in general it will lie with the consumer.

367. Considering the above-mentioned function of the presumption and its influence on the systems of private law of the jurisdictions investigated, it appears that the presumption of non-conformity has not received as much attention as was expected. The authors of the *EC Sales Directive Commentary* stated that within six months from the time of delivery, the application of the presumption is close to full warranty, because as they say '*(...) evidence to the contrary is very difficult to assemble*'. They continued that even after the expiry of six-month period, the protection provided by Article 3 (and Article 6) of the Directive continues to alleviate the consumers' evidential position. This view appears to suggest that the consumers are fully protected within six months from the delivery as well as after the expiry of that period.[5]

Micklitz regards the presumption of non-conformity as a kind of cut-off period, which will put the consumer under pressure to put forward his claim or to investigate whether there is lack of conformity.[6] Others see it as an 'all-risk insurance' weighing upon the seller to prove that the lack of conformity was caused by the buyer.[7] The majority of the presented opinions indicate that the expectations regarding the role, function and effectiveness of the presumption of non-conformity from Article 5 (3) of the Consumer Sales Directive were high.

Although this would be an ideal situation, one may question whether the above views are supported by the legal practice in the jurisdictions that are evaluated in this study. In the latter part of this chapter I will try to prove that the application of the presumption is far from being easy and that in some circumstances the outcome of the application of the presumption is not always favourable for the consumer.

368. According to Staudenmayer's view, the provision of Article 5 (3) of the Consumer Sales Directive is one of the major steps of the Directive.[8] Until enacting the Consumer Sales Directive, the European legislator has not addressed the issues regarding burden of proof on a large scale. The regulation of the burden of proof was limited only to very specific topics, for example, the burden of proof regarding unfair advertising.[9] The differences among the Member States prevented the European legislator from trying to unify rules on burden of proof.[10] The matters of allocation of the burden of proof have been therefore

5 Massimo Bianca and Grundmann 2002, p. 69.
6 Micklitz 1999, p. 486; Reich, Micklitz, Rott and Tonner 2014, p. 177.
7 Schafer and Pfeiffer 1999, p. 1835.
8 Staudenmayer 2000, p. 557.
9 For example: Article 6 (a) of the Directive on misleading advertising, 97/55/EC, OJ L 290/18, 23.10.97, amending the Directive of 1984.
10 Staudenmayer 2004, p. 272.

left to the national legislators to solve. Article 5 (3) of the Consumer Sales Directive is the first provision in the field of private law of all Member States which determines on such a large scale the allocation of the burden of proof.[11] It must be said that the European legislator has made a significant step in recognising the importance of rules on the burden of proof as a tool which can increase the level of consumer protection. Although the abovementioned steps have been taken to the advantage of consumer protection, the drawbacks of Article 5 (3) should not be disregarded. In the following paragraphs, both positive and negative consequences of the implementation of Article 5 (3) of the Consumer Sales Directive into national legal systems will be presented.

369. A further issue regarding Article 5 (3) of the Directive considers its real character, which in practice may have a serious impact on the outcome of the dispute. There is uncertainty as to whether Article 5 (3) constitutes a legal presumption of non-conformity or rather shifts the burden of proving essential facts from the buyer to the seller. The problem has been already identified by the doctrine. For example, Dutch scholars and practitioners have discussed the character of Article 5 (3) of the Directive and Article 7:18 (2) BW. There are contrary opinions regarding the issue. One view states that the provision of Article 5 (3) is constructed as a rebuttable presumption of non-conformity.[12] Another opinion states that although it is formulated as a presumption it shifts the burden of proof in favour of the consumer. Recognising the problems in determining the character of Article 5 (3), it seems that on the European level it is both unnecessary and impossible to define its effects on the allocation of the burden of proof. Firstly, the Directive does not have to be followed word for word by the Member States, only the effect of the Directive has to be achieved through the implementation. Furthermore, there is a lack of legal grounds to discuss the theory of the burden of proof on the European level. Finally, the cases are to be solved by applying national rules of the burden of proof, which may belong to procedural or substantive law, as discussed in chapter 2. The difference in approach to the character of Article 5 (3) does not substantially affect the conditions for its application however, depending on its adopted construction it may affect its legal consequences.[13]

370. Taking into account factors mentioned in this section, the application of the presumption does not seem to be as straightforward as one might think. It also seems that the operation of the presumption may be less favourable to the consumers than was intended, especially taking the objectives and function of the presumption into consideration. The analysis of particular elements of the presumption varying between jurisdictions will provide

11 Staudenmayer 2000, p. 557.
12 Massimo Bianca and Grundmann 2002, p. 62.
13 Staudenmayer 2000, p. 557.

information necessary to establish whether the national legislation facilitates and simplifies the consumer's burden of proof and brings balance to the disputes between professionals and consumers.

5.2.3 *Conditions for the application of the presumption*

5.2.3.1 Non-conformity

371. To make use of evidential advantages resulting from the application of the presumption of non-conformity, the consumer has to provide the court with evidence supporting the occurrence of facts on which operation of the presumption depends. Pursuant to Article 5 (3) of the Consumer Sales Directive, the consumer must prove that the goods do not conform to the contract and that this non-conformity became apparent within six months from the time of delivery.

372. Article 2 (2) (a)-(d) of the Consumer Sales Directive provides for the criteria determining the goods' conformity.[14] For the consumer to prove that the product does not conform to the contract it should be sufficient to deny the existence of one of the factors from Article 2 (2) (a)-(d) and provide supporting evidence. It should be noted how significant for the application of the presumption the criteria of non-conformity from Article 2 (2) of the Directive are. In fact, they determine whether the first condition for the application of the presumption has been met. They also determine the scope of seller's liability in general.[15] In some cases, where for example there are obvious, external defects in the product, further proof that the goods do not conform to the contract may not be necessary. In other cases an extended expert opinion may be required. The level of precision of proving defects will depend on the complexity of the non-conformity alleged.

5.2.3.2 Six-month period

373. The second condition for the application of the presumption requires the consumer to show that the non-conformity in question has become apparent within six months from the time of delivery. The Directive does not provide further information regarding the six-month period and the proof that the consumer has to present in this respect. However, it recognises uncertainties that may occur due to the different notions (delivery and the passing of risk) used by the national legislators. Recital 14 of the Consumer Sales Directive states that references to the time of delivery do not imply that Member States should change

14 Chapter 4, para 219.
15 Massimo Bianca and Grundmann 2002, p. 69.

their laws on the transfer of risk.[16] Taking above into consideration, there may be differences among the Member States regarding the beginning and expiry of the six-month period.

To fulfil the second condition of the presumption, the consumer may send notice or otherwise provide information about the defects. He may also produce evidence to support the claim by taking a photo of the product's defects with an indication of the date.

374. The European legislator already recognised several decades ago that it is necessary to determine the general rules applicable to periods, dates and time limits to attain the objectives of the Communities.[17] Given that there are potential differences between the national legislation regarding the beginning of the periods, its length and expiry, the question arises whether the provisions of the Council Regulation determining the rules applicable to periods, dates and time limits should not apply in this respect. Article 3 (1) of the Regulation states '*where a period, expressed in days, weeks, months or years is to be calculated from the moment at which an event occurs or an action takes place, the day during which that event occurs or that action takes place shall not be considered as falling within the period in question*'. It seems that where there is uncertainty regarding the beginning of the six-month period the above provision might provide a solution. Following this rule, the period for application of presumption of non-conformity begins to run from the day after delivery or passing of risk.

5.2.4 *Construction of Article 5 (3) of the Consumer Sales Directive*

375. In this sub-section the chart illustrating the possible application of the presumption of Article 5 (3) of the Consumer Sales Directive will be presented. It explains the conditions and subsequent stadiums in the application of the presumption of non-conformity. The analysis of the application of the presumption of non-conformity within the national frameworks will also be performed in the order presented in the chart.

16 Recital 14 of the Consumer Sales Directive '*Whereas the references to the time of delivery do not imply that Member States have to change their rules on the passing of the risk*'.

17 Regulation (EEC, Euratom) No 1182/71 of the Council of 3 June 1971 determining the rules applicable to periods, dates and time limits.

Chart 5.1

Conditions for the presumption		
1. Non-conformity	→	burden of proof on the consumer
2. Six months	→	burden of proof on the consumer
Presumption applies		
3. Goods lack conformity at the time of delivery		
Rebuttal		
4. Evidence to the contrary	→	burden of proof on the seller
Exclusion criteria		
5. Nature of the goods	→	burden of proof on the seller
6. Nature of the non-conformity	→	burden of proof on the seller

376. The above chart illustrates the operation of the presumption of Article 5 (3) of the Consumer Sales Directive. Below, an outline of a model construction of this presumption will be presented. It takes into account various options regarding possible evidence and probable outcome of the dispute. The line of reasoning that can be applied in solving consumer sale disputes will be presented to answer the questions of how the burden of proof is allocated. It should be observed that, in this chapter the notion of presumption and expressions such as 'reversed burden of proof' and 'shift of the burden' are generally used as an indication that the duty to provide evidence has been altered, no other specific legal meaning should be given without direct reference.

The prerequisites for the application of the presumption of Article 5 (3) of the Directive are as follows:

1. Existence of non-conformity.
2. Appearance of non-conformity within six months from the time of delivery.

When the above criteria have been met it is presumed, pursuant to Article 5 (3) of the Directive, that the defect existed at the time of delivery. The first uncertainty concerns the question when the non-conformity can be regarded as proven. Article 2 (2) (a)-(d) of the Directive provides the criteria of non-conformity. Based on these criteria the consumer tries to convince the judge of the existence of the non-conformity. The judge has discretion regarding the recognition of whether a party provides sufficient evidence to prove the facts within the meaning of Article 2 (2) (a)-(d).[18]

18 Chapter 2, Standard of proof, sections: 2.2.4, 2.3.4, 2.4.4, 2.5.4.

377. In the majority of cases of the application of the presumption of non-conformity, the consumer will be a claimant and therefore the onus is on him to present facts and provide sufficient evidence regarding the facts that he relies on.[19] In general, the consumer has to state and prove the existence and content of a contract and that the goods lack conformity, for example, a car does not drive. At this stage it is important to determine what exactly has happened to the product and whether that amounts to non-conformity as described in Article 2 (2) (a)-(d) of the Consumer Sales Directive. The often asked question is whether the fact that the goods do not work (properly) automatically constitutes non-conformity in the sense of Article 2 (2) (a)-(d) of the Consumer Sales Directive. It is in the consumer's interests to provide as much information and evidence as possible. To convince the court that the defects must have resulted from the internal defects, a consumer can also provide evidence that he used the goods in accordance with the manuals, and that he did not use them in an abnormal or negligent way.[20] The national scope of the notion of non-conformity or defect will determine what facts the buyer must show exactly to prove its existence. The national rules on the burden of proof and law of evidence, as presented in chapter 2, will determine the process and requirements of an assessment whether the proof provided was satisfactory.

378. Following the presentation of facts provided by the consumer, the seller gets a chance to reply. Depending on the allegations that the goods lack conformity he may try to prove that the current state of the product is what the consumer could have reasonably expected from it, taking the content of the contract into consideration. In other words, there is a lack of non-conformity. Regarding sale of the second-hand car, for instance it is common that some parts have reduced functionality over time and distance covered by the car. The seller can state that the consumer buying a used car with a high mileage should have expected certain defects to occur. Therefore, there is nothing wrong with the product (car), and the fact that some of the parts do not work or do not work as well as in the beginning is a natural consequence. Furthermore, the seller can claim that the defect was caused by the consumer, for instance by incorrect usage or storage. When it comes to the second-hand cars, the seller may specifically argue that particular defect has been caused by the incompetent use of the vehicle, misuse or lack of proper maintenance. Finally, the seller can allege that defect has been caused by an external independent event or fault of the third party. The last two arguments are used to convince the judge that the non-conformity does not originate from the product and that it has occurred only after the goods were delivered.

19 Alternatively the consumer is a defendant, when sued for a lack of payment in cases when he relies on the rescission of contract. In such cases he has to prove that the rescission was legitimate, including that the goods delivered by the seller were defective.

20 Sivesand 2005, p. 196.

379. On the basis of the claim and the reply, the judge has to take a first decision whether he has been convinced by the presented there arguments. It will depend on the individual case and national practice. In general at this stage there are several possibilities, for example:

1. No (sufficient) evidence that the goods lacked conformity (within six months). The consumer loses the case.
2. Inconclusive evidence of non-conformity – the consumer may receive an additional opportunity to prove his case, but most probably based on *non liquet* will lose the case.
3. Evidence that the goods lacked conformity within six months is conclusive and the presumption of Article 5 (3) of the Directive applies (given that the second condition has been fulfilled).[21]

The judge may find that the consumer has provisionally proven the facts showing that the goods lacked conformity, and ask the seller to provide evidence that the goods conform to the contract (or in any case did so at the time of delivery). There are several possibilities regarding the seller's evidence:

1. No evidence – presumption of non-conformity applies.
2. Inconclusive evidence. The seller sheds doubts as to the facts that were provisionally proven by the consumer, without proving that the goods conform to the contract (or that they did at the time of delivery). Principle of *non liquet* applies – the consumer probably loses the case because of the lack of successful proof of the non-conformity. The outcome may depend on the jurisdiction.
3. Successful evidence that the goods conform to the contract (or that they did at the time of delivery) – the consumer loses the case.

380. In a situation where it is established that there is a non-conformity and that it appeared within six months from the time of delivery, the presumption of non-conformity applies. The seller may rebut the presumption. To be successful thereof, he must provide evidence to the contrary. The content of evidence to the contrary depends on domestic legislation and its interpretation. As seen later in this chapter, evidence to the contrary requires proof that the goods were in conformity at the time of delivery, or that the defects occurred later. The following possibilities exist for the outcome of the case.

1. No evidence to the contrary – the seller loses the case.
2. Inconclusive evidence to the contrary. Principle of *non liquet* applies – the seller most probably loses the case because of the lack of successful evidence to the contrary. The outcome may depend on the jurisdiction.
3. Successful evidence to the contrary – no liability for the non-conforming goods.

21 See point 3 on Chart 5.1.

381. Regarding the possibilities for excluding the application of the presumption, Article 5 (3) of the Directive provides that the presumption does not apply if it is incompatible with the nature of the goods or the nature of the non-conformity. The Directive does not provide for further explanations of these terms. Their scope and application depend entirely on the domestic law and the national interpretation of the above terms. Due to the fact that there are considerable differences between Member States, the detailed analysis of the exclusion criteria will be provided for each national system separately.

5.2.5 *Conclusions*

382. Based on information presented concerning the construction and application of Article 5 (3) of the Consumer Sales Directive, several conclusions can be drawn. There are multiple possibilities for the consumer sale case to be resolved depending on the way the burden of proof of particular elements of the claim is allocated. In particular, it is important whether certain issues – and the facts pertaining to these issues – are allocated at the stage of establishing the non-conformity, or at the stage of rebutting the presumption, or other stage of establishing whether the presumption does (not) apply. A correct application of the presumption of non-conformity is crucial for consumer protection, as it simplifies the consumer's burden of proof. Whether facts presented by the consumer satisfy the burden of proof depends on national law. There are no indications in the Directive regarding this aspect. The Directive provides for a framework, but its execution depends on national substantive and procedural law. Taking into account the objectives of the Directive, it seems that it would be more favourable for the consumer if the national judge would allow the broad scope of the term 'non-conformity', and if he would apply the presumption as a rule. The seller could still challenge presumed fact by providing evidence to the contrary or referring to the exclusion criteria.

5.3 Presumption of non-conformity in Polish law

5.3.1 *Introduction*

383. This section presents the application of the presumption of non-conformity in Polish law. It begins with the general information of the scope of the presumption of non-conformity in Polish law (5.3.2). The central questions regard the conditions (5.3.3), rebuttal (5.3.4) and the exclusion criteria (5.3.5) of the presumption of Article 5 (3) of the Consumer Sales Directive implemented in the Polish system in Article 4 (1) of the Consumer Sale

Act. Article 4 (1) has been substituted by Article 556^2 (2) of the Civil Code.[22] The new provisions that entered into force in December 2014 seem to include a higher level of consumer protection, especially when referring to the extended period for the application of the presumption of non-conformity.[23] The analysis of the above-mentioned topics will answer whether the presumption has been correctly implemented, whether the objectives of the presumption of non-conformity have been achieved, and whether a Polish consumer can easily take advantage of the simplifications in supply of evidence designed for him by the European legislator.

5.3.2 *Scope of the application of the presumption*

384. According to the Consumer Sale Act, the existence of non-conformity of goods at the time of delivery is a condition for the seller's liability. When applying general rules on the allocation of the burden of proof from Article 6 of the Civil Code, the buyer, in order to be able to make use of the remedies for non-conforming goods, will have to prove that there are defects and that they existed at the time of delivery. Proving the existence of non-conformity at the time of delivery can be difficult, especially when there is no duty to inspect the goods at the time of delivery, as said for example by Jezioro and Pecyna.[24] The Consumer Sales Directive does not contain such a duty, although it can be found among the provisions of the CISG.[25]

Article 4 (1) of the Consumer Sale Act implements Article 5 (3) of the Directive and provides that if non-conformity of goods becomes apparent within six months from the time of delivery, it is presumed to have existed at that time. Following the European legislator, the Polish legislator describes the most important objectives of the presumption to ease the burden of proof that lies with the consumer, and to increase consumer's chances of receiving legitimate protection in case of the delivery of non-conforming goods.[26]

22 The Consumer Rights Act amending the Civil Code and repealing the Consumer Sale Act entered into force on 25 December 2014.

23 Article 556^2 '*if a buyer is a consumer, and a defect has become apparent within one year from the time of delivery, it is presumed the defect or its origin has existed at the moment of passing of risk to the consumer*'. (Article 44 (13) of the Consumer Rights Act, implementing the Directive on Consumer Rights and amending provisions on consumer sale and incorporating them into the Civil Code); Chapter 5, para 384, 388, 395, 397, 398.

24 Jezioro 2010, p. 135 *et seq*; Pecyna 2003, p. 33.

25 Article 38 of the CISG. It is said that the notion of non-conformity from the Directive has been modelled on the notion of non-conformity from the CISG, however the Directive does not follow the CISG regarding the duty to investigate the goods which in fact could be favourable because the consumer's attention must have been drawn to the apparent defects of the goods or could help to accommodate the evidence that the goods were defective at the time of delivery; See also Pecyna 2003, p. 5 *et seq*.

26 Sejm RP 2014, Statute justification.

The main objective of the presumption of non-conformity is to facilitate the buyers' position with regard to evidence. One question is whether this aim could not have been successfully achieved by other means. Some commentators state that in comparison with the previous regulation, the simplification facilitated by the presumption reverses the burden of proof and only temporarily helps the consumer to supply evidence.[27] Following the expiry of six months, the consumer must present proof that the legislator has already found to be a very burdensome duty in the first six months. It may seem illogic that the legislator reduces burdens of evidence which consumer needs to bear in the first six months, explaining that otherwise it is too difficult to obtain protection, and at the same time requires the consumer to satisfy the same burdens after six months, when it will be even more difficult to achieve, due to the time lapse.

The new amendments to the consumer sale state in Article 556^2 of the Civil Code that when the defect becomes apparent within one year from the time the risk was passed, it is presumed that this defect or its origin have existed at that time. The new provision extends the period for the application of the presumption of non-conformity, which will positively affect consumers' position and considerably increase the level of protection. It will also silence some of the criticism of the current regulation, since the one year period of the presumption may in some cases be equal to limitation period, in particular in cases of second-hand goods.

385. Regarding the interpretation of the presumption, there has been an attempt to read the presumption of Article 4 (1) of the Consumer Sale Act as meaning that if the non-conformity became apparent after the expiry of the six-month period it is presumed not to exist at the time of delivery. Fortunately, the above interpretation has been denied by the Consumer Arbitration Court in a decision of 22 March 2006, and ruled to be incorrect.[28] Had that not been the case, that line of interpretation could provide the seller with an excuse to not proceed with the consumer complaint if it has been lodged after six months from the time of delivery. Following the above interpretation the seller could dismiss the complaint without substantially considering it. The assumptions of above-mentioned interpretation deserve rejection.

386. Having presented the main characteristics of the presumption of Article 4 (1) of the Consumer Sale Act, it can be stated that the first reason for introducing the presumption was to fulfil the implementation duties. Another reason for introducing the presumption was to protect the consumer and ensure that he will be able to benefit from the remedies

27 Radwański 2006, p. 113; Jezioro 2010, p. 135; Pecyna 2003, p. 5 *et seq.*

28 Polubowny Sąd Konsumencki przy Zachodniopomorskim Wojewódzkim Inspektorze Inspekcji Handlowej w Szczecinie, 22.03.2006, sygn. akt. 26/2006 (Consumer Arbitration Court by the Regional Trade Inspectorate).

in case of delivery of non-conforming goods. The European legislator recognised the difficulties related to the classic allocation of the burden of proof. The Polish legislator wanted to support and to encourage consumers to make use of the rights provided in the Directive. The reason for choosing the presumption was to simplify consumer's obligations concerning evidence and to facilitate application of the protective rights in case of the delivery of non-conforming goods, to enhance consumers' participation in the common market.[29] Although the Polish legislator was aware of the fact that the new regulations were less favourable than the protection available under the Civil Code,[30] it seemed that the legislator wanted all implemented provisions to reflect the European provisions, without evaluating the state of domestic legislation.[31] It has been stated that the legislator did not make use of minimum harmonisation. Eventually it was decided that the application of the Civil Code should be excluded from relationships between consumers and professional sellers, what resulted in decreasing the level of protection. The legislator responded that too high a level of consumer protection could disturb balance on the market.[32]

387. Summing up, the objectives of the presumption introduced by Article 5 (3) of the Directive and implemented in Article 4 (1) of the Consumer Sale Act are to ease the burdens regarding evidence that the consumer has to satisfy in order to make use of the remedies for the delivery of non-conforming goods. It does not mean that it provides for the most favourable solution for the consumer. Taking into account the Polish Supreme Court approved interpretation of the application of factual presumption providing that the defects existed at the time of delivery (not restricted to the time period), the previous regulation was more beneficial for consumers.[33]

5.3.3 *Conditions for the application of the presumption*

5.3.3.1 Non-conformity

388. In order for the consumer to be able to invoke the presumption of non-conformity he has to prove the existence of non-conformity and the fact that it has become apparent within six months from the time of delivery. These conditions are the same as those provided by Article 5 (3) of the Consumer Sales Directive. The notion of non-conformity and its criteria found in Article 4 (2) and 4 (3) are indispensable for the application of the

29 Łętowska 2004, p. 362.

30 Chapter 3, para 114-116.

31 Radwański 2006, p. 105, 110; Kołodziej 2010, p. 62, Łętowska, Jagielska, Lis, Miklaszewicz and Wiewiorówska-Domagalska 2007, p. 875; Włodarska-Dziurzyńska 2009, p. 476.

32 Sejm RP 2014, Statute justification, p. 14-16.

33 Given interpretation was also applicable to contracts under the Civil Code, for example to C2C and B2B.

presumption. As already stated,[34] the content of definition of the non-conformity is amended in accordance with Article 556^1 of the Civil Code, which entered into force on 25 December 2014. In practice it repeals the notion of non-conformity and introduces a modernised notion of defect applicable to all types of contracts of sale. On the other hand, a new definition of defects is explained by the existence of non-conformity to the contract, which may lead to conclusion that factual content of 'non-conformity' and 'defect' is close to identical, at least based on the definition of 4 (2) and (3) of the Consumer Sale Act and new Article 556^1 of the Civil Code. Any simplification regarding the proof of the existence of non-conformity may affect operation of the presumption and as a consequence it may affect the application of the remedies for non-conforming goods.

389. According to the main rule on the allocation of the burden of proof (Article 6 of the Civil Code), the consumer would have to prove the existence of defects at the time of delivery, it could have meant the impossibility of holding the seller liable because of the burden of such proof.

The main reason for the proof of the existence of defects at the time of delivery being so difficult to provide is the fact that most often the defects become apparent sometime after the delivery. In case the defects were visible at that time, the consumer would probably have not accepted them.[35] Without the presumption of non-conformity, the consumer would have to present arguments and provide supporting evidence regarding the facts about which he was not aware of at the time.[36] Sometimes, the defects of goods are not only invisible to the consumer, but they may be objectively (temporarily) undetectable. Expecting for the consumer to succeed in providing the proof of such non-conformity is difficult.[37]

390. The presumption of non-conformity only concerns the circumstances that the consumer has relied upon and not every defect that is possible to be ascertained during the period of six months.[38] For example, when a consumer states in his claim that the display of his MP3 player is defective and shows that it appeared within six months from the time of delivery, the presumed fact is that at the moment of delivery the MP3's display was defective. It does not concern any other possible defect of the device. For instance, when later it occurs that the battery does not work properly and this defect also appeared within six months, the originally ascertained presumption (regarding the display) will not be dependent on the latter malfunction. For every defect, a separate presumption must apply.

34 Chapter 5, para 244 *et seq.*
35 Pecyna 2003, p. 33.
36 Habryn 2010, p. 45.
37 Szczotka 2007, p. 46.
38 Pecyna 2003, p. 33.

Where multiple defects appear in the purchased product every single defect must be proved separately according to the rules of Article 4 (2) or 4 (3) of the Consumer Sale Act in order to be able to make full use of the presumption, unless the multiple defects have the same origin. Furthermore, every defect must have become apparent within six months from the time of delivery. The existence of a defect may not be assumed only because of the appearance of another defect.[39]

391. According to the interpretation of the Polish Civil Code,[40] the defects were traditionally divided into visible defects and hidden defects, including defects originating in the product. Although Article 4 (2) and (3) of the Consumer Sale Act does not mention the above division, both categories of defects can be recognised.[41] When referring to this division, it should be stated that the applicability of the presumption is only justified in the case of the second and third type of defects. The visual defects should normally be discovered and objected to, otherwise they will be deemed to have been accepted by the buyer.[42]

392. In recent case law it can be observed that the proof of the existence of the defect is often easily accepted by the court. For example, in the case regarding the sale of living-room furniture, the consumer successfully complained about the defects of the delivered goods.[43] According to the consumer, delivered goods did not conform to the contract because the stuffing of pillows belonging to the set was unsatisfactory the seats were uneven, and the upholstery was unacceptable. According to the expert opinion, these characteristics constituted non-conformity, which could have been easily and quickly cured without extensive costs.

Also in another case regarding the defects of living-room furniture, the consumer was able to prove relatively easily the existence of non-conformity. He claimed that the furniture was made from a type of natural leather, unfit for furniture, which stretched and lost colour.[44] The seller's argument, that alleged characteristics are normal for natural leather, was not satisfactory.

393. In another case, direct questions on the allocation of proof were raised.[45] The consumer bought a pair of shoes together with a bag and both of them became defective within six months. The seller refused to repair the goods. He claimed that the repair of the bag was

39 The court could probably use these facts to construct the factual presumption of the defectiveness of goods.
40 Szczotka 2007, p. 48; Jezioro 2010, p. 141.
41 Kołodziej 2006, p. 116.
42 Szczotka 2007, p. 47.
43 SO Lublin 08.08.2013, II Ca 438/13; See also SR Złotoryja 23.04.2013, I C 461/12, SR Wrocław-Śródmieście 29.10.2013, VIII C 1030/13; SR Klodzk 14.06.2013, I C 203/12.
44 SR Wrocław-Krzyków 20.06.2013, I C 846/11.
45 SO Wrocław 30.01.2013, II Ca 1425/12.

impossible. With regard to the shoes he stated that the defects were irrelevant (trivial), and consequently there were no remedies available. The court stated that the seller's arguments were not satisfactory. He failed to provide evidence to the contrary to rebut the presumption of the non-conformity of goods. Furthermore, based on Article 8 (4) of the Consumer Sale Act (defects *de minimis*), the seller has the burden of proving the facts justifying the refusal of remedies based on irrelevant defects. The court decided that the seller did not show sufficient evidence regarding the character of defects. As a result, the application of the presumption of non-conformity was permitted.[46]

394. Another case regarded a defective mobile phone, which had been repeatedly and unsuccessfully serviced. The court stated that the fact the consumer did not state that the phone did not conform to the contract due to several malfunctions having its origin in the defective battery is irrelevant.[47] In cases of complex electronic devices, a consumer cannot be required to point out the concrete element/part of this device which is defective and that this specific part causes the non-conformity of the device. The duty to establish the above facts lies with the seller, who can use technical facilities, know-how and experience to determine the origins of the malfunction of complex devices. Because the mobile phone appeared to be defective within six months from the time of delivery, the consumer was given the benefit of the presumption of non-conformity. This approach regarding consumer's statements and evidence must be assessed positively. In comparison for example, with the approach of German courts,[48] the Polish approach can be regarded as more lenient and overall more consumer-friendly.

In other case of the sale of a mobile phone, the consumer made sure to convince the judge about the existence of defects at the time of delivery.[49] She provided an expert opinion explaining that the phone showed no signs of mechanical defects. According to the expert the phone was afflicted with hidden defects caused during the manufacture process. Moreover, there were other defects which must have been caused by the seller during previous attempts to repair the phone. The judge concurred to the report and decided the case in favour of the consumer. It shows that providing similar expert rapport may be a safeguard of positive outcome. However, one should observe that the costs of expert opinions often exceeds the value under litigation and only wealthy consumers may be willing to invest in such evidence before starting litigation.

395. The Consumer Sale Act contains a provision related to the proof of the existence of defects which is extremely favourable to consumers. Article 8 (3) of the Consumer Sale

46 See: ECJ 03.10.2013, C-32/12 *Soledad Duarte Hueros v Atoiciba et al.*, not yet published.

47 SR Wrocław Śródmieście 08.03.2013, VIII 170/12; See also: SR Wrocław Fabryczna 11.02.2013, XI C 695/12.

48 Presented in para 441-449.

49 SR Wrocław Śródmieście 01.10.2013, VIII C 318/13.

Act states that if the seller does not reply to the consumer complaint and request for remedies within fourteen days from the complaint, the seller is regarded as having acknowledged the grounds for a complaint and admits the consumer's request for remedies.[50] Article 8 (3) provides a rebuttable presumption that if the seller does not react within fourteen days he is deemed to have admitted the merits of the complaint. The seller can rebut this presumption by informing that he cannot substantially reply to the complaint because the goods have been handed over to the expert for an examination.[51] The consequence of Article 8 (3) is that the seller loses the chance to challenge the consumer's claim before the court if he ignored the initial complaint. The objective of this provision was to discipline the seller and prevent situations where the seller could postpone the complaint procedure.[52] The consumer rights from Article 8 (3) of the Consumer Sale Act are regarded as a counter-part to the duty to inform from Article 9 (1). According to the latter provision, a consumer loses the right to remedies if he does not inform the seller of the non-conformity within two months from the time he discovered it.

Above interpretation is approved in the literature[53] and confirmed by the Polish Supreme Court.[54] The Supreme Court expressly stated that when the seller does not respond to consumer's complaint within fourteen days, and the complaint was sent within six months from the time of delivery, the seller can no longer challenge his liability before the court. If the consumer's complaint regarded the defects that became apparent after the expiry of six months and the presumption of non-conformity ceases to apply, the seller is allowed to prove that at the time of delivery the goods in question were free from defects. The consequences of this interpretation may be controversial.[55] Where a complaint is sent within six months, even if the seller successfully proves that the delivered goods were in conformity at the time of delivery, he still loses the case due to the lack of response within fourteen days to the consumer's original complaint.[56]

Since the Civil Code has been redrafted the rights resulting from Article 8 (3) of the Consumer Sale Act are located in Article 561^5 of the Civil Code. It provides that if the consumer demands a replacement, repair or a price reduction, and the seller does not substantially respond to these demands within fourteen days, it is assumed that he considers the demands legitimate. Given that the new provisions provide for the presumption of non-conformity applicable within one year from the time of delivery, the interpretation of the Supreme Court regarding the consumer's complaint shall be adapted accordingly.

50 Acknowledged facts do not require proof, Article 229 k.p.c.

51 Szczotka 2004, p. 50.

52 Pecyna 2003, p. 39.

53 Szczotka 2004, p. 53.

54 SN 05.07.2012, IV CSK 75/2012.

55 An example of the case where the consumer did not prove the non-conformity and won the dispute due to the lack of seller's timely response – SO Wrocław 28.05.2013, II Ca 259/13.

56 SR Wrocław Śródmiescie 23.20.2013, VIII C 797/13.

396. There are also cases where the consumer was not able to convince the judge about the existence of the defects.[57] This might have resulted from better evidence material provided by the seller which convinced the judge about the lack of the first condition for the application of the presumption, excluding the liability for the delivery of non-conforming goods.

397. Taking a new reform of the consumer sale into consideration, in particular the regulation of the presumption of non-conformity, the content of the first requirement for the application of the presumption will not be directly affected. The courts have lately shown tolerance in accepting consumer's proof of the existence of non-conformity and it seems that they will not change their approach, in particular because the new reform is drafted in a consumer-friendly tone.

5.3.3.2 Six-month period

398. To invoke the rights from Article 4 (1) of the Consumer Sale Act the defect must become apparent within six months from the time of delivery. It does not mean that the statement in question must be communicated or received by the seller within this time.[58] Furthermore, according to Article 9 (1) of the Consumer Sale Act the consumer is obliged to notify the seller of the non-conformity within two months of the defects being detected, otherwise he loses the right to remedies.[59]

As already stated, under the new Article 556^2 of the Civil Code, the presumption of non-conformity will apply if the defect became apparent within one year from the time of the passing of risk. The proposed reform does not contain two-month time notice about the defects, which did apply under the Consumer Sale Act. The proposed provisions contain the duty to inspect and to inform only with regard to the contract of sale between professionals.[60]

399. The Recital 17 of the Directive allows Member States to limit the time in which the seller is liable for non-conformity, when appropriate.[61] Accordingly, the Consumer Sale Executive Act (Ministry Resolution) provides in Article 1 (1) that in cases of perishable

57 See: SR Zgorzelec 14.01.2013, I C 842/12; SR Oleśnica 25.02.2013, I C 100/12; SO Tarnów 05.11.2013, I Ca 288/13.

58 Pecyna 2003, p. 35.

59 SO Białystok 29.08.2013, II Ca 567/13.

60 Article 563 states that '*in contracts of sale concluded between professional parties, the buyer loses his rights to remedies when he did not inspect the goods within a period, and in a manner, common for particular type of goods, and if he did not inform the seller within the reasonable time; if the defect became apparent later – immediately after the defect became apparent.*'

61 Recital 17 of the Consumer Sales Directive '*Whereas it is appropriate to limit in time the period during which the seller is liable for any lack of conformity which exists at the time of delivery of the goods (...)*'.

goods the period in which the consumer can claim non-conformity amounts to three days.[62] The seller can be liable only for the non-conformity that becomes apparent during this time and about which (during this time) the buyer has informed the seller. Subsequently, the period in which the presumption operates must also amount to three days. For example, when the consumer buys milk and after two days it becomes sour, it is presumed to have been sour on the day of delivery. Alternatively, it could be stated that the presumption does not apply in respect of those goods. These specific terms apply only to the products indicated in the Act.

I *Beginning of the period*

400. A professional seller is liable for non-conformity that existed at the time of delivery. The time of delivery is also the moment when the period of six months that grants the consumer the presumption of non-conformity begins to run. To be able to state whether the defects have appeared within six months from the time of delivery, it is necessary to determine the beginning and the end of this period. For both parties to the contract, it is important to establish the exact moment of delivery.

401. There are several opinions regarding the question of the moment of delivery for the purpose of consumer sales. According to the first view, delivery should be understood as a simple act of handing over the product, even when the documents necessary for disposal of the product have not yet been handed over.[63] Another view states that delivery means handing over the product, in a manner that the buyer obtains actual power over the goods.[64] These views regard the delivery for the purpose of a consumer sale as obtaining possession of the goods. According to Article 348 of the Civil Code the transfer of possession is exercised by the delivery, which entails handing over the goods and all other things that enable the person to use the goods.

Another opinion is that the seller's liability starts only after the risk of accidental loss has passed to the buyer. It is not always the moment of the passing ownership or (possession) of goods or actually receiving it, for example, in case of the shipment of goods.[65] Article 544 of the Civil Code provides that when the shipment of goods is carried out by a third party, the delivery occurs at the moment the goods are handed to the carrier. The above understanding of the delivery could make the proof regarding existence of non-

62 Rozporządzenie Ministra Gospodarki, Pracy i Polityki Społecznej z dnia 30 stycznia 2003 r. w sprawie terminów zawiadomienia sprzedawcy o stwierdzeniu niezgodności towaru żywnościowego z umową, Dz. U. Nr 31 poz. 258 (Regulation of the Minister of Economy, Labour and Social Policy about the notice of non-conformity of the food products).

63 Gniewek 2013, p. 34 *et seq.*

64 Pecyna 2003, p. 112.

65 Szczotka 2007, p. 47.

conformity at the moment of delivery close to impossible. In such cases application of the presumption seems to be the only possibility of satisfying the burden of proof.

The discussion seems to be irrelevant, taking into account that the Civil Code provides for the general rule on delivery. As long as there is no specific definition for the purpose of the consumer sale, the definition of Article 348 of the Civil Code must apply.

402. The provision of Article 556^2 of the Civil Code repealing Article 4 (1) of the Consumer Sale Act states that if the defect becomes apparent within a year from the time the risk passed, it is presumed that this defect or its origin has existed at that time. The legislator also provided a specific provision determining the moment of the passing of risk for the purpose of (consumer) sales contract. Article 548 (1) of the Civil Code provides that at the moment of delivery, the handing over of the goods, the risk passes to the buyer. When the goods are delivered to the consumer by carriage of goods performed by a third party, the risk passes to the consumer at the time of actual delivery. The exception applies when the seller has no influence on the method of carriage chosen by the consumer. In such a situation, the delivery takes place at the time of the goods are handed to the carrier.

403. Regarding the start of the six-month period (after the reform – one year), there is uncertainty over whether the day of delivery is the first day of the period or rather the period starts to run the day after the delivery. If the statute or the parties' agreement does not determine how the period should be calculated, the matter can be considered by looking at the general provisions of the Civil Code:

1. Article 111 (2) of the Civil Code applies to periods counted in days. It states that when a particular event causes the period to run, the day after the event is to be the first day of the period.
2. Article 112 of the Civil Code states that the periods counted in months expire at the end of the day corresponding by name or date with the starting day.

The period of the presumption of non-conformity is to be counted in months, therefore Article 111 (2) is inapplicable. Accordingly, Article 112 of the Civil Code will apply. It has been agreed that the event/day that designates the start of the period should be regarded as the first day of the period.[66] Furthermore, as already said, the general rules apply only when the statute or the agreement do not determine the calculation of the period. The question may arise whether Article 4 (1) of the Consumer Sale Act does not indicate the moment of the beginning of the period. It states that the presumption applies regarding the defects discovered during the six months from the time of delivery. Consequently, it seems that based on Article 112 of the Civil Code or Article 4 (1) of the Consumer Sale

66 Rudnicki and Trzaskowski/Kodeks Cywilny 2014, Art. 112, nr. 1, p. 781.

Act, the date of delivery is to be calculated as the first day of the period.[67] This seems to be different from the Regulation on rules determining the time periods.[68] In theory there is a discrepancy between Polish calculation and the calculation established in the Regulation. In practice, the problem seems to be insignificant as it seems that if the consumer is able to prove the existence of defects within six months from the time of delivery, including that day, the court most probably will accept the proof also when de period will run from the following day.

II Length of the period

404. Pursuant to Article 4 (1) of the Consumer Sale Act, the period for the operation of the presumption amounts to six months. In the proposed reform, the operation of the presumption of non-conformity is extended to one year. There are two rules regarding the periods counted in months or years. Article 112 of the Civil Code states that in cases where the term is expressed in months or years, it ends at the end of the day which corresponds with the name or date of the initial day. If there is no such day in this month, it ends the on last day of the month. For example, if the day of delivery was 30 August, the expiry of the period will be 28 or 29 February.

Article 114 of the Civil Code states that if the period is expressed in months or years and the continuity of period is not required the period of one month shall be counted as thirty days. The question is what the continuity of a period means. It can be easily explained using a timeshare agreement as an example. Where an owner is obliged to make the property available for six months in one year and the property does not have to be available for six months straight, given that one month of availability counts as thirty days, the owner must make his property available 180 days per year in order to fulfil the obligation.[69]

Taking the function of the presumption of non-conformity into account, it is clear that the six-month period (after the reform – one year) requires a continuity. Consequently, regarding the period of the operation of the presumption, Article 114 of the Civil Code does not apply.

III Expiry of the period

405. There is an opinion that in particular cases the period for the operation of the presumption can extend the statutory period.[70] Although it is only an idea open to interpretation, given the relevance of this subject, it deserves attention. Szczotka expressed that in case of groceries, chemical products, and cosmetics, if there is an expiry date stated on the

---

67 According to Article of 556^2 of the Civil Code, the period starts at the time of passing of risk, which pursuant to Article 548 takes place at the time of delivery, handing over the goods.

68 Chapter 5, para 374.

69 Gniewek 2011, p. 182.

70 Szczotka 2007, p. 49.

product, any defect that became apparent before the expiry date, should be presumed to have existed at the time of delivery.[71] According to Szczotka, the above interpretation should apply regardless of the fact that the expiry date is longer than the statutory period.[72] This situation could be regarded as a modification of the statutory period. The seller could rebut the presumption by providing evidence to the contrary, for example, by arguing that the consumer has not kept the above-mentioned goods as advised, which resulted in the existence of non-conformity.[73] Despite the lack of any general rules modifying the period for the presumption, the Consumer Sales Directive allows Member States to set different periods regarding certain categories of goods.[74]

406. One may doubt whether the manifestation of defects after the expiry of the statutory period but before the end of the expiry date prolongs the period for the operation of the presumption of non-conformity. Another opinion could be that the date on the packaging constitutes specific characteristics of the product that parties agreed upon. The second view has, however, one disadvantage. While proving non-conformity will not be problematic as in given circumstances the agreed term (usable by) has not been met, the six-month period has already expired. The consumer will not be able to make use of the presumption of non-conformity because the second requirement is missing. To receive remedies the consumer will be required to prove that non-conformity has existed at the time of delivery. However, the court may help the consumer by applying a factual presumption. Bearing in mind objectives of the presumption, the first interpretation seems to be much more favourable for consumers.[75]

IV Application of the presumption after the expiry of the statutory period

407. The presumption of non-conformity of Article 4 (1) of the Consumer Sale Act applies to the defects which become apparent within six months from the time of delivery. According to Article 556^2 of the Civil Code the presumption will apply in relation to the defects that become apparent within one year from the time the risk passed. After its expiry, a presumption of non-conformity does no longer apply. The burden of proof of the existence of non-conformity at the time of delivery is restored in accordance with the general rule of the burden of proof of Article 6 of the Civil Code and lies with the consumer.

The question arises whether the presumption can apply if the consumer discovers the defects after expiry of the statutory period, even if the discovery was objectively possible

71 New Article 568^1 states that '*if the expiry date falls after two years from the time of delivery, the seller is liable for defects which became apparent before the expiry of that date*'. According to this Article the expiry date may extend the limitation period, which normally amounts to two years from the time of delivery.

72 Szczotka 2007, p. 49.

73 For example, most of the cosmetic products must be kept in a dark and dry environment.

74 Recital 21 of the Consumer Sales Directive.

75 Szczotka 2007, p. 49.

within that time. The subjective approach requires a consumer to discover the defects within the statutory period. In case the defects were ascertained after the expiry regardless of whether it was possible to discover them earlier, the consumer might not be able to benefit from the presumption.[76] The objective approach requires the defects to appear within six months even when for the consumer they became apparent only after this period.

Furthermore, it is uncertain what exactly the consumer would have to prove in case the defects, which must have objectively existed before, were discovered after the lapse of the statutory period. The possible options are:

1. The exact moment when the non-conformity became apparent.
2. Non-conformity became apparent at any moment within the statutory period.
3. (High) probability that the non-conformity appeared within the statutory period, shifting burden to prove otherwise to the seller.

It would be too burdensome to expect the consumer to prove exact date of the non-conformity. He is not obliged to do so when the defect occurs within the statutory period and he notifies the seller after the expiry of that time. Regarding the third option, it seems that it will depend on the judge whether probability presented by the consumer is sufficiently convincing to, for example, apply a factual presumption. Therefore, the second option seems to be most suitable one. In a given case, the consumer will have to prove that the particular non-conformity has become apparent at any time within six months from the time of delivery, regardless of when it came to his attention.

408. There is a view that consumers should be required to carry out 'sort of inspection'[77] during six months after the delivery and in case of discovering the defect they should immediately undertake action.[78] Such an approach could help to reduce the number of cases where, after the expiry of the statutory period the consumer realises that the product is defective, although it was possible to discover it before the six-month period elapsed. Such an approach facilitates the use of the simplifications in the duty to supply evidence from Article 4 (1) of the Consumer Sale Act and Article 556^2 of the Civil Code. Despite its practical advantages, taking the legal certainty as to the timely operation of the presumption and the allocation of the burden of proof into account, neither the Directive nor the Consumer Sale Act imposes a duty on the consumer to inspect the goods. There is another measure to discipline the consumer regarding the duty to inform the seller of the defects. As already stated, Article 9 (1) of the Consumer Sale Act provides that the consumer loses

76 Pecyna 2003, p. 112.
77 Not necessarily equal with duty to inspect with all its consequences.
78 Jezioro 2010, p. 142.

his right to claim remedies if he does not inform the seller about the defects within two months from the time of their discovery.

409. In practice, after the expiry of the statutory period the consumer's position becomes particularly difficult concerning evidence. Starting court proceedings seems to be inevitable in order to be able to receive remedies.[79] It has been observed that currently, if the defects become apparent within six months the sellers more often offer remedies since they know that before the court they are in a more difficult position.[80] After the expiry of the six-month period, the sellers often reject the complaints regarding non-conforming goods and wait for the consumer to initiate the proceedings.[81] The reason for that is the fact that the burden of proof that the goods were defective at the time of delivery lies with the consumer. Consequently, there is a higher probability that the consumer will fail. The question remains whether this trend will continue after the new statute enters into force. The new provisions extend the operation of the presumption to one year from the moment risk is passed, which in some cases will be equal to the limitation period.

5.3.3.3 Conclusions

410. Article 4 (1) of the Consumer Sale Act imposes two requirements for the presumption of non-conformity. The first requirement of application of the presumption is existence of non-conformity. It is also a main condition for the seller's liability for non-conforming goods. Where the consumer cannot prove the defects, the claim against the seller will be unsuccessful. The criteria of non-conformity from Article 4 (2) and (3) of the Consumer Sale Act play an important role. They determine whether the consumer will make use of the presumption of non-conformity. In the near future the content of first requirement will change. The redrafting of the Civil Code introduces one notion of defects applicable to all types of contracts of sale.[82]

411. Based on the case law it can be concluded that the Polish courts are relatively lenient in assessing consumer's proof of the existence of defects. In practice, this should have a positive effect on the frequency of the application of the presumption of non-conformity.

A construction facilitating consumer protection, which does not exist in other jurisdictions, is provided by Article 8 (3) of the Consumer Sale Act and the new Article 561^5 of the Civil Code. When the consumer sends a complaint about a defect, which became

79 It is already difficult during the six months and in general taking the legal action in Poland is often the only possibility to receive remedies.

80 Jezioro 2010, p. 146.

81 Polubowny Sąd Konsumencki przy Zachodniopomorskim Wojewódzkim Inspektorze Inspekcji Handlowej w Szczecinie, 22.03.2006, sygn. akt. 26/2006. (Consumer Arbitration Court set by the Regional Trade Inspectorate).

82 Chapter 4, para 244-247.

apparent within six months (the period of operation of the presumption of non-conformity) and the seller does not substantially respond to this complain within fourteen days, he is regarded as liable for the defects. This precludes the seller's right to challenge the grounds of liability before the court. In cases where the consumer's complaint regards the defects appearing after the expiry of six months, the seller still has the right to challenge the grounds for liability. He is allowed to provide the proof before the court that at the time of delivery the goods were in conformity. The above interpretation has been confirmed by the Polish Supreme Court. Given that the proposed reform extends the period of the presumption, the interpretation of Article 8 (3) of the Consumer Sale Act approved by the Supreme Court will most probably be adopted in accordance with the new provisions.

412. The second requirement concerns the proof that the defects have become apparent within six months. To begin with, there is some uncertainty with regard to when the six-month period begins to run and how it is to be counted. The main issue arises in the situation when the defects are only discovered when the six months have expired. There is uncertainty over what the consumer must prove in order to be successful in his claim. Whether it is sufficient to rely on the non-conformity which objectively existed, but has not been discovered within six months, remains to some extent unanswered. According to the Consumer Sale Act, it seems that as long as the consumer is able to prove that the non-conformity appeared within six months, the presumption that it existed at the time of delivery must be applied.

The next issue concerns whether the period of six months can be extended due to the specifically stated expiry date. It seems logical that when a producer promises that the certain product is to be usable until a given date the consumer can assume that if the goods are defective before that date, they were defective from the beginning.[83] On the other hand, the protection given by the guarantee that the goods are usable by the expiry date seems to be a more appropriate solution. By all means, it provides higher level of legal certainty.

413. Taking the complexity of the presumption into account, in cases regarding remedies for the non-conformity of goods, it is ultimately the consumer who has the burden of proving essential facts. Therefore, although there is no legal duty to do so, the consumer should always take care of this own interests and ideally inspect the goods within the first six months. After the presumption expires it becomes difficult to provide evidence that the goods were defective at the time of delivery. As a result the time is of the essence since after the expiry of six months, the chances of receiving remedies for the delivery of non-conforming goods significantly diminish.

83 Szczotka 2007, p. 49.

5.3.4 *Rebuttal of the presumption*

414. The statutory presumptions are either rebuttable or non-rebuttable.[84] According to Article 5 (3) of the Consumer Sales Directive, the presumption applies unless proven otherwise. Below, the characteristics and content of proof to the contrary under Polish law will be presented. In particular, it will be discussed what facts the seller has to present to prove that the defects, whose existence within six months from the time of delivery has been proven by the consumer, occurred after that time.

415. In order to rebut the presumption of non-conformity found in Article 4 (1) of the Consumer Sale Act, the seller has to provide evidence to the contrary. He must show that although the basic facts have occurred (there is non-conformity which became apparent within six months from the time of delivery), the presumed fact (non-conformity existed at the time of delivery) is incorrect. Evidence presented by the seller must demonstrate that the product was in conformity at the time of delivery or that the defects were caused only after that time, for example due to the consumer's fault or accidental events.[85] The seller can use all available means of evidence, including other (factual) presumptions.[86] In particular, the seller can claim that the consumer used the product incorrectly, or against directions provided in the manuals supplied together with the product. Furthermore, arguments such as interference with producers' safeguards or breaking protective seals may support the seller's arguments to convince the court that at the time of delivery the product was in conformity and that the defects occurred only later, and/or potentially they were caused by the consumer.[87] If seller's evidence is successful he will not only prevent the application of the presumption, but he cannot be held liable for the non-conformity of goods.

416. There are other means available to the seller for preventing the application of the presumption as such. He can achieve it by showing that the defects could not have become apparent within six months from the delivery, or that at the moment indicated by the buyer the product was in conformity. The seller can therefore challenge the second condition of the application of the presumption. Where the seller successfully argues that the defect became apparent after the expiry of the six-month period, he will successfully prevent the application of the presumption. Accordingly, the burden of proof that the goods were defective at the time of delivery will be shifted back to the consumer and allocated in

84 Piasecki 2010, p. 90; Dolecki 1998, p. 141; Chapter 2, para 35, 36.

85 Szczotka 2007, p. 50; Jezioro 2010, p. 145; Pecyna 2003, p. 115; SR Świdnica 04.06.2013, I C 741/11 - an unsuccesful rebutal.

86 Piasecki 2010, p. 90.

87 Stefanicki 2006, p. 204.

accordance with the general rule on the burden of proof found in Article 6 of the Civil Code.

417. The seller may use strategies other than evidence to the contrary to prevent the application of the presumption. He may undermine the grounds for the application of the Consumer Sale Act in general. If the seller is successful, the application of the presumption will be excluded. In general, if the court decides that the Consumer Sale Act applies, the seller has to provide evidence excluding application of the Consumer Sale Act. He can use arguments that the buyer does not act in the capacity of a consumer, that the sold goods are not consumer goods, or that the seller is not a professional seller. The seller has the burden of proving these facts and bears the risk of being unable to prove them. Finally, the seller may argue that there was no contract between the parties. Each of the above-mentioned facts, if proven, will prevent the application of the presumption of non-conformity.

5.3.5 *Exclusion of the application of the presumption*

418. Article 5 (3) of the Consumer Sales Directive excludes the application of the presumption if the presumption is incompatible with the nature of the goods or with the nature of the non-conformity. There is no general definition determining '*the nature of the goods*' or '*the nature of the non-conformity*', at least for the purposes of consumer sales.

Contrary to the Directive and the national implementations examined in this study, the provisions of the Polish Consumer Sale Act do not contain exclusion criteria.[88] This means, at least in theory, that the presumption of non-conformity is unconditional and every time the basic prerequisites for the application have been met, the court must allow the application of the presumption.

419. The lack of reservations seems to be favourable to the consumers, since the presumption will apply (at least in theory) even when it is incompatible with '*the nature of the goods, or the nature of the non-conformity*'. As long as the conditions for the presumption are met, the seller must provide evidence to the contrary to rebut the presumption, or provide facts excluding application of the Consumer Sale Act.

On the other hand, implementing exclusion criteria would unquestionably be in line with the Consumer Sales Directive. Other Member States have implemented the criteria and although it is difficult to categorise particular circumstances and accurately determine

88 Luxembourg and Slovenia also did not implement the exclusion criteria; See Schulte-Nölke, Twigg-Flesner and Ebers 2008, p. 684.

the legal character of the exclusion criteria, they may correctly prevent the application of the presumption.[89]

420. In the literature there is discussion regarding the importance of the exclusion criteria and their practical consequences.[90] Habryn supports the choice made by the legislator to not implement the criteria. She argues that the possibility of excluding the application could unfairly narrow the scope of protection and diminish the role of the presumption of non-conformity.[91] Furthermore, she continues that the lack of uniform definitions of '*incompatibility with the nature of the good and the nature of the non-conformity*' supports the legislator's choice. Finally, it has been stated that it does not matter whether the reservations have been implemented or not, because their application depends on existence of facts and evidence which must be provided by the seller.[92]

421. Another opinion states that the 'unconditional' application of the rebuttable presumption should not be allowed.[93] Łętowska describes situations where the presumption of non-conformity should not apply as it is incompatible with the nature of the goods and the nature of the defects. The first situation concerns the sale of animals, which are infected with a disease and where the incubation period proves to be shorter than six months. In practice, the cases regarding this specific type of non-conformity may indicate that said non-conformity has developed within a short period of time after the delivery. In such circumstances, the judge should have discretion to rule out the presumption as incompatible or incorrect. The second situation regards second-hand goods, specifically when non-conformity falls within the scope of wear and tear.[94] Above reasoning is approved in the literature.[95]

To prevent the application of the presumption in cases where an animal is infected with the disease the legislator could classify particular diseases as a characteristic for certain animals. Such list would mean that if the listed disease occurs it confirms that the animals lack non-conformity. The animals are living organisms and therefore the risk of becoming infected with a virus is a natural (common) characteristic of such organisms. Certain features belong to the particular group of goods and therefore its existence should not be recognised automatically as non-conformity. This construction would probably require (a statutory) catalogue of respective diseases. Otherwise, the court would have to rule

89 Schulte-Nölke, Twigg-Flesner and Ebers 2008, p. 683 *et seq.*
90 Habryn 2010, p. 44-50; Pecyna 2003, p. 112-117; Łętowska 2004, p. 386.
91 Habryn 2010, p. 47.
92 Pecyna 2003, p. 114.
93 Łętowska 2004, p. 386.
94 Łętowska 2004, p. 386.
95 Łętowska 2004, p. 386; Pecyna 2003, p. 115.

individually in every case, which in practical terms would not differ from the current construction.

One may observe that the above examples regard the characterisation of goods and defects. Relying on the above arguments, the seller is not arguing that the presumption is incompatible with the nature of the goods or the nature of the non-conformity, but simply that the particular diseases or deficiencies of second-hand goods do not constitute non-conformity as such. Consequently, the presumption of non-conformity should not apply because its first condition (the existence of a non-conformity) has not been successfully fulfilled.

422. The issue of exclusion criteria has not been addressed in the official statute justification to the draft of the Consumer Sale Act. The Polish courts also have not spoken up about revealed problems regarding the exclusion criteria. The fact that the exclusion criteria are not implemented into the Consumer Sale Act does not mean that the seller may not use similar arguments during the proceedings. One of the arguments supporting the Polish legislator's choice to not introduce exclusions points out that the seller is allowed to use similar arguments as a way to rebut the presumption of non-conformity.[96] The consequences of the above solution may affect the allocation of the burden of proof. As presented in chapter 2, the distribution, content of proof and the standard of proof may differ depending on whether the argument is used to challenge the existence of non-conformity as a condition of the presumption, to provide evidence to the contrary, or to prove the exclusion of the application of the presumption.

The recently amended provision on the presumption of non-conformity, Article 556^2 of the Civil Code, also omits the issue of exclusion criteria. Similarly to the statute justification of the Consumer Sale Act dated from more than ten years ago, the current amendments' justification is also silent on the reasons why the legislator refrains from regulating the matter.

423. Summing up, the Polish legislator decided not to implement the exclusion criteria of the application of the presumption due to its incompatibility with the nature of the goods and the nature of the non-conformity. Omitting these provisions is not necessarily in line with Article 5 (3) of the Consumer Sales Directive, which explicitly provides exclusion criteria. However, the character of the Directive as a minimum harmonisation measure allows for such a solution. Due to the lack of case law regarding this topic, one may speculate on what the courts' line of reasoning would be. I estimate that most probably the court would not directly regard the incompatibility of the presumption as a reason for its exclusion. The fact that the presumption of Article 4 (1) of the Consumer Sale Act is

96 Habryn 2010, p. 48.

rebuttable and the seller may use all available means of evidence including other (factual) presumptions indicates that the incompatibility arguments can be used to rebut the presumption of non-conformity.

5.3.6 *Road map of the presumption*

424. In this sub-section the scheme of how the presumption is constructed and how it might be applied will be discussed. Furthermore, the relationship between particular stages of the presumption as well the defences available to both parties will be presented. Some of the elements have been already discussed but will be repeated for the purpose of creating some kind of roadmap of the presumption of Article 4 (1) of the Consumer Sale Act. The reference will be also made to the amendments provided in the recently enacted article 556^2 of the Civil Code.

425. Article 4 (1) of the Consumer Sale Act provides that if the non-conformity became apparent within six months from the time of delivery it is presumed to have existed at that time. The consumer must meet two conditions to be able to benefit from the presumption. He has to prove the existence of non-conformity and the fact that it existed within six months from the time of delivery. Additionally, a consumer must inform the seller of the non-conformity within two months from the moment it has been discovered otherwise the consumer loses the right to remedies.

The burden of proof regarding the two conditions (non-conformity within statutory period) lies with the consumer. The Polish courts are relatively lenient in their evaluation of the existence of non-conformity. The consumer does not have to provide specific information when the case regards complex goods. Due to the seller's experience and knowledge he is required to provide technical data regarding the goods and their defects.

A similar approach is taken when it comes to the six-month period. It has been argued that when the defects become apparent after the statutory period lapses, it is sufficient to prove that the goods were objectively defective within six months, even when the consumer discovered the defects after that time.

426. If the two requirements have been met, the presumption of non-conformity applies and the burden of proof reverses to the seller. To rebut the presumption the seller has to prove that the goods were in conformity at the time of delivery. He can also undermine the evidence supporting the existence of the presumption's prerequisites. In the latter situation the presumption will not apply and the burden of proof that the goods were defective at the time of delivery lies with the consumer. Other options for challenging the presumption are to prove that the defects occurred only after the goods were delivered. Finally, the

seller can try to disprove that the contract amounts to a consumer sale, consequently excluding the application of the Consumer Sale Act. It should be remembered that the exclusion of protective provisions does not entail a decrease in protection. The regulation and interpretation of rules found in the Civil Code are regarded as more favourable to the consumer than the protection provided by the Consumer Sale Act.

427. The Polish Consumer Sale Act does not provide for exclusion criteria. In theory, the presumption will also apply when it is incompatible with the nature of the goods or the nature of the non-conformity. The legislator seems to ignore the issues of exclusion. It does not provide for exclusion criteria and it does not address these issue in the statutes' justifications. The question arises whether the Polish legislation deliberately refrained from exclusion criteria. Regardless of the lack of exclusion criteria in the statute, it has been agreed that the arguments of incompatibility can still be used by the seller to rebut the presumption. This proves the close connection between exclusion criteria and the content of the evidence to the contrary, necessary to rebut the presumption.

428. Article 556^2 of the Civil Code, which entered into force on 25 December 2014 extends the period within which the presumption may apply. It states that if the non-conformity applies within one year from the time the risk was passed it is presumed to have existed at that time. Other changes that may affect the application of the presumption regard the new definition of defects. Taking into consideration that this definition uses very similar criteria, in practical terms, it seems the scope of application should not change. Similarly to Article 4 (1) of the Consumer Sale Act, its successor, Article 556^2 of the Civil Code does not contain the exclusion criteria. Summing up, except the extension of the statutory period for the application of the presumption of non-conformity, which will considerably increase consumer protection, no considerable changes were introduced. Finally, it is unclear whether the consumer will be able to benefit from the application of the factual presumption as presented in chapter 3, para 114 and 115. It seems that the construction developed before the implementation of the Consumer Sales Directive will not play a significant role, at least within the statutory period for the application of the presumption of non-conformity of Article 556^2 of the Civil Code. The statutory presumption cannot be disregarded for the benefit of the application of the factual presumption. The role of the factual presumption after the expiry of the statutory period will depend on the individual case and the judge's opinion of its applicability. It seems that in particular circumstances the factual presumption as presented in chapter 3, para 114 and 115 may still be used for the benefit of the buyer.

5.3.7 *Conclusions*

429. This section presents information about the presumption of non-conformity of Article 5 (3) of the Consumer Sales Directive as implemented in Polish law in Article 4 (1) of the Consumer Sale Act. The main focus was on the conditions and the legal consequences of the presumption, on the rebuttal and the exclusion criteria. To be able to make use of the simplifications in the supply of evidence, the consumer must first prove the existence of non-conformity of goods. Secondly, he has to prove that this non-conformity appeared within six months from the time of delivery. As a consequence, the general rules on the allocation of the burden of proof are altered. Pursuant to the general rule of Article 6 of the Civil Code, the burden of proof of the existence of non-conformity at the time of delivery would normally lie with the buyer/consumer. Thanks to the presumption, in the first six months after the delivery the burden that at the time of delivery the goods were free from defects lies with the seller.

430. The seller can rebut the presumption by providing evidence to the contrary. He can argue that the defects proven by the consumer were caused only after the delivery, for example, due to incorrect usage, the fault of a third party, or an accident for which the seller is not responsible. In cases of successful evidence rebutting the presumption, there is no ground for liability and claim will be dismissed. Additionally, the seller can challenge the second condition of the presumption that is the expiry of six-month period. If he is successful in claiming that the six months have expired, the presumption will not apply, and the burden of proof will be allocated according to the general rule of Article 6 of the Civil Code.

431. The Polish legislator decided not to implement the exclusion criteria because of its incompatibility with the nature of the goods and the nature of the non-conformity. As a result, there is uncertainty over whether the presumption can be excluded in the above-mentioned circumstances. It seems that the presumption of non-conformity will be applied regardless of its incompatibility with the nature of the goods or the nature of the non-conformity. On the other hand, the incompatibility arguments could be accepted as the arguments forming the rebuttal.

Having said that, there are nonetheless claims that not implementing the exclusion criteria is an omission on the part of the legislator.[97] To avoid legal uncertainty the legislator may want to close this lacuna and ensure that the rights and obligations of the parties to the consumer sale are comprehensible. Unfortunately, in the new statute, the matters of exclusion criteria are again left aside, without further explanation.

97 Habryn 2010, p. 48; Pecyna 2003, p. 115 *et seq.*

432. It must be stated that the presumption facilitates the consumer's position only temporarily, within the first six months from the time of delivery. Following the expiry of that period, the consumer is in a more difficult position regarding the probability of satisfying the burden of proof and obtaining remedies. The seller has numerous possibilities challenging a consumer's claim, while consumer must rely on the applicability of the presumption otherwise his chances to win the case are rather weak. It has been said that the period in which the presumption operates should be longer because of the difficulties in providing evidence after the expiry of the six months. A consumer does not have the same knowledge or resources as a seller. For a seller, to prove the contrary will probably not be as difficult as for the consumer.[98] The last suggestion has been recently introduced and will enter into force in the near future. The new statute provides in Article 556^2 for a one-year presumption of non-conformity, which will considerably improve consumers' chances of obtaining remedies.

433. It should be underlined that the rules on the allocation of the burden of proof have proven to be a significant tool for consumer protection. Generally, they may soothe the inconvenience of the substantive regulations. The national legislators should therefore be aware of this fact and use rules on the allocation of the burden of proof to restore balance between the parties. For this reason, the presumption of non-conformity has been one of the most controversial instruments of the Consumer Sales Directive. Although the requirements for the application and its consequences have been transposed into Polish law in line with the Directive, it seems that the expectations as to the role and function of this provision may have been overestimated. The consumer still bears the burden of supplying information and evidence regarding the non-conformity which may be difficult at times.

5.4 Presumption of non-conformity in German law

5.4.1 *Introduction*

434. This section describes the application of the presumption of non-conformity in German law. It begins with the general information of the scope of the presumption of non-conformity in German law (5.4.2). The central issues in this section regard the conditions for the application of the presumption (5.4.3), rebuttal of the presumption (5.4.4) and the exclusion criteria (5.4.5). Information on the above-mentioned topics will lead to the conclusions on whether the objectives of the presumption of non-conformity have been

98 Pecyna 2003, p. 116.

achieved and whether a German consumer can easily take advantage of the simplifications in supply of evidence designed for him by the European legislator.

5.4.2 *Scope of the application of the presumption*

435. The German legislator implemented the presumption of non-conformity of Article 5 (3) of the Consumer Sales Directive in § 476 BGB. Following Article 5 (3) of the Directive, § 476 BGB states that if a material defect becomes apparent within six months from the time of the passing of risk, it is presumed that the defect existed at that time, unless the presumption is incompatible with the nature of the goods or the nature of the defects. In other words, § 476 BGB contains a presumption of the existence of material defects at the time the risk was passed, if the defect becomes apparent within six months from that time.

§ 476 BGB belongs to the new regulations on the German law of obligations. It alters the general rule regarding the allocation of the burden of proof in consumer sale cases. Before the modernisation of the German law of obligations, when the parties were in conflict, regardless of whether the goods were defective at the time the risk was passed (old § 459 BGB), the burden of proof was allocated in accordance with § 363 BGB. § 363 BGB contains the general rule of the burden of proof in cases of non-performance of obligations. It states that '*if the obligee has accepted performance offered to him as performance of contract, he bears the burden of proof if he does not wish to have the performance considered as performance of contract because it was different from the performance owed or because it was incomplete*'.[99] After the implementation of the Consumer Sales Directive, the general rule still applies to contracts of sale other than consumer sales. § 476 BGB is therefore a *lex specialis* of § 363 BGB. The special rule on the burden of proof shifts the burden to the seller provided the defect appeared within six months from the time the risk was passed and its existence is proven by the consumer.[100]

Amendments regarding the allocation of the burden of proof have led to an interesting debate over the prerequisites and consequences of the application of the presumption, as well as the exclusion of its application. Taking into account the number of consumer sale contracts concluded every day, the practical implications of the presumption of § 476 BGB are important. It comes as no surprise that the new regulations have attracted broad attention among legal scholars. Also the BGH had ruled on the application of the presumption of non-conformity in a considerable number of cases and it has established a certain line of interpretation of § 476 BGB.

99 Translation http://www.gesetze-im-internet.de/englisch_bgb/englisch_bgb.html#p1473 (23.10.2014); See also: Baumgärtel, Laumen and Prütting 2009, p. 86; Schinkels 2007, p. 1; Reinicke and Tiedtke 2009, p. 273.

100 Beckmann 2013, p. 344; Dauner-Lieb and Langen 2012, p. 1754; Hoeren and Martinek 2002, p. 184.

436. The German legislator justifies the wording and purpose of § 476 BGB by pointing out that the professional seller is at an advantage in terms of knowledge, know-how and experience in comparison to the consumer and is better placed to supply evidence that the goods were not defective at the time the risk was passed.[101] Taking into account the inequality between the parties, the disadvantageous allocation of the burden of proof exacerbates the differences between the parties. The presumption of non-conformity is designed to simplify the burden borne by the consumer and to make obtaining remedies for defective goods easier. Regarding the aim of § 476 BGB, some describe the presumption of non-conformity as a significant improvement and important tool granted to consumers.[102] Others describe it as a *quasi-guarantee* of the six-month period.[103] In German literature it is underlined that although at first glance it would appear that the presumption only favours the consumer, in fact, for the sake of legal certainty, its proper application is in the interests of all parties involved.[104]

437. The presumption of non-conformity concerns defects that appeared within six months after the passing of risk and whose existence is proven by a consumer. It does not concern defects which became apparent after the expiry of the period, even if complaints had already been expressed regarding other defects. The only exception is when the defects that occurred later are a consequence of the defects which the consumer proved to be existent within the first six months.[105] Each defect must be proven separately. Unless all conditions are met in relation to each particular defect, the consumer will not be granted protection respectively. It must be concluded that the presumption concerns only the actual condition of the goods and not the existence of defects in general.[106] This could have significant consequences for the necessary evidence the consumer must present in a courtroom. The question is whether a consumer would have to provide precise evidence proving a particular defect or whether he would be allowed to show that the purchased product does not work properly as such. The above issue will be discussed in sub-section 5.4.3.1.

438. The presumption of non-conformity applies only to material defects and not to the legal defects from § 435. Regarding the latter, the general principle of the allocation of the burden of proof applies.[107] One might ask whether § 476 BGB should not cover legal defects. The question is interesting for several reasons. First, the BGB distinguishes two types of defects, material and legal defects. The definitions in § 434 and § 435 BGB may be regarded

101 Deutscher Bundestag 14/6040, p. 245; Mausltzsch 2006, p. 3092.
102 Faust 2011, § 476 Rn. 1-21.
103 Hoeren and Martinek 2002, p. 657.
104 Maultzsch 2006, p. 3092.
105 Becker 2009, p. 87.
106 Maultzsch 2006, p. 3093.
107 Beckmann 2013, p. 344, 345; Lorenz 2012, § 476 Rn. 7.

as reflecting the criteria of non-conformity of Article 2 (2) (a)-(d) of the Consumer Sales Directive. On the other hand § 476 BGB expressly mentions only material defects as its scope of application. This raises the question whether presumption of non-conformity should be interpreted as exclusively applicable to material defects or it could be extended by analogy to cover legal defects respectively. As already stated, the liability for legal defects is not regarded as liability for non-conformity.[108] It constitutes an independent ground for liability not associated with the physical state of goods. Consequently, § 476 BGB must be strictly interpreted as applying only in cases involving material defects of consumer goods.[109]

Another question is whether the presumption of non-conformity should apply to all types of goods or only to the new ones. After engaging in debate, the literature and jurisprudence have concluded that the presumption of § 476 BGB must apply to both new and second-hand goods.[110] Consequently, the presumption has been applied numerous times to the second-hand goods with varying degrees of success, especially in the sale of used cars.[111]

439. The issues concerning the application of § 476 BGB have received a great deal of attention in both literature[112] and the courtroom.[113] The presumption of § 476 BGB has been recognised as having a real significance for consumer protection. Any inconsistencies should be clarified and eliminated through legal and judicial interpretation. In contrast to some other European countries, where there is little to no case law, in Germany there is a distinct line of interpretation of the new sales law. Nevertheless, it still appears that German courts and scholars are mostly concerned with the domestic legal system when interpreting the provisions in question. There is criticism that the BGH does not try to look into other jurisdictions at how the comparable issues have been dealt with.[114] Therefore, despite many

108 Chapter 4, para 284.

109 Lorenz 2012, § 476 Rn. 7.

110 Baumgärtel, Laumen and Prütting 2009, p. 86; See also: BGH 14.09.2005, VIII ZR 363/04, NJW 2005, 3490, 3492; OLG Köln 11.11.2003, 22 U 88/03, NJW-RR 2004, 268; OLG Stuttgart 31.01.2005, 5 U 153/04, ZGS 2005, 156, 158.

111 See: AG Aachen 10.12.2003, 14 C 161/03, Beck RS 2005, 06814; AG Berlin-Charlottenburg 10.10.2008, 232 C 196/07, Beck RS 2009, 12941; LG Halle/Saale 18.10.2012, 4 O 1417/10; OLG Düsseldorf 23.06.2008, 1 U 264/07, Beck RS 2008, 15373.

112 For example: Pfeiffer 2002; Massimo Bianca and Grundmann 2002; Grundmann 2001; Grundmann 2005; Maultzsch 2006.

113 For example: BGH 11.07.2007, VIII ZR 110/06, NJW 2007, 2619; BGH 18.07.2007, VIII ZR 259/06, NJW 2007, 2621; BGH 14.09.2005, VIII ZR 363/04, NJW 2005, 3490; BGH 08.11.2007, VII ZR 183/05, BGHZ 174, 110; BGH 10.10.2007, VIII ZR 330/06, NJW 2008, 53; BGH 02.06.2004, VIII ZR 329/03, BGHZ 159, 215; BGH 29.03.2006, VIII ZR 173/05, BGHZ 167, 40; BGH 23.11.2005, VIII ZR 43/05, NJW 2006, 434; BGH 22.11.2004, VIII ZR 21/04, NJW 2005, 283; BGH 11.11.2008, VIII ZR 265/07, NJW 2009, 580.

114 Rühl 2009, p. 913.

commentaries and thorough interpretation, a question remains over whether the German provisions are true to the intention and the direction set by the European legislator.[115]

5.4.3 Conditions for the application of the presumption

5.4.3.1 Non-conformity (*Sachliche Komponente*)

440. To be able to enjoy the benefits of the presumption of § 476 BGB, the consumer must prove that the seller's performance diverged from what had been agreed upon by the parties, or that the product did not possess the characteristics as mentioned in the latter part of § 434 BGB.[116] The consumer has to present the basic facts, that there is a material defect in the sense of § 434 BGB and that it became apparent within six months from the time of the passing of risk, in order the presumed fact, that the goods were defective at the time of the passing of risk, could be inferred.

The prerequisites of the presumption of non-conformity under § 476 BGB are the same as those set out in Article 5 (3) of the Consumer Sales Directive. Some German authors try to distinguish a third prerequisite, namely that the contract between the parties must constitute a consumer sales contract as set out in § 474 BGB.[117] The fact that a contract between the parties is a consumer sale contract constitutes a condition for the application of any provision introduced by the Directive, of which § 476 BGB is but one. However, as observed in the case law, the question of whether there was a consumer contract is considered relatively frequently.[118]

441. To prove the product is defective, the buyer has to present the facts provided in § 434 BGB. For example, a consumer will have to provide evidence that the product does not possess the specific quality that was individually agreed upon or it does not meet the standard quality expected in goods of the same kind. In some cases the consumer will also be expected to present evidence of exactly what the parties have agreed upon. That may be particularly burdensome, especially in cases where the parties only agreed orally or when the consumer did not save the confirmation document (receipt). There are also cases where the consumer does not have to specify how the defect occurred. In such cases it is sufficient to prove that it existed within six months from the passing of risk.[119]

---

115 Schulte-Nölke, Twigg-Flesner and Ebers 2008, p. 646.
116 Chapter 4, para 277-283.
117 Schürnbrand 2008, p. 1.
118 OLG Koblenz Hinweisbeschluss 8.01.2013, 2 U 1066/12, JurionRS 2013, 35008; OLG Bremen 11.03.2004, 2 U 99/03, JurionRS 2004, 17711; BGH 29.03.2006, VIII ZR 173/05, BGHZ 167, 40.
119 Grundmann and Ochmann 2007, p. 457.

442. There is uncertainty as to when the product can be regarded as proven to be defective. There can be various approaches to this issue. Based on the case law there are three instances of defects that can be distinguished.

First of all, in relatively simple cases, the product may possess a defect in the sense of § 434 BGB. That means one of the circumstances expressly stated in § 434 BGB has been encountered by the consumer. The defect is concrete, identified, and proven by the consumer. The exact origins of the defect may be unclear. It might have existed at the time the risk was passed and remained temporarily undiscovered or it might have occurred later, however its existence is undisputed. In such cases the presumption will apply, unless rebutted or incompatible with the nature of the goods or the nature of the non-conformity.[120] For instance, a laptop is delivered with a clearly, visible defective display, or it has different than agreed parameters.

Moreover, there are two further instances of the defects reaching beyond what is literally stated in § 434 BGB. The first is considered by the doctrine as a *Grundmangel.*[121] It is a problem with purchased goods not existing at the time the risk was passed. To consider such issue as a defect for the purpose of § 476 BGB it must have resulted from the internal defective factors present at the time of the passing of risk. For example, the consumer complains that the display on a laptop, which at the time of the passing of risk was working, does not function properly. The inspection shows that the cables connected to display were not sufficiently tight and they loosened up more over time causing the display to fail. In this situation it is clear that the problem with the purchased goods resulted from the internal factors (incorrectly installed cables) present at the time of the risk passing.

The last instance of the defect is considered by the doctrine as a *Folgemangel.*[122] It is a problem with purchased goods not existing at the time the risk was passed. It can be caused by the presence of the *Grundmangel* as explained above, or it might have other external origins. The link between the existence of the problem and the existence of a *Grundmangel* must be proven by the consumer. The proof of such link is often difficult to provide. If the consumer provides sufficient evidence it might be presumed that the problem with the goods has been caused by a defect resulting from the defective factors existing at the time the risk was passed. To consider a *Folgemangel* as a defect for the purpose of § 434 and § 476 BGB other potential origins such as wear and tear and misuse of the goods must often be excluded by the consumer. For example, the incorrectly functioning display made the owner of the laptop use more power when working with touch-screen what caused the touch-screen functions to fail.

120 AG Hamburg 25.03.2009, 7c C 53/08.

121 Becker 2009, p. 87; Beckmann 2013, § 476 Rn. 19.

122 Becker 2009, p. 87, Beckmann 2013, § 476 Rn. 19; Lorenz 2004, p. 3022.

The detailed examples of the case law regarding the *Grundmangel* and *Folgemangel* are provided in the following paragraphs.

443. As stated above there are situations when the problem with the goods becomes apparent sometime after the passing of risk and it is clear that this problem did not exist at that time, for example damage to the engine of a car. Generally, it may be caused by the defective factors existing at the time the risk was passed (the situation considered as a *Grundmangel*), or it could be caused by the product's misuse or other external factors. The situation can be compared with the facts of BGH case of 18 July 2007 (*Zylinderkopfdichtung*).[123] In this case, the second-hand car broke down four weeks after the passing of risk. After examination it was undisputed that the cooling system of the car contained too little water caused by a defective head gasket and a torn valve crosspiece (*a Grundmangel*). It was unclear when and how the defects of the parts occurred. The defects in the head gasket and a valve crosspiece might have existed at the time of sale or appear later due to the faulty operation of the car. The question was whether in the given circumstances the presumption from § 476 BGB can be applied. Factually, it comes down to the question of whether the consumer has successfully proven the existence of defects. The court stated that the presumption applies only with respect to the moment at which the defect had occurred. Therefore, before applying the presumption, the existence of a defect has to be positively established by the consumer. The court stated that in the present case the consumer has identified and proven the existence of defects and only the time when the defects were caused remained unknown. Consequently, the consumer was allowed to rely on the presumption of non-conformity.

444. In other situations the problems with the goods, which become apparent after some time from the passing of risk, may be even more complex. These problems are referred to as *Folgemangel*. Such problem can concern an engine defect, which might have resulted from another defect whose origins were in the defective factors present at the time the risk was passed (caused by the existence of a *Grundmangel*) or it might have been a consequence of the consumer's misuse of goods or other external factors. In these types of cases the position of the consumer is much more complex. He is not able to prove the existence of a defect as provided in § 434 BGB, for example due to the lapse of time, complexity of the defect or multi-source character of the defect. To help the consumer, the court may allow the factual presumption that the final defect (*Folgemangel* – the engine does not work) constitutes the defect resulting from the defective causes present at the time of the passing of risk (*Grundmangel*). However, to be able to benefit from such a factual presumption,

123 BGH 18.07.2007, VIII 259/06.

the consumer must provide sufficient evidence, very often including the extended examination regarding origins of the defects carried out by the expert.[124]

The above-illustrated situation can be found in several of the BGH's decisions. The first noteworthy case in this respect is case of 2 June 2004 (*Zahnriemenfall*).[125] It concerned the sale of a second-hand car, which less than six months after the passing of risk broke down (*Folgemangel*). It sustained engine damage and there was uncertainty over what the cause of this defect (engine damage) was. At the same time it was undisputed that at the time the risk was passed the defect had not existed (the car as such was good to drive). The consumer provided the court with an expert opinion that the engine damage was attributed to a defective drive belt. However, the expert opinion was inconclusive as to the origins of this defect. The drive belt defect might have already been present at the time the risk was passed. Alternatively, it might either have been caused by the mere exploitation of the car, or by the driver's inability to drive properly. The BGH stated that in this case the application of the presumption from § 476 BGB depends on whether the consumer is able to prove that the engine damage was attributable to a cause stemming from the car. Taking into consideration the fact that the consumer was unable to convince the court that the engine damage caused by the defective drive belt was due to the material defects existing in the car, the BGH decided that the consumer had failed to prove the existence of defect and therefore the application of the presumption from § 476 BGB was denied.

Following the court's decision, the consumer was supposed to prove not only the defect (engine damage, defective drive belt) but also he was supposed to exclude incorrect driving as a possible cause of the motor damage in order to win the case. Furthermore, he had to prove causality of other factors existing in the car itself and the final defect of the car. Taking into account the facts of this case, the factual presumption that the consumer wanted to rely on was that the engine damage was caused by the *Grundmangel* (defective drive belt) caused by the defective factors existing at the time of the passing of risk. Consequently, in order to be able to use the benefit of presumption of non-conformity the consumer must not only prove that the engine and drive belt were damaged but also prove all possible causes of the damage, or at least address them in order to exclude the possibility that the damage has been caused by his misuse of the car and by the wear and tear. Critics state that when comparing above interpretation to the wording of Article 5 (3) of the Directive, the consumers' burdens are much heavier than the ones from the Consumer Sales Directive. Consequently, the level of consumer protection under the BGB seems to be lower than the one emerging from the Directive.[126]

---

124 Junker, Beckmann and Rüßmann 2013, § 476 Rn. 19; Rühl 2009, p. 916.

125 BGH 02.06.2004, VIII ZR 329/03, BGHZ 159, 215; See also AG Berlin-Charlottenburg 10.10.2008, 232 C 196/07, Beck RS 2009, 12941.

126 Lorenz 2004, p. 3020; Reinking 2004, p. 607-611; Gsell 2004, p. 903-904; Roth 2004, p. 2025-2027; Saueressig 2008, p. 2075.

445. In another decision of BGH (*Turbolader*),[127] the consumer purchased a second-hand car in January 2003. In July 2003 the turbocharger of the car broke down and by letter of 13 August 2003 the consumer demanded a free repair. The seller refused to do so and the consumer had the turbocharger replaced by another company. The consumer subsequently requested the reparation price from the seller. In December 2003 the car suffered a further defect – engine damage, and the consumer decided to rescind the contract and claimed payment matching the initial purchase price. The case ended up before the BGH, which stated that the consumer failed to provide sufficient evidence that the car was defective and therefore had no claim against the seller. According to the BGH, it is clear that the turbocharger could not have been defective at the time the risk was passed, therefore to ensure success the consumer would have had to prove that the turbocharger defect resulted from a cause that constituted a material defect in the sense of § 434 BGB or have been caused by the defective factors present at the time the risk was passed. According to the expert opinion, the actual causes of the turbocharger's defectiveness could not have been established. The company which replaced the defective turbocharger had disposed of it, and it was no longer available for investigation. The experts expressed that it was possible but not very likely, that the defects were caused by the material defects existing at the time the risk was passed. Moreover, taking the age and the kilometre reading into account, ordinary wear and tear was a more probable cause. As a result, the BGH decided that the presumption of § 476 BGB does not apply and that the general rules on the allocation of the burden of proof apply. Since the consumer was unable to provide sufficient evidence, he did not succeed in his claim.

446. The last case discussed in the context of the consumer's obligation to prove the existence of defects considers the sale of a horse (*Sommerekzem*).[128] A consumer purchased an Arabian horse on 18 February 2002. On 17 September he informed the seller that in August 2002 the horse suffered from an allergic reaction and that the contract due to this health-related defect is to be rescinded. The seller objected to the consumer's claim and the case ended before the court. The consumer has provided proof – a medical examination dated on 30 August 2002 stating that a horse suffers from the above-mentioned allergy. He therefore claimed that because the defect has become apparent within six months from the time the risk was passed, the presumption of § 476 BGB applies. Before the BGH the question arose whether § 476 BGB can apply in the present circumstances. From the expert opinion heard by the court, it emerges that *Sommerekzem* does not amount to a hidden disease, but rather to a seasonal allergy. It is a specific reaction of an immune system trig-

127 BGH 23.11.2005, VIII ZR 43/05, NJW 2006, 434.
128 BGH 29.03.2006, VIII ZR 173/05, BGHZ 167, 40.

gered by the mosquito bites, including an inflammation of skin and itch.[129] The BGH decided that in the given circumstances the presumption from § 476 BGB cannot apply. Accordingly, the court stated that it was not possible to determine that the allergic reaction, which occurred months after the passing of risk, in fact resulted from the excessive sensitiveness of the horse (*Grundmangel*) existing at the time of sale, or developed later on. In the court's view, the consumer did not provide sufficiently satisfactory evidence regarding the existence of defects to enable the application of the presumption.[130]

447. In the above-presented decisions, it should be noted that in proving the existence of defects, attention is drawn to the sale of second-hand goods in particular. To be able to enjoy the benefits ensured by the application of § 476 BGB, it is not sufficient to state that the purchased product is defective as such or that it does not work properly. The product must be defective within the meaning of § 434 BGB. What must be taken into consideration when assessing whether a defect has been successfully proven is mainly what the consumer could expect from the purchased product, whether the defect in question is common/probable with respect to this kind of product, whether it is only wear and tear or factually a defect, and whether the consumer was involved in some way that could influence the existence of defect. In any case, it is insufficient to show that the product's quality has deteriorated since being purchased by the consumer. To be successful the consumer has to show that the deterioration in quality amounted to a material defect in the sense of § 434 BGB.[131] Based on decisions presented, it must be underlined that the consumer very often will have to provide additional evidence to challenge the seller's defences. Where the seller casts doubts on the nature of the defects, the consumer has to take initiative to secure the successful application of the presumption. In some cases, the consumer is expected to prove not only the existence of the defects, but also that these defects have not been caused by the ordinary wear and tear of the product, or his misuse of goods. In case of doubt as to the source of the final defect (*Folgemangel*), using the principle of *non liquet*, the court will rule against the consumer and prevent the application of the presumption, or it will rule on the absence of defects and exclude the seller's liability.

448. It should be stated that the BGH's approach to the defectiveness of goods as a requirement for the application of the presumption has been criticised by some scholars.[132] They point out that the current interpretation is not as favourable for consumers as one

129 In its deliberations the BGH first extensively described the application of the exclusion criteria in contracts of sale of animals, what will be presented in chapter 5, para 477, 478.

130 Rühl 2009, p. 917.

131 Lorenz 2012, § 476 Rn. 7.

132 Lorenz 2004, p. 3020; Reinking 2004, p. 607-611; Gsell 2004, p. 903-904; Roth 2004, p. 2025-2027; Saueressig 2008, p. 2075.

might have expected. Namely, in cases where the defects are internal and the causes of the defects are unknown, the consumer cannot rely on the presumption because it is unclear what the origins of the defect are.[133] Very often, the court finds that in the given circumstances the consumer has not proven the existence of a defect and as a consequence the presumption cannot apply. The opposite approach is also possible. In case of doubt, the court could allow the application of the presumption for exactly the same reasons. The objective and function of § 476 BGB is to protect consumers, and in doubtful circumstances, the seller – who has better means of obtaining evidence – could be required to do so.[134] That would also fit the aim and the purpose of Article 5 (3) of the Consumer Sales Directive.

Taking AG Sharpston's[135] opinion into account, which seems to present a different approach to the burden of proof and the specificity of proof of the existence of non-conformity, there are grounds for claiming that in particular circumstances the German approach may indeed be undermining the objectives of Article 5 (3) Consumer Sales Directive and a high level of consumer protection. AG Sharpston suggests that in case of destroyed goods, unavailable for an inspection, a consumer should not be required to prove the cause, or that the fact the goods are destroyed is attributable to the seller. AG Sharpston states that it would be impracticable to place such a burden of proof on the consumer because it is reasonable to assume that, in principle, the seller has more knowledge and information on the product and the state it was delivered in. In other words, a consumer cannot be required to provide the proof that is unavailable to him.[136] If the above view is confirmed by the ECJ, the German courts may be required to reconsider their current approach to the consumer's evidential burdens in cases where the object of sale is destroyed and no longer available for an inspection.

449. Based on the above it is possible to draw the following conclusions. First, the presumption of non-conformity from § 476 BGB can apply exclusively in cases of concrete material defects, or when the consumer can prove that the consequential defects have resulted from the defective factors existing at the time of the passing of risk.[137] That means it is not sufficient to state that the product possesses some undefined, general defects. The defect must be determined and proven by the consumer.

The main problem regarding the first condition for the application of the presumption is the question of when the defects can be regarded as satisfactorily proven. There is no standard approach on this issue. The more complex the defect means the more difficult

133 Martis 2010, p. 842, 843.

134 BT-Dr 14/6040, p. 245; Klöhn 2007, p. 2811-2812.

135 Opinion of Advocate General Sharpston delivered on 27 November 2014, C-497/13, *Fraukje Faber v Autobedrijf Hazet Ochten BV*, see chapter 3, para 207.

136 Opinion of AG Sharpston, para 88.

137 Faust 2011, § 476 Rn. 6.

evidence, what reduces the chances for the application of the presumption of non-conformity. Taking all relevant facts into consideration, in particular, a possibility of buyer's fault, ordinary wear and tear, and the moment when the defect appeared or was discovered, the judge is obliged to assess the evidence freely to decide whose evidence is more convincing.[138] If neither of the parties has convinced the judge, the case will be decided against the consumer since he bears the burden of proving the existence of defects.[139]

5.4.3.2 Six-month period (*Zeitliche Komponente*)

450. The second requirement for the application of the presumption of § 476 BGB is that the defects occurred within six months from the time of passing the risk.[140] One question that emerges is what it means that the defect is apparent. That can mean it is visible, but it can also involve other senses such as touch or hearing. Furthermore, the defects must be detected by the consumer and the seller must be notified about them in time.[141] When the defects became apparent just one day after the lapse of six months starting from the moment the risk was passed, in principle the allocation of the burden of proof reverses as according to the general rule.[142] Consequently, to be able to exercise his rights after the lapse of six-month period, the consumer must prove that the goods were defective at the time the risk was passed.

To be able to state that the buyer has successfully proven the existence of a defect within the six-month period it is necessary to determine when the six-month period begins to run, when it expires, and whether there are any special rules regarding its postponement, suspension or any other rules applicable to the prescription periods affecting the statutory period for the application of the presumption.

I Beginning of the period

451. According to § 476 BGB, the moment the risk was passed is the determinant for the beginning of the six-month period. In the BGB the term passing of risk is a counterpart of the time of delivery found in Article 5 (3) of the Consumer Sales Directive.[143] Based on § 446 BGB '*the risk of accidental destruction and accidental deterioration passes to the buyer upon delivery of the sold goods. From the time of delivery the emoluments of the goods accrue to the buyer and he bears the charges on them. If the buyer is in default of acceptance of delivery, this is to be considered equivalent to delivery*'.[144] In other words, the moment of the passing of risk is when the consumer acquires possession and independent control

138 Chapter 2, para 54.

139 Chapter 2, para 43, 44.

140 OLG Hamm 04.08.2006, 11 U 142/05, Beck RS 2007, 04385.

141 Beckmann 2013, § 476 Rn. 24; Staudinger 2004, § 476 Rn. 12-14.

142 Eggert 2002, p. 175.

143 Saenger and Schultze (Hk BGB) 2010, § 476 Rn. 1-4.

144 Translation http://www.gesetze-im-internet.de/englisch_bgb/englisch_bgb.html#p1473 (23.10.2014).

over the goods, unless the consumer is in default in accepting the delivery. In such case, the risk passes at the time of buyer's default. Based on this definition, it can be stated that in the majority of cases the passing of risk is identical to the moment of delivery.

452. When the consumer does not accept performance the risk passes at the moment of his default. If he decides to accept performance after all, the question arises of at what moment does the risk actually pass and which moment must be taken into account when applying the rules on the burden of proof, the moment of late acceptance or the moment of the default of acceptance. § 446 BGB expressly states that the risk passes at the time when the buyer should have accepted the delivery, therefore it should not matter whether afterwards the performance has been accepted or not.[145] Consequently, the six-month period will begin to run at the moment of the consumer's default. While the evidence that the consumer must provide does not change, the defences available to the seller may differ slightly. Firstly, the seller has to prove that the consumer was in default in accepting performance. He can do so by showing that the actual offer under § 294 BGB was rejected and that the performance offered was free from defects. Furthermore, the seller can prove that he made a verbal offer pursuant to § 295 BGB and the consumer rejected it. Taking the specific rules on the passing of risk into account to determine the starting moment of the operation of the presumption, the following rules apply:

1. If the consumer can prove the existence of defects, it means that the risk passed while handing the product over and the time for the operation of presumption begins to run from that moment on.
2. If the consumer cannot prove the existence of defects at the time set out in § 294, § 295 or § 296 BGB, it means that he was in default in accepting performance but it does not prove that the product was free from defects. The § 476 BGB presumption begins to run from the moment of the consumer's default.[146]

Summing up, the buyer's default in accepting performance cannot delay the beginning of the six-month period.

453. § 447 BGB provides a specific regulation of the passing of risk where shipment or the carriage of goods is involved. In such cases the risk passes to the buyer '*as soon as the seller has handed the goods over to the forwarder, carrier or other person or body specified to carry out the shipment*'.[147] Originally, § 474 (2) BGB explicitly stated that the rule on the passing of risk set out in § 447 BGB did not apply to contracts between professional sellers and

145 Faust 2011, § 476 Rn. 6.

146 Doehner/*diss* 2004, p. 217.

147 Translation: http://www.gesetze-im-internet.de/englisch_bgb/englisch_bgb.html#p1473 (23.10.2014).

consumers. Accordingly, in consumer contracts where shipment or the carriage of goods was involved, the risk passed at the time of actual delivery.[148] After the changes that entered into force on 13 June 2014, pursuant to § 474 (4) BGB, § 447 (1) applies to consumer contracts only when the consumer did choose the carrier which has not been made available by the seller.[149]

454. In case of supplementary performance by providing another defect-free product (replacement), the period described in § 476 BGB begins when the risk was passed in relation to the replaced item.[150] When the subsequent performance has been rendered by repair of the defective product, the six-month period begins when the repair is completed and the risks regarding the improved product are passed to the consumer. Finally, when the defect is a result of incorrect installation, the six-month period begins with the completion of the installation.[151]

455. Based on what has been presented, there are at least three possible moments for the passing of risk and two possible moments for the start of the period for the application of the presumption:

1. Delivery.
2. Buyer's fault in accepting the goods.
3. The moment of handing over the goods to a carrier (not applicable to consumer contracts).

Furthermore, different types of contracts or different types of products and defects could also be of importance in indicating the start of the six-month period. For example, where there is supplementary performance, delivery by instalments or when a defect concerns installation errors.

II Length of the period

456. The BGB provides general rules for counting time periods in civil law. To establish the beginning of a period § 187 BGB applies. § 187 (1) BGB states that '*if a period commences on the occurrence of an event or at a point in time falling in the course of a day, then the day on which the event or the point in time occurs is not included in the calculation of the period*'. Furthermore, § 187 (2) states that '*if the beginning of a day is the determining point of time for the commencement of a period, then this day is included in the calculation of the*

148 Becker 2009, p. 82.

149 Wendehorst 2014, p. 583.

150 Staudinger 2004, § 476 Rn. 25.

151 Staudinger 2004, § 476 Rn. 24; Lorenz 2008, § 476 Rn. 1; OLG Saarbrucken 25.10.2011, 4 U 540/10, NJW-RR 2012, 285.

period'.[152] Therefore, it would appear that the six-month period begins to run on the day following the day the risk was passed pursuant to § 187 (1) BGB. The Directive and the national implementation of Article 5 (3) state that the six-month period starts at the time of delivery (or at the time the risk was passed). Such wording does not indicate whether the day of delivery should be included into the calculation of six-month period. It is arguable that the provision from the Directive constitutes a specific rule on counting the time periods excluding the general rule of § 187 (1) BGB. It must be remembered that the Consumer Sales Directive is a minimum harmonisation measure, which allow national legislators to introduce other periods provided they are more favourable to the consumers than the ones from the Directive.

III Expiry of the period

457. The expiry of period is governed by § 188 (2) BGB, according to which '*a period of time specified by (...) months (...) ends, in the case of § 187 (1), on the expiry of the day (...) of the last month which, in its designation or its number, corresponds to the day on which the event or the point of time occurs*'. § 188 (3) BGB states that if the period is determined by months and the day on which it is due to expire does not occur in the last month, the period ends on the expiry of the last day of this month.[153]

According to Article 3 (2) of the Regulation determining the rules applicable to periods, dates and time limits expressed in months '*shall end with the expiry of the last hour of whichever day (...) in the last month falling on the same date, as the day from which the period runs. If, in a period expressed in months or in years, the day on which it should expire does not occur in the last month, the period shall end with the expiry of the last hour of the last day of that month.*' Regarding the moment of expiry of periods the German and European provisions are alike.

458. § 193 BGB provides that if the last day of the period falls on a Saturday, on Sunday or on a public holiday officially recognised at the place of the declaration or performance, then the next working day should be considered as the last day of the period.[154] However, in case of the six-month period from § 476 BGB, § 193 does not apply. § 476 BGB does not concern situations where the declaration of intent or an act of performance must be done on a particular day or within a specific period. Consequently, the six-month period in which the presumption of non-conformity applies can expire on any of the above-mentioned days.[155]

152 Translation: http://www.gesetze-im-internet.de/englisch_bgb/englisch_bgb.html#p1473 (23.10.2014).

153 Translation: http://www.gesetze-im-internet.de/englisch_bgb/englisch_bgb.html#p0540 (23.10.2014).

154 Laumen 2007, p. 271.

155 Grothe 2001, § 476 Rn. 2-4.

IV Application of the presumption after the expiry of statutory period

459. The question arises whether the presumption can apply if the consumer discovers the defects after expiry of the statutory period, even if the discovery was objectively possible within that time. There is also uncertainty as to what must be proven if the consumer discovers the defects after the expiry of six months. The options are as follows:

1. The exact moment of when the defects became apparent.
2. Defects became apparent at any moment within the statutory period.
3. (High) probability that the defects appeared within the statutory period, shifting burden to prove otherwise to the seller.

It should be underlined that a professional seller cannot challenge evidence regarding the time of appearance of defects by simply stating and proving that he did not receive a notification within six months from the time the risk was passed.[156] Therefore, the six-month period is not treated as the period within which the presumption must be applied. It is the period within which defects became apparent, not necessarily to the consumer.[157] Therefore, it seems that it is unnecessary to prove the specific date at which the defect occurred. As long as it is possible for the consumer to prove that the defects occurred within six months from the time the risk was passed, he will be able to benefit from the presumption.[158] Taking consumer interests into account the second option sounds most reasonable. Furthermore in practice, depending on the other party's submissions, the court has discretion as to whether the facts and evidence regarding the time of occurrence of the defects presented by the consumer are sufficiently persuasive.

460. Finally, it should be noted that the six-month period should not be mistaken for the contractual durability guarantee set out in § 443 BGB.[159] There might be some difficulties in drawing a clear line between these two.[160] At first, both instruments might seem similar however, the durability guaranty refers to defects that become apparent after the passing of risk, while § 476 BGB requires the existence of defects at the time of the passing of risk

156 Baumgärtel, Laumen and Prütting 2009, p. 87.

157 Baumgärtel, Laumen and Prütting 2009, p. 87.

158 Lorenz 2008, § 476 Rn. 8; Baumgärtel, Laumen and Prütting 2009, p. 87.

159 Art 443 BGB (1) '*If the seller or a third party gives a guarantee for the quality of the thing or that the thing will have a specified quality for a specified period (guarantee of durability), then, if there is a claim under the guarantee, the buyer, notwithstanding his statutory claims, has the rights given by the guarantee upon the terms set out in the declaration of guarantee and in the relevant advertising in relation to the person who granted the guarantee.*
(2)*To the extent that a guarantee of durability has been given, there is a presumption that a material defect which appears during the guarantee period triggers the rights under the guarantee.*' Translation: http://www.gesetze-im-internet.de/englisch_bgb/ (23.10.2014).

160 Beckmann 2013, p. 346; Büdenbender 2005, § 476 Rn. 4; Baumgärtel, Laumen and Prütting 2009, p. 86; Maultsch 2006, p. 3096; Dauner-Lieb 2006, p. 430.

and it merely eases the consumer's duty to prove that fact.[161] The guarantee of durability provides different benefits protecting consumer interests. If a material defect appears during the guarantee period, it triggers the rights under the guarantee.

5.4.3.3 Conclusions

461. Based on information provided above, it can be concluded that both requirements for the application of the presumption of non-conformity have been implemented in accordance with Article 5 (3) of the Consumer Sales Directive. Conditions for the application of the presumption from § 476 BGB – (I) the existence of defects (II) apparent within six months – are counterparts to the conditions provided in the Directive. There are some minor differences, but they seem not to change the scope of the requirements that the consumer must meet in order to rely on the presumption. One of such differences between the Consumer Sales Directive and BGB concerns the moment when the six-month period begins to run. According to § 476 BGB, the period starts at the time of the passing of risk and not necessarily at the time of delivery. In practice, in the majority of cases these two moments will overlap.

462. Based on the BGH's decisions investigated there are some practical and theoretical difficulties when it comes to the burden of proving the existence of defects. To meet the first condition for the application of the presumption, the consumer must prove that the goods are afflicted with a defect in the sense of § 434 BGB. For the purpose of § 476 BGB, the defect from § 434 BGB may be understood broadly, including defects as stated in § 434 BGB, *Grundmangel*, and in some cases *Folgemangel*. In short, the application of the presumption may depend on the type of the defect:

1. A defect in the strict sense of § 434 BGB, possible doubts as to the time of occurrence and the cause. Presumption from § 476 BGB applies.
2. A defect not existing at the time the risk was passed, for the presumption to apply the consumer has to prove that the defect is a consequence of the internal defective factors present at the time the risk was passed (*Grundmangel*).
3. A defect not existing at the time the risk was passed, there is a possibility that this defect is a consequence of another defect resulting from defective factors existing at the time the risk was passed (*Grundmangel*). If the consumer provides sufficient evidence it might be presumed that the defect has been caused by another defect resulting from the defective factors existing at the time the risk was passed (*Folgemangel*). If that is the case the presumption applies.[162]

161 Faust 2011, § 476 Rn. 2.
162 Beckmann 2013, § 476 Rn. 19.

The application of the presumption is therefore not equally straightforward, since it depends on the instance of defect. In specific situations the application of the presumption is relatively complex. There are situations where the consumer may have serious difficulties in proving the existence of a defect in the first place. One of the reasons is that in cases described as *Grundmangel* and *Folgemangel* it is clear that the defects could not have existed at the time the risk was passed. Secondly, there is a risk that there are multiple origins of a particular defect, which must be excluded by the consumer in order to prove the existence of these defects.

463. The second condition for the presumption to apply is that the defect must have become apparent within six months. There is some uncertainty over what happens when the defects were objectively apparent and not yet known or detected by a consumer.[163] Based on the discussion above it can be concluded that the presumption applies even if the defects became visible for the consumer only after the expiry of six months, provided that he can prove they became objectively apparent within that period. This opinion has been approved by the doctrine.[164]

Finally, there are some minor uncertainties regarding the counting of the six-month period. The beginning and length of the period are important for the consumer, as only proof of the defects that occurred within six months can be simplified by § 476 BGB. For some it can be unclear whether the day that risk passes to the buyer or rather the following day should be regarded as the first day of the six-month period. Following § 187 (1) BGB it appears that the day of passing of risk is not included into calculation of the period. Furthermore, it seems that in case of doubts as to the beginning of the period, the provisions of the European Regulation determining the rules applicable to periods, dates and time limits could provide an additional argument. In practice, a one-day difference does not appear to have much significance. If the consumer can prove the defects occurred before the expiry of six months counting from the time the risk was passed, or from the following day, the court should probably recognise evidence given as satisfactory and allow the application of the presumption. Therefore, although the uncertainty surrounding the legislation remains, the issues regarding the six-month period should not cause practical problems.

5.4.4 *Rebuttal of the presumption*

464. This sub-section describes the seller's options for challenging the presumption of § 476 BGB when its applicability has already been granted. This is when the consumer has

163 Dauner-Lieb and Langen 2012, p. 1755.
164 Prütting, Wegen and Weinreich 2014, § 476 Rn. 4, 5; Saueressig 2008, p. 2076.

successfully satisfied the two conditions for its application. He has provided evidence of the existence of defects becoming apparent within six months from the time of the passing of risk. According to Article 5 (3) of the Consumer Sales Directive, the presumption applies unless 'proved otherwise'. Below I will illustrate what facts the seller has to present to prove that the defects, whose existence within six months from the time of the passing of risk has been proven by the consumer, occurred after the time the risk was passed.

465. Once the conditions for the application of the presumption presented in the previous section have been met, the presumption of § 476 BGB can be invoked. To escape liability for defective goods the seller has to provide evidence contradicting the presumed facts. Consequently, the seller has to prove that at the time of the passing of risk the product was free from material defects. In other words, he has to provide evidence to the contrary.[165]

§ 292 ZPO states that to rebut the presumption, the essential facts showing the contrary must be provided.[166] The evidence presented by the seller is expected to show that the product was factually free from defects at the time the risk was passed. Merely undermining the grounds for the presumption is at this stage insufficient. Evidence to the contrary is interpreted strictly. Presenting *prima facie* evidence that the defects occurred after the moment that risk passed is considered unsatisfactory.[167]

466. There are several options available to the seller for proving the contrary. It can be sufficient to offer in evidence an examination issued not long before or not long after the time of the passing of risk, showing the absence of the alleged defects.[168]

Similar use can be made of an acceptance receipt confirming that the consumer received a defect-free product. § 309 (12) BGB regarding unfair standard terms states that a provision by which the party modifies the burden of proof to the disadvantage of the other party, in particular by imposing on the latter the burden of proof for circumstances lying outside of his sphere of responsibility, or having the other party to the contract confirm certain facts, is void. The second example does not apply to acknowledgements of receipt that are signed separately or provided with a separate qualified electronic signature. The buyer can refuse or cancel the acceptance receipt if he realises that it was submitted to him only for a signature without any common examination of the product.[169]

Finally, to rebut the presumption of § 476 BGB, the seller may prove that the defects occurred after the passing of risk and that they were caused by the consumer himself due to the misuse or lack of proper maintenance, or that the defects were caused by a third

165 Faust 2011, § 476 Rn. 14; Becker 2009, p. 86.
166 Lorenz 2012, § 476 Rn. 23, 25-27.
167 Becker 2009, p. 88; Maultzsch, p. 3095.
168 Becker 2009, p. 89.
169 Becker 2009, p. 90.

party or *force majeure*. Following the decision of the Amtsgericht Hamburg of 25 March 2012, the seller can rely on certain omissions in the maintenance of goods only if particular instructions were clearly stated in the manuals provided to the consumer.[170]

467. The seller will be successful in his pleadings and will rebut the presumption if he demonstrates that the defect, which became apparent during the six-month period could not have occurred at the time the risk was passed.[171] Based on what the seller (and the consumer) presents, the judge will decide whether he is convinced that the goods were free from defects at the time of passing the risk. In case of doubts, the consumer may be entitled to submit additional statements for example that there was no incorrect usage.[172] All in all, it is for the seller to prove the contrary. If this is not achieved, the judge will rule in the consumer's favour.

Where one of the parties frustrates evidence or impedes the obtaining of evidence by the other party, the court can ease the burden of proof of the suffering party by ordering a reversal of burden of proof.[173] It may regard the initial burden of proving the existence of defects, which lies with the consumer or it may regard evidence to the contrary which is supposed to be provided by the seller. Finally, it seems that the same facts and evidence that the seller relies on while trying to rebut the presumption could have already been presented or challenged by any of the parties when presenting or challenging evidence on the existence of defects or its occurrence within the six-month period.

5.4.5 *Exclusion of the application of the presumption*

468. Article 5 (3) of the Consumer Sales Directive states that the presumption of non-conformity cannot apply if it is incompatible with the nature of the goods or the nature of the lack of conformity. Following the Directive, in § 476 BGB the German legislator implements both criteria for the exclusion of the presumption. The aim of these criteria is essentially to prevent unreasonable and unfair results.[174] There is a dearth of European-level interpretation of incompatibility with the nature of the goods and the nature of the non-conformity. Therefore, it is for the national legislators, academics and judges to determine the meaning of this term in accordance with its function and purpose. Generally, the exclusion criteria must be applied exceptionally and interpreted strictly to ensure that the function and objective of the presumption is guaranteed. In every case, the grounds

170 AG Hamburg 25.03. 2009, 7c C53/08, Beck RS 2008, 12681.

171 Bamberger and Roth 2012, § 476 Rn. 4.

172 Lorenz 2012, § 476 Rn. 24; BGH 02.06.2004, VIII ZR 329/03, BGHZ 159, 215; BGH 23.11.2004, VIII ZR 43/05.

173 OLG Naumburg 11.10.2012, 1 U 2/12, Beck RS 2013, 05532.

174 Lorenz 2008, § 476 Rn. 14.

for exclusion of the presumption must be considered individually.[175] Furthermore, the exclusion criteria must not interfere with the main purpose of the operation of the presumption, which is facilitation of the burden of proof set out by the legislator to protect consumer interests.[176]

469. There are many uncertainties regarding the exclusion of the presumption, some of them are due to the lack of definitions and explanations as to what exactly incompatibility with the nature of the goods and the nature of the defects entails. Although there are in principle two exclusion criteria, in practice there is also no clear division between them and it is difficult to draw a clear line, as they may often overlap. Moreover, in one jurisdiction a particular case might be considered as concerning the nature of the goods while in another as concerning the nature of the lack of conformity.

470. Further uncertainties as to the application of the exclusion criteria concern issues of evidence. Questions such as who is obliged to provide and prove particular facts, to what extent must the incompatibility be proven and what is the content of the notion of incompatibility often causes difficulties. It has been argued that regarding the burden of proof of the presumption's incompatibility with the nature of the goods or the nature of the defects, there is no *objektive Beweislast.*[177] As a result, none of the parties bear the objective burden of proof for these facts. On the other hand, if the seller invokes the issues of exclusion, he imposes the burden of proof of above facts upon himself.[178] The *subjektive Beweislast* lies therefore with the seller. Below, the case law where the issues of incompatibility have been considered will be discussed. I will also try to categorise courts' decisions and come up with a scheme illustrating in which circumstances the presumption of non-conformity can be regarded as incompatible with the nature of the goods and in which with the nature of the defects.

5.4.5.1 Incompatibility with the nature of the goods

471. There are no general exclusions regarding the incompatibility of the presumption with the nature of the goods. There are however, some groups of products, which are often regarded as increasing the chances of such incompatibility. The first category of goods mentioned in the literature whose nature can be considered incompatible with the presumption consists of perishable goods, such as foods or cosmetics.[179] The fact that food or

175 Lorenz 2004, p. 3021.

176 Lorenz 2004, p. 3021.

177 Chapter 2, para 43, 44.

178 Liepold 2008, p. 86; OLG Stuttgart 18.1.2005, 10 U 179/04, ZGS 2005, 276, 277.

179 Lorenz 2008, § 476 BGB Rn. 16.

other 'organic' products are consumed or spoiled between the time the risk was passed and six months after that time is usually a normal consequence of the lapse of time.[180]

The characteristics of perishable goods often prevent the parties from being able to prove that the goods were defective at the time of the passing of risk. Similarly, it can be difficult to prove that food or other similar products conformed to what was agreed upon, or that they do not meet a specific standard of quality. To put it simply, it is common for most food products to spoil within six months' time, and this does not allow for assumptions that these products were already spoiled at the time of the passing of risk. For these reasons the application of the presumption of non-conformity to the contracts of sale of perishable goods is challenging. The character of perishable goods may often indicate the presumption's incompatibility with the nature of the goods.

472. German courts of various instances have dealt with the issue of the presumption's incompatibility with the nature of the goods. The majority of the decisions regard two categories of goods, animals and second-hand goods.

Regarding the cases of the sale of animals, it is difficult to establish the incompatibility because of the nature of the goods and the nature of the defects.[181] Regarding the first criterion it is undisputed that there is a lack of general exclusion of the presumption in relation to animals. § 90a BGB expressly states that although the animals are not regarded as goods, they are governed by the provisions applicable to goods with necessary modifications, unless provided otherwise. Similar conclusions regarding the application of consumer sales provisions to the sale of animals can be drawn from the statute's justification.[182] Finally, the BGH has also confirmed that there is no general exclusion of the presumption in cases regarding sales of animals.[183] The situation is the complete opposite when it comes to the sale of 'second-hand animals' bought by public auctions. The BGH based on § 474 (1) s. 2 confirmed that presumption of non-conformity from § 476 BGB does not apply to horses purchased by public auctions.[184]

473. The next category of goods often regarded as incompatible with the presumption due to their nature are second-hand goods.[185] Also with respect to second-hand goods there is no general exclusion of the application of the presumption. On the contrary, the second-hand goods cannot be considered as defective merely because they have been used in the

180 Except the products with long expiry date, for example rice, dried pasta, etc.

181 Faust 2011, § 476 Rn. 18.

182 Deutscher Bundestag 14/6040 p. 207.

183 BGH 29.3.2006, VIII ZR 173/05.

184 BGH 24.02.2010, VIII ZR 71/09, NJW 2010, 8, followed by the OLG Celle 22.11.2010, 20 U 8/10, NJW 2011, 132.

185 Lorenz 2012, § 476 Rn. 16; Mankowski 2003, p. 465; Faust 2011, § 476 Rn. 18; Arlt 2010, p. 115.

past, or that they are not brand new.[186] Accordingly, it was confirmed that the presumption § 476 BGB applies to the purchase of second-hand goods just as it does to the purchase of new goods.[187] During and after the implementation process there was controversy over whether the § 476 BGB presumption can apply to second-hand cars. Some academics argued that the reversed burden of proof in consumer sales cannot apply, due to the nature of the goods as being used. This opinion was rejected by the courts in cases where used cars had defects that were not due to their long-term use. For instance, the Oberlandesgericht Köln[188] approved the application of the presumption to the purchase of used cars, where a ten-year-old Porsche had a very specific engine defect which became apparent one day after the time the risk was passed, after the buyer has driven the vehicle for approximately 700 km. The court stated that the presumption applies regardless of whether the product is new or used. Its application will be restricted only if the goods are defective due to normal long-term use, but it cannot be restricted for unusual, rare defects such as those in the case in question.[189] Summing up, the presumption of § 476 BGB applies to the purchase of second-hand goods just as it does to the purchase of new goods.[190]

474. The presumption regarding second-hand goods can exceptionally be considered as incompatible if the facts of the case indicate so, and if the seller successfully persuades the court of the existence of these facts. The matters that must be taken into account when assessing second-hand goods are: the state of the goods, the degree of wear and tear at the time the risk was passed, and the character of the defects. The crucial question to establish is whether the particular defect in the specific product could have reasonably occurred at the time of the passing of risk, and whether the particular defects are common regarding the type of goods and the amount of time passed from the moment of sale.[191] In addition, the important question is what the consumer could have expected from the second-hand goods. It is reasonable to say that the buyer cannot expect the goods to be as good as new, unless they are described thus. Ordinary wear and tear does not constitute a defect in the sense of § 434 BGB and as a result § 476 BGB does not apply to such deficiencies.[192]

The Oberlandesgericht Bremen decided in a judgement that the presumption of § 476 BGB does not apply in relation to defects resulting from the extraordinary wear and tear

186 Lorenz 2008, § 476 Rn. 16; Arlt 2010, p. 116.

187 Baumgartel, Laumen and Prütting 2009, p. 86; Lorenz 2008, § 476 Rn. 16; Arlt 2010, p. 116; Müller 2003, 1975, 1976.

188 OLG Köln 11.11.2003, 22 U 88/03, (ZGS) 2004, 40.

189 BGH 14.09.2005, VIII ZR 363/04, NJW 2005, 3490.

190 Baumgärtel, Laumen and Prütting 2009, p. 86; Lorenz 2008, § 476 Rn. 16; Arlt 2010, p. 116; Müller 2003, 1975, 1976.

191 Lorenz 2004, p. 3021.

192 AG Schäbisch Hall 20.12.2011, 5 C 557/11, Beck RS 2012, 12524.

of a ten year old boat.[193] The buyer submitted that the boat's engine after very short time lost power and had been inoperable since. The defects discovered resulted from very specific causes, and due to the usage and age of the boat, they deteriorated extremely quickly. This case illustrates that when it comes to the second-hand goods it is also difficult to determine exactly the criterion that should be applied in particular case to exclude the presumption. In the present case, both the nature of the goods (ten-year old, second-hand boat), and the nature of the non-conformity (extraordinary wear and tear) contributed to the exclusion of the presumption.

475. The next category of goods that might be considered as incompatible with the presumption because of their nature includes goods requiring installation.[194] This might be somewhat controversial since according to § 434 BGB, incorrect installation constitutes a material defect and therefore if this type of material defect becomes apparent within six months, the presumption of § 476 BGB will apply. However, there was uncertainty as to whether the presumption can apply if the installation has been performed by a third party – a professional – not related to the seller and for whom the seller is not responsible. According to the BGH,[195] the presumption applies even if the goods were installed by a third party for which the seller is not responsible. In this case the consumer purchased a water pond and had it installed by an independent company. The water pond appeared to be leaking. It must be underlined that it was not determined that the leakage was a result of incorrect installation. The BGH stated that the wording of § 476 BGB does not provide a basis for an argument that the reversal of the burden of proof could be excluded because of the above-mentioned reason. Consequently, if the goods installed by a third party become defective within six months from the time of the passing of risk, the presumption from § 476 BGB cannot be excluded because of its incompatibility with the nature of the goods.

476. Potentially, the last category of goods whose nature in some cases might be regarded as incompatible with the presumption includes art, for example paintings, sculptures, music pieces and other artistic objects.[196] In general, there are several possible difficulties in applying the consumer sales provisions to contracts of sale of pieces of art.[197] First of all, the specific characteristics of a piece of art, which is almost always an original, unique

193 OLG Bremen 11.03.2004, 2 U 99/03, JurionRS 2004, 17711.

194 Faust 2011, § 476 Rn. 20.

195 BGH 22.11.2004, VIII ZR 21/04, NJW 2005, 283.

196 Also in Poland the sale of art has been recognised as problematic in comparison to contracts of sale of 'manufactured' goods. Article 3 of the Act on general terms of the sale contracts and guarantees of 1983 excluded sale of art from the application of the Act. (*Uchwała z dnia 13 czerwca 1983 w sprawie ogólnych warunków umów sprzedaży detalicznej towarów oraz ogólnych warunków gwarancyjnych dotyczących towarów trwałego użytku, sprzedawanych przez jednostki handlu uspołecznionego*).

197 Mangold/*diss.* 2008, p. 4 *et seq.*

object differs from the average goods normally purchased by a consumer in everyday transactions. The majority of contracts regard products manufactured on a large scale. Furthermore, what can cause further problems are the possible defects of these goods. For example, a painting can have the following defects: it is a copy and not the original, there is some physical damage to the canvas, paint, or frame, individual expectations of the buyer are not fulfilled or it differs from what has been agreed upon. Finally, taking into account the specific defects there are also limited remedies available to the defective piece of art. The piece of art can only be replaced very rarely as most often it is the only one that exists. A repair is also rather restricted remedy. Therefore the most common remedies are price reduction and rescission of the contract.[198]

As discussed throughout this book, the evidence that a contract amounts to a consumer sale and that the goods are defective are normally provided by a consumer, pursuant to the general rule on the allocation of the burden of proof.[199] In case of sale of art the first mentioned evidence should not be a problem, as the contract is often concluded by an individual through/with a gallery.[200] The issue may arise with respect to the moment when the defect became apparent, and whether it existed at the time the risk was passed. There is no reason why the presumption should not apply if the consumer can prove the existence of the defect within six months from the passing of risk. In practice there may be some specific difficulties. For example, if the consumer can prove that the painting is an imitation, no proof of the time of defect will be necessary, as it is clear that it must have been an imitation from the beginning. Furthermore, concerning the subjective expectations of the buyer and criteria of defectiveness such as intended or customary use, it might be difficult to convince a judge of the existence of these defects, consequently affecting the application of the presumption of § 476 BGB. Taking the above into account, in some circumstances of the sale of art, the presumption could be regarded as incompatible with the nature of the goods, and not applied even when both conditions for its application have been met.[201]

5.4.5.2 Incompatibility with the nature of the defects

477. The second criterion for the exclusion of the presumption of non-conformity of § 476 BGB is incompatibility with the nature of the defects. As already observed, in many cases it is impossible to draw a line between the two exclusion criteria. Generally, the BGH analysed the issue of incompatibility with the nature of the defects from the perspective of two groups of goods and their specific defects. The first category again includes animals. In particular, certain types of animal diseases, where there is uncertainty regarding the moment of the infection and the outbreak of the disease. In order to regard a disease as a

198 Mangold/*diss.* 2008, p. 113 *et seq.*
199 Faust, § 474 Rn. 22; Lorenz, § 474 Rn. 26.
200 § 474 (1) BGB, Consumer sale provisions do not apply to art pieces bought on public auctions.
201 Mangold/*diss.* 2008, p. 129 *et seq.*

defect its existence cannot be doubted, the only unknown must be the time of the outbreak.[202] In the sale of horses, the following diseases have occurred in cases regarding the incompatibility of the presumption: skin tumours such as *sarkoid*, *Sommerekzem*, blood circulation diseases, chronic bronchitis, kissing spine syndrome, arthritis, and many more.[203] The list provides for types of diseases where the exclusion criteria were considered but not necessarily applied. The second group of defects (goods) distinguished by the BGH regards goods with external defects, usually external defects of the second-hand goods.

478. Regarding the animal diseases, the presumption may be held to be incompatible with the nature of the defects, in particular, due to uncertainty about the moment of infection and the moment of the disease's outbreak. The exclusion will not necessarily apply for all types of diseases/conditions occurring with animals. Examples of the diseases when the presumption will apply, if their existence is successfully proven, are for example genetic sicknesses and chronic diseases.[204]

The BGH has stated that the appearance of seasonal allergic reaction triggered by mosquitos bites (*Sommerekzem*) does not form a sufficient ground for the exclusion of the presumption because of its incompatibility with the nature of the defect. In fact, in this case there was also a question of insufficient proof that the allergy constituted a defect within the meaning of § 434 BGB. Hence, the presumption of non-conformity did not apply in the first place.[205]

Furthermore, the Oberlandesgericht Köln decided that *Podotrochlose* (navicular necrosis), a condition which is often caused by excessive weight on hooves does not constitute a type of disease that would be incompatible with the presumption found in § 476 BGB.[206]

479. Another case where the BGH considered the exclusion criteria because of its incompatibility with the nature of the defect regarded the sale of a cat.[207] Several weeks after the passing of risk the cat was diagnosed with fungal disease (ringworm, a kind of skin parasite), caused by the infection of *microsporum canis* (an organism that causes a ringworm). According to the expert witness at the time of the passing of risk the cat was most probably already infected with *microsporum canis*. However, as observed by the court, an infection does not necessarily lead to the outbreak of the disease. In this case the infection was categorised as a *Grundmangel*, and the final disease a result of this infection, since there has

202 OLG Celle 31.05.2006, 7 U 252/05, OLGReport Celle 2006, 577.

203 https://www.oexmann.de/Publikationen/publikationen_artikel.php?id=Mg==&date=MjAwNzAx (23.10.2014); Neuman/*diss*. 2006, p. 94; Dauner-Lieb 2012, p. 1974.

204 Beckmann 2013, p. 352.

205 BGH 29.03.2006, VIII ZR 173/05, BGHZ 167, 40.

206 OLG Köln 08.08.2007, 11 U 23/7, VersR 2012, 1008.

207 BGH 11.07.2007, VIII ZR 110/06, NJW 2007, 2619.

been further harm caused by it to the cat.[208] The fact that the subject matter of the infection was undetectable at the time of the passing of risk is insufficient for the exclusion of the application of the presumption due to incompatibility with the nature of the defect.

The opposite outcome was reached in a case adjudicated by the Oberlandesgericht Hamm. The case again regarded the sale of a horse.[209] Sometime after the passing of risk, the horse suffered unidentified lameness (equine). Twenty-two days after the delivery, the animal was examined by a vet who found that the lameness was caused by a traumatic dislocation of the sacroiliac joint related to an asymmetry of the cross hump. Neither upon the delivery or arrival at the stables was this condition discovered, and nor did the defect manifest itself during the examination carried out four days after the delivery. The court stated that taking into consideration the nature of the animal as being a living creature and the nature of the defect presumably resulting from a spontaneous event, the application of the presumption from § 476 BGB was excluded.

Another case regarding the sale of a horse where the court refused to apply the presumption concerned *Hemiplegia laryngis* (roaring) disease caused by the paralysis of nerves in vocal cords manifesting by a whistling in the throat. The disease occurred more than five months after the delivery.[210] In this case the court decided that the presumption did not apply because of its incompatibility with the nature of the goods as well as with the nature of the defect.[211]

Finally, the courts are also reluctant to allow application of the presumption when it comes to the behavioural disorders of animals. Mainly because the causes of the changes in the behaviour may be the result of various factors, for example, the new environment, an unfamiliar jockey or disease. In such cases the courts prefer to rule that the defect itself has not been sufficiently proven or that the presumption of non-conformity is excluded because of its incompatibility with the nature of the defect.[212]

480. Summing up, due to the fact that an animal is a living creature, its conformity depends on many external factors, such as the environment in which it lives and the care it receives. An animal may be very sensitive to any changes in its environment and the treatment received from its carers. In a situation where the care provided is not optimal the chances of non-conformity developing are significantly higher than for example taking similar factors (for example maintenance) in the sale of second-hand cars or other manufactured goods.[213] For this and other reasons there is discussion of whether the application of the

208 Schinkels 2007, beck-online 240778.

209 OLG Hamm 03.05.2005, 19 U 123/04, NJW-RR 2005, 1369.

210 Neumann/*diss.* 2006, p. 198.

211 Neumann/*diss.* 2006, p. 198.

212 For example: OLG Saarbrucken 24.05.2007, 8 U 328/06, OLGReport Frankfurt 2007, 645; OLG Celle 31.05.2006, 7 U 252/05, OLGReport Celle 2006, 577; AG Schleswig 18.06.2010, 2 C 21/10, NJW 2010, 2893.

213 Neumann/*diss.* 2006, p. 188.

presumption should be generally excluded from the sale of animals. One opinion is that § 90a BGB creates the possibility for excluding animals from consumer goods category by providing adequate reservation in § 474 BGB.[214] However, this suggestion was not sufficiently convincing and consequently the last word whether the presumption should apply in particular cases of the sale of animals belongs to the courts.

481. Regarding the second-hand goods, a question that often arises is whether the defect in a second-hand product constitutes a material defect in the sense of § 434 BGB. As already explained, the second-hand products cannot be considered as defective merely because they have been used in the past, or that they are not brand new.[215] The cases of ordinary wear and tear of second-hand goods do not amount to defects in the sense of § 434 BGB and therefore § 476 BGB cannot apply to such cases.[216] Additionally, in some instances there are particular defects for which the presumption may be considered as incompatible.

482. The presumption may be incompatible with the nature of the defects if it concerns an external defect, which should have been discovered by a layman at the time of the passing of risk. A case decided by the BGH concerned the sale of a car with visible body defects, which should have been evident to the inexperienced consumer.[217] The consumer objected to the defect only after the car had been handed over and the risk of accidental damage had been passed to the consumer. The court stated that where the buyer first inspected and accepted the goods, the applicability of the presumption for external defects is ruled out as a result of the incompatibility of such a presumption with the nature of the defects.[218] To sum up, where the defects could have easily been detected by a non-professional at the time of the passing of risk, the application of the presumption is excluded because of its incompatibility with the nature of the defects.[219]

483. The incompatibility of the presumption with the nature of the defects can also be invoked in cases where the defects are too general, or multi sourced such as engine damage. The presumption of § 476 BGB applies only in relation to concrete material defects.[220] If the consumer fails to prove such concrete defects but does prove general dysfunction, the court may rule that in the given circumstances the presumption does not apply because

214 Neumann/*diss.* 2006, p. 190.

215 Lorenz 2008, § 476 Rn. 16; Arlt 2010, p. 116.

216 AG Schwäbisch Hall 20.12.2011 5, C557/11.

217 BGH 14.09.2005, VIII ZR 363/05.

218 Martis 2010, p. 842.

219 The situation resembles the lack of liability because of the knowledge of the defects, except the fact a different time reference applies. Regarding the knowledge of defects, the time of the conclusion of the contract is of importance, while in the incompatibility of external defects – the time of passing of risk.

220 Maultzsch 2006, p. 3093.

the defect has not been sufficiently proven or that the presumption is incompatible with the nature of the defects (too general).[221] According to the BGH, arguing that a defect is of such a character that it can occur at any moment and it is not likely that it existed at the time of the passing of risk, is not sufficient to exclude the presumption. In the interests of effective consumer protection the presumption from § 476 BGB should apply even when the defects are potentially not directly associated with the product itself and their original cause cannot be determined, as long as they amount to the material defects in the sense of § 434 BGB.[222]

5.4.5.3 Conclusions

484. Based on the above analysis, it must be stated that the German legislator followed Article 5 (3) of the Consumer Sales Directive and implemented the exclusion criteria in § 476 BGB. Pursuant to § 476 BGB, the presumption of non-conformity does not apply if it is incompatible with the nature of the goods or the nature of the defects. There are no general exclusions of the presumption under German law. The scopes of both criteria are not clear and jurisprudence plays a significant role in their interpretation and application.

The BGH has repeatedly ruled that the presumption of § 476 BGB should be applicable for the benefit of a consumer. For this reason the presumption should only be excluded in exceptional cases. Nevertheless there is a considerable number of case law where the possibility to exclude the presumption was addressed and subsequently applied, potentially at the expense of consumer interests. Based on this case law, there are several categories of goods distinguished as having an increased chance of being incompatible with the presumption thanks to their nature. Examples of such goods are: perishable goods, animals, second-hand goods, goods requiring installation and pieces of art. It should be underlined that these categories of goods do not constitute any general exclusion. They represent the types of goods where the incompatibility might be considered more often because of specific characteristics of above goods.

485. Regarding the incompatibility of the presumption with the nature of the defects there are no general exclusions. There are however, specific defects that may bring along the issue of incompatibility. For example, specific animal diseases or external defects in second-hand goods. Regarding the latter, the presumption might be incompatible with the nature of the defects when they are noticeable by a non-professional at the time of the passing of risk. In such cases the consumer is expected to object in due time (at the time the risk was passed). If the consumer accepts the product without objection, this invites the assumption that there were no defects in the first place. Furthermore, the presumption cannot apply

221 Faust 2011, § 476 Rn. 18, 19.
222 Klöhn 2007, p. 2814.

to an unidentified defect. It must concern proven and concrete defects. The cases of overly broad, general defects may be regarded as incompatible with the presumption because of the nature of the defects.[223]

According to Maultzsch, from the systematic and teleological interpretation of § 476 BGB it can be concluded that the presumption is not compatible with the nature of the defect if the seller can provide *prima facie* evidence that the particular defect occurred only after the time the risk was passed. This seems to be in contradiction to the wording of § 476 BGB, which requires evidence to the contrary to rebut the presumption. In any case, when the exclusion criteria are permitted, the general rule on the allocation of the burden of proof applies, meaning the consumer must prove that at the time of the passing of risk the goods were already defective.[224]

Regarding the incompatibility of the presumption with regard to certain animal diseases, there is no clear interpretation regarding the application of the exclusion criteria that can be provided. There are some types of diseases where the application of the presumption will be allowed such as genetic or chronic diseases. In other cases when the presumption is not applied, for example, in spontaneous conditions occurring after the passing of risk, the question arises whether there is incompatibility or simply insufficient proof of the existence of the defects. In some cases the BGH seems to conflate these two situations making the understanding of the construction and application of the presumption difficult. In the end it seems that the question of how the parties performed in providing the evidence while pleading the existence or lack of existence of defects distinctly affects the application of the exclusion criteria.

Summing up, the scope of the exclusion criteria is difficult to determine, the German courts sometimes depart from the principle of protecting the consumer interests by allowing the exclusion. Furthermore, the case law regarding the matter seems to be somewhat inconsistent and challenging to study.

5.4.6 *Road map of the presumption*

486. This sub-section discusses how the scheme of the presumption is constructed and how it might be applied. Furthermore, the relationship between the particular stages of the presumption as well as the arguments and defences available to both parties is be presented. Some of the elements have been already discussed but will be repeated for the purpose of creating some kind of roadmap of the presumption of § 476 BGB.

223 Alternatively the court can decide that the consumer has not proven the existence of defects and therefore the presumption cannot apply.

224 Maultzsch 2006, p. 3097.

§ 476 BGB states that '*if, within six months after the date of the passing of risk, a material defect manifests itself, it is presumed that the thing was already defective when risk passed, unless this presumption is incompatible with the nature of the thing or of the defect.*'[225] Before the presumption can apply, the consumer must state and prove if needed the existence of defects and the fact that they occurred within six months from the passing of risk. There are several instances of defects demanding various degrees of consumer's initiative and invention to meet the duty to provide evidence. Based on the discussion presented in para 441-449 and 462 of this chapter, it must be stated that the level of certainty of the existence of defects which is required from the consumer is rather high, in particular, in complex cases of technically complex goods and multi-sourced problems.

Discharging the burden of proof of the existence of defects and supplying evidence thereof is the most important phase of litigation in consumer cases, not only for the applicability of the presumption but also for receiving remedies in general. Regarding the proof of defects, German courts require a strong and clear evidence as to their existence. The arguments available for the seller at this stage regard the origins of defects. Most often they concern the facts that the defect has been caused by the factors lying in the sphere of a consumer, for example, misuse of goods or incorrect maintenance. They may also regard ordinary wear and tear, or external sources, such as the fault of third parties or *force majeure*. In the complex cases referred to as *Grundmangel* and *Folgemangel* it is not sufficient to comprehensively present the existing problems with the goods, it is often necessary to exclude the above-mentioned potential sources of defects.

487. If two requirements have been met, the presumption of non-conformity applies and the burden of proof is reversed. The seller may attempt to prevent its application by challenging the existence of any of the necessary conditions. As well as the lack of evidence of defects, he can rely on the fact that the defects became apparent after the expiry of the six-month period. If successful, the burden of proof will be allocated as according with the general rule. The seller may also argue that the contract is an ordinary sale, not a consumer sale and therefore the presumption of § 476 BGB is not applicable.

488. Even when the presumption is applied, the seller can rebut the presumption. As a consequence he will not be liable for the delivery of defective goods. To achieve this, the seller must provide evidence to the contrary, showing that the goods were defect-free at the time of the passing of risk. § 292 ZPO requires full proof to the contrary. *Prima facie* evidence and undermining the grounds of the presumption will at this stage no longer be successful to fight the presumption. Interestingly, the cases that have been reviewed for

225 Translation: http://www.gesetze-im-internet.de/englisch_bgb/englisch_bgb.html#p1607 (10.10.2014).

the purpose of this study did not directly deal with the issues of rebuttal. The most common problems considered are proving the existence of defects or the exclusion criteria.

In the literature[226] it is indicated that § 476 BGB is to be interpreted so that if the exclusion criteria do not apply then the seller must provide evidence to the contrary as set out in § 292 ZPO in order to win his case. It might be understood in such a way that the necessity of evidence to the contrary depends on the applicability of the exclusion criteria. In Dauner-Lieb and Langen, when talking about the presumption, the order of discussion is as follows: the conditions for application, the legal consequences, incompatibility, and lastly rebuttal of the presumption.[227] This order might indicate that in every case where the presumption is invoked, the possible application of the exclusion criteria must also be assessed. Such order is not necessarily favourable for the consumer. Although it is not considerably different from other jurisdictions, such an explicitly stated relationship between these two instruments (exclusion and rebuttal) might indicate that if the criteria for the presumption are met, then excluding its application must be tested, and it is a consumer who is expected to provide evidence that the criteria for the exclusion do not apply. On the other hand, since a judge assesses each case after hearing all the facts presented by the parties, in practice the above-mentioned order may seem less relevant. Nevertheless, it may incorrectly indicate that the consumer carries the burden of negating the applicability of the criteria for the exclusion of the presumption, which is not the case. The burden of proving the existence of these criteria, when invoked, lies with the seller, since he relies on the legal consequences of their existence.[228]

Some have argued that the exclusion of the presumption because if its incompatibility with the nature of the goods or the nature of the defects is not as burdensome as proving evidence to the contrary. Due to the burdensomeness of the evidence to the contrary there is a danger that the exclusion of the presumption may be awarded too easily, just because '*proof to the contrary is too burdensome*'.[229] Such interpretation would mean that the seller's interests would prevail and the consumer may not be able to entirely rely on the benefits of the presumption of § 476 BGB.

5.4.7 *Conclusions*

489. This chapter discussed the presumption of non-conformity of Article 5 (3) of the Consumer Sales Directive as implemented in the German law in § 476 BGB. The main

226 Lorenz 2012, § 476 Rn. 27; Maultzsch 2006, p. 3092; Dauner-Lieb and Langen 2012, p. 1961.
227 Dauner-Lieb and Langen 2012, p. 1961.
228 Chapter 2, para 45, 46, 48; Chapter 5, para 470.
229 Maultzsch 2006, p. 3092.

focus was given to the conditions, legal consequences, rebuttal and exclusion of the application of the presumption of § 476 BGB.

To be able to rely on the simplifications in rules on evidence provided by the legislator, the consumer has to prove that the delivered goods are defective and that the defects appeared within six months from the time the risk was passed. As a consequence of the application of the presumption, the general rules on the allocation of the burden of proof are altered. According to the general rule in cases of non-performance of obligations found in § 363 BGB, the burden of proving the existence of defects at the time the risk was passed will normally lie with the creditor/buyer. Thanks to the presumption, in the first six months following the passing of risk the burden of proving that the goods were free from defects at that time lies with the seller. Therefore, the conditions of the presumption are in accordance with Article 5 (3) of the Consumer Sales Directive.

490. Although the conditions are implemented correctly, German law uses different notions from those adopted by the Consumer Sales Directive. First of all, instead of non-conformity the German consumer must prove the existence of material defects. Secondly, instead of from the moment of delivery, the period for the application of the presumption is counted from the time of the passing of risk. The scope of the notions used by the BGB and the Consumer Sales Directive are very similar however, in some circumstances their content may cause uncertainty.

491. To meet the first condition the consumer has to prove that there is a defect in the sense of § 434 BGB. As provided in this section this is not always as easy as it may appear, even when it is clear that the goods are not working properly. Based on the decisions of the BGH it can be concluded that the ability to prove the defects depends on the instance of defect. Namely, there are three instances distinguished by the BGH: defect interpreted strictly, as stated in § 434 BGB. The consumer usually has no difficulty in proving the circumstances described in the above paragraph, even when their source is unknown. The second instance is referred to as *Grundmangel*, it is clear that the problem did not exist at the time the risk was passed. To be regarded as material defect in the sense of § 434 BGB it must result from the defective factors present at that time, often difficult to prove. The third instance is referred to as *Folgemangel*, where similarly to *Grundmangel* it did not exist at the time risk was passed and its origins are unclear. It might be caused by the existence of a hidden *Grundmangel*, or other factors such as misuse, wear and tear or a combination of both. The last two instances of defects are more difficult to prove. The case law regarding this complex topic remains rather inconsistent. Finally, it should be underlined that the majority of issues on the applicability of the presumption from § 476 BGB

are inevitably and directly connected to the notion of defects and a sufficient proof of their existence.[230]

492. The consumer must make sure that evidence as to the existence of defects has been satisfied. The court will assess evidence from the perspective of what the consumer may reasonably expect from the purchased goods. In particular, it can be concluded that proving that second-hand goods are defective is not at all easy due to the character of goods and the fact that they have been previously used. The role of the presumption of non-conformity should be to simplify and ease the burden of proof however, in some cases the burdens that a consumer must carry to benefit from the presumption are just as heavy as burdens to prove that at the time of passing the risk the goods were already defective. Regarding the particular topics the question remains whether the presumption is applied correctly and achieves its goals as set out by the European legislator. In particular the interpretation of the notion of *Folgemangel* indicates a lower standard of protection than the one emerging from Article 5 (3) of the Consumer Sales Directive. One may argue that the above-mentioned notion regards the assessment of evidence and the means of evidence necessary to prove the defects from § 434, which belongs to the autonomic national provisions.

493. Other issues regarding the presumption from § 476 BGB consider the exclusion criteria. The German legislator has implemented them in line with the Directive and the BGH has repeatedly applied and interpreted them. The BGH stated that the criteria must apply exceptionally however, there are many decisions where the presumption was excluded and the burden of proving that the defects were present at the time of passing the risk fell on the consumer. Based on the case law discussed in this part, it can be concluded that in the majority of cases where the presumption was not permitted, the consumer lost the case. It shows how important the application of presumption from § 476 BGB is for achieving remedies and the protection of consumer interests.

5.5 Presumption of non-conformity in English and Welsh law

5.5.1 *Introduction*

494. This chapter describes the implementation of the presumption of non-conformity from Article 5 (3) of the Consumer Sales Directive into English and Welsh law. As with the previous sections first the general information about the scope of the presumption of

230 Bachmeier 2008, Rn. 997.

non-conformity will be provided (5.5.2). Subsequently, the focus will be on the requirements for the application of the presumption (5.5.3), rebuttal (5.5.4) and exclusion criteria (5.5.5). The analysis of the above-mentioned topics will provide answers to whether the presumption has been correctly implemented into the English system, whether the objectives of the presumption of non-conformity have been achieved and whether an English consumer can easily take advantage of the simplifications in supply of evidence designed for him by the European legislator.

495. To begin with, it should be stated that the English legislator, law practitioners and scholars do not seem to pay the same attention to the presumption of non-conformity as their German, Polish or Dutch counterparts do. The issue of the burden of proof does not generally receive attention in English commentaries or debates regarding sales law, and in particular consumer sales law. However, the idea of introducing the reversed burden of proof in consumer sale cases has been welcomed in the literature.[231] It has been confirmed that the seller more often has access to information which helps to establish that the goods are in conformity (or they were at the time of delivery) than there is a chance that consumer will have access to information allowing him to establish the existence of non-conformity at the time of delivery.[232] Unfortunately, there is very little written about the role, conditions and consequences of the application of the presumption of non-conformity, also sometimes referred to as the presumption of disconformity.[233] Despite the lack of information on this matter, the most important aspects of the application of the presumption of non-conformity in English law will be presented and as far as possible it will be explained why the presumption does not seem so important under English law.

5.5.2 *Scope of the application of the presumption*

496. The consumer's right to receive remedies depends on whether the goods were defective at the time of delivery. This is true for the rights found in the Directive and it also counts for all national systems discussed in this study, including England and Wales. Proving the existence of non-conformity at the time of delivery can be challenging, in particular, when the defects have been discovered long after the delivery.[234] The European legislator has decided to ease the burden of proof by introducing a presumption of non-conformity, which has been followed by the English legislator.

231 Willett and Morgan-Taylor 2004, p. 102; Macleod 2007, nr. 14.02-14.05.

232 Willett and Morgan-Taylor 2013, p. 412.

233 Benjamin's sale of goods 2010, nr. 12-075.

234 Macleod 2007, nr. 14.01.

497. The presumption of non-conformity was implemented into English law in the Sale and Supply of Goods to Consumers Regulations 2002, Part 5A s. 48A (3) and (4) and incorporated in the Sale of Goods Act 1979. Section 48A (3) of the Sale of Goods Act 1979 states that '*the goods which do not conform to the contract of sale at any time within the period of six months starting with the date on which the goods were delivered to the buyer must be taken not to have conformed at that date.*' The subsequent provision of 48A (4) states that Section 48A (3) does not apply if:

1. It is established that the goods did conform at that date.
2. Its application is incompatible with the nature of the goods or the nature of the lack of conformity.

To make use of the presumption, a consumer claiming that the goods lack conformity must prove a breach of an express term or breach of one of the implied terms from Sections 13-15 of the Sale of Goods Act 1979.[235] Furthermore, a consumer must prove that the lack of satisfactory quality (non-conformity) has become apparent within six months from the time of delivery. After the expiry of six months, the burden of proof that the goods were defective at the time of delivery will be shifted back on to the consumer.

498. When the presumption is applied, the *prima facie* formal effect should be to reverse the burden of proof regarding the state of goods during the first six months after purchase, so that the burden that the goods were not defective at the time of delivery is on the seller.[236] As already stated, after six months, it is again for the consumer to prove that the goods were defective at the time of delivery.[237] The purpose of Section 48A (3) and (4) of the Sale of goods Act 1979 has the same purpose as the respective provisions in other Member States,[238] to assist consumers by simplifying the supply of evidence in the disputes against professionals. The presumption of non-conformity is a way to equalise powers between the parties.

499. In English law, the presumption of non-conformity applies to consumer contracts and only in relation to the statutory remedies in the scheme of Part 5A of the Sale and Supply of Goods to Consumers Regulations 2002, incorporated into the Sale of Goods Act 1979 in sections: 48A (2), 48B and 48C. These remedies are: repair, replacement, price reduction and the rescission of contract. The presumption of non-conformity does not

235 *Leicester Circuits Ltd v Coates Brothers Plc*, 2002 EWCA Civ 290, para 62.
236 Chapter 2, para 69.
237 Macleod 2007, nr. 14.06; Benjamin's sale of goods 2010, nr. 12-075.
238 Article 4 (1) of the Polish Consumer Sale Act; § 476 BGB; Article 7:18 (2) BW.

apply to the traditional remedies for example, the right to reject and damages, which are also applicable to consumer contracts.[239]

When claiming traditional remedies, the burden of proving a lack of satisfactory quality also in the first six months following the delivery lies with the consumer. One might observe that such distinction is not desirable and may cause uncertainty, especially for inexperienced market participants. The issue has been recognised by the Law Commissions[240] which expressed that in the interests of simplicity the same presumption should apply when consumer chooses to rely on one of the traditional remedies.[241] On the other hand, it seems that the effects of the above distinction could be waived by a court, willing to infer on relevant facts that goods, which were found defective within a short period of time, were probably similarly defective at the time of delivery. However, although in practice possible, such inference would not be based on the statutory six-month presumption as such, but on the *prima facie* evidence or factual presumption.[242]

500. In the context of future reform there will also be some changes regarding the presumption of non-conformity. The Consumer Rights Bill provides in Section 19 (14) that for the purposes of Sections 19 (3) (b) and (c), 19 (4) (remedies), goods which do not conform to the contract at any time within the first six months, beginning on the day on which the goods were delivered to the consumer, must be treated as not having conformed on the day of delivery. The presumption does not apply if it is established that the goods did conform to the contract on that day, or its application is incompatible with the nature of the goods or with how they fail to conform to the contract.

Looking at the wording of Section 19 (14) of the new Consumer Rights Bill it can be stated that the scope of the presumption is limited. It does not apply to all remedies. Similarly to the presumption from Section 48A (3) of the Sale of Goods Act 1979 it applies only in the context of repair, replacement, price reduction and final right to reject (rescission of contract), which are available to the consumer if the goods do not conform to the contract because of a breach of the terms regarding satisfactory quality, fitness for purpose, description, sample, model and incorrect installation. The presumption does not apply if the consumer chooses the short-time right to reject. The most problematic characteristic of the application of the presumption in English law is the difference in the application of the presumption depending on the chosen remedy. This will not be changed after the new Bill enters into force.

239 Naidoo 2011, p. 3.
240 The Law Commission and the Scottish Law Commission.
241 The Law Commission and the Scottish Law Commission 2009, Consumer Remedies for faulty goods, Summary, para 1.42.
242 Benjamin's sale of goods 2010, nr. 12-075, 14-015.

501. There is a concern regarding the diversity in application of the presumption of non-conformity and whether the diversity interferes with the system of protection provided in the Consumer Sales Directive. The Directive introduced the presumption of non-conformity to simplify the duty to produce evidence in order to be able to receive remedies for non-conforming goods. One might observe that this simplification should be used regardless of the type of remedy available to the consumer. Regardless of the remedy, the initial burden of proof lying with the consumer is alike. Normally, the buyer/consumer must prove that the goods did not conform to the contract at the time of delivery. Only allowing the operation of the presumption of non-conformity to consumer remedies may lead the consumers no longer rely on the traditional remedies because of the disadvantageous allocation of the burden of proof.[243]

On the other hand, the Consumer Sales Directive is a minimum harmonisation measure, and national systems may contain additional instruments to secure protection of consumer interests. The traditional remedies may be considered as such additional protection,[244] which the English legislator may freely regulate as long as the minimum protection stemming from the Directive has been implemented correctly. The issue may arise in relation to the Directive on Consumer Rights, which provides for maximum harmonisation and will be soon implemented in the Consumer Rights Bill.

502. For the lack of conformity that becomes apparent after the statutory six months, it is for the consumer to provide evidence that the goods did not conform to the contract at the time of delivery. One way to do so might be to obtain an expert opinion confirming that the item must have been poorly manufactured or designed, or that it contained defects that were likely or certain to make the product flawed at some future date.[245] It is agreed that it is hard to provide convincing evidence that the goods were defective at the time of delivery, and sometimes such proof requires knowledge and experience that only a professional seller possess.

503. Regarding the presumption of non-conformity, there has been a tendency to regard this provision as creating a compulsory guaranty of quality for six months after the delivery.[246] It is however the wrong approach. The central point of the presumption is the question of the burden of proving the existence of defects at the time of delivery. It should

243 On the other hand the traditional remedies are well-known and well-established in the English system, therefore a consumer may feel more confident to ask for the remedies he is acquainted with.

244 Looking from the perspective of the Consumer Sales Directive, from the perspective of English law, remedies from the Consumer Sales Directive might be regarded as additional ones.

245 Department of Trade and Industry, Consumer and Competition Policy Directorate, the Sale and Supply of Goods to Consumers Regulations 2002, A Brief Introduction – Full Version, p. 13. Available online at: http://www.secola.org/db/2_12/gb_noteslong.pdf (23.10.2014).

246 Benjamin's sale of goods 2010, nr. 14-015.

be also noted that the disputes very often arrive much later than six months, which may undermine the role that the presumption of non-conformity was set out to fulfil.

Taking the above facts into account it can be stated that the current situation causes uncertainty for the consumers and creates inconsistency within the English system. It can be misleading for consumers and could lead to consumers no longer being able to rely on the remedies such as rejection and damages, thanks to the disadvantageous allocation of the burden of proof, and instead using remedies included in the Consumer Sales Directive. In this regard further clarification of the operation of the presumption of non-conformity within English system is desirable.

5.5.3 *Conditions for the application of the presumption*

5.5.3.1 Non-conformity

504. Section 48A (3) of the Sale of Goods Act 1979 stipulating the presumption of non-conformity states that '*the goods which do not conform to the contract of sale at any time within the period of six months starting with the date on which the goods were delivered to the buyer must be deemed not to be conforming to the contract at that date.*' The goods do not conform to the contract if the express or implied term from 13-15 of the Sale of Goods Act 1979 is breached.[247] To be able to benefit from the presumption of non-conformity, the consumer has to prove that the purchased goods do not possess characteristics specifically agreed upon, that the goods are not of satisfactory quality, they are not fit for purpose, or do not correspond to the model or sample shown to him by the seller. The consumer must prove his claim on a balance of probabilities, which in England is considered 50% + 1 of probability.[248] In comparison to the German standards it seems that in England and Wales it is relatively easy to initially convince a judge of the non-conformity and subsequently shift the burden to the buyer, even without the operation of statutory presumption of non-conformity. In particular, the notion of durability may simplify the consumer's position in convincing the court about the existence of unsatisfactory quality or unfitness for purpose.[249]

505. The new reform provides more specific regulation of what the consumer must prove, without considerably changing his duties. Section 19 (3) of the new Consumer Rights Bill expressly states that the goods do not conform to the contract if there is a breach of the terms described in sections 9, 10, 11, 13 and 14 of the Bill. Furthermore, it seems that Section 19 (3) – which provides for remedies in cases of non-conformity and Section 19

247 Chapter 4, para 300-315.

248 *Leicester Circuits Ltd v Coates Brothers Plc*, 2002 EWCA Civ 290, para 5.

249 Chapter 4, para 301.

(14) – which provides for a presumption, apply also to digital content that does not conform to what has been agreed under the contract. In this context, compared to the current legislation, the new Consumer Rights Bill will provide a broader scope of application of the presumption of non-conformity.

5.5.3.2 Six-month period

506. The second condition for the application of the presumption concerns the time at which the non-conformity became apparent. Following Article 5 (3) of the Consumer Sales Directive, Section 48 (3) of the Sale of Goods Act 1979 states that this period amounts to six months from the time of delivery. This element was initially implemented identically in all the Member States' domestic laws that were analysed and it is also provided in the Consumer Rights Bill. However, the interpretation of the beginning and expiry of the period may already be different. Below, the English view on the six-month period will be presented.

I Beginning of the period

507. As already said, the goods must be in conformity at the time of delivery. It seems that when the European legislator used the term delivery it meant the actual handing over the goods. This is one of the reasons why the English legislator decided to modify the rules regarding the passing of risk in the consumer sales. Under the previous rules, in some circumstances, the goods might have been at the buyer's risk even before the actual delivery.[250] If this rule had been left unchanged, it could have made the application of the presumption of non-conformity challenging, in particular, when the six-month period began to run much earlier than the date on which the actual delivery of goods took place. Furthermore, when the seller agreed to deliver through a third party to a buyer's home and the goods were damaged, the buyer could not claim non-performance as the risk had not remained with the seller. The buyer was left only with a claim of negligence against the carrier.[251] In cases where there was no negligence on the carrier's part, the consumer could be left without remedies. This rule was considered too strict for the purpose of consumer sales, and was therefore amended. Under the Section 32 (4) of Sale of Goods Act 1979, the risk will not pass until the goods are physically delivered to the consumer.[252] As a result, the beginning of the operation of the presumption of non-conformity is the moment of actual delivery.

250 Watterson 2001, p. 203.
251 Watterson 2001, p. 204.
252 Macleod 2007, nr. 22.01.

508. The moment the risk was passed is also expressly provided for in the new Consumer Rights Bill. Section 29 (2) states that the goods remain at the seller's risk until they come into the physical possession of the consumer or a person identified by the consumer to take the possession of the goods. The above provision does not apply if the goods are delivered to a carrier who is commissioned by the consumer to deliver the goods and the seller has not designated the carrier as one of the transport options. Consequently, the physical delivery serves as a general rule for the moment of delivery, with possible exceptions involving the delivery by a carrier. However, the majority of the cases fall within the general rule.

II *Length of the period*

509. Regarding the way the six months should be counted there is an indication in the Consumer Rights Bill that it should be counted from the date of delivery and including this date. Section 19 (14) states that the non-conformity must appear at any time within the period of six months beginning with the day on which the goods were delivered to the consumer. There are no further general rules regarding time periods in civil cases. For this reason there could be a necessity to refer to the European Regulation on the rules determining the dates and time periods.[253]

III *Expiry of the period*

510. The wording of 48A (3) of the Sale of goods Act 1979 indicates that the period of six months is interpreted strictly, and that after this period, it is for the consumer to prove the existence of non-conformity at the time of delivery. It has been expressed that it is in the line with the Consumer Sales Directive that '*when the consumer reported defectiveness after the expiry of the first six months, the presumption still might apply. However, the onus to prove that non-conformity exhibited itself within the six months will be on the consumer. It is advised for the consumer to report non-conformity as soon as it is discovered*'.[254] Therefore, it seems that in any case the consumer will be able to prove the existence of non-conformity within six months, even when it appeared to him and has been reported after the expiry of six months, the court should admit the application of the presumption. Furthermore, the court may give the consumer the benefit of the doubt and extend the operation of simplifications in the duty to supply of evidence.[255]

253 Chapter 5, para 374.

254 Department of Trade and Industry, Consumer and Competition Policy Directorate, the Sale and Supply of Goods to Consumers Regulations 2002, A Brief Introduction – Full Version, p. 14. Available online at: http://www.secola.org/db/2_12/gb_noteslong.pdf (23.10.2014).

255 Macleod 2007, nr. 14.06.

IV Application of the presumption after the expiry of statutory period

511. Although the statutory period is fixed both under the Consumer Sales Directive as well as under English law, it is possible for similar protection to be available for longer than the statutory six months. In principle, below presented options are available also in other jurisdictions, however it seems that in England they are used more often than elsewhere. First of all, under English law the parties may and often do regulate the matter differently.[256] The seller may issue a special warranty, which extends a statutory period and improves consumer's position. In a case described in *The Guardian*,[257] the seller stated in the terms of contract regarding the purchase of a computer that the warranty provides that within twelve months of the delivery the seller will investigate faulty product claims without the consumer having to provide any further evidence. After the twelve months following delivery, where the cause of the defect is unclear, the consumer is required to provide an independent report on the product and the possible defects. If this report confirms a manufacturing defect the seller will recover the costs of the report and receive an appropriate remedy.[258] Pursuant to the above agreement, it is the seller who bears the burden of proof of the cause of the defects within twelve months from the time of delivery.

Another eventuality is to extend the time and possibly the scope for the application of the presumption of non-conformity at the judge's discretion. It has already been indicated that the judge can use a similar construction to that of the presumption of non-conformity if the consumer claims traditional remedies instead of statutory remedies. Therefore, it seems reasonable to believe that the judge could also extend the period in which in particular circumstances the presumption of non-conformity should operate for longer than six months, for example applying the notion of durability.[259]

Finally, as already stated, the presumption of non-conformity applies in cases when the consumer discovered the existence of non-conformity after the expiry of the statutory period, even when the defect objectively could have been discovered within the first six months. Ultimately, the application of the presumption of non-conformity depends on the proof of the non-conformity appearing within six months from the time of delivery.

5.5.3.3 Conclusions

512. Based on information provided above, it can be concluded that both requirements for the application of the presumption of non-conformity have been implemented in accordance with Article 5 (3) of the Consumer Sales Directive. Conditions for the application of the presumption from Section 48A (3) of the Sale of Goods Act 1979 – (I) the existence of non-conformity (II) apparent within six months – are counterparts to the

256 However, not in the way to infringe the minimum standard set out in the Consumer Sales Directive.
257 Tims 2011.
258 Tims 2011.
259 Chapter 4, para 301.

conditions provided in the Directive. Similarly, proposed Section 19 (14) of the Consumer Rights Bill contains two requirements for the application of the presumption, which are in line with the Consumer Sales Directive. Due to the lack of cases regarding the matter it is impossible to conclude how the courts deal with the conditions of the presumption. However, taking into account the standard of proof required before English courts, it seems that it should be relatively easy for a consumer to prove the existence of non-conformity. Moreover, even without the operation of the presumption, the consumer may be relieved from the requirement to prove the existence of the non-conformity at the time of delivery through the application of the notion of durability.

513. As to the second condition, the appearance of the non-conformity within six months from the time of delivery, following conclusions can be made. The English legislator provides the same period for the operation of the presumption as the European legislator. It also adopted the European concept of actual delivery applicable to consumer contracts, without which the operation of the presumption might have been problematic. Furthermore, there are no specific rules regarding the calculation of legal periods, what in theory may cause uncertainty. However, the lack of these rules does not seem to have any significant consequences, since in practice the presumption of non-conformity as such is not being applied, nor has been extensively discussed in the literature.

5.5.4 *Rebuttal of the presumption*

514. According to Article 5 (3) of the Consumer Sales Directive, the presumption applies unless 'proved otherwise'. Below it will be illustrated what the elements of proof to the contrary under English law are and what facts the seller has to present to prove that the defects, whose existence within six months from the time of delivery has been proven by the consumer, occurred after that time.

515. In Section 48A (4) (a) of the Sale of Goods Act 1979, it is stated that the presumption of non-conformity does not apply when it is established that the goods did conform to the contract at the time of delivery. The burden to provide this fact lies with the seller. Firstly, he will most probably try to challenge the statement that there is insufficient proof of the existence of non-conformity in the sense of Sections 13-15 of the Sale of Goods Act 1979. The seller can also claim that even though the goods are defective at the time of dispute, they were free from defects at the time of delivery. Accordingly, in order to rebut the presumption the seller has to provide evidence to the contrary.[260] To do so he could allege that any defects that occurred, resulted from natural wear and tear, misuse, lack of sufficient

260 Chapter 2, para 69.

care, failure to maintain or service the goods, or other causes occurring after the delivery. The presumption makes the above arguments more difficult to defend. If the judge is convinced by one of the arguments presented by the seller, a consumer would probably need to call for expert evidence to disprove the seller's arguments, confirming that a particular product was of poor quality or design, or of insufficient durability, and that these features were present at the time of delivery.[261] The matter of rebuttal remains unchanged under the new Consumer Rights Bill.

5.5.5 *Exclusion of the application of the presumption*

516. Section 48A (4) (b) of the Sale of Goods Act 1979 excludes the application of the presumption of non-conformity in the situations where:

1. The presumption is incompatible with the nature of the goods.
2. The presumption is incompatible with the nature of the lack of conformity.

The criteria for the exclusion are identical to the criteria formulated in Article 5 (3) of the Consumer Sales Directive. There is a lack of case law regarding this matter however, there is an argument among English scholars that the presumption of non-conformity is incompatible with short-lived goods such as flowers or food products (perishable goods).[262] As a consequence, the buyer who consumes food or other products after the recommended expiry date, which is shorter than six months, may be left without a remedy.[263]

517. The Consumer Rights Bill provides for the same exclusion criteria, only they are formulated slightly differently. Section 19 (15) (b) states that the presumption of non-conformity does not apply if its application is incompatible with the nature of the goods or with how they fail to conform to the contract. In practice, the scope of exclusion criteria remains the same as under the Sale of Goods Act 1979.

518. It seems that in England there is less need to separate the rebuttal and exclusion of the presumption than in other jurisdictions. In England the exclusion criteria are not that distinguished or categorised as they are in other jurisdictions investigated. The proof to the contrary and the incompatibility of the presumption with the nature of the goods and the nature of the non-conformity are generally regarded as circumstances when the presumption does not apply.[264]

---

261 Benjamin's sale of goods 2010, nr. 12-075.

262 Benjamin's sale of goods 2010, nr. 12-075; Shears 2000, p. 269.

263 Woodroffe and Lowe 2013, p. 109, 110.

264 Section 48 (4) of the Sale of Goods Act 1979: '*Sub-section (3) does not apply if:*
(a) it is established that the goods did so conform at that date;

In general, the parties are expected to take the initiative and provide as many facts and evidence as possible to convince the judge. Where the consumer initiates the proceedings he will have the final chance to speak. The reason why the claimant ends is that this party bears the burden of proof and should have the last word.[265] There is no further case law (known to me) regarding the requirements for application, rebuttal or exclusion of the presumption from Section 48A (3) and (4) of the Sale of Goods Act 1979.

5.5.6 *Road map of the presumption*

519. After the analysis of the English implementation of the Consumer Sales Directive in the context of the presumption of non-conformity and the future amendments found in the Consumer Rights Bill, it can be stated that the presumption of non-conformity is of little practical significance. There seem to be a several reasons for this. Before discussing these reasons, a brief summary of the construction of the presumption will be presented.

Theoretically, in order to invoke the presumption of non-conformity the consumer must prove that the goods do not conform to the contract. He can do this by proving that one of the express terms of the contract or one of the implied terms from Sections 13-15 of the Sale of Goods Act 1979 was breached. The second requirement is that the non-conformity (breach of one of the terms mentioned above) becomes apparent within six months from the time of delivery. To rebut the presumption the seller must provide evidence to the contrary showing that the goods were in conformity at the time of delivery or became defective only after that time. Where the application of the presumption is incompatible with the nature of the goods or the nature of the non-conformity, it can be excluded. The burden of proof to provide the criteria of exclusion and the elements of evidence to the contrary lies with the seller.

520. As repeatedly mentioned, the presumption of non-conformity does not yet have practical importance in English law. There are no decisions where it has been applied, and its application and interpretation is not being discussed in the literature. There are several possible reasons explaining the insignificance of the presumption under English law. First of all, the standard of proof is relatively low (50% + 1)[266] and therefore easier to meet. In cases when it is reasonable, the judges tend to shift the burden to the seller applying factual presumption or allowing *prima facie* evidence. Furthermore, there is an important role of the notion of durability, which also carries a factual presumption that the goods were defective at the time of delivery in cases where they break within an unreasonably short

(b) its application is incompatible with the nature of the goods or the nature of the lack of conformity.'

265 Andrews 2008, p. 59.

266 *Leicester Circuits Ltd v Coates Brothers Plc*, 2002 EWCA Civ 290, para 5.

period of time. Finally, taking into account the very high costs of litigation it seems that an English consumer litigates much less than the consumers in Germany, the Netherlands, or in Poland. There is well-developed practice of disputes being solved amicably by the consumer and seller and filing the court claim remains a last resort. Alternatively, the consumers who do litigate may rely on the traditional remedies to which the presumption of non-conformity does not apply. Taking the above possibilities into account, the presumption of non-conformity is an unpopular construction, possibly without any practical relevance at this point.

5.5.7 Conclusions

521. Based on the available information it can be concluded that the English legislator has correctly implemented presumption of non-conformity. The provisions regarding the prerequisites for application of the presumption, rebuttal and the exclusion criteria have been implemented in line with the Consumer Sales Directive. However, due to a lack of case law or scholarly debate, it is difficult to state whether the presumption is being applied correctly within the English legal framework.

From the limited attention that the presumption of non-conformity received it is difficult to draw any detailed conclusions. Only by regarding the issues surrounding six-month period and the burden of providing evidence connected to it, is it clear that the English regulation brings similar uncertainty regarding the matter as observed in other jurisdictions. There was some uncertainty regarding delivery and the passing of risk, which the English legislator has clarified while implementing the Directive. This simplifies establishing the moment of the passing of risk and potential application of the presumption. Comparing the function of the presumption with other jurisdictions, it seems that until now the presumption has had little practical importance and little interest from the market participants and legal practitioners. The lack of case law concerning the matter prevent from any (detailed) comparison between England and other jurisdictions regarding the application of the presumption.

522. The general purpose of the presumption is assessed positively. It has been admitted that the burden of proof of the existence of non-conformity at the time of delivery would be too burdensome for consumers, and therefore the reversed burden of proof should have improved the consumers' position. On the other hand, it counts only for the statutory remedies. Apparently, when it comes to traditional remedies for example, the rejection of goods or damages, the traditional allocation of the burden of proof is not considered as too burdensome.

In the absence of case law there are a number of areas regarding the application of the consumer sale provisions in general and the application of the presumption in particular that need further clarification. Moreover, there is also a lack of serious debate and literature on the interpretation of Section 48 (3) of the Sale of Goods and its place within the English system, which makes discussing this subject particularly challenging. It also considerably restricts the possibility of comparing the English system to other jurisdictions in the context of the presumption of non-conformity.

5.6 PRESUMPTION OF NON-CONFORMITY IN DUTCH LAW

5.6.1 *Introduction*

523. This section describes the application of the presumption of non-conformity in Dutch law. It begins with the general information of the scope of the presumption of non-conformity in Dutch law (5.6.2). The main issues that will be dealt with regard the prerequisites for application of the presumption and its consequences (5.6.3), rebuttal (5.6.4) and the exclusion criteria (5.6.5). Information on the above-mentioned topics will lead to the conclusions on whether objectives of the presumption of non-conformity set by the European legislator have been achieved and whether a Dutch consumer can easily take advantage of the simplifications in supply of evidence designed for him by the European legislator.

5.6.2 *Scope of the application of the presumption*

524. Article 5 (3) of the Consumer Sales Directive was implemented by Article 7:18 (2) BW. Article 7:18 (2) BW states that if the non-conformity of goods becomes apparent within six months from the time of delivery, it is presumed that the goods lacked conformity at that time, unless the presumption is incompatible with the nature of the goods or the nature of the non-conformity.[267] Article 7:18 (2) BW came into force on 1 May 2003 together with other provisions implementing the Consumer Sales Directive.[268] Although before the implementation Dutch law already provided for protective sales provisions, it was unfamiliar with the presumption of non-conformity. On the ground of Article 7:6 (1), Article 7:18 (2) – introducing presumption, belongs to the mandatory law applicable

267 Article 7:18 (2) BW, '*Bij een consumentenkoop wordt vermoed dat de zaak bij aflevering niet aan de overeenkomst heeft beantwoord indien de afwijking van het overeengekomene zich binnen een termijn van zes maanden na aflevering openbaart, tenzij de aard van de zaak of de aard van de afwijking zich daartegen verzet.*'

268 Stb 2003, 110 (*aanpassingswet*); Stb 2003, 151 (*inwerkingtreding*).

exclusively to contracts concluded between professional sellers and consumers.[269] It is clear from the *Parlementaire Geschiedenis*[270] that the implementation of Article 5 (3) of the Directive triggered an interesting debate about the shape and place of the presumption of non-conformity in Dutch sales law.[271]

525. As with the other legal systems analysed above, the implementation of Article 5 (3) of the Consumer Sales Directive has been justified by the fact that it can be extremely difficult for the consumer to prove that the goods were non-conforming at the time of delivery. In particular, when the non-conformity becomes apparent after that time and when the seller claims that the defect results from, for example, incorrect usage of goods.[272] Article 7:18 (2) BW follows the Consumer Sales Directive and simplifies the burden of proof borne by a consumer. It offers statutory protection from the overly burdensome obligation to prove the existence of non-conformity at the time of delivery. This protection is only valid for six months. After that time the burden of proof shifts back to the consumer and is allocated in accordance with the general rule on the allocation of the burden of proof found in Article 150 Rv.[273] Consequently, the burden of proof that the defects which became apparent after the expiry of six months, existed at the time of delivery, lies with the consumer. Summing up, Article 7:18 (2) BW introduces a time-restricted presumption of non-conformity applicable only to consumer sales.

526. During the implementation process, a debate regarding the applicability of the presumption of non-conformity to the sale of animals took place. There were arguments supporting a general exclusion of the application of the presumption of non-conformity to sales of animals.[274] It has been explained that the animals may suffer from unprofessional care given by the buyer, or even from a change in the environment and treatment. This may already result in the subsequent non-conformity (for example behavioural disorders – *stalgebreken*). The animals can also suffer from hidden or genetic diseases. Furthermore, almost all evidence supporting or denying non-conformity requires very costly expert opinion.[275] According to the advocates of such exclusion, due to the above facts animals should not be treated in the same way as manufactured goods.[276] However, in the end, just

269 Definition of consumer sales in the Netherlands; Chapter 3, para 195.

270 Further referred to as legislative documents.

271 Hijma 2011, p. 31, 32.

272 MvT *Kamerstukken* 2000-2001, 27 809 nr. 3, p. 3; Castermans and Krans 2013 (T&C Vermogensrecht), art. 7:18, aant. 4; Asser/Hijma 7-I* 2013, nr. 332a; Frenk 2003, p. 957.

273 Chapter 2, para 83.

274 NMvA *Kamerstukken I* 2003 27 809, nr. 32, p. 3, 4.

275 NMvA *Kamerstukken I*, 2003 27 809 nr. 32, p. 3, 4.

276 Van Dongen and De Feijter 2010, sub 7, p. 8; Van Eerten 2008, p. 60.

as in Germany, it was decided not to exclude the sale of animals from the scope of consumer sale and the scope of the presumption of non-conformity of Article 7:18 (2) BW.

527. The presumption of non-conformity found in Article 7:18 (2) BW appears to have been excluded from the sale of perishable goods. According to the legislative documents, when a consumer discovers defects in perishable goods and informs of the non-conformity within two months, which falls after the expiry date provided on the packaging and before the end of six-month period, it seems that the consumer is required to prove that the goods were already defective at the time of delivery.[277] Consequently, in this specific situation Article 7:18 (2) BW seems to not apply.[278]

528. Regarding the second-hand goods, the presumption of non-conformity of Article 7:18 (2) BW applies just as it applies to new goods.[279] The differences might appear while proving the existence of non-conformity, especially in respect of what the consumer was reasonably entitled to expect from the purchased goods, taking into account the nature of the goods and the seller's statements about the goods. It seems that in case of second-hand goods the expectations towards the goods are lower than towards the same new goods. The fact that the particular goods are not new cannot constitute non-conformity in the sense of Article 7:17 (2) BW.

529. There has been discussion surrounding the essence of Article 7:18 (2) BW, namely whether it constitutes a statutory presumption causing the reversal of the burden of proof, or whether it affects the burden of proof in another less serious manner.[280] The wording of Article 7:18 (2) BW '*wordt vermoed*'[281] indicates that this provision constitutes a statutory rebuttable presumption.[282] It alters the general rule on allocation of burden of proof of Article 150 Rv. Article 150 Rv provides that the party who claims the existence of certain facts and relies on the legal consequences of these facts must prove their existence, unless on the ground of special legal provisions or the requirements of reasonableness and equity (*redelijkheid en billijkheid*), a different allocation of burden of proof is required.[283] In normal circumstances, in cases of non-conformity it is the buyer who relies on the legal consequences of the existence of defects at the time of delivery and therefore he should

277 NMvA *Kamerstukken I* 2003, 27 809, nr. 32, p. 3, 4.
278 Smits 2003, p. 20.
279 Smits 2003, p. 7.
280 Valk 2010 (II), sub. 7, p. 4.
281 It is presumed.
282 Asser/Hijma 7-I* 2013, nr. 332a; van Rossum 2012, BW 7 Article 18, para 4.
283 Chapter 2, para 84, 85.

provide satisfactory evidence of these facts.[284] When a contract constitutes a consumer sale, thanks to the application of the presumption of Article 7:18 (2) BW, a buyer is released from the duty to prove the existence of defects at the time of delivery, if he has successfully established that the defects of goods became apparent within six months from the time of delivery. Consequently, the burden of proof that the goods were free from defects at the time of delivery lies with the seller.[285]

530. There is some uncertainty over what the importance of Article 7:18 (2) BW is. According to Hijma, in cases of non-conformity apparent within six months from the time of delivery, and even without the statutory presumption of Article 7:18 (2) BW introduced by the implementation of the Directive, in certain circumstances it would be possible to (factually) presume that at the time of delivery the goods did not conform to the contract according to Article 150 Rv.[286] Moreover, for many types of goods and defects such a presumption would not have to be restricted by time limit of six months. Therefore, according to the author, the scope of the application of the presumption, which could not have been covered by the general rule of 150 Rv is not too excessive. On the other hand, the fact that the European legislator decided to explicitly enact the presumption may lead to more frequent and systematic application of the presumption of non-conformity.[287]

5.6.3 *Conditions for the application of the presumption*

531. According to Article 7:18 (2) BW to be able to benefit from the presumption of non-conformity a consumer has to prove that the delivered goods do not conform to what has been agreed upon, in the sense that the goods do not possess characteristics that the buyer is entitled to expect and that this non-conformity has become apparent within six months from the time of delivery. If these facts are successfully shown, the judge must allow the presumption that at the time of delivery the goods were defective. Consequently, the burden of proving that the goods were free from defects at the time of delivery will shift to the seller.[288] The two conditions for the application of the presumption are identical to the Consumer Sales Directive as in all jurisdictions analysed in this study. Nevertheless, the content of these conditions may be different especially due to the different scope of the notion of non-conformity or different assessment of proof of the existence of non-con-

284 Rb Zwolle 21.05.2003, ECLI:NL:RBZWO:2003:AH8762; Asser/Hijma 7-I* 2013, nr. 332a; Van Dongen and De Feijter 2010, sub 1, p. 1.

285 For the answers on what does it mean for a seller see chapter 5, para 546 *et seq*.

286 Asser/Hijma 7-I* 2013, nr. 332b.

287 Asser/Hijma 7-I* 2013, nr. 332b.

288 Castermans and Krans 2013 (T&C Vermogensrecht), art. 7:18, aant. 4; Asser/Hijma 7-I* 2013, nr. 332a.

formity. The content of conditions for application of the presumption under Dutch law will be presented below.

5.6.3.1 Non-conformity

532. The first prerequisite for the application of the presumption is the proof of the existence of non-conformity. Articles 7:17 and 7:18 BW provide the respective criteria.[289] For the purpose of this section it is sufficient to say that in order to benefit from the presumption a consumer must provide evidence of (or lack thereof) the existence of circumstances provided in Article 7:17 and 7:18 BW. The important part in proving non-conformity is to determine what the consumer was reasonably entitled to expect under the contract and subsequently to demonstrate that these justifiable expectations have not been met.[290] The defect in question can also regard the incorrect installation.[291] In general, the courts seem to be rather lenient in accepting the consumer's proof of non-conformity. For example, in the case concerning the sale of a mobile phone, which two weeks after delivery appeared to have a crack on the display, the consumer was able to rely on the presumption of Article 7:18 (2) BW.[292] He successfully claimed the costs for repair of the display. Although the seller claimed that the defect must have occurred due to a fall, or unsuitable usage of the phone, evidence provided by the seller was insufficient. There are many cases when the consumer without having to provide complex evidence was able to convince the judge about the existence of non-conformity.[293]

533. For a considerable period of time, the issues of origins of defects and specificity of proof have not been considered by the courts. For example, in the case before the Rechtbank Utrecht, which regarded the sale of a horse, one day after the delivery the horse showed difficulties in walking.[294] The seller stated that because before the delivery the symptoms were not present, they must have occurred after the delivery. The court was of the opinion that the fact that the non-conformity did not appear before, or at the time of delivery does not necessarily lead to the conclusion that the origins of non-conformity did not exist at that time. In this case the court decided that the non-conformity resulted from the defective

289 Chapter 4, para 335 *et seq.*

290 Justified expectations in relation to the characteristics of delivered goods.

291 Hof Arnhem-Leeuwarden 26.11.2013, ECLI:NL:GHARL:2013:8982.

292 Rb Arnhem 09.01.2012, ECLI:NL:RBARN:2012:BV3827.

293 Rb Haarlem 24.01.2007, ECLI:NL:RBHAA:2007:AZ74480; Hof Amsterdam 01.03.2007, ECLI:NL:GHAMS: 2007:BA9978; Rb Haarlem 17.02.2010, ECLI:NL:RBHAA:2010:BM3339; Rb Arnhem 10.11.2010; WCLI:NL: RBARN:BO4047; Rb Alkmaar 20.06.2011, ECLI:NL:RBALK:2011:BR1997.

294 Rb Utrecht 25.03.2009, ECLI:NL:RBUTR:2009:BI1714, para 4.13; also Hof Arnhem-Leeuwarden 10.09.2013, ECLI:NL:GHARL:2013:6635; Rb Leeuwarden 26.04.2011, ECLI:NL:RBLEE:2011:BQ3070; Rb Limburg 07.08.2013, ECLI:NL:RBLIM:2013:4796.

factors which must have been present at the time of delivery. However, the defective factors were not identified or named.

534. There are also cases where the courts took more strict approach with respect to the possible cause of the defect. In some cases the consumer was successful after providing extensive evidence of the existence of non-conformity.[295] In other cases the court decided that the condition of non-conformity was not met.[296] The case decided by the Gerechtshof Leeuwarden regarded the purchase of a second-hand car, which after the delivery underwent numerous minor (standard) repairs. Several months after the delivery, the car suffered engine damage due to the insufficient amount of oil, caused by a leak in the crankcase. Based on the examination of the car, given the location of the leak, it was argued that it could have occurred while placing the jack just under the crankcase during one of the previous repairs. Accordingly, the court came to the conclusion that the consumer's proof of the existence of non-conformity was not sufficient. Consequently, the presumption of Article 7:18 (2) BW did not apply.

Also in the case of the sale of a young horse the court decided that the consumer had not sufficiently proven the existence of non-conformity.[297] Before the delivery the consumer had ridden the horse twice. Following delivery it became clear that it would no longer be possible to ride it, since the horse became stressed and dangerous when ridden. The consumer claimed rescission of the contract due to non-conformity. Allegedly the seller ensured the consumer that the horse was calm and very easy to ride. The seller denied such assurance and argued that the consumer was aware that the purchased horse was young, inexperienced and that only recently it has been ridden for the first time. Taking all the arguments of the parties into account, the court stated that the consumer had not sufficiently proven that the seller assured her that the horse was easy to ride. Consequently, she had not sufficiently proven the existence of non-conformity. As a result, the application of the presumption was refused.

535. A recent question arose within Dutch literature and jurisprudence wondering how detailed and certain the consumer's proof of the existence of non-conformity must be. This issue has been recognised in relation to the sale of animals. Is it sufficient for the purpose of Article 7:18 (2) BW to state (and prove) that the animal in question is dead, or is some further information on the cause of death necessary?[298] The same problem but in

295 Rb Midden-Nederland 10.07.2013, ECLI:RBMNE:2013:3233; Rb Midden-Nederland 09.01.2013, ECLI:NL:RBMNE:2013:BY8341; Rb Groningen 21.12.2011, ECLI:NL:RBGRO:2011:BU9714; Hof 's-Hertogenbosch 02.08.2011, ECLI:NL:GHSHE:2011:BR5909.

296 Hof Leeuwarden 18.05.2010, ECLI:NL:GHLEE:2010:BM6766; See also: Rb Rotterdam 06.10.2010, ECLI:NL:RBROT:2010:BO4071; Rb Groningen 19.08.2009, ECLI:NL:RBGRO:2009:BJ6974.

297 Rb Dordrecht 12.01.2011, ECLI:NL:RBDOR:2011:BP0723.

298 Loos 2004, p. 52.

the context of second-hand cars has been recently discussed by Hijma.[299] Furthermore, the Rechtbank Breda indirectly dealt with the described problem.[300] The court stated that the fact a speedboat sunk does not necessary mean it did not conform to the contract. In order to answer the question of non-conformity, it must be established whether the sinking was caused by the lack of characteristics which the consumer was reasonably entitled to expect or by the external conditions. In other words, it must be established whether the sinking was caused by the defect existing at the time of delivery.

As discussed in chapter 3, the Gerechtshof Arnhem-Leeuwarden referred preliminary questions to the ECJ.[301] One of these questions specifically regarded the degree of certainty that the consumer must establish with regard to the goods' non-conformity. The court asked to what extent a consumer must prove the facts and circumstances concerning the causes of the non-conformity in question. Whether it is sufficient for a consumer to state and prove that the product does not (properly) function, or is it required that he provides the source(s) of the defects and factors that have caused the final malfunction.

536. A similar problem was presented by Loos on the occasion of a dispute decided by the *Geschillencommissie Voertuigen* on 2 April 2009.[302] The case regarded the sale of a second-hand car *Fiat Stilo* delivered on 29 February 2008. After about two and a half months the car stopped working. The cause appeared to be a damaged engine block due to the staggered drive and timing belts. The causes of the staggered timing belts were unclear. The consumer relied on Articles 7:17 and 7:18 (2) BW and claimed the repair costs or alternatively rescission of the contract. The seller objected to the existence of the non-conformity stating that it is unreasonable for the consumer to expect that a car, sold without guarantee, with a kilometre reading at the time of delivery of 159,270, did not possess any defect. Furthermore, the seller pointed out that the consumer failed to carry out the purchase inspection. Consequently, based on Article 7:17 (2) and (5) BW the purchased car cannot be regarded as defective.[303] The *Geschillencommissie* decided in favour of the consumer and ordered the seller to repair the defective car free of charge. Loos observed that the seller had a point relying on the lack of non-conformity and stated that the members of the *Geschillencom-*

299 Hijma 2013, p. 259, 260.

300 Rb Breda 29.06.2011, ECLI:NL:RBBRE:2011:BR1086.

301 Hof Arnhem-Leeuwarden 09.04.2013, ECLI:NL:GHARL:2013:BZ6346 (Hof Arnhem-Leeuwarden 10.09.2013, ECLI:NL:GHARL:2013:6635), para 8.2, question 5. The question regarded the second-hand car which has been destroyed in the fire; Chapter 3, para 205 *et seq.*

302 Loos 2009 (de Geschillencommissie), p. 5, 6.

303 Article 7:17 (2) BW '*A thing is not in conformity with the contract if it does not have the characteristics which the buyer was entitled to expect under the contract, taking into account the nature of the thing and the statements made by the seller about it (...)*'.
Article 7:17 (5) BW '*The buyer may not invoke non-conformity of the thing to the contract if he was, or reasonably ought to have been aware of it at the time the contract was concluded (...)*'. Translation: Warendorf, Thomas and Curry-Sumner 2009.

missie did not sufficiently consider the above argument. According to Loos, based on Article 7:17 (2) and (5) BW there is serious uncertainty over whether the car can be regarded as defective. Pursuant to 150 Rv it is the responsibility of the buyer to prove the existence of non-conformity in accordance with Article 7:17 BW. Article 7:18 (2) BW does not facilitate this proof. It can only be applied when the proof of the existence of non-conformity has been satisfied, which according to Loos in this case was not obvious. He has criticised the *Geschillencommissie* for overlooking the above argument and for not providing sufficient justification and reasoning behind its decision.[304]

537. Upon investigation of the case law it seems that Dutch courts generally accept the proof of non-conformity provided by the consumer much more readily than for example German courts. As discussed in chapter 5, sub-section 5.4.3.1, German courts, especially in complex cases, often require the consumer to prove the origins of defects, or to exclude the possibility that he was a source of the defect.[305] Without distinguishing the instances of defects as it is done under German law,[306] several Dutch courts recognised the complexity of specific circumstances in proving non-conformity.

538. Summing up, it seems that under the Dutch law, especially in comparison to Germany, non-conformity is relatively easy to prove. This may significantly affect the frequency with which the application of the presumption of non-conformity is permitted. In general, the consumer must prove that the goods do not work properly, which is usually sufficient to meet the first requirement for the application of the presumption. Having said that, in several cases the complexity of defects amounting to non-conformity and the problem of certainty of proof offered by the consumer over the existence of non-conformity has been recognised. All in all, the courts consider the role and objectives of the provisions – protection of consumer interests seem to be lenient in accepting the consumer's proof of the non-conformity. Nevertheless, as mentioned, the issue of different instances and the complexity of non-conformity has also been recognised. Taking into consideration that there has been a preliminary question referred to the ECJ regarding this topic, the ECJ's decision will hopefully offer a more systematic interpretation of how detailed the evidence on non-conformity should be. Until then, the differences between different court decisions regarding the proof of the existence of non-conformity may well remain considerable.[307]

304 Loos 2009 (de Geschillencommissie), p. 5, 6.

305 *Sachmangel, Grundmangel, Folgmangel*; Chapter 5, para 441-449.

306 Hijma 2013, p. 259; Chapter 5, para 535.

307 It should also be borne in mind that the specificity of proof of non-conformity depends on the facts of particular case. In some simple cases no evidence will be required, also when the non-conformity not objected by the seller, in other complex (technical) cases detailed proof requiring expert report will be necessary.

5.6.3.2 Six-month period

539. Article 7:18 (2) BW states that the consumer must prove that the non-conformity became apparent within six months from the time of delivery to be able to benefit from the presumption of non-conformity. To be able to state that the buyer has successfully proven the existence of defect within the six-month period, it is necessary to determine when the six-month period begins to run, when it expires, and whether there are any special rules regarding its postponement, suspension or any other rules applicable to the limitation periods affecting the statutory period for the application of the presumption.

I Beginning of the period

540. Article 7:18 (2) BW states that the consumer must prove that the non-conformity became apparent within six months from the time of delivery to benefit from the presumption. According to Article 7:9 (2) BW the delivery should be understood as a transfer of the possession of goods to the buyer.[308] Furthermore, according to Article 7:10 (1) BW at the moment of delivery the risks connected to the goods are transferred to the buyer even if the ownership has not yet passed. Article 7:10 (2) states that if the consumer is in default of the acceptance of delivery the risk passes at that time. In cases when the contract regards goods in kind to be specified by the consumer, the risk passes at the time the seller has made the goods in question available for the selection and he notified the consumer thereof. Additionally, Article 7:11 (1) BW states that where the goods must be delivered by carriage by the seller or a third person to the consumer, the risks related to the goods pass at the moment of actual delivery. The seller is liable for defects existing at the time of delivery, even when apparent only after that time. He is no longer liable for the loss or any defects caused after the delivery.[309]

II Length of the period

541. To establish whether the consumer has actually proven the existence of defect during the six-month period, the provisions on counting periods in civil law must be examined. Compared to Germany and Poland, Dutch law does not contain specific rules on the beginning and length of the periods in civil law. There is a general Act on legal periods (*Algemene termijnenwet*)[310] which determines when the periods can expire, but it does not contain provisions regarding calculation of the periods as such. A general principle regarding the legal periods shared by the scholars and jurisprudence provides that a period starts on the day after the day on which the triggering event occurred.[311] Therefore, it

308 Castermans and Krans 2013 (T&C Vermogensrecht), art. 7:9, aant. 3.

309 Hijma 2013, p. 258; Hijma 2011, p. 33, 34; Asser/Hijma 7-I* 2013, nr. 332a.

310 Algemene termijnenwet 25.07.1964.

311 Asser/Hartkamp and Sieburgh 6-II* 2013, nr. 400; Verbintenissenrecht (Wissink) 2014, nr. 320; Opinion of the advocate general F.F. Langemeijer of 08.07.2011 ECLI:NL:PHR:2011:BQ3890, para 2.3.

appears that the day of delivery should not be calculated within the six months when the presumption of non-conformity applies.

Finally, the question arises of whether in case of a lack of Dutch provisions regarding the periods the Council Regulation determining rules applicable to periods should apply.[312] Article 3 (1) of the Regulation states that the periods expressed in months are to be calculated from the moment at which an event occurs or an action takes place. The day during which that event occurs or that action takes place shall not be considered as falling within the period. The above provision is in line with the general principle applicable in the Netherlands.

III Expiry of the period

542. As stated above there are no specific rules on the calculation of periods in civil law. The general Act on legal periods (*Algemene termijnenwet*) provides in Article 1 (1) that if the last day of the period falls on a Saturday, Sunday or public holiday, the period should be postponed until the first day that is not a Saturday, Sunday or public holiday. Nonetheless, Article 4a states that the Act on legal periods does not apply to the periods described as longer than three months. In this case, it is questionable whether the application of the Act should be excluded regarding the six-month period, or longer periods are to be treated in the same way by analogy. Furthermore, there seems to be a possibility to apply the Council Regulation determining the rules applicable to periods, as presented in the previous paragraph.

Based on the above, regarding the length and the expiry of the six-month period in the Netherlands the conclusions may be somewhat unclear. There are no express rules regarding the matter. On the other hand, it seems that up until now there have been very few practical problems with counting the periods. Furthermore, in cases of dispute it seems that in this context the court may have to establish which rules apply and how they should be interpreted with respect to the presumption of non-conformity.

IV Application of the presumption after the expiry of statutory period

543. The questions that arose while analysing other jurisdictions and which are also relevant for Dutch law are: what is the character of the six-month period, and what exactly must the consumer prove in terms of time of defects becoming apparent? The six-month period is interpreted as a period in which the defects must become apparent. It is not necessary for the consumer to complain or give notice of the discovered defects within this period. The question that arises is whether this counts also for the defects which the consumer discovered only after the six-month period expired but which already existed before that

312 Regulation (EEC, Euratom) No 1182/71 of the Council of 3 June 1971 determining the rules applicable to periods, dates and time limits; Chapter 5, para 374.

time. For example the consumer buys a leaf blower during the January sales. He uses it for the first time in the autumn, after the period of six months expires and it turns out to be defective. In general, it is accepted that even when the consumer discovers defects after the expiry of six months, but they objectively existed before and the consumer is able to prove it, the presumption of non-conformity shall apply.[313] However, it must be stated that according to the Dutch law, the above situation may prompt the question of whether the consumer has fulfilled the duty to inform stipulated in Article 7:23 (1) BW.[314] Consequently, the presumption of non-conformity applies to defects which objectively existed within the first six months and the consumer informed the seller of the defects within the reasonable time as provided in Article 7:23 (1) BW, even when that is after the expiry of six months.

5.6.3.3 Conclusions

544. Based on information provided above, it can be concluded that both requirements for the application of the presumption of non-conformity have been implemented in accordance with Article 5 (3) of the Consumer Sales Directive. Conditions for the application of the presumption from Article 7:18 (2) – (I) the existence of non-conformity (II) apparent within six months – are counterparts to the conditions provided in the Directive. Regarding the first requirement – the existence of the non-conformity – there are many cases when the consumer did not have any difficulties with convincing the court about the existence of non-conformity. On the other hand, the uncertainty arose of how detailed the consumer's proof of the existence of non-conformity must be. It resulted in the preliminary question regarding the degree of certainty that the consumer must establish in the context of the goods' non-conformity, referred to the ECJ. Summing up, although the courts seem to be rather lenient in accepting consumer's proof of non-conformity and allowing the application of the presumption, the uncertainty of the specificity of consumer's proof should not be disregarded.

545. Regarding the second condition for the application of the presumption, the existence of non-conformity within the six-month period, there may be uncertainty as to how the statutory period of six months should be calculated. The Dutch law does not contain clear rules on how to count the time periods in civil law. The interpretation of the matter provided by the doctrine appears to clarify the indicated problem. Furthermore, the question may arise as to what the consumer must prove in the context of the statutory period when the non-conformity was objectively existent but not detected by a consumer within six months

313 Asser/Hijma 7-1* 2013, nr. 332a.

314 In case of consumer sales, a notification within two months after the discovery will always be regarded to be within reasonable time.

from the time of delivery. In general, if the consumer afterward is able to prove that the goods lacked conformity at any point of time within the statutory period, the presumption of non-conformity should be allowed, regardless of the fact that he became aware of the existence of non-conformity after the expiry of six months. Summing up, although the uncertainty regarding the second condition for the application of the presumption remains, it should not cause practical problems.

5.6.4 *Rebuttal of the presumption*

546. This sub-section describes the seller's options for challenging the presumption of Article 7:18 (2) BW when its applicability has already been permitted. This is when the consumer has successfully satisfied the two conditions for its application and provided evidence of non-conformity becoming apparent within six months from the time of delivery. According to Article 5 (3) of the Consumer Sales Directive, the presumption applies unless 'proved otherwise'. Below I will illustrate what the characteristics of proof to the contrary under Dutch law in this particular situation are, and consequently what facts the seller must demonstrate to prove that the defects, whose existence within six months from the time of delivery has been proven by the consumer, occurred after that time.

547. In the legislative documents, the Dutch legislator explained that the seller does not have to provide positive and full evidence to the contrary to rebut the presumption of non-conformity of Article 7:18 (2) BW.[315] It has been stated that it is sufficient to cast enough doubt regarding the presumed facts for the statutory presumption to be impossible to stand.[316] Consequently, if sufficient doubts have been cast by the seller, the burden of proof that the goods were defective at the time of delivery should be shifted back to the buyer.[317] This view on the rebuttal of presumption of non-conformity has received mixed reactions, some showing support,[318] and others severe criticism.[319]

548. According to the Gerechtshof Arnhem, bearing the scope and objectives of the Consumer Sales Directive in mind, the seller's evidence that the goods were free from defects at the time of delivery must amount to full evidence to the contrary. *Prima facie* evidence

315 Explanation of *tegenbewijs* and *bewijs van het tegendeel*; Chapter 2, para 89.

316 MvA *Kamerstukken I*, 2002/2003, 27 809, nr 32a, p. 3. However, in earlier stage of the debate, the legislator assumed that the proof to the contrary was required by the Directive. See MvT *Kamerstukken II*, 2000/2001, 27 809, nr. 3, p. 19.

317 Asser/Hijma 7-I* 2013, nr. 332a.

318 Biemans 2007, p. 322.

319 Valk 2010, sub. 7, p. 5.

or a demonstrative probability of the lack of non-conformity will not suffice to rebut the presumption.[320] In the present case, approximately two weeks after the delivery, the horse appeared to make strange sounds and was diagnosed with *luchtzuigen.*[321] The seller submitted that this condition develops within two to three days, and therefore it is highly probable that the condition did not exist at the time of delivery. The court referring to legislative documents and the debate regarding application of the presumption to the sale of animals confirmed that the presumption applies equally to ordinary goods as to living goods. The seller claimed, using arguments based on legislative documents, that it is sufficient to rebut the presumption by casting enough doubt on the presumed facts so that the presumption becomes untenable. The court, after looking into the wording of the Directive, and comparing it with other national implementations stated that in order to provide sufficient consumer protection, evidence to the contrary cannot be understood as casting doubt, but it must be regarded as full evidence to the contrary. In the end, the seller was able to provide sufficient evidence to prove that at the time of delivery the horse did not suffer from *luchtzuigen.*

The above decision differs from the presented opinion of legislative documents in the final stage of the legislative process, which state that casting enough doubt on the claim that the goods were defective upon delivery is sufficient to rebut the presumption of non-conformity.[322]

Interpretation of the evidence to the contrary presented by the Gerechtshof Arnhem, rejecting the view emerging from the legislative documents, has been confirmed and followed in other cases.[323] The general reaction to the decision from Dutch scholars and practitioners was positive. First of all, the wording of the Directive clearly provides that the presumption that the goods were defective at the time of delivery applies unless proved otherwise. Furthermore, allowing the seller to cast doubt in order to make the presumption untenable would entail a lower level of consumer protection than the one emerging from the Consumer Sales Directive and other national legislation, for example German and English statutes.[324] Moreover, to rebut the presumption of non-conformity, Article 7:18 (2) BW must be read in light of the Directive as requiring full evidence to the contrary, not just casting doubt.[325]

---

320 Hof Arnhem 2.05.2006, ECLI:NL:GHARN:2006:AX6541.

321 *Luchtzuigen* – (cribbing) an abnormal, compulsive behavior or stereotypy seen in some horses, and considered a stable vice. It involves the horse grabbing a solid object such as the stall door or fence rail with its incisors, then arching its neck, pulling against the object, and sucking in air (Wikipedia).

322 MvA *Kamerstukken I*, 27 809, nr. 32a, p. 3.

323 Hof Amsterdam 23.11.2010, ECLI:GHAMS:2010:BP5515; Rb Almelo 05.12.2012, ECLI:NL:RBALM:2012:BY8124; Hof Arnhem-Leeuwarden 10.09.2013, ECLI:NL:GHARL:2013:6635; Hof Den Haag 03.12.2013 ECLI:NL:GHDHA:2013:4492; Hof Arnhem-Leeuwarden 25.02.2014, ECLI:NL:GHARL:2014:1388.

324 Hijma 2011, p. 37.

325 Krans 2010, p. 50.

549. The courts have ruled on the rebuttal of the presumption of non-conformity numerous times. In many of these cases the seller was not successful in proving his case.[326] Below, several examples of cases are given when the proof provided by the seller was insufficient to rebut the presumption of Article 7:18 (2) BW. The first case concerned the sale of a shower and steam cabin, which within six months from the time of delivery appeared to be defective.[327] The consumer discovered the damages, including scratches on the acrylic surface of the shower tray. In order to rebut the presumption the seller argued that the consumer must have used specific cleaners including chemical substances that affected the surface of a shower tray. Alternatively, he must have used incorrect luting (materials). The court decided that assumptions claiming the consumer misused the goods were insufficient to prove the contrary and prevent the presumption from applying.

Another decision, regarding the rebuttal of the presumption, concerned the sale of a second-hand car.[328] After the delivery, a vehicle appeared to have numerous incidents with the oil sensor and other parts of the engine. Leaving aside the technical details, the Gerechtshof Arnhem-Leeuwarden confirmed that to rebut the presumption of Article 7:18 (2) BW the full proof to the contrary is required and simply casting doubt on the character of the defects by providing unintelligible expert report is insufficient to rebut the presumption of non-conformity.

Another case where the seller was unable to rebut the presumption regarded bedroom furniture.[329] The consumer claimed that furniture that was delivered differed in colour from the ones displayed in the showroom, the installed locks were defective, wood used for furniture lost colour, and substance and resin rubbed onto the consumer's clothing and bedding. The court decided that the last factor in particular amounted to the non-conformity in the sense of Article 7:17 (2) BW. The seller had an opportunity to rebut the presumption, but the facts and proof that was provided were insufficient. The court found the seller's argument that the consumer should have expected that furniture made from natural (raw) wood might lose substance and colour, unsatisfactory. According to the court, the seller should inform the consumer that furniture made from a particular type of wood may lose substance and colour and in this respect cause damage to clothing and bedding. The seller did not make similar statements and therefore the consumer was entitled to claim that the goods did not possess the characteristics which he could have expected under the contract.

---

326 See: Hof Leeuwarden 25.09.2012, ECLI:NL:GHLEE:2012:BX9126; Rb Noord-Holland 13.05.2013, ECLI:NL: RBNHO:2013:10061; Rb Maastricht 20.07.2010; ECLI:NL:RBMAA:2010:BQ6158; Hof Den Haag 03.12.2013, ECLI:NL:GHDHA:2013:4492; Hof Den Haag 19.03.2013, ECLI:NL:GHDHA:2013:BZ6596.

327 Rb Breda 4.06.2008, ECLI:NL:RBBRE:2008:BD5195.

328 Hof Arnhem-Leeuwarden 13.08.2013, ECLI:NL:GHARL:2013:5954.

329 Rb Haarlem 10.06.2009, ECLI:RBHAA:2009:BJ2323.

550. Regarding the rebuttal of the presumption of non-conformity, the court can order the seller to provide specific statements and evidence to prove the contrary.[330] In the case decided by the Gerechtshof Arnhem-Leeuwarden,[331] the seller was ordered in the preliminary decision to provide evidence that the defects occurring in the second-hand car which appeared two days after the delivery were due to the faulty driving (including changing of the gears while driving too fast).[332] According to the Gerechtshof Arnhem-Leeuwarden, the seller did not provide sufficient evidence regarding the evidence order. Consequently, the original favourable to the consumer decision was upheld.

551. Summing up, to rebut the presumption of non-conformity of Article 7:18 (2) BW the seller is required to provide the proof to the contrary. Although the legislative documents in the end suggested that merely casting doubt to make the presumption of non-conformity untenable is sufficient to rebut the presumption, the case law rejected this interpretation. It was stated that the above understanding of 7:18 (2) BW would reduce the level of consumer protection in comparison with the Consumer Sales Directive and other European legislation. Consequently, as confirmed in presented case law[333] to rebut the presumption of non-conformity, the full proof to the contrary is required.

5.6.5 *Exclusion of the application of the presumption*

552. Article 5 (3) of the Consumer Sales Directive states that the presumption of non-conformity cannot apply if it is incompatible with the nature of the goods or the nature of the lack of conformity. Following the Directive, in Article 7:18 (2) BW the Dutch legislator implements both exclusion criteria. The Directive does not provide any explanation regarding these criteria. Similarly, the Dutch legislator with the exception of several examples given in the legislative documents, does not provide definitions or what the scope of the term 'nature of the goods or nature of the non-conformity' is.[334] According to Hijma, the European origins of the provision and the provided exceptions contribute to the peculiar character of Article 7:18 (2) BW. He continues that the exceptions from the application are formulated very broadly, which may contradict with the objectives of

330 Art. 22 Rv '*De rechter kan in alle gevallen en in elke stand van de procedure partijen of een van hen bevelen bepaalde stellingen toe te lichten of bepaalde, op de zaak betrekking hebbende bescheiden over te leggen (...).*'; For example: Rb Arnhem 07.03.2007; ECLI:NL:RBARN:2007:BA1777; See also Rb Almelo 14.02.2012, ECLINL:RBALM:2012:BV9721; Rb Arnhem 19.12.2007, ECLI:NL:RBARN:2007:BC2718; Rb Haarlem 21.05.2008, ECLI:NL:RBHAA:2008:BD2453.

331 Hof Arnhem-Leeuwarden 19.03.2013, ECLI:NL:GHARL:2013:BZ4794.

332 Alternatively, he had to prove that there was an agreement that the price for the replacement of the cylinder block was to be covered by the consumer.

333 Presented decisions are of first and second instance.

334 Asser/Hijma 7-I* 2013, nr. 332a.

Article 5 (3) of the Consumer Sales Directive and Article 7:18 (2) BW. Hijma also observes that the wording of the exceptions leaves plenty of room to the judges to apply the exceptions every time when it would be unreasonable to allow the application of the presumption and when the burden of proof should be applied in accordance to general rules of the allocation of burden of proof. Summing up he is an advocate of the reasonable interpretation and application of exclusion criteria contrary to.[335]

553. What makes defining the exclusion criteria difficult is the fact that there is no clear difference between the nature of the goods and the nature of the non-conformity. In practice they often overlap and what in one case might be regarded as simply the nature of the goods in another might be regarded as constituting non-conformity.[336] The presumption can be also incompatible partially because of the nature of the non-conformity and partially because of the nature of the goods. In fact, as explained further in this section (para 545, 546, 553), the issues of exclusion criteria correspond to whether the non-conformity in question may, with a sufficient degree of probability, be led back to a defect that already existed at the time of delivery.[337]

554. The task of determining the meaning of the term 'nature of the goods and nature of the non-conformity' has been laid at the feet of the domestic courts and the ECJ. In the legislative documents it has been observed that any specification included in the national statute might have been considered as contrary to the objectives of the Directive.[338] The main aim of the exclusion criteria must remain as preventing unreasonable and unfair results. As observed in other jurisdictions, especially in Germany and in Poland, there is a great deal of uncertainty regarding the application of the exclusion criteria. Below, the available interpretations of the exclusion criteria under the Dutch law will be discussed. The focus will be given to their function, and the examples of their application will be presented. The issues of exclusion criteria are presented in the context of several types of goods: perishable goods, animals, plants, second-hand goods, and certain types of animal diseases.

555. The Dutch legislator has addressed the questions of exclusion of the presumption of non-conformity in the legislative documents. The types of goods, which could in particular, justify the exclusion of the presumption are perishable goods with a short expiry date, plants, and particular types of animals with short life expectancy or requiring special living

335 Asser/Hijma 7-I* 2013, nr. 332a.
336 Asser/Hijma 7-I* 2013, nr. 332b.
337 Asser/Hijma 7-I* 2013, nr. 332b.
338 NMvA *Kamerstukken I* 2003, 27 809, nr. 32, p. 3, 4.

conditions and care.[339] It has been observed that especially in cases of the sale of animals the statutory presumption may lead to the irresolvable evidence issues for the seller, in particular, when it comes to hidden defects or health conditions.[340] The majority of case law touching upon non-conformity of animals regards the relatively expensive sale of horses or ponies. The purchase price sometimes reaches thousands of euros often leading to very expensive and time-consuming litigation, especially when a detailed expert report is required, which is almost always a case (not only in cases of the sale of horses).[341] Furthermore, horses (as well as other animals) are very sensitive to changes in their environment, training, treatment and care, which easily can lead to changes in their behaviour. Finally, in the case of horses, it is most often the change of stables and their transportation that can potentially trigger 'non-conformity'.

However, the evidence that a horse did or did not conform to the contract might be successful by providing clinical examination including x-rays, stating whether the condition constituting non-conformity was present at the time of the delivery or occurred after that time (*antidateren*).[342] Some conditions such as *luchtzuigen*, other behavioural conditions and some infectious diseases can develop within very short periods of time. When it comes to the conditions with short incubation periods, only becoming apparent after longer periods from the time of delivery, will be regard to not exist at the time of delivery.[343]

5.6.5.1 Incompatibility with the nature of the goods

556. As with the other systems analysed, general exclusions are nowhere to be found in Dutch law. In theory, the presumption of Article 7:18 (2) BW applies to all types of goods and all types of defects, unless it is incompatible with the nature of the goods or the nature of the non-conformity.

As stated above, according to the Dutch legislator the examples of the goods whose nature might be incompatible with the presumption are perishable goods,[344] plants and animals,[345] especially with regard to certain diseases.[346] However, it has been observed that the fact that the Consumer Sales Directive applies to the sale of animals in the same way as it does to the sale of other goods should not prevent the (relatively frequent) application of exclusion criteria where appropriate.[347] There are some types of animals for example

339 NMvA *Kamerstukken I* 2003, 27 809, nr. 32, p. 3, 4.
340 Van Dongen and De Feijter 2010, sub 1, p. 1.
341 Loos 2004, p. 52.
342 Van Dongen and De Feijter 2010, sub 2.1, p. 2.
343 The question remains whether the reason for that should be an insufficient proof of the existence of non-conformity or application of the exclusion criteria.
344 MvT *Kamerstukken II* 2000/01, 27 809, nr. 3, p. 20.
345 MvA *Kamerstukken I* 2001/02, 27 809, nr. 323b, p. 8, 9.
346 Loos 2003, p. 52; NMvA *Kamerstukken I* 2003, 27 809, nr. 32, p. 3, 4.
347 Asser/Hijma 7-I* 2013, nr. 332b.

animals with short life expectancy (six months or less) when the application of the presumption seems to be impossible. For example, if such an animal dies within six months there is nothing to indicate that the death has been caused by non-conformity. On the contrary, it was expected to happen within six months, given the character of the particular animal (character of the goods).[348] If certain characteristics are to be expected taking the character of the goods into account, based on Article 7:17 (2) BW these characteristics shall not be regarded as non-conformity.[349]

Another example of where the presumption of non-conformity might be regarded as incompatible with the nature of the goods regards the sale of food products. In particular, when the expiry date is shorter than six months, or when products' long expiry date falls within six months from the time of delivery. In above cases, it seems that the presumption should be regarded as incompatible with the nature of the goods.[350] Perishable goods with an expiry date shorter than six months should not be treated too differently from animals with life expectancy that is shorter than six months. In my opinion both of these situations could constitute grounds for the exclusion of the presumption based on the incompatibility with the nature of the goods (or nature of the non-conformity).[351]

557. According to Hijma, other goods whose nature may be incompatible are very sensitive animals requiring special care and particular conditions.[352] This example is less obvious than previous examples. In the latter situation if the consumer proves that he provided the necessary care then the burden of proof that an animal was free from defects at the time of delivery remains with the seller.

558. The jurisprudence already seems to have established a line of interpretation rejecting the exclusion of the presumption in cases of the sale of animals, confirming the statements found in the legislative documents. Below, there are several examples which support the above-mentioned interpretation of Article 7:18 (2) BW. The first case regards the sale of parrots.[353] After a veterinary check in the middle of September 2007, on 4 October 2007 the exotic birds were delivered to the consumer. On 26 November 2007, one of the birds appeared to be less active, and two days later it was taken to the vet. The condition of the bird deteriorated and on 24 December 2007 it has had to be put down. The post mortem examination showed that the parrot suffered from pneumonia and severe respiratory (and other) bacterial infections. The seller claimed that due to the fact that the parrot is a living

348 Hijma 2011, p. 39.

349 Again the question concerns whether there is a lack of non-conformity or the exclusion of the presumption because of the nature of the goods.

350 Valk 2010 (II), sub. 7, p. 4.

351 It does not mean that there must be a statutory exclusion of any kind.

352 Hijma 2011, p. 39, 40.

353 Hof Amsterdam 23.11.2010 ECLI:GHAMS:2010:BP5515, Rb Alkmaar 19.08.2009 ECLI:RBALK:2009:BJ5668.

creature and that it suffered from the condition of a relatively short incubation period, the application of the presumption of non-conformity of Article 7:18 (2) BW should be rejected on the ground of its incompatibility with the nature of the goods and the nature of the non-conformity. The court decided that the arguments provided by the seller were not satisfactory and that the presumption cannot be excluded only because the contract of sale regarded living creatures.

559. Another example regards the sale of a second-hand car concluded in September 2009.[354] Sometime after the delivery it transpired that the gearbox of the car was defective. The seller performed the reparation in his garage but demanded the consumer to cover the repair costs which amounted to € 1.459,47. The consumer stated that the car became defective within six months from the time of delivery, and therefore he relied on the presumption of non-conformity of Article 7:18 (2) BW. The seller argued that at the time of delivery the car was free from any defects, claiming that shortly before the conclusion of the contract the car passed an APK (a test for car and road safety – MOT test in England). Furthermore, taking the nature of the goods into consideration and given the fact that the second-hand car was six year old, the consumer cannot expect the car to possess the same characteristics as a brand new car, and therefore the presumption of non-conformity should not be applicable. The court did not share the above view and rejected the seller's claim for payment of the repair costs.

560. In light of the following example it may be observed that with respect to second-hand cars as well as other used products the application of the exclusion criteria may be justified.[355] In February 2009 a consumer purchased a caravan and then stored it for the winter months having only driven it for 150 km. In May 2009, in order to prepare the vehicle for the summer season, the buyer had the caravan examined. It turned out that the caravan had bent chassis beams. Claiming rescission of the contract the consumer stated that considering the time of non-conformity he is entitled to rely on the presumption of Article 7:18 (2) BW. Consequently, no further evidence is necessary.[356] The seller stated that regarding the age and state of the caravan (second-hand) the consumer cannot expect the same quality as a new caravan. Furthermore, the ANWB's report (Dutch Automobile Association) provided that there was a possibility that the buyer caused the defect himself while driving it from Friesland to his place of residence. Moreover, it was established that the consumer had thoroughly examined the caravan before the purchase and did not detect bent chassis beams. The court stated that the fact that the caravan is a second-hand product

354 Rb Leeuwarden 26.04.2011, ECLI:NL:RBLEE:2011:BQ3070; See also Hof Den Haag 19.03.2013, ECLI:NL:GHDHA:2013:BZ6596.

355 Rb Haarlem 19.05.2010, ECLI:NL:RBHAA:2010:BN0550.

356 Since the defects became apparent within six months from the time of delivery.

cannot as such exclude the application of the presumption because of its incompatibility with the nature of the goods. However, the combination of both criteria in the context of the facts and evidence led to the conclusion that the presumption should not apply due to the nature of the goods and non-conformity. Consequently, the consumer had to prove the existence of non-conformity at the time of delivery. Since he did not succeed in proving this, the case was dismissed.[357]

561. Based on the above case law, it can be stated that the question of the incompatibility of the presumption with the nature of the goods arises relatively often. The courts often state that although the issues of living organisms and their potential incompatibility with the presumption have been recognised in the legislative documents, it did not lead to a general exemption for animals from the scope of application of the presumption. The above justification is to be found in almost every decision denying the exclusion of the presumption as a result of its incompatibility with the nature of the goods.[358] Furthermore, in other cases where the issues of exclusion criteria have been raised, there is uncertainty over whether they actually touch upon the exclusion of the presumption or rather relate to the basic question of (a lack of) sufficient evidence as to the existence of non-conformity.

5.6.5.2 Incompatibility with the nature of the non-conformity

562. The second criterion for the exclusion of the presumption of non-conformity of Article 7:18 (2) BW is the incompatibility of the presumption with the nature of the non-conformity. As already observed, in many cases it is impossible to draw the line between the two exclusion criteria. According to the Dutch legislator, damage to a video recorder undoubtedly caused by a fall is an example of the situation when the presumption should be excluded because of incompatibility with the nature of the non-conformity. In the given case it is apparent that the defect has been caused by the buyer's use/misuse of the goods.[359] The presumption will still apply where there is doubt concerning the origins of the defect.[360] It is not clear whether a given example should be treated as an exclusion criterion or the lack of consumer's proof of the existence of the defect.

563. In the pre-implementation debate on the exclusion criteria for the application of the presumption, animal diseases were discussed in the context of the nature of the goods.[361]

357 The question remains whether the decision should be based on the lack of sufficient evidence as to the existence of non-conformity or rather on the exclusion of the presumption and lack of the proof that the caravan was already defective at the time of delivery.

358 For example: Rb Utrecht 25.03.2009, ECLI:NL:RBUTR:2009:BI1714; Rb Arnhem 10.06.2009, ECLI:NL:RBARN:2009:BJ4349; Rb Zutphen 15.02.2008, ECLI:NL:RBZUT:2008:BC4965.

359 MvT *Kamerstukken II* 2000/01, 27 809, nr. 3, p. 20.

360 Hijma 2013, p. 261.

361 NMvA *Kamerstukken I* 2003 27 809, nr. 32, p. 3, 4.

In Germany, the issue of diseases with an incubation period shorter than six months are covered by the scope of the nature of the defects.[362]

In the jurisprudence there are various decisions regarding the question of the incompatibility of certain animal diseases with the nature of the non-conformity. Interestingly, there are some contradictory decisions regarding the same non-conformity, namely *luchtzuigen*. The district court in Arnhem decided that due to the fact that the condition can develop in a period much shorter than six months it might be regarded as incompatible.[363] It ruled in favour of the seller however, stating that the seller was able to provide proof to the contrary based on the extensive medical examination carried out before the delivery. Nevertheless, the argument that *luchtzuigen* may be incompatible with the presumption because of the nature of the non-conformity has also been brought forward.

The Gerechtshof Arnhem decided in another case that the *luchtzuigen* could not be regarded as incompatible with the presumption.[364] In this case the court referred to the pre-implementation debate and the legislative documents, which did not mention animal diseases as a ground for the exclusion of the presumption due to its incompatibility with the nature of the non-conformity. The decision has been followed by the same court in the case of the sale of a pony also suffering from *luchtzuigen* just one day after delivery.[365] In the end, the court found the seller's argument that *luchtzuigen* develop within a very short time (up to seventy two hours) to be insufficient.

564. Another decision where the court refused to apply the exclusion criteria also regards the sale of a horse.[366] The horse was originally offered for sale for € 9,000. Before the contract was concluded the horse underwent a veterinary examination and was diagnosed with a bone abnormality. Accordingly, the parties agreed on a purchase price of € 6,000 – € 3,000 less than the asking price. Sometime after the delivery, the buyer claimed a rescission of the contract due to non-conformity. According to the consumer the horse was not suitable for dressage exercises at Z level or higher, the horse refused to do exercises and when forced to do so, became dangerous. The seller did not challenge the fact that at the time of the dispute the horse was not able to do the dressage routine, but claims that this non-conformity occurred after the delivery due to incorrect training. Pursuant to Article 7:18 (2) BW the burden of proving the lack of defects at the time of delivery fell on the seller. The court decided that the exclusion criteria, necessary for finding the presumption with the nature of the non-conformity incompatible, do not apply. In order to rebut the presumption the seller must provide that at the time of delivery the horse was in conformity with the contract.

362 Van Dongen and De Feijter 2010, sub 5.2, p. 5.
363 Rb Arnhem 24.05.2004, ECLI:NL:RBARN:2004:AP4372.
364 Hof Arnhem 2.05.2006, ECLI:NL:GHARN:2006:AX6541.
365 Rb Arnhem 18.01.2012, ECLI:NL:RBARN:2012:BV3590.
366 Rb Arnhem 11.10.2006, ECLI:NL:RBARN:2006:AZ2929.

565. In the following case the court also refused to apply the exclusion criteria.[367] The case regarded the purchase of a fish, which shortly after delivery appeared to suffer from a bladder infection. The seller claimed that at the time of delivery the fish was free from defects and became defective only after delivery. According to the vet, from 19 September 2007 onwards it was apparent that the fish suffered from health problems, which was cured thanks to the treatment it underwent. On 5 January 2008 it was established that the fish suffers from a bladder infection, of which the seller had been informed on 15 January 2008. According to the seller, based on the symptoms existing already in September and October 2007, it was clear what was wrong with the fish. The parties did not dispute the fact of the infection and consequently the existence of non-conformity. The dispute regarded whether the fish was already defective at the time of delivery in August 2007. The seller claimed that due to the fact that the fish is a sensitive living creature, and that the bladder infection can develop within a very short time from the infectious parasites and bacteria present in any water tank, the application of the presumption should be excluded. Both the nature of the goods and the nature of the non-conformity must be taken into account. According to the court, none of the criteria apply and the examples provided by the legislative documents do not correspond to the facts in question. Therefore, to win the case the seller must provide full evidence to the contrary proving that the fish did not suffer from the bladder infection at the time of delivery.

566. The Gerechtshof Leeuwarden[368] also decided not to apply the exclusion criteria and consequently allowed the presumption of Article 7:18 (2) BW. In the present case the horse, bought for the seller's disabled daughter turned out to be disobedient and difficult to manage, thus unsuitable for the purpose for which it had been purchased. During the proceedings the seller has pointed out that before the delivery there were no indications of the behavioural problems (the horse won the Dutch Championships in the higher class for ponies). Furthermore, the seller argued that a horse is a living creature and these behavioural problems can develop within very short time, especially taking into account the long journey to Finland, the change of environment (much lower temperatures) and different training. The court decided that these arguments are insufficient to exclude presumption of non-conformity. Consequently, the burden of proof that at the time of delivery the horse was in conformity fell on the seller. The evidence regarding the lack of non-conformity at the time of delivery was assessed as unsatisfactory.

567. Looking at the amount of case law touching upon the issues of the exclusion criteria, it must be said that the Dutch courts are very reluctant to apply them, which seems to be

367 Rb Arnhem 10.06.2009, ECLI:NL:RBARN:2009:BJ4349.
368 Hof Leeuwarden 12.03.2008, ECLI:NL:GHLEE:2008:BC8175.

favourable to the consumer.[369] Below I will present the cases where the seller was allowed to rely on the exclusion criteria and the application of the presumption was successfully excluded because of its incompatibility with the nature of the non-conformity. Both cases regard the sale of dressage horse.

568. The first case concerns the sale of a pony (Pony 'N') which successfully participated in the national and international dressage competitions, including the European Championships.[370] The pony was delivered to the buyer in 2003. Shortly afterwards, as the owner's daughter had decided to retire from competitive sport, he decided to sell the pony. The new owner had insufficient expertise and therefore concluded a contract with an intermediary to find a buyer for the pony. In June 2003 the pony was sold. In November 2003, within a period of six months from the time of delivery, a new owner demanded (from the company and previous owner) a rescission of the contract due to non-conformity. The pony demonstrated serious behavioural problems, disobedience and insubordination making it unsuitable for dressage competitions. Pursuant to Article 7:18 (2) BW the burden of proof that at the time of delivery the pony was free from defects fell on the seller. The court concurred with the seller's arguments and concluded that because the pony is a living creature, with its own energy, character, and interaction with the environment, it must be treated differently to that of a manufactured product. The existence of behavioural problems, which develop mostly due to a change in the environment, living conditions and care and treatment provided, cannot be presumed to exist at the time of delivery. Due to the incompatibility of the presumption and because of the nature of the goods (animal) and the nature of the non-conformity (behavioural problems) the application of the presumption was excluded. Consequently, the burden of proof that at the time of delivery the pony was afflicted with defects lies with the consumer.

569. In the second case[371] the parties concluded a contract of sale for a horse on 28 June 2008. Two days before the contract was signed the horse was examined and approved by a vet. On 3 July 2008 the horse was transported to England at the expenses of the buyer. Upon delivery some problems with the horse were encountered. On 7 August 2008 the horse was again examined by a vet. It was diagnosed with lameness, and swelling which might have been caused by the current lameness, an old injury or strain, or could be insignificant. On 14 August the horse was examined by another vet, who confirmed that the horse was partially lame, and there was swelling. The horse was prescribed a box rest with gradual return to work. By e-mail of 18 August 2008 the buyer informed the seller

369 Other cases where the seller (unsuccessfully) tried to rely on the exclusion criteria: Rb Amsterdam 09.11.2011, ECLI:NL:RBAMS:2011:BV2833.

370 Rb Arnhem 6.09.2006, ECLI:NL:RBARN:2005:AT2927.

371 Rb Haarlem 12.05.2010, ECLI:NL:RBHAA:2010:BN1607.

that from the time of the horse's arrival they had been unable to do anything with the horse due to the persistent lameness. The buyer demanded rescission of contract due to the non-conformity. The court ordered a veterinary investigation which was carried out on 20 July 2009 (almost one year later). The report stated that based on the photos and tests dating from August 2008 it was inconclusive as to whether the horse suffered from the injury. From then on no further tests were carried out, and in July 2009 it was no longer possible to discover the cause of the lameness that occurred in 2008. The buyer claimed non-conformity because the horse did not correspond to what the buyer was entitled to expect from a dressage horse. According to the claimant, the horse suffered from an injury and was therefore not healthy. The non-conformity became apparent within six months from the delivery and the consumer relied on the presumption of Article 7:18 (2) BW. The seller admitted that at the moment of dispute the horse suffered from an injury. However, he claimed that at the time of delivery the horse was healthy and therefore in conformity and it became defective only after that time. Furthermore, he claimed that the presumption should be excluded because its incompatibility with the nature of the goods or the nature of the non-conformity. The seller claims that the horse is a living creature and that this fact justifies the exclusion of the presumption. Furthermore, the injury in question can have multiple sources, such as changes of environment, care and treatment, a long journey and, unprofessional care. This supports the argument that the presumption should be excluded due to the nature of the non-conformity. The court denied the exclusion because of the nature of the goods, as in accordance with the legislative documents the application of presumption cannot be excluded merely because the sale regards animals. However, the court considered the nature of the non-conformity and took following facts under consideration:

1. According to medical examination made on 26 June the horse was healthy and suitable to compete.
2. On 17 May the seller has competed and the horse won one 'proof'.
3. The buyers saw and rode the horse on 21-22 June.
4. The horse had been on a very long journey with very little space.
5. Normally, the horse trained every day but during the journey it stood still.
6. The horse kicked the walls of the stable upon arrival.
7. None of the medical tests after discovery of injury were conclusive whether the injury has existed before or occurred after 3 July 2008.

The court stated that the presumption would be excluded because of its incompatibility with the nature of the non-conformity, and therefore the general rule on allocation of the burden of proof from 150 Rv should apply. Accordingly, to win the case, the buyer must prove that the injury existed on 1 July 2008 (delivery – payment).

Regarding the above case, again uncertainty exists over whether there was a sufficient evidence of the existence of defects at the time of delivery. The seller was not able to convince the judge that the horse was defect-free at the time of delivery, otherwise, he would be able to rebut the presumption. On the other hand, arguments provided by the seller brought sufficient degree of probability that the non-conformity in question has not existed at the time of delivery. For this reason the judge decided to exclude the presumption of non-conformity and apply the general rule of the burden of proof.

5.6.5.3 Conclusions

570. The Dutch legislator has implemented the exclusion criteria in light of the Directive. Nevertheless in practice the application of the exclusion criteria causes considerable problems. One of the reasons is a lack of a clear definition of the nature of the goods and the nature of the non-conformity and the fact that they very often overlap. As with other jurisdictions, Dutch law does not provide for general exclusions of application of the presumption. It means that in cases which increase the chances of incompatibility such as the sale of perishable goods, plants, second-hand goods and animals, the exclusion criteria must be considered individually.[372]

571. Based on discussed case law it can be concluded that the Dutch judges are hesitant to allow the application of the exclusion criteria. From the presented case law analysis there are only a handful of cases where the application of presumption was excluded because of its incompatibility with the nature of the goods or the nature of the non-conformity. More often than not, the claims relying on the exclusion criteria are rejected.

572. Dutch courts often refuse the application of the exclusion criteria by referring to the legislative documents. For example, regarding the sale of animals, the legislative documents provide that there should not be any general exclusion of the application of presumption because of the incompatibility of the presumption with the nature of the goods. On the other hand, such exclusion should not be prevented in cases where the circumstances indicating incompatibility occur, for example, animals with a short life expectancy. In my opinion, standing by the legislative documents does not always ensure the correct results. First of all, these documents were drafted before any case law regarding the application of the presumption was ever adjudicated, making it impossible to predict all potential situations regarding the nature of the goods or the nature of the non-conformity that may arise. Furthermore, the fact that in the legislative documents it is stated that the application of the presumption cannot be generally excluded because of the nature of the goods and the nature of the non-conformity, does not mean that in the particular circumstances of the

372 Van Dongen and De Feijter 2010, sub 5.1, p. 5.

sale of animals or plants (or other goods) the application of presumption must not be excluded due to such incompatibility. In other words, it does not mean that the exclusion criteria may never be applied because of the nature of the goods when it comes to the sale of animals.

573. Finally it should be noted that the jurisprudence regarding the exclusion criteria covers somewhat inconsistent results, which may require further clarification. In the case known as Pony 'N' the court of first and second instance in Arnhem approved the exclusion of the presumption, while in other comparable cases regarding the same non-conformity (*luchtzuigen*), the same court refused such exclusion. There are further differences in courts' decisions and their justifications regarding the application of the exclusion criteria throughout the country. At this point, it seems that the level of legal certainty as to the scope of application of the exclusion criteria is not satisfactory.

The line of reasoning in cases of incompatibility with the nature of the non-conformity has been criticised by the doctrine, by practitioners in particular.[373] Contrary to the legislative documents and case law, some authors believe that there should be a general exclusion of the application of presumption of non-conformity regarding the sale of animals.[374]

5.6.6 *Road map of the presumption*

574. This sub-section will discuss how the scheme of the presumption is constructed and how it might be applied. Furthermore, the relationship between the particular stages of the presumption as well as the defences/arguments available to both parties will be presented. Some of the elements have been already discussed but will be repeated for the purpose of creating some kind of roadmap of the presumption of Article 7:18 (2) BW.

Article 7:18 (2) BW provides that if the non-conformity of goods appears within six months from the time of delivery, it is presumed to have existed at that time, unless it is proven otherwise, or the presumption is incompatible with the nature of the goods or the nature of the non-conformity. To benefit from the presumption, the consumer must prove the existence of non-conformity and the fact that it became apparent within six months from the time of delivery. The notion of non-conformity corresponds to the lack of reasonable expectations of the consumer towards the goods that he might have under the contract, taking the nature of the goods and the statements about the goods made by the seller into account. Consequently, the consumer must show what he is entitled to expect and that these expectations have not been met. The Dutch approach to evidence of the existence of non-conformity is quite lenient. In particular, in comparison to the German approach,

373 Van Dongen and De Feijter 2010, sub 7, p. 8; Van Eerten 2008, p. 60.
374 Van Dongen and De Feijter 2010, sub 7 p. 8.

it is relatively easy to prove that the goods do not possess characteristics meeting justifiable expectations the consumer has. Having said that, there are also several cases, including the decision referring preliminary questions to the ECJ,[375] where the issues of specificity of proof appeared and the degree of certainty of the existence and origins of defects were considered. Based on this case law, at this point the tolerant approach appears to prevail.

At the stage of conditions for the presumption, the sellers often try to challenge the existence of non-conformity and the rights to remedies by claiming that the consumer did not inform the seller about the defects soon enough. Article 7:23 BW provides that the buyer must inform the seller about the non-conformity within the reasonable time from its discovery. In any case, notice about the defects given within two months is to be regarded as given within a reasonable time.

575. When the presumption applies, the seller can rebut it by providing evidence to the contrary. This has been confirmed by the case law. A judicial interpretation of the rebuttal of the presumption differs from the final opinion about the matter presented by the legislator in the legislative documents. The Dutch legislator stated that casting enough doubt over the presumed facts so that the presumption is untenable is sufficient to rebut the presumption of non-conformity. This view on rebuttal was eventually rejected by the judiciary as it decreased the level of consumer protection in comparison to the one emerging from the Directive and national legislation, for example English and German statutes. Summing up, to rebut the presumption of non-conformity the seller must provide positive evidence to the contrary, that the goods were in conformity at the time of delivery or that the non-conformity occurred after the delivery.

576. According to Article 7:18 (2) BW, the presumption of non-conformity can be excluded when it is incompatible with the nature of the goods or the nature of the non-conformity. There are no general exclusions. The seller can attempt to prove that in particular circumstances the nature of the goods or the nature of the non-conformity require exclusion of the presumption. The exclusion criteria are rarely allowed and the courts have not yet established a uniform interpretation where the above-mentioned arguments will be sufficient to prevent the application of the presumption. Regarding the nature of the goods, the types of goods discussed most are animals (with a short life expectancy, and requiring special care), second-hand goods, and perishable goods. Interestingly, in the legislative documents it is provided that the presumption cannot be excluded because of the incompatibility with the nature of the goods merely because the contract of sale regards animals. The Dutch courts refer to the above statement almost every time the exclusion of the presumption is denied and a case regards the sale of animals. Regarding the nature of the non-

375 Hof Arnhem-Leeuwarden 09.04.2013, ECLI:NL:GHARL:2013:BZ6346.

conformity, the legislator mentioned the defects, which have been caused by the consumer (a damaged video recorder). In this case it seems that the example rather refers to the failure to prove the existence of defects or successful evidence to the contrary, instead of the argument for exclusion of the application of the presumption of non-conformity as such.

5.6.7 *Conclusions*

577. The introduction of a six-month presumption of non-conformity in Dutch law has broadly been accepted. After analysing the application of the presumption of non-conformity of Article 7:18 (2) BW it can be stated that in practice there is a great deal of uncertainty regarding, in particular, questions of the proof of the existence of non-conformity, rebuttal and exclusion criteria. Over the decade of Article 7:18 (2) BW applying to consumer contracts no clear interpretation of this provision has been achieved. It can be however observed that the Dutch courts have been so far relatively lenient in accepting consumer's proof as the existence of non-conformity. This practice positively affects the frequency in which the presumption of non-conformity applies.

578. The clear scope of the application and uniform interpretation of Article 7:18 (2) is necessary for the proper functioning of consumer sales law. First of all, the above-mentioned provisions alter general rules on the allocation of the burden of proof, which may have significant influence on the final results of litigation. Furthermore, the rule of Article 7:18 (2) BW touches upon the interests of all involved parties, consumers as well as sellers. It aims principally to ease the burden of proof borne by the consumers, but at the same time it includes reservations, which protect sellers from the obligation to provide impossible or unreasonable statements. Therefore, it must be concluded that the clear and uniform application of Article 7:18 (2) BW is in the best interests of both parties to the contract.

579. To rebut the presumption the seller has to provide evidence to the contrary. What that exactly means in practice depends on the capacity of the term 'evidence to the contrary'. The Dutch legislator adopted in the end of the legislative process the view that the presumption can be rebutted by casting sufficient doubts about the possibility of the defect at the time of delivery. This view has been rejected by the Dutch judiciary who stated that taking the function and purpose of the presumption into account the full positive evidence that the goods were defect-free at the time of delivery must be provided.

580. It has been observed that in some cases of sale of animals, suffering from specific diseases (or in cases of the sale of plants) a requirement of full evidence to the contrary is

difficult. Additionally, the exclusion criteria are rarely applied in the sale of animals. This leads to the question of whether the presumption should apply generally to sales of living creatures.[376] The issue could be solved by introducing a general exclusion for the sale of animals from the scope of consumer sale to Article 7:5 BW, or determining the scope of the exclusion criteria that covers the sale of animals suffering from certain diseases making the presumption incompatible due to the nature of the goods or the non-conformity.

Regarding the application of the exclusion criteria because of the incompatibility with the nature of the goods or the nature of the non-conformity, there is a considerable number of cases considering the application of the criteria. They most often regard the sale of animals and second-hand goods. At this point there is no uniform interpretation of the exclusion criteria and their applicability is entirely at the judges' discretion.

581. The implementation of the presumption of non-conformity has serious consequences for the general (national) rules on the burden of proof as they are altered by the European legislator. Taking the frequency of the conclusion of consumer sale contracts and potential number of cases where the presumption of non-conformity can be applicable into consideration, the presumption of Article 7:18 (2) BW has great practical and legal importance.[377]

5.7 Conclusions

582. The provision introducing the presumption of non-conformity has proven to be one of the most important provisions of the Consumer Sales Directive. Its correct implementation is crucial for consumers' ability to obtain remedies for the delivery of non-conforming goods. After comparing the regulation of the presumption of non-conformity in four jurisdictions it must be stated that in general all the Member States examined implemented Article 5 (3) of the Directive correctly. Had that not been the case, the Commission would have undertaken appropriate measures against the Member States' governments to ensure correct implementation. On the other hand, there are considerable differences in application of the presumption between Member States and there is much uncertainty regarding the proper functioning of Article 5 (3) in the domestic legal systems, affecting the frequency of the application of the presumption of non-conformity and the level of consumer protection in the context of the delivery of non-conforming goods.

583. One of the main failures on the part of the Polish legislator was to exclude the application of the Civil Code and introduce a separate notion of liability for non-conforming goods in consumer sales. Regarding the substantive issues, the Polish statute has a distinctive

376 Traditionally animals have been treated as goods when it comes to the legal transactions
377 Krans 2010, p. 49.

definition of non-conformity, which despite matching criteria found in the Directive, caused uncertainty as to its application. This uncertainty was caused mainly by the introduction of the division on contracts where the characteristics of goods are, or are not, individually negotiated. Furthermore, Article 4 (1) of the Consumer Sale Act does not contain the exclusion criteria. Theoretically, the presumption of non-conformity may also apply where such presumption is incompatible with the nature of the goods or the nature of the non-conformity. To some extent Polish scholars have resolved the above issue. Although there is no exclusion criteria, the same arguments should be admitted while supplying evidence to the contrary. Although this solution is convincing there are still some questions which can only be resolved by the legislator. The lack of specific case law regarding the exclusion of the application of the presumption makes it impossible to say whether or how these criteria operate in practice. A recently promulgated reform incorporates the presumption of non-conformity into the Civil Code and provides a much longer period where the presumption may be enjoyed. According to Article 556^2 of the Civil Code, the new presumption of non-conformity applies to defects which have become apparent within one year from the time of risk being passed. The new provisions remain silent concerning the possibilities for excluding the presumption. The introduced changes increase the level of consumer protection and simplify the application of consumer sales law, however they do not clarify all issues arising under Polish law in respect to the application of the presumption of non-conformity.

584. The introduction of the presumption of non-conformity in § 476 BGB has attracted a great deal of attention from German scholars, judges and practitioners. The application of § 476 BGB has also been discussed extensively by the BGH. In particular, the issues of the proof of the existence of defects and the issues of the exclusion of the presumption have received attention. Based on the above-mentioned case law it can be stated that to meet the conditions for the application of the presumption, a consumer must present solid, convincing evidence, often excluding the consumer's misuse of goods as a cause of the defects. This results from the extensive theory of defects and evidence, which is required to prove their existence. It can be stated that the application of the first requirement of the presumption cannot be regarded as favourable to the consumer, especially when comparing to Polish or Dutch legal practice. Regarding the exclusion criteria, there is still uncertainty regarding their application. There is no clear interpretation clarifying when the presumption is incompatible with the nature of the goods and the nature of the defects. Finally, it can be concluded that the judges tend to interpret the presumption strictly. It seems that this strict approach sometimes strips the consumer of his chances to benefit from the presumption.

585. The English implementation of the presumption of non-conformity raises many questions regarding its functioning within the English legal framework. Firstly, the presumption of non-conformity applies only to statutory remedies introduced after the Directive. With regard to the traditional English remedies, the application of the presumption of non-conformity is excluded. This means that to make use of one of them the consumer must prove that at the time of delivery the goods were not of satisfactory quality or that they were unfit for purpose. Consequently, there are two sets of remedies available to the consumer, and to each of them different rules on the burden of proof apply. This may cause legal uncertainty regarding the content of the consumer's/buyer's rights and the process of receiving these rights. Interestingly, for both sets of remedies, traditional and statutory, the same limitation period of six years applies. Another reason why the assessment of the implementation and application of the presumption in England is difficult is the lack of case law regarding the issue. Although the enactment of the presumption was generally welcomed in the literature, the matters of its application are not particularly popular among legal scholars. The recently proposed Consumer Rights Bill will simplify many issues regarding consumer sales, in particular implied terms and some issues of remedies but it does not provide direct changes to the presumption of non-conformity.

586. The Dutch legislator implemented the presumption of non-conformity in Article 7:18 (2) BW. The elements of the presumption align with the Directive. To benefit from the presumption a consumer must prove the existence of non-conformity which is formulated in the way that it makes providing the proof easier than for example under German law. The consumer must prove that the goods do not possess the characteristics that he was entitled to expect under the contract taking the characteristics of the goods and the statements made by the seller about the goods into account. Based on the case law it can be concluded that the presumption is applied relatively often. Initially, most uncertainty with respect to the presumption regarded the rebuttal of the presumption and the content of evidence to the contrary as well as the application of the exclusion criteria. Regarding the rebuttal, the Dutch legislator at some point of the legislative process stated that it is sufficient to rebut the presumption by casting sufficient doubt on the presumed facts. The jurisprudence rejected this view. The decisions in numerous cases of the courts of first and second instance confirmed that to rebut the presumption, the full evidence to the contrary is required and casting doubt is not sufficient to rebut the presumption. Currently, the most problematic matter seems to be the exclusion of the presumption. There are many questions concerning situations where the presumption should be excluded. Until now the possibility to exclude the presumption has been mostly considered in cases of the sale of animals and of second-hand goods. The legislative documents also mention perishable goods and goods whose defects were caused by the consumer. Looking at the number of cases it must be said that the presumption of non-conformity has an important practical

implication for Dutch consumers and although questions surrounding the exclusion criteria remain unanswered, the construction of the presumption and the way it is being applied by the Dutch courts seems to be rather favourable to the consumers.

587. There are many differences between the jurisdictions when it comes to the practical importance of the presumption. In England, there is very little information on the functioning of the presumption. The impression is given that the presumption and easing of the consumer's burden of proof were not necessary for consumer protection and that it was introduced merely to meet the implementation duties. In Germany, § 476 BGB plays a significant role. The scope of application of the presumption of § 476 has been discussed repeatedly by scholars, judges and practitioners. Despite the broad discussion and attention § 476 BGB received, to benefit from the presumption a German consumer may have to meet some heavy burdens regarding, in particular, the existence of material defects. In Poland, there were initially far fewer cases than in the Netherlands and Germany and the impact on actual consumer protection was lower than in those countries. Recently, the first decisions regarding the application of the Consumer Sales Act in general, and the operation of the presumption in particular, have emerged. In numerous cases, a consumer was readily allowed to benefit from the presumption. In the Netherlands, the presumption has great practical importance. It is applied relatively often and relatively easily. The general assessment of the application of the presumption, from the perspective of a Dutch consumer, must be a positive one.

588. Summing up, it is clear that the European legislator tried to ensure better consumer protection by enacting Article 5 (3) of the Consumer Sales Directive. In my opinion the presumption of non-conformity has potential to be a powerful protective measure. At this point it has significant practical importance, in particular in Germany and Netherlands, with the reservation that its application (especially in Germany) seems not always be favourable to the consumer. The required specificity of the proof to successfully show the existence of defects and a high standard of proof that a consumer must meet to demonstrate the existence of defects may prevent consumers from fully enjoying the rights contained in the Consumer Sales Directive. In Poland, the role of the presumption also gradually increases and with the extension of the six-month period to one year it may become one of the most important tools in consumer protection.

Finally, taking the functions and objectives of the presumption of non-conformity set out by the European legislator, it can be stated that the national legislators could have gone further in order to ease the consumer's duty to produce evidence. Regardless of this fact, there is still space for national judges to adapt the existing law to a high level of consumer protection. It seems that having the provisions as they are, in many cases the judges are still the last resort in the consumers' battle for fair protection against professionals.

6 Comparative conclusions

589. This chapter presents the results of the comparative study on the burden of proof in consumer sales based on the Consumer Sales Directive and its national implementations in four Member States: Poland, Germany, England and Wales and the Netherlands. After an analysis of the issues of national rules on the allocation of the burden of proof (chapter 2), the notion of non-conformity (chapter 4); and implementation, application and interpretation of the presumption of non-conformity (chapter 3 and 5), several topics proved to be particularly interesting given their potential significance for effective consumer protection in the area of sales law.

Alongside the focus on the presumption of non-conformity found in Article 5 (3) of the Consumer Sales Directive, the role and the influence of national rules on the allocation of the burden of proof (and other procedural rules) will be presented. Throughout this book the presumption has been analysed in the order presented in Chart 5.1. The discussion of national provisions regarding the presumption of non-conformity began with requirements for the application of presumption, accompanied with their consequences for the allocation of the burden of proof. It was followed with the possibilities to rebut the presumption, showing various options that a seller has to fight the presumption on the merits. The last element of each analysis regarded an application of the exclusion criteria, their character, and the consequences for the allocation of the burden of proof. This concluding chapter begins with several general remarks and continues in the same way as the analysis of the presumption of non-conformity presented above.

6.1 Aims and objectives of the presumption of Article 5 (3) of the Consumer Sales Directive

590. The classic allocation of the burden of proof[1] in relation to the non-conformity of goods in disputes regarding consumer sales was regarded by the European legislator as too burdensome. The European legislator emphasised the experience, knowledge and resources that a professional seller has and decided that the seller (rather than the consumer) should provide evidence that at the time of delivery the goods were in conformity with the contract. The presumption of non-conformity was enacted to simplify and to ease the consumer's duty to supply evidence in order to receive remedies for non-conforming goods. It applies under two conditions; where the consumer successfully proves the existence

1 *Actori incumbit probation.* The burden of proof of the existence of defects at the time of delivery/passing the risk (common for all analysed systems) lies on the buyer.

of defects and the fact that these defects became apparent within the first six months from the time of delivery. The application of the presumption of non-conformity can be excluded if it is incompatible with the nature of the goods or the nature of the non-conformity.

The presumption of non-conformity applies only to defects that have become apparent within six months from the time of delivery. The initial burden as to the existence of non-conformity as such and the fact it became apparent within the first six months lies with the consumer. Following the expiry of six months the burden of proof is allocated in accordance with the general rules, which will entail a consumer receiving remedies for the non-conforming goods once it is proven that the non-conformity existed at the time of delivery.

The presumption of Article 5 (3) of the Consumer Sales Directive is the first European provision, which affects national general rules on the allocation of the burden of proof on such a large scale. Until the implementation of the Directive, the rules on the allocation of the burden of proof belonged to the autonomy of national legislators. Bearing the above in mind, it should be a priority to establish a clear scope of application and uniform interpretation of Article 5 (3) of the Consumer Sales Directive as well as its national counterparts.

591. From the beginning, expectations of the presumption of non-conformity were high. Article 5 (3) of the Consumer Sales Directive has been initially regarded by some commentators as providing full protection for a consumer within the first six months (chapter 5, para 367, 368). The reality transpired to be quite different with respect to the actual application and the uniform interpretation of the presumption still needs to be improved. The reason for this may be that the presumption of Article 5 (3) of the Directive must be applied using the national legal framework. The four jurisdictions that were examined differ in many ways; such as how the Article 5 (3) presumption has been implemented. These differences were presented in chapter 3 and 5. They also differ in the scope of the notions on which the application of the presumption depends, for example non-conformity, discussed in chapter 4. Finally, there are differences in Member States' rules and theories on the burden of proof and the ways the issues of burden of proof are dealt with in litigation, as seen in chapter 2. The most striking differences affecting the application of the presumption of non-conformity will be presented in the latter part of these conclusions.

592. The implementation of the presumption of Article 5 (3) of the Consumer Sales Directive has received predominant acceptance in all of the systems presented in this study. The national legislators recognised the need to ease the burdens of evidence lying with the consumer in order to receive remedies for the delivery of non-conforming goods. Numerous times it has been mentioned in national legislative documents that the professional sellers' know-how, experience and access to the technical resources indicate that

the seller should be the one to bear the burden of proof for some time after the delivery (at least within six months). In this manner the legislators have tried to balance the interests of the parties and to ensure an equal position in pursuing their respective rights.

It must be said that not all aims and expectations of the legislation on the presumption have been fully achieved. The presumption of non-conformity turned out to be a complex legal construction whose application depends on many and varying factors and which may be particularly unsuitable when applied to the sale of certain goods. Summing up, it must be stated that the presumption of non-conformity does not always provide the level of protection originally expected, and in some circumstances fails to assist the consumer seeking proof.

6.2 Conditions for the application of the presumption

593. To be able to benefit from the presumption of non-conformity, the consumer must meet two requirements. He must prove the existence of *non-conformity* and that this non-conformity became apparent within *six months* from the time of delivery.

These two conditions for the application of the presumption have been implemented in all the legal systems studied.[2] Looking closely at the national legislation, it must be stated that although the wording of these requirements is to a great extent alike, based on case law and interpretations thereof there are considerable differences in applying (and interpreting) these requirements. The existing differences may affect the scope of the application of the presumption of non-conformity and the level of protection which is dependent on the correct application of the presumption.

6.2.1 *Non-conformity*

594. The notion of non-conformity is indispensable for the application of the presumption. Any simplification or impediment regarding the proof of the existence of non-conformity may influence the operation of the presumption, affecting the availability of remedies, and consequently, the level of consumer protection. The concluding remarks on national notions of non-conformity (defects) and evidence of its existence, required for the seller's liability and necessary to be able to rely on the presumption of non-conformity, will be presented below.

2 The recent amendments in Poland introduced a period of one year for the operation of the presumption; i.e. chapter 5, para 398.

6.2.1.1 Poland

595. The notion of non-conformity applicable under the Consumer Sale Act is understood rather broadly. It includes defects of second-hand goods and it covers legal defects, which is exceptional in comparison to other legal systems that were examined. The new reform of consumer sale, discussed in chapter 3, transposes provisions on the consumer sale to the Civil Code. It harmonises consumer sales and ordinary sales provisions and returns to the 'traditional' notion of defects.[3] The new definition of defects found in Article 556^1 of the Civil Code (in force as of 25 December 2014) fully covers the scope of non-conformity applicable under the Consumer Sale Act, with the exception of matters of legal defects. The legal defects are regulated separately in Article 556^3 of the Civil Code.

To increase the chances of successfully proving the existence of defects, the consumer should take the initiative and provide as many facts as possible. However, normally the consumer is not required to provide specific or detailed information about the origins of defects. For example, in cases of complex electronic goods, the consumer is not required to prove which part of the goods was defective and what the origin of the defect is. Taking into consideration both the know-how and technical services available to the seller, he is expected to provide or deny facts regarding detailed technical problems of the goods.[4]

Based on recent case law, it appears to be relatively easy for the consumer to prove the non-conformity of goods, yet it still depends on the facts and evidence provided by the seller. An expert opinion is often needed in the hearing of evidence to assess the state of goods at the time of delivery.

596. Under Polish law there is an additional construction (chapter 5, para 395, 411), providing protection for consumers against professional sellers. It is closely connected to the admissibility of a seller's proof challenging the existence of defects. There is no similar legal construction being interpreted in comparable manner in other jurisdictions examined in this study. Article 8 (3) of the Consumer Sale Act provides that if the seller does not reply to the consumer's complaint within fourteen days,[5] the seller is regarded as having accepted the facts, constituting the grounds for liability and consumer's demands concerning remedies. Given the complaint was sent within the statutory period, the seller can no longer challenge the grounds for liability before the court.[6] If the complaint was sent following the expiry of the statutory period for the application of the presumption, the seller will be allowed to provide evidence that the goods were in conformity at the time of

3 It returns to the notion of defects based on the Civil Code, which has been modernised in the light of the Consumer Sales Directive; Chapter 4, para 244-247.

4 Chapter 5, para 394.

5 The complaint must be concrete, it should point out specific defects of the goods or describe in which way the goods do not conform to the contract and it should demand a remedy (repair, replacement).

6 Pursuant to Article 8 (3) of the Consumer Sale Act, the consumer will win the case.

delivery. Article 8 (3) of the Consumer Sale Act and its interpretation gives the consumer an advantage in cases where the seller ignored a complaint and did not respond to it in time.

A similar provision will be transposed into Article 561^5 of the Civil Code after the consumer sales reform enters into force (25 December 2014). Given the fact that the presumption of non-conformity will then apply to defects which have become apparent within one year from the time of delivery, the interpretation of Article 561^5 of the Civil Code will most probably be adopted in accordance with the new period for operation of the presumption.

6.2.1.2 Germany

597. The presumption found in § 476 BGB applies to new goods as well as to second-hand products and the sale of animals. It does not apply to the legal defects of goods. The presumption of § 476 BGB concerns only the specific condition of the goods and not the existence of defects in general. This may have consequences for what evidence the consumer must provide in relation to the existence of defects. Accordingly, it is not sufficient to state that the product possesses some unidentified defects, the consumer must show the existence of the concrete defects in the sense of § 434 BGB.

598. In the German system there are many questions accompanying the first prerequisite, the proof of the existence of defects. The most important issue is when the existence of defects can be regarded as successfully proven. The uncertainty concerns mostly technically complex goods and their defects. Based on case law, the uncertainty appears mainly in cases of the sale of second-hand cars and animals.

Several categories (instances) of defects have emerged from the relevant jurisprudence. In order to meet the requisite level of proof, varying degrees of certainty are required. The first instance is an ordinary (common) defect in the sense of § 434 BGB. The existence of the circumstances outlined in § 434 BGB are indisputable, although the exact origins of this defect might be unclear. The existence of a defect is relatively easy to prove which (given that the second requirement has been met) allows the presumption to apply.

The second instance is referred to as a *Grundmangel*. The problem with the goods is said not to exist at the time of the passing of risk. To consider it as a defect for the purpose of § 434 BGB and § 476 BGB, it must result from the internal defective factors which were present at the time of the passing of risk. For example, engine damage caused by the malfunction of electronic sensors.

The third instance of the defect is referred to as a *Folgemangel*, which is also described as a problem with the goods that did not exist at the time of the passing of risk. It might have been caused by the presence of a *Grundmangel*, or it might have resulted from an external cause (misuse, wear and tear, accidental damage or through the fault of a third party). An example would be that the engine damage was caused by an insufficient amount of engine oil. The latter could have been caused by poorly executed oil changes, oil leaks, or by putting the wrong, or poor quality oil in the engine. For the presumption of § 476 BGB to apply (and to regarded a *Folgemangel* as a defect in the sense of § 434 BGB) a consumer must prove that the final problem with the goods results from a presence of a *Grundmangel* which had its origins in particular defective factors existing at the time of the passing of risk. In the given example, that could be a defective oil installation causing a leak. The court may allow a factual presumption that the *Folgemangel* constitutes this kind of defect. To be able to benefit from this factual presumption, a consumer must provide sufficient evidence that very often entails extended examination regarding possible causes of defects, in order to exclude the consumer's fault or misuse of goods. In the given example, that constitutes providing proof that the oil has been regularly checked and refilled when necessary.

It should be underlined that the German courts often consider which instance of defect took place in a particular case, and whether the consumer successfully discharged the burden of proof of the elements necessary for the non-conformity to apply. The burdens and duties of the consumer are treated strictly. What complicates the matter is the fact that there are no clear differences between *Grundmangel* and *Folgemangel*. Their scopes may differ depending on the complexity of goods and characteristics of defects.[7]

599. The literature on the subject contains some criticisms of the approach regarding the first requirement that could potentially decrease the level of protection in comparison to the level emerging from Article 5 (3) of the Consumer Sales Directive and the law of other Member States. Consequently, there are doubts over whether the German interpretation of defects indeed facilitates the correct application of the presumption of § 476 BGB.

Taking this criticism into account, an alternative solution could allow the application of the presumption found in § 476 BGB, even if doubts regarding the origins of defects remain. Where these doubts are well founded the seller could, using his knowledge, experience, resources and access to technical services, still be able to prove the contrary, or that the origins of the defect are the consumer's fault. Such an approach would still conform to Article 5 (3) of the Consumer Sales Directive and would ensure a high level of consumer protection.

6.2.1.3 England and Wales

600. The notion of non-conformity is defined as an infringement of express or implied term. The notion is understood broadly and in principle the presumption of non-conformity applies to the sale of animals and second-hand goods. It does not apply to legal defects,

7 Compare to chapter 6, para 595.

which constitutes a separate ground for the seller's liability. The legislator provides a separate section on non-conformity (Section 48F of the Sale of Goods Act 1979) which mainly refers to Sections 13-15 of Sale of Goods Act 1979 determining satisfactory quality and fitness for purpose.

Considerably less attention is given to the matter of the presumption of non-conformity in England and Wales as opposed to other legal systems investigated. Generally, introducing the reversed burden of proof in consumer sales has been welcomed in English literature and policy reports. The requirements for the application of the presumption are the same as in the Directive and other national legislative acts.

The recently proposed Consumer Rights Bill amends the provisions of the Sale of Goods Act 1979. Section 19 (3) of the Consumer Rights Bill expressly states that the goods do not conform to the contract if there is a breach of the terms described in sub-sections 9, 10, 11, 13 and 14 of the Bill. These sections resemble implied terms from the Sale of Goods Act 1979, however they are more detailed in determining specific circumstances when the goods do not conform to the contract. The presumption of non-conformity is located in Section 19 (14) of the new Consumer Rights Bill.

501. The definitions of non-conformity (satisfactory quality and fitness for purpose) are very descriptive helping the consumer to formulate arguments and provide evidence of the alleged non-conformity. These descriptions are even more specific in the new Consumer Rights Bill. The presumption of non-conformity applies only when claiming one of the statutory remedies: repair, replacement, price reduction, and rescission. The remedies available to consumers have been amended in the Consumer Rights Bill. If a consumer is not satisfied with delivered goods he is entitled to invoke a short-time rejection, rejection (rescission of contract), repair or replacement of goods or a reduction in price.

The presumption is not available to the traditional common law remedies, such as rejection of goods and damages, which (most probably) might be relied on much more often than the new remedies, because of the consumers' familiarity with these remedies. Under the Consumer Rights Bill, the presumption applies to all remedies that are available to a consumer according to the Consumer Rights Bill except the short-time rejection. As a result, the current situation provides there are differing allocations of the burden of proof depending on the remedy the consumer relies upon. This situation may cause legal uncertainty and confusion regarding available remedies and required evidence.

6.2.1.4 The Netherlands

602. The notion of non-conformity necessary for the application of the presumption of non-conformity is regarded as quite broad. The presumption applies to all kinds of movables, regardless of whether they are new or second-hand. It also applies to the sale of animals. As with other examined jurisdictions (except Poland under the Consumer Sales

Act), the legal defects are regulated separately and are not covered by the notion of non-conformity. Consequently, the presumption of non-conformity does not apply to legal defects.

Regarding the proof of non-conformity, in accordance with Article 7:17 (2) BW the consumer must show that the goods do not possess characteristics he was entitled to expect based on the nature of the goods and the statements made by the seller about the goods. The Dutch courts seem to be lenient in their assessment and acceptance of the proof offered by the consumer. The lenient approach may stem from how the non-conformity is formulated in the Dutch Civil Code. Specifically, the factor of reasonable expectations of the goods based on the nature of the goods and seller's statements about the goods may play a role. The issue of the origin of the defects has so far rarely been considered by Dutch courts. Recently, a question arose: how detailed and certain the consumer's proof must be in order satisfy the application of the presumption of non-conformity. A preliminary question regarding this matter has been referred to the ECJ. The ECJ's decision should give more clarity on how detailed the consumer's proof regarding non-conformity must be. The ECJ's decision may have an impact on the German interpretation of defects. Furthermore, until now Dutch courts have, in several cases, recognised the complexity inherent in proving whether the goods are defective. However, up until now it seems to have not affected the overall relatively tolerant assessment of evidence regarding the existence of non-conformity. This tolerant approach positively influences the frequency of application of the presumption of non-conformity.

6.2.1.5 Comparative remarks

603. The first requirement for the application of the presumption is successfully proving the existence of non-conformity. In theory, the requirement is the same for all examined Member States. In practice, there are considerable differences in how the notion of non-conformity is defined, interpreted and applied. In particular, there are differences in answering the question of whether the consumer has successfully proven the existence of a defect. A single simplification in the content of the facts and proof may substantially affect the frequency of application of the presumption.

As seen above, in comparison to other systems, under German law the consumer is in a relatively difficult position when proving the existence of defects, in particular where instances of defects: *Grundmangel* and *Folgemangel* are concerned.

The Polish and Dutch courts seem to be more lenient in assessing and accepting the consumer's proof, in particular when compared to German courts. The Polish court stated that in case of complex goods and their defects, a consumer does not have to prove which part specifically is defective or how it came to be defective. The seller is regarded as possessing sufficient knowledge and experience to provide the essential facts and necessary evidence explaining the details of the defective goods.

The recently formulated preliminary questions put to the ECJ by the Dutch Gerechtshof in Arnhem-Leeuwarden regarding the specificity of defects could be very important for the future approach towards the proof of the existence of non-conformity. Given the strict assessment of the existence of defects adopted by the German courts, the ECJ's decision may challenge German practice.

From the analysis presented in this study, it can be concluded that among the Member States discussed there are considerable differences regarding the first requirement for the application of the presumption, in particular regarding the facts that must be proven and to what degree of certainty they must be proven in order to satisfy the burden of proving the existence of non-conformity. These differences affect the application of the presumption and consequently they may result in an unequal level of consumer protection among the Member States in the area of sales law.

6.2.2 *Six-month period*

604. The second requirement of the presumption is the appearance of non-conformity within six months from the time of delivery. This regards a factual situation, the existence of non-conformity within a six-month period. This time does not constitute a period available for an activity or declaration of will on the part of consumer. As a result, the notice of defects does not necessarily have to be dispatched or received within this time.

There are several questions regarding the six-month period. First of all, when it begins to run and when it expires. Whether there are national rules governing time periods in civil law. Whether it is possible to modify (extend) the length of this period, or what happens when the non-conformity has been discovered following the expiry of six months, but it objectively existed within the statutory period.

6.2.2.1 Poland

605. According to Article 4 (1) of the Consumer Sale Act, the period of six months begins to run from the time of delivery. The new provision of Article 556^2 of the Civil Code extends the period to one year from the time of passing of risk, which in the majority of cases is the same as the time of delivery. This is an exceptionally long period in comparison to other countries studied. Article 112 of the Civil Code, which is one of the general rules on the counting of legal periods in civil law, states that periods counted in months end on the final day corresponding by name or date with the starting day. Therefore, the day of the delivery seems to be included into calculation of the period.

Regarding the possibility for modification of the period of application of the presumption, the Ministry of Economy issued a regulation (secondary executive act) providing that the time available for the consumer to claim non-conformity of perishable goods amounts to three days. It seems that in this situation the presumption also operates within the given three days, or alternatively its application can be regarded as being excluded as a result of the incompatibility with the nature of the goods.

There is a suggestion in the literature that if the expiry date is longer than the statutory period and the goods become defective after the statutory period but before the expiry date it could be presumed that they were defective at the time of delivery. Consequently, this would allow for a possible extension of the statutory period.[8]

In the situation when the consumer discovers a defect after the expiry of six months, there is an opinion that if he is able to prove that the non-conformity factually existed before the expiry of this period, the presumption of non-conformity should apply. Finally, in cases when the defects have been discovered after the expiry of statutory period and when the circumstances allow, the court may apply a factual presumption that the goods were not in conformity at the time of delivery and shift the burden of proving otherwise to the seller.

6.2.2.2 Germany

606. In Germany the period begins to run at the time of the passing of risk, which is when the consumer acquires possession and independent control over the product, unless the consumer is in default of accepting delivery. In practice, the moment of passing the risk essentially means the moment of delivery. Based on the general provision on counting the periods in civil law, § 187 (1) BGB it seems that the day of the delivery is not included in the time period. The expiry of the period is governed by § 188 (2) BGB, according to which '*A period of time specified by (...) months (...) ends, in the case of § 187 (1), on the expiry of the day (...) of the last month which, in its designation or its number, corresponds to the day on which the event or the point of time occurs*'. The six-month period may expire on Saturday, Sunday or public holiday. There are no available possibilities for extending or modifying the period of six months, however as already observed in Poland there may be some issues with the delimitation between six month period and the guarantee of durability found in § 443 BGB.[9]

Regarding the issues of proof that the defects existed within six months, even when discovered later, it seems that as long as the consumer is able to prove this fact, even if he discovered the defects following the expiry of statutory period, the presumption of non-conformity shall apply.

8 There is an uncertainty whether the mentioned modification should not be covered by the guarantee, consequently regarding the defects which became apparent after the delivery. The questions remains – further clarification desired.

9 Chapter 5, para 460.

6.2.2.3 England and Wales

607. When implementing the Consumer Sales Directive, the English legislator decided to amend the rules on the passing of risk to fit the character of the consumer sales provisions, including the presumption of non-conformity. In accordance with these amendments, in consumer sale contracts the risk passes at the time of factual handing over the goods. Consequently, the six-month period begins to run at the time of delivery. There are no general rules applicable to counting legal periods in civil law. The wording of Section 48A (3) of the Sale of Goods Act 1979, which implemented the presumption of non-conformity, and Section 19 (14) of the Consumer Rights Bill, indicates that the period shall be interpreted strictly. However, the parties seem to be able to extend the period in the contract. Furthermore, the English courts have discretion as to whether to extend the effects of the presumption of non-conformity in relation to the defects that appeared following the expiry of six months. If there are circumstances indicating the validity of such a solution supported by parties' pleadings and appropriate evidence the judge may formulate a similar factual presumption shifting burden of proof of the lack of existence of defects to the seller, even when the defects became apparent only after the expiry of the statutory period.

Regarding the defects discovered six months after the handing over of the goods, if the consumer is able to show that the non-conformity in fact has appeared within six months even when discovered later, the presumption will be allowed. Eventually, it comes down to whether the consumer's proof of the existence of non-conformity within six months from the passing of risk is convincing. Taking the notion of durability and the limitation period of six years into account, the practical importance of a six-month period seems to be moderate.

6.2.2.4 The Netherlands

608. According to Article 7:9 (2) BW the delivery should be understood as the transfer of the possession of goods to the buyer. Furthermore, pursuant to Article 7:10 (1) BW at the time of delivery the risks connected to the goods are transferred to the buyer even if the ownership has not yet passed. The six-month period begins to run at the time of the handing over of the goods.

There is uncertainty over the calculation of the six-month period. First of all, there are no statutory provisions on time periods in civil law. The general principle regarding the beginning of the period is that the day of delivery does not fall within the six-month period. Furthermore, there is a general statute regarding the legal periods which deals merely with the expiry of the periods. It provides that if the last day of the period falls on Saturday, Sunday or a public holiday, the period should be postponed until first day not being Saturday, Sunday or a public holiday. However, there is uncertainty over whether this statute applies to the six-month period, and if not whether there are any other rules applicable to the six-month period. There is no further debate regarding the six-month period. This may indicate that the practical questions that may arise from this topic have not yet been experienced by Dutch courts.

As to the discovery of defects following the expiry of six months, the application of the presumption does not require the consumer to complain or to give notice of non-conformity within six months. This counts for the defects discovered within six months as well as for the defects discovered following the expiry of six months. The only condition is that the consumer is able to provide evidence about their objective existence within the first six months from the time of the passing of risk.

In some cases, the seller could have a defence against the consumer that the latter did not meet the duty to inform him about the non-conformity found in Article 7:23 (1) BW. Although the requirements to invoke Article 7:23 BW have recently been set quite high by the Dutch Supreme Court, in some cases even when the consumer is able to prove the necessary facts, the presumption will not be allowed and the right to remedies could be excluded if the notice of the non-conformity was not given within the reasonable time after the consumer discovered the non-conformity.

6.2.2.5 Comparative remarks

609. Regarding the length of the statutory period for the application of the presumption there were originally very few differences between the Member States. In December 2014 the Polish amendments of the consumer sale, which provide the extension of the period of the presumption up to one year following the time of the passing of risk, entered into force. They considerably improve the consumer's position.

In all examined jurisdictions the consumer is able to benefit from the presumption even when he discovered the defect after the expiry of the statutory period, but he is able to prove that the defect must have existed before the expiry of the period. Additionally, there is room for a judge to apply presumptions of fact that the defective goods were defective at the time of delivery/passing of risk, even when the defect became apparent after the statutory period. Although in the jurisdictions investigated different factors may be taken into account, all jurisdictions recognised the judge's discretion in applying factual presumptions in the mentioned context.

There are several minor differences regarding for example, the start of the period (delivery, passing of risk) and counting of the period. However, they appear to be irrelevant for the protection of the consumer.

Summing up, the differences in respect of the statutory time for the application of the presumption found among the Member States did not seem to affect the level of consumer protection. The recent amendments to the Polish consumer sale act provide for much longer period for the application of the presumption. Starting from 25 December 2014 the presumption of non-conformity applies to defects that have become apparent within one year from the time of the passing of risk. Consequently, this provides for a considerably longer facilitation of the burden of proof which in practice means a higher level of consumer protection in case of the delivery of non-conforming goods.

6.3 REBUTTAL

610. Article 5 (3) of the Consumer Sales Directive provides that the presumption of non-conformity applies unless it is proven otherwise. There is uncertainty over what exactly the seller must prove to successfully rebut the presumption. What facts and evidence can be regarded to sufficiently proving otherwise, and whether there are differences in the possibilities for rebutting the presumption, which might have an influence on the frequency of the application of the presumption?

6.3.1 *Poland*

611. According to Article 4 (1) of the Consumer Sale Act, confirmed by case law, in order to rebut the presumption the seller must provide evidence to the contrary. In the first instance the seller can try to challenge the consumer, by proving that the goods are not defective. In case the existence of defect is undisputed, the seller must provide evidence that at the time of delivery the goods were in conformity and that the defect occurred after that time. The seller can make use of all available means of evidence, including factual presumptions. If the seller does not succeed in providing evidence to the contrary, or after providing evidence the doubts regarding the existence of defects at the time of delivery remain, pursuant to the principle of *non liquet*, the consumer will win the case. The issues of rebuttal as such will not be affected by the amendments to the new Civil Code, entering into force on 25 December 2014.

612. Pursuant to Article 8 (3) of the Consumer Sale Act the seller loses his right to challenge the grounds for liability (in particular the existence of defects) if he did not respond to the consumer's complaint within fourteen days regarding defects that occurred within the first six months, and therefore during the time of the operation of the presumption. This is based on the assumption that through a lack of a substantive response the seller accepts the facts constituting grounds for liability. The seller can still prove that the lack of response did not constitute acceptance of the facts in the sense of Article 229 k.p.c. For example, the seller can state he could not substantially assess the complaint because he handed the goods over to an expert for investigation. This interpretation has been confirmed by the Polish Supreme Court but only concerns complaints regarding defects that became apparent within the statutory period of the presumption. Following the reform of the consumer sales law, the above presented provision will be transposed to the Civil Code in

Article 561[5]. As the period of the presumption will be extended to one year, the above interpretation will most probably be adjusted accordingly.

6.3.2 *Germany*

613. To rebut the presumption of non-conformity the seller is required to provide evidence to the contrary in the sense of § 292 ZPO. The seller can provide this evidence in two ways; firstly, by showing that the goods were free from defects at the time of the passing of risk. Secondly, by stating that the defects occurred after the time of the passing of risk. The case law demonstrates that the seller can rely on the consumer's poor maintenance of goods only if specific instructions regarding the necessary maintenance have been stated in the manuals or safety rules delivered to the consumer together with the purchased goods.

Merely undermining the grounds for presumption or providing *prima facie* evidence is insufficient to fight the presumption on its merits. Evidence to the contrary is interpreted strictly. If the seller is unable to prove the contrary and no exclusion criteria apply, the presumption applies and the consumer receives remedies for the delivery of defective goods. The risk of *non liquet* lies with the seller. It should be stated that cases dealing directly with a rebuttal are rare. The main focus is given to the existence of defects or the exclusion criteria, which to a certain extent concerns questions of the existence of defects.

6.3.3 *England and Wales*

614. According to Section 48A (4) (a) of the Sale of Goods Act 1979 the presumption will not apply if it is established that the goods conformed to the contract at the time of delivery. In the proposed Consumer Rights Bill a similar rule is found in Section 19 (15) (a). Initially, it would appear that the seller must prove that the goods were in conformity at the time of delivery. In practice, he can meet this obligation by providing that the non-conformity can only have occurred after the time of the delivery. For example, the consumer or a third party caused the defect. The seller can also argue that the defects constitute ordinary wear and tear. The persuasive burden of proving that the goods were free from defects lies with the seller. He also bears the risk of being unable to prove his case, therefore in case of inconclusive evidence, the consumer will enjoy remedies.

6.3.4 *The Netherlands*

615. According to Article 7:18 (2) BW, if the non-conformity occurs within six months from the time of delivery it is presumed that it existed at that time. Dutch law does not

indicate how the presumed facts should be rebutted. In principle there are several ways to rebut the presumption.[10]

In legislative documents, the Dutch legislator eventually expressed the opinion that to rebut the presumption the seller does not have to provide full evidence to the contrary. It was said to be sufficient to rebut the presumption of Article 7:18 (2) BW by casting sufficient doubt regarding the presumed facts, so that the statutory presumption cannot stand. Consequently, according to the legislator, if sufficient doubts have been cast by the seller, the burden of proving that the goods were defective at the time of delivery should remain with the consumer. The above view received mixed reactions and has been subsequently discredited by case law. The Gerechtshof Arnhem stated that the seller's evidence that the goods were free from defects at the time of delivery must amount to full evidence to the contrary. *Prima facie* evidence or casting doubt is insufficient to rebut the presumption of Article 7:18 (2) BW. After comparing the Dutch wording of Article 5 (3) of the Directive with other language versions the court stated that rebutting the presumption with anything less than full proof to the contrary would lead to a lower level of consumer protection than the level given by the Consumer Sales Directive. This interpretation has been broadly accepted and followed in the decisions of other courts of lower instances. So far, the Hoge Raad has still not given a decision regarding the topic of rebuttal.

616. The seller can prove the contrary in two ways: by providing evidence that the goods were in conformity at the time of the passing of risk, or that the non-conformity occurred after the passing of risk, for example it was caused by the consumer's misuse of the goods. Mere assumptions that the consumer misused the goods are insufficient to prove the contrary and prevent the application of the presumption.

Regarding the rebuttal, the court can order the seller to prove specific statements and provide particular evidence to prove the contrary. The judge may play an important role in determining the precise content of the facts that must be proven and the evidence that should be submitted in support. In other words, in certain cases the judge may determine the content of evidence to the contrary and the means of evidence necessary to satisfy this proof. If the seller fails to provide evidence to the contrary, following the principle of *non liquet*, the consumer will win the case.

6.3.5 *Comparative remarks*

617. Eventually in all jurisdictions investigated it was agreed that in order to rebut the presumption of non-conformity the seller must provide full and positive evidence to the contrary. In this respect, all of the jurisdictions in question use the same interpretation. It

10 Chapter 2, para 89.

is also the only element of the presumption that is interpreted in the exact same way. In general, to satisfy evidence to the contrary the seller must prove that the goods were in conformity at the time of delivery or that the non-conformity occurred after the time of delivery. Still, there are possible differences with respect to the assessment and evaluation of proof in the context of rebuttal.

6.4 Exclusion

618. Article 5 (3) of the Consumer Sales Directive provides that the presumption of non-conformity does not apply if it is incompatible with the nature of the goods or the nature of the non-conformity. There are no further explanations regarding the scope of these reservations. What in one Member State might be regarded as the nature of the goods in another Member State may be regarded as the nature of the defects. The exclusion criteria allow the reversal of burden of proof to be disregarded as a result of the special characteristics of goods or defects. When the above criteria apply, the presumption of non-conformity is not applicable. Consequently, the burden of proof of the existence of defects at the time of delivery is allocated in accordance with the general rules on the burden of proof.

6.4.1 Poland

619. The Consumer Sales Act does not contain the exclusion criteria mentioned in the Consumer Sales Directive, as the Polish legislator decided not to implement them. In theory, the presumption of non-conformity also applies when it is incompatible with the nature of the goods or the nature of the non-conformity. There is no specific case law regarding this matter. Following the opinions of the doctrine, it can be argued that the non-implementation of the exclusion criteria is an omission on the part of the legislator. In practice the judge will most probably refuse to apply the exclusion criteria as they appear in the Directive. The arguments normally reserved for the exclusion of the presumption could be used while challenging the consumer's proof of the existence of non-conformity or as additional arguments supporting the rebuttal of the presumption. This indicates the close connection between the exclusion criteria and evidence regarding the existence of non-conformity.

620. The literature provides for different types of goods where the presumption might be incompatible because of the nature of the goods. The types of goods increasing the chances of incompatibility are animals, perishable goods and second-hand goods. Regarding the incompatibility of the presumption with the nature of the non-conformity the literature mentions certain animal diseases, with short or very long incubation periods.

621. The lack of exclusion criteria under Polish law, while they are expressly provided under the Directive, may cause uncertainty as to the scope of the presumption. When it comes to consumer protection, there is a need for comprehensive regulations. Unfortunately, new amendments to the consumer sale do not provide any clarification regarding this matter. Article 556^2 (2) of the Civil Code, which will replace Article 4 (1) of the Consumer Sale Act as of 25 December 2014, does not contain the exclusion criteria either. Once again there is no explanation in the justification to the proposed reform as to why the drafters chose to give up the exclusion criteria. This triggers a question whether not including exclusion criteria was intentional, or whether the drafters of the new consumer sale overlooked this issue once again. After years of preparing the reform, the first option is more probable. However, if dropping the exclusion criteria was a deliberate step, given that it differs considerably from the Directive, it should be clarified in the statute explanations. The rules on the burden of proof have always been regarded as a very important tool. They are said to be able to soothe the inconveniences of substantive law and for these reasons they should be regulated with care.

6.4.2 *Germany*

622. The BGB implements the exclusion criteria as provided in Article 5 (3) of the Consumer Sales Directive. There is uncertainty about the application of the exclusion criteria, which mostly regard the terminology and scope of the criteria, caused by a lack of definitions for the nature of the goods and the nature of the defects. There is no clear line between the two exclusion criteria, and they often overlap. Additionally, it is unclear what facts and means of evidence are required to prove the existence of exclusion criteria. Finally, what particularly draws attention in the context of the construction of § 476 BGB is the relationship between the rebuttal of the presumption and the exclusion criteria.

623. There are no general exclusions for the application of the presumption. It is accepted that the exclusion criteria must be applied exceptionally and interpreted strictly. In cases of the sale of animals, which has started most discussions on the subject, the presumption applies just as it applies to other goods. § 90 BGB states that although animals are not to be regarded as goods, they are governed by the provisions applicable to goods. An exception is the sale of animals bought in public auctions, which is excluded from the scope of application of the consumer sale pursuant to §474 (1) s. 2 BGB.

6.4.2.1 Incompatibility with the nature of the goods

624. In the literature, the first types of goods recognised as increasing the chances for the incompatibility are perishable goods as long as their life expectancy is shorter than six

months. This is because it is nearly impossible to prove that the goods were defective at the time of the passing of risk. Moreover, it is common for these goods to spoil within six months, which bars an assumption that they were defective at the time of the passing of risk.

625. Another group of goods that may be problematic in relation to this topic are second-hand goods. In general, the second-hand goods must not be considered defective simply because they have been used in the past or because they are not new. The BGH confirmed that the application of the presumption may be restricted only if the goods are defective due to normal long-term use, but not in case of unusual, rare defects. In fact, this leads to the question of whether the consumer was able to prove existence of a defect in a second-hand good, where normal wear and tear is not regarded as a defect.

626. Another group of goods raising uncertainty and increasing the chance of incompatibility are goods requiring installation carried out by a (third) professional party for which the seller is not responsible. The BGH confirmed that there is no reason the presumption should be excluded because the installation was performed by a professional third party (installation itself not defective). If such goods became defective within six months from the time of the passing of risk, the presumption cannot be excluded because of its incompatibility with the nature of the goods.

6.4.2.2 Incompatibility with the nature of the defects

627. The criterion of the nature of the defects is examined by courts mainly from the perspective of two types of goods/characteristics of defects. The first group includes animals, particularly specific animal diseases.

The courts are particularly reluctant to apply the presumption of non-conformity to behavioural disorders in animals. These types of disorders often develop from changes to an animal's environment, living conditions, training, nourishment, experiencing uncomfortable travel, or the existence of other diseases.[11] In these cases the courts often find that the existence of defects has not been sufficiently proven. Alternatively, when the existence of defects has been successfully proven the courts may exclude the application of the presumption because of its incompatibility with the nature of the defects. Given the strict rules regarding the existence of the defects, the first of the above-mentioned solutions occurs more often.

628. A second group of goods increasing chances of incompatibility because of the nature of the defects includes second-hand goods with visible defects. The BGH confirmed that

11 Other than chronic disease or a genetic one.

in cases of the sale of goods with external defects that should have been discovered by an inexperienced consumer, the seller may invoke the incompatibility with the nature of the defects.

629. The incompatibility may also be invoked in cases when the defects are too general, for example regarding multi-sourced problems such as engine defects, which again touches on evidence of the existence of the defects and a complex interpretation of the instances of defects regarding the notions of *Grundmangel* and *Folgemangel.*

Furthermore, there was an argument that the presumption should be excluded because of the nature of the goods where a defect proven by the consumer could have occurred at any time and it is not likely to have existed at the time of the passing of risk. The BGH rejected this view and stated that the presumption where the existence of a defect is successfully proven within six months it must have existed at the time of passing of risk is a core element of the doctrine. The argument that it could have occurred at any time cannot suffice to exclude the application of the presumption.

6.4.2.3 Relationship between rebuttal and exclusion of the presumption

630. § 476 BGB might be interpreted to mean that, once the requirements for the application of the presumption are met, the criteria for its exclusion should be tested for their applicability.[12] This could result in a different understanding of the role of the exclusion criteria in various Member States. For example, in Poland where the exclusion criteria have not been implemented at all. On the other hand, the facts presented to challenge the prerequisites could easily serve as facts and evidence to support the exclusion of the presumption. The BGH considered a case[13] where the origins of a defect were indeterminable at the time of sale. The seller argued that there were no material defects, or alternatively that the defects were not sufficiently proven by the consumer.

Finally, in case of undefined defects, the seller could also argue that the fact that the goods did not work in general constitutes a type of non-conformity with which the presumption is incompatible as such. This is because it is said that the presumption should refer to a concrete defect and the fact that for example a car does not drive is too broad. Although in practice this would probably be regarded as the lack of proof of the existence of defects, both interpretations are not particularly beneficial for the consumer.

631. The findings on the exclusion criteria lead clearly to the conclusion that their application is closely connected to how the parties performed in providing evidence of the existence of defects, or their lack of existence. The question arises whether it was a goal of the German

12 Chapter 5, para 488.
13 Chapter 5, para 479.

legislator or it is simply a side effect of the particular construction of the presumption of Article 5 (3) of the Directive and the application of national rules on burden of proof, which in the end focus on whether the existence of defects at the time of the passing of risk has been proven or disproven.

6.4.3 *England and Wales*

632. Section 48A (4) (b) of the Sale of Goods Act 1979 stipulates the exclusion of the presumption if it is incompatible with the nature of the goods or the nature of the lack of conformity. In the recently proposed Consumer Rights Bill, amending the English consumer sale, Section 19 (15) (b) states that the presumption does not apply if its application is incompatible with the nature of the goods or how they fail to conform to the contract. The slightly altered wording of the new provision does not affect the scope of the exclusion criteria.

The criteria are implemented in accordance with Article 5 (3) of the Consumer Sales Directive. Regarding the scope of the exclusion criteria, English and Welsh law also lacks definitions explaining the nature of the goods and the nature of the non-conformity. It seems that the division on the incompatibility due to the nature of the goods and the nature of the non-conformity is much less sharp than it is in Germany or the Netherlands. The two criteria are often regarded together.

633. In the literature it is stated that the presumption would be excluded due to its incompatibility (because of the nature of the goods or the nature of the non-conformity) in contracts of sale of short-lived goods such as flowers, plants, and perishable goods. In particular, a consumer who consumes the goods after the expiry date but before the end of the six-month period may be left without remedies. The solution resembles the Polish regulation which for perishable goods provides a very short period where the consumer may claim non-conformity. A similar interpretation regarding perishable (short-lived) goods can be found in Dutch law.

634. It seems that under English and Welsh law the necessity to separate the rebuttal of the presumption from the exclusion criteria is much less important than in other jurisdictions (especially Germany and the Netherlands).[14] It may result from the duties the parties have in litigation. First of all, they should initially provide as many facts and provide as much evidence as possible to convince the judge of their claim. The judge has a minor role in navigating the hearing of evidence in litigation. Without intervening, the English judge

14 In Poland there are no statutory exclusion criteria, in practice similar arguments may be used as arguments rebutting the presumption; Chapter 6, para 619.

decides on the application of the presumption and the liability for delivery of non-conforming goods based solely on the parties' submissions. Furthermore, it seems that the presumption as such does not have too much practical significance in England and Wales, therefore the detailed construction of its application does not seem to have much importance either. Finally, there is a lack of case law regarding this topic, and there is almost no scholarly debate about the structure and function of the presumption of non-conformity.

6.4.4 *The Netherlands*

635. Article 7:18 (2) BW implements the exclusion criteria in accordance with Article 5 (3) of the Consumer Sales Directive. As with other jurisdictions there are no definitions of the nature of the goods and the nature of the non-conformity. The task of determining the meaning of the terms is given to national legislators and judges. In the legislative documents the Dutch legislator provided several examples of such criteria. It is said that the Consumer Sales Directive provides broad exceptions from the application of the presumption, which may contradict the objectives of Article 5 (3) of the Consumer Sales Directive and its national counterparts. For these reasons the exclusion criteria should be interpreted narrowly and applied exceptionally, however this has been challenged by the doctrine. The Dutch legislator has observed that any specification included in the national statutes might have been considered as contrary to the Directive. Finally, there is no clear line between both exclusion criteria and in practice they may often overlap.

636. In general, the issues of exclusion criteria are presented in the context of particular types of goods: perishable goods, animals, plants, second-hand goods, and certain animal diseases. The Dutch legislator has specifically discussed possibilities of the presumption's incompatibility in the situation of perishable goods with short expiry dates, plants, and animals with short life expectancy or requiring special conditions and care.

There was also discussion focusing on the possibility of a general exclusion of the presumption for the sale of animals. It has been observed that the presumption's unrestricted application may lead to very complex evidence issues. The purchase price of certain animals reaches thousands of euros and often requires very expensive and time-consuming litigation, especially when a detailed expert report is required (which is almost always the case). Finally, animals are very sensitive to changes in their environment, training, treatment and care, all of which can easily lead to changes in behaviour (or other non-conformity). Although there were some very strong arguments to exclude the sale of animals from the consumer sale, just as in Germany they failed and the presumption of non-conformity applies to sales of animals just as it applies to manufactured goods.

6.4.4.1 Incompatibility with the nature of the goods

637. The examples given by the legislator indicate which situations may increase the chances of incompatibility: perishable goods (especially with short expiry date), plants, animals (especially in cases of particular diseases). Regarding animals the matter is very unclear. The legislator has emphasised that the application of the presumption is not excluded in the sale of animals, and it applies to these cases just as it applies to any other good. It seems that a possible exception to this interpretation would be animals with very short life expectancy, less than six months, or animals requiring special conditions and care, though this still remains somewhat doubtful.

Based on Dutch case law, the question of the incompatibility of the presumption with the nature of the goods arises relatively often. However, the courts are very reluctant to apply this exception. Regarding the exclusion of animals, their potential incompatibility has already been recognised in legislative documents. Nevertheless, as already stated it did not lead to any general exclusion. This argument is to be found in the majority of cases refusing the possibility of the incompatibility of animals with the presumption of non-conformity because of the nature of the goods.

The most important uncertainty that may be deduced based on the case law where the questions of exclusion criteria are raised, is whether these questions actually regard the exclusion of the presumption as such, or rather they exclusively deal with questions of the burden of proof and evidence regarding the (non)existence of non-conformity as such.

6.4.4.2 Incompatibility with the nature of the non-conformity

638. The analysis of case law confirms that sometimes it is very difficult to distinguish the nature of the goods from the nature of the non-conformity. The Dutch legislator provides a specific example of when the presumption shall be considered as incompatible because of the nature of the non-conformity. The example regarded damage to a video recorder caused by a fall. Consequently, the legislator stated that in cases where it is clear that the defect has been caused by the buyer's use/misuse of the goods the presumption is incompatible. The presumption still applies if the doubts about the origins of the defects remain.

The example given by the legislator seems to be incorrect, especially if we look at this situation from the perspective of the requirements of the presumption: proof of the existence of non-conformity and the six-month period. If it is clear that the defect was caused by the consumer's use/misuse, the presumption cannot apply because of unsuccessful evidence as to the existence of non-conformity (or successful evidence to the contrary – the defect occurred after the delivery) and not because of the exclusion criterion regarding the nature of the non-conformity.

639. The courts repeatedly considered the possibility of exclusion in the context of certain animal diseases, in particular *luchtzuigen*.[15] As previously stated in cases of the sale of animals the application of the presumption will not be excluded due to the nature of the goods. The question remains whether it can be excluded due to the incompatibility with the nature of the non-conformity. In one of these decisions, the court admits the possibility of the exclusion because of the incompatibility with the nature of the non-conformity. On the other hand, when assessing evidence presented by the seller, it appears he provided extended evidence about the lack of non-conformity. In the end it was stated that the seller was able to rebut the presumption, rather than relying on the exclusion criteria. Another decision regarded the case of *luchtzuigen* which occurred just one day after delivery. The seller's argument that the disease can develop within seventy-two hours and therefore the presumption should be excluded, was insufficient. This means that in order to assess whether the particular disease or other defect constitutes a criterion of the nature of the goods, things such as the time of discovery can be of great importance, as it can indicate whether there is a possibility that the defect – a disease – existed at the time of delivery or occurred later.

640. Summing up, under Dutch law there is still uncertainty about the correct application of the exclusion criteria. There is a lack of uniform interpretation and there are differences between the courts decisions regarding similar legal problems. Having said that, it must be stated that the courts' reluctance in applying exclusion criteria seems to favour consumers.

There are a handful of decisions where the exclusion criteria were applied by Dutch courts and consequently the application of the presumption of non-conformity was prevented. As repeatedly highlighted, there is significant uncertainty over whether these cases in fact regard the exclusion criteria (incompatibility with the nature of the non-conformity) or whether they rather regard successful evidence to the contrary rebutting the presumption of non-conformity.[16] In my opinion the details of the majority of cases support the second argument.

Concluding, based on Dutch case law significant uncertainty arises over whether we can state that there is a real possibility of excluding the application of the presumption. In the majority of cases it seemed that the crucial factor was the success, or lack thereof, of evidence proving the existence of defects or evidence to the contrary.

15 Chapter 5, para 548, 563.

16 This question can be answered by looking at the consequences in particular litigation, i.e. whether after the presumption has been denied the consumer has a possibility to prove the existence of defects at the time of delivery (that would be an exclusion) or the consumer loses the case (this is a situation when the seller successfully provide for evidence to the contrary).

6.4.4.3 Relationship between rebuttal and exclusion of the presumption

641. After analysing Dutch case law it must be stated that there are many decisions exclusively concerning the question of rebuttal. The decisions taken in these cases determined the content of the notion of evidence to the contrary when it comes to the presumption of non-conformity. It indicates that the construction of the presumption and the order in which the elements are taken into account is as follows: requirements, rebuttal, and exclusion. This differs from the German approach, which rarely answers the questions of rebuttal as such. The German courts mostly consider issues of the existence of defects and exclusion criteria. This may stem from a different approach to the assessment of certain elements of the presumption of non-conformity and different constructions of notions of non-conformity and defects.[17]

6.4.5 Comparative remarks

642. All Members States except Poland implemented the exclusion criteria in accordance with Article 5 (3) of the Consumer Sales Directive. The Polish legislator did not implement the exclusion criteria at all, which in theory is advantageous to the consumers, as the presumption cannot be excluded because of its incompatibility with the nature of the goods or the nature of the non-conformity.

It must be observed that in the jurisdictions where the exclusion criteria have been implemented, the interpretation of the incompatibility with the nature of the goods and the nature of the non-conformity is to some extent alike and inconsistent in a similar way. In all the jurisdictions investigated, including Poland and England, examples of goods suggesting that the application of the presumption of non-conformity may be problematic are similar. The doctrine mentions animals, second-hand goods, perishable goods, and plants. The sale of animals attracts the most controversy, in particular in the Netherlands and Germany. In both Member States some were of the opinion that the sale of animals should be excluded from the scope of consumer sales.

The presumption of non-conformity in cases of the sale of horses seems to be applied much less frequently in Germany than in the Netherlands. One of the reasons is that German courts, in cases of animal diseases, will often find there is a lack of proof of the existence of a defect. In the same cases the Dutch courts may accept the evidence of the existence of non-conformity and consequently shift the burden of proof that the goods were free from defects at the time of delivery.

Dutch courts' reluctance to apply the exclusion criteria appears to favour consumers. In this respect the situation also seems to differ from German practice, where the exclusion

17 For example assessment of the existence of non-conformity, or more frequent application of the exclusion criteria.

criteria are regularly allowed. Consequently, the presumption of non-conformity does not apply and the burden of proof is allocated in accordance with the general rules on the burden of proof. In practice, it essentially deprives consumers of the benefit of the presumption. Regarding the function and characteristics of the exclusion criteria, the case law suggests that in both the German and Dutch systems, the issues of the exclusion criteria in fact amount to whether the non-conformity in question may, with a sufficient degree of probability, be led back to a defect already existing at the time of delivery.

6.5 FINAL REMARKS

643. All the jurisdictions examined have a similar approach to the allocation of the burden of proof, differing at times in the standard of certainty the judge must obtain in reaching the final decision. In general, the initial allocation of the burden of proof in consumer sale cases is similar. The burden of proving the existence of non-conformity at the time of delivery lies with the buyer. The presumption of non-conformity simplifies the second element, the moment of the existence of non-conformity. Within each jurisdiction there are measures to facilitate the burden of proof: factual presumptions, *prima facie* evidence and the reversed burden of proof. Before the implementation of the Consumer Sales Directive, the application of these measures was at the sole discretion of the national judge. In theory, the presumption of non-conformity ensured the institutional application of the presumption every time a consumer successfully proves the existence of non-conformity within six months from the time of delivery, unless it is incompatible with the nature of the goods or the nature of the non-conformity. In the majority of cases discussed in this study when a consumer was unable to benefit from the presumption he would lose the case. This proves the importance of the presumption for the consumer's ability and his chances of receiving remedies for the delivery of non-conforming goods.

644. In general, all the Member States studied ensured the correct implementation of the presumption of non-conformity, although the provisions transposing the presumption into national law often differed. All the Member States apply the same prerequisites for the application of the presumption, the existence of non-conformity and the six-month period, except Poland where the statutory period has been extended to one year as of 25 December 2014. In all the Member States the presumption can be rebutted. In Germany, England and Wales, and the Netherlands the presumption can be excluded if incompatible with the nature of the goods or the nature of the non-conformity, whereas the Polish legislator did not introduce these exclusion criteria.

Despite almost identical conditions, comparing the analysed jurisdictions, there is a lack of uniform interpretation and application of the presumption of non-conformity. The concepts and notions the presumption consists of in different systems are eventually governed by the national law. Each Member State has its own definition of non-conformity or independent concept of defects. Anyhow they are supposed to include the criteria of non-conformity found in Article 2 (2) of the Consumer Sales Directive. As analysed in this study, the circumstances and facts that constitute the defects or non-conformity differ between the Member States. In particular, there are discrepancies regarding facts the consumer must state to prove non-conformity and when the defects or non-conformity is regarded as having been proven. Consequently, the core issue regards the question of what the consumer must provide to prove the existence of non-conformity. It covers the substantive content of the notion of non-conformity and the procedural aspect of a sufficient standard of proof.

As to the rebuttal of the presumption, the questions that may arrive regard the content of the rebuttal such as what the seller must provide to successfully fight the presumption on its merits. There were initial differences between the Member States, but recently all jurisdictions agreed that in order to rebut the presumption the seller must provide full and positive evidence to the contrary. It basically entails the seller proving that the defects were in conformity at the time of delivery, or that they were caused only after that time.

Alongside the existence of non-conformity, the topic causing the most problems regards the exclusion of the presumption for which there are several reasons. First of all, the exclusion criteria are not implemented throughout the jurisdictions in the same way, Polish legislation does not provide for the exclusion criteria at all. Second of all, the content of the criteria is vague and their interpretation is left for the national legislators and judges. This may result in a different understanding of the exclusion of the presumption, and the terms: nature of the goods and nature of the non-conformity. Finally, when analysing the exclusion criteria it was clear that almost all the cases considering the exclusion criteria were closely connected to the issue of proving the existence of non-conformity, whether unsuccessful evidence of the existence of non-conformity or satisfactory evidence to the contrary. This brings back the above argument that the national legislation regulating circumstances and facts, which constitute non-conformity and the sufficient proof thereof, differ between the Member States. As long their interpretation, content and the necessary evidence to prove the existence of non-conformity differ, there will be no uniform application of the exclusion criteria. Accordingly, the uniform application of the presumption of non-conformity depends heavily on the uniform notion of non-conformity, its content, and the equal assessment of evidence as to the existence of non-conformity.

Literature

Ancery 2012
Ancery A.G.F., Ambtshalve toepassing van EU-recht, Serie Burgerlijk Proces & Praktijk, nr. XIV, Deventer: Kluwer 2012.

Andrews 2003
Andrews N., English Civil Procedure. Fundamentals of the New Civil Justice System, Oxford University Press 2003.

Andrews 2008
Andrews N., English Civil Proceedings: A Synopsis, Ritsumeikan Law Review, 25/2008, pp. 25-61.

Apps 1994
Apps A., The right to cure defective performance, (1994) LMCLQ 525.

Arlt 2010
Arlt C., Verbraucherschutz im reformierten Kaufrecht. Die Umsetzung der neuen Vorschriften durch Rechtsprechung und Unternehmenspraxis, Peter Lang 2010.

Asser/Procesrecht/Asser 3 2013
Asser W.D.H., Mr. C. Assers Handleiding tot de beoefening van het Nederlands Burgerlijk Recht. Procesrecht Deel 3. Bewijs, Deventer: Kluwer 2013.

Asser/Hartkamp and Sieburgh 6-III* 2014
Hartkamp A.S., Sieburgh C.H., Mr. C. Assers Handleiding tot de beoefening van het Nederlands Burgerlijk Recht. 6. Verbintenissenrecht. Deel III. Algemene leer der overeenkomsten, Deventer: Kluwer 2014.

Asser/Hartkamp and Sieburgh 6-II* 2013
Hartkamp A.S., Sieburgh C.H., Mr. C. Assers Handleiding tot de beoefening van het Nederlands Burgerlijk Recht. 6. Verbintenissenrecht. Deel II. De verbintenis in het algemeen, Deventer: Kluwer 2013.

Asser/Hijma 7-I* 2013
Hijma J., Mr. C. Assers Handleiding tot de beoefening van het Nederlands Burgerlijk Recht, Bijzondere overeenkomsten, deel 7-1 (Koop en ruil), achtste druk, Deventer: Kluwer 2013.

Atiyah/Adams and Macqueen 2010
Atiyah P.S., Adams J. N., Macqueen H., The Sale of Goods, 11th Edition, Pearson Longman 2010.

Bachmeier 2008
Bachmeier W, Rechtshandbuch Autokauf, München: CH Beck 2008.

Baumgärtel, Laumen and Prütting/Grundlagen 2009
Baumgärtel G., Laumen H-W., Prütting H., Handbuch der Beweislast. Grundlagen, Köln: Carl Heymans Verlag 2009.

Baumgärtel, Laumen and Prütting 2009
Baumgärtel G., Laumen H-W., Prütting H., Handbuch der Beweislast. Bürgerlisches Gesetzbuch Schuldrecht Besonderer Teil I, §§ 433-610 mit UNKR, Köln: Carl Heymans Verlag 2009.

Beale 2009
Beale H., The Draft Directive on Consumer Rights and UK Consumer Law – Where now?, in Howells G., Schulze R. (Ed.), Modernising and Harmonising Consumer Contract Law, European Law Publishers Selier 2009.

Beale and Howells 1997
Beale H., Howells G., EC Harmonisation of Consumer Sales Law – A missed opportunity?, (1997) 12 Journal of Contract Law, pp. 21-46.

Becker 2009
Becker Ch., in Baumgärtel G., Laumen H-W., Prütting H., Handbuch der Beweislast. Bürgerlisches Gesetzbuch Schuldrecht Besonderer Teil I, §§ 433-610 mit UNKR, Köln: Carl Heymans Verlag 2009.

Beckmann 2013
Beckmann M. in Junker M., Beckmann R.M., Rüßmann M., Juris Praxiskommentar BGB Band 2: Schuldrecht, Saarbrücken: Juris 2013.

Bemberger and Roth 2012
Bemberger H.G., Roth H., Kommentar zum Bürgerlichen Gesetzbuch: BGB, C.H. Beck 2012.

Benjamin's sale of goods 2010
Benjamin J.P., Benjamin's Sale of Goods, Guest A.G. (gen. ed.), London: Sweet & Maxwell 2010.

Berger and Jauernig 2011
Berger Ch., Jauernig O., Bürgerliches Gesetzbuch, 14 Auflage, München: Verlag C.H. Beck 2011.

Biemans 2007
Biemans J.W.A., Richtlijn 99/44/EG betreffende bepaalde aspecten van de verkoop van en de garanties voor consumptiegoederen, in Hartkamp A.S., Sieburgh C.H., Keus L.A.D., De invloed van het Europese recht op het Nederlandse privaatrecht, Deel II, Deventer: Kluwer 2007.

BIS 2014
Department of Business Innovation and Skills, Implementing the Alternative Dispute Resolution Directive and Online Dispute Resolution Regulation - Impact Assessment, March 2014.

BIS 2014, Consumer Rights Bill - Explanatory Notes
Department of Buisiness Innovation and Skills, Consumer Rights Bill - Explanatory Notes, http://www.publications.parliament.uk/pa/bills/cbill/2013-2014/0161/en/14161en.htm (10.10.2014).

Bradgate 2004
Bradgate R., Remedying the unfit fitted kitchen, (2004) 120 Law Quarterly Review, pp. 558-563.

Bridge 2002
Bridge M. G., in Massimo Bianca C., Grundmann S., EU Sales Directive. Commentary, Antwerp-Oxford-New York: Intersentia 2002.

Bridge 2003
Bridge, M.G., What is to be done about sale of goods? (2003) 119 Law Quarterly Review, pp. 173-177.

Brown 1999
Brown I., Sales of goods in the course of a business, (1999) 115 Law Quarterly Review, pp. 384-389.

Brownsword and Howells 1999
Brownsword R., Howells G., When surfers start to shop: Internet commerce and contract law, (1999) Legal Studies 19 (3), pp. 287-315.

Bruder 2007
Bruder F., Burden of proof and the Unfair Terms in the Consumer Contracts Directive, (2007) 15 European Review of Private Law, Issue 2, pp. 205-231.

Büdenbender 2005
Büdenbender U., Anwalt Kommentar BGB. Gesamtausgabe, Deutscher Anwaltverlag & Institut der Anwaltschaft GmbH 2005.

Bussani and Werro 2009
Bussani M., Werro F., European Private Law, A Handbook, Berne: Stäpfli Publishers Ltd 2009.

Castermans 2009
Castermans A.G., De burger in het burgerlijk recht – of De eigenschappen van perensap, Den Haag: BJu 2009.

Castermans and Krans 2013 (T&C Vermogensrecht)
Castermans A.G., Krans H.B., Koop en Ruil, Boek 7, Title 1, Vermogensrecht. Tekst en Commentaar, edt. Nieuwenhuis J.H., Stolker C.J.J.M., Valk W.L., Wissink M.H., Deventer: Kluwer 2013.

Choo 2012
Choo A.L-T., Evidence, Oxford University Press 2012.

Clermont and Sherwin 2002
Clermont K.M., Sherwin E., Comparative view of standards of proof, The American Journal of Comparative Law Vol. 50, No. 2 (Spring 2002).

Commission 1993
Green Paper of 15 November 1993 on guarantees for consumer goods and after-sales services, OJ C 338, 15.12.1993.

Cross and Tapper 2010
Cross A.R.N., Tapper C.F., Cross and Tapper on evidence, 12th edt., Oxford University Press 2010.

Dauner-Lieb 2006
Dauner-Lieb B., Viereinhalb Jahre Gezetz zur Modernisirung des Scchuldrechts. Das neue Schultrecht und der BGH – eine Zwischenbilanz, AnwBl 7/2006, pp. 430-434.

Dauner-Lieb, Konzen and Schmidt 2003
Dauner-Lieb B., Konzen H., Schmidt K., Das neue Schuldrecht in der Praxis, Cologne: Heymans 2003.

Dauner-Lieb and Langen 2012
Dauner-Lieb B., Langen W., BGB Schuldrecht Nomos Kommentar §§ 241-610, Baden-Baden: Nomos Verlagsgesellschaft 2012.

Demendecki 2012
Demendecki, in Jakubecki A. (edt.), Kodeks postępowania cywilnego. Komentarz, Wolters Kluwer Polska 2012.

Dimroth/*diss.* 2007
Dimroth J., Die Umsetzung der Verbrauchsgüterkaufrichtlinie (44/99/EG) in Deutschland und den Niederlanden, Ein Rechtsvergleich, Driesen 2007.

Doehner/*diss.* 2004
Doehner R., Die Schuldrechtsreform vor dem Hintergrund der Verbrauchsgüterkauf-Richtlinie, die Richtlinie des Europäischen Parlaments und des Rates zu bestimmten Aspekten des Verbrauchsgüterkaufs und der Garantien für Verbrauchsgüter und ihre Auswirkungen auf das deutsche Recht, Baden-Baden: Nomos-Verlag-Ges 2004.

Dolecki 1998
Dolecki H., Ciężar dowodu w Polskim procesie cywilnym, Warszawa: Wydawnictwa Prawnicze PWN 1998.

Van Dongen and De Feijter 2010
Van Dongen M.C.P., De Feijter A., 'Ontsnappingssprongen' met paard or pony inzake het wettelijke vermoeden ex art 7:18 lid 2 BW, NTBR 3/2010, pp. 11-17.

DTI 1999
DTI Modern Markets: Confident Consumers, Cm 4410, The Stationary Office, London, July 1999.

Duivenvoorde 2010
Duivenvoorde B.B., Consument of handelend in de uitoefening van beroep of bedrijf? Het Bundesgerichtshof doet uitspraak, Tijdschrift voor Consumentenrecht en handelspraktijken 2010/4, pp. 176-180.

Van Eerten 2008
van Eerten H.M., Bewijslastverdeling 'verborgen gebreken' bij verkoop van dieren, Agrarisch Recht Nr 2/2008, pp. 57-60.

Eggert 2002
Eggert Ch., Die Beweislastumkehr beim Verbrauchsgüterkauf, Verkehrsrecht aktuell 12/2002, p. 175.

Elßner and Schirmbacher 2003
Elßner Ch., Schirmbacher M., Die Gesellschaft bürgerlichen Rechts als Verbraucher?, Verbraucher und Recht 7/2003.

Ervine 2004
Ervine W.C.H., Satisfactory quality, what does it mean?, Journal of Business Law 2004, pp. 684-703.

Faust 2011
Faust F., in Bamberger H., Roth H., Kommentar zum Bürgerlichen Gesetzbuch: BGB, Band 1, München: Verlag CH Beck 2011.

Frenk 2003,
Frenk N., Herziening van de regeling van de consumentenkoop, AA (52) 12/2003, pp. 953-959.

Gajda-Roszcynialska 2012
Gajda-Roszczynialska K., Sprawy o ochronę indywidualnych interesów konsumentów w postępowaniu cywilnym, Warszawa: Wolters Kluwer 2012.

Gajek 2003
Gajek M., Niezgodność z umową jako przeslanka odpowiedzialności sprzedawcy towaru konsumpcyjnego, Monitor Prawniczy 5/2003, pp. 207 *et seq.*

Galetta 2010
Galetta D.U., Procedural Autonomy of EU Member States: Paradise Lost? A study on the 'functionalized procedural competence' of the EU Member States, Springer 2010.

Gebauer 2009
Gebauer M., Der Durbruch zur richtlinienkonformen Rechtsfortbildung: Anmerkung zu BGH, Urteil vom 26.11.2008, VIII ZR 200/05 - Qelle, GPR 2/2009, pp. 82-86.

Giesen/*diss.* 2001
Giesen I., Bewijs en aansprakelijkheid. Een rechtsvergelijkend onderzoek naar de bewijs-risico-omkering in het aansprakelijkheidsrecht (diss. Tilburg), Tilburg-Den Haag: BJu 2001.

Goode/McKendrick 2010
Goode R., McKendrick E., Commercial Law, 4th ed., London: Penguin 2010.

Gniewek 2011
Gniewek E., Kodeks Cywilny. Komentarz, Warszawa: C.H. Beck 2011.

Gniewek 2013
Gniewek E., System Prawa Prywatnego, Prawo rzeczowe, Warszawa: C.H. Beck 2013.

Grochowski 2013
Grochowski M., Wada prawna jako postaci niezgodności towaru konsumpcyjnego z umową, Monitor Prawniczy 7/2013, pp. 379-382.

Grothe 2001
Grothe H., Münchener Kommentar zum BGB, 4. Auflage, C.H. Beck 2001 at https://beck-online.beck.de/?vpath=bibdata%2Fkomm%2FMuekoBGB_Band1_4%2FBuch%2Fcont%2FMuekoBGB%2EBuch%2ETitel%2Ehtm.

Grundmann 2001
Grundmann S., European Sales Law — Reform and Adoption of International Models in German Sales Law (2001) 9 European Review of Private Law, Issue 2/3, pp. 239-258.

Grundmann 2005
Grundmann S., Germany and the *Schuldrechtsmodernisierung* 2002, ERCL 1/2005, pp. 129-148.

Grundmann and Ochmann 2007
Grundmann S., Ochmann F., German Contract Law Five Years After the Fundamental Contract Law Reform in the Schuldrechtsmodernisierung, European Review of Contract Law 2007, Volume 3, Issue 4, pp. 450-467.

Grundmann and Uhlig 2011
Grundmann S., Uhlig S., German Contract Law – Nearly a Decade After the Fundamental Reform in the *Schuldrechtsmodernisierung*, European Review of Contract Law 2011, Volume 7, Issue 1, pp. 78-94.

Gsell 2001
Gsell B., Kaufrechtsrichtlinie und Schuldrechtsmodernisierung, JZ 2001, pp. 65-75.

Gsell 2004
Gsell B., Beweislast des Käufers für Vorliegen des Sachmangels nach Entgegennahme der Kaufsache, Kurzkommentar zu BGH, Urt. v. 2.6.2004 – VIII ZR 329/03, EWiR, § 437 BGB 1/2004, pp. 903-904.

Gsell 2011
Darlegungs- und Beweislast für das arglistige Verschweigen eines Mangels, Anmerkung zu BGH, Urt. v. 12.11.2010, V ZR 181/09 (OLG Celle, LG Lüneburg), ZJS 2011, pp. 86-87.

Haas 1998
Haas P. M., Compliance with EU directives: insights from international relations and comparative politics, Journal of European Public Policy, 5/1 March 1998, pp. 17-37.

Habryn 2010
Habryn E., Niezgodność towaru konsumpcyjnego z umową sprzedaży konsumenckiej, Wolters Kluwer Polska 2010.

Hardy 2009
Hardy R.R.R., Differentiatie in het (Europees) contractenrecht: rechtsvergelijkende studies naar de consument, de ondernemer en hun overeenkomsten, Den Haag: BJu 2009.

Hawes and Twigg-Flesner 2010
Hawes C., Twigg-Flesner Ch., Sales and guarantees, in Howells G., Ramsey I., Wilhemsson T., Kraft D. (edt), Handbook of Research on International Consumer Law, Edward Elgar 2010.

Heinrich 1996
Heinrich C., Die Beweislast bei Rechtsgeschäften, Köln: Carl Heymanns Verlag 1996.

Hente 2005
Hente V., The Recent German Law, Implementing a Modernisation of German Contract Law, International Business Law Journal, pp. 359-372.

Heymans and Bartels 2012
Heyman H.W., Bartels S.E., Vastgoedtransacties: koop, Den Haag 2012.

Hijma 1992
Hijma J., Consumentenkoop of gewone koop?, WPNR 1992/6051, pp. 387-388.

Hijma 2011
Hijma J., Bewijsperikelen rond een uitgemergelde parkiet (wetsvoorstel 27 809), in Signora Senatrice over Recht, Onderwijs en Politiek (Opstellen aangeboden aan Ankie Broekers-Knol bij haar afscheid van de Faculteit der Rechtsgeleerdheid van de Universiteit Leiden), pp. 31-41, Boom Den Haag 2011.

Hijma 2013
Hijma J., Consument en non-conformiteitsbewijs, Tijdschrift voor Consumentenrecht en handelspraktijken (TvC) 2013/6, pp. 257-261.

Hodges, Benöhr and Creutzfeld-Banda 2012
Hodges Ch., Benöhr I., Careutzfeld-Banda N., Consumer ADR in Europe, Oxford: Hart Publishing 2012.

Hoeren and Martinek 2002
Hoeren T., Martinek M., Systematischer Kommentar zum Kaufrecht, Recklinghausen: ZAP, Verlag für die Rechts- und Anwaltspraxis 2002.

Van Hooijdonk and Eijsvoogel 2012
Van Hooijdonk M., Eijsvoogel P., Litigation in the Netherlands, Wolters Kluwer 2012.

Hondius 2006
Hondius E., The Notion of Consumer: European Union versus Member States, Sydney Law Review 2006, vol. 28: 29, pp. 89-98.

Hondius 2008
Hondius E., Principles of European Law on Sales (PELS), European Law Publishers Selier 2008.

Hondius and Schelhaas 2001
Hondius E., Schelhaas H., In conformity with the Consumer Sales Directive? Some remarks on transposition into Dutch law, 2001 European Review of Private Law, 2 & 3, pp. 327-336.

Honsell 2001
Honsell H., Die EU-Richtlinie über den Verbrauchsgüterkauf und ihre Umzetung ins BGB, JZ 6/2001, p. 276.

Howells and Weatherill 2005
Howells G.,Weatherill S., Consumer Sales Law, Ashgate 2005.

Howells and Wilhelmsson 1997
Howells G., Wilhelmsson T., EC Consumer Law, Ashgate Dartmouth 1997.

Jagielska 2001
Jagielska M., in Pazdan M., Konwencja Wiedeńska o umowach w międzynarodowej sprzedaży towarów. Komentarz, Kraków: Zakamycze 2001.

Jankowski 2000
Jankowski J., Postępowanie uproszczone w procesie cywilnym, Monitor Prawniczy, 10/2000, pp. 2-3.

Jezioro 2010
Jezioro J., Ustawa o szczególnych warunkach sprzedaży konsumenckiej, Komentarz, C.H. Beck Warszawa 2010.

Junker, Beckmann and Rüßmann 2013
Junker M., Beckmann R.M., Rüßmann M., Juris Praxiskommentar BGB Band 2: Schuldrecht, Saarbrücken: Juris 2013.

Kakouris 1997
Kakouris C.M., Do the Member States Possess Judicial Procedural 'autonomy'?, (1997) 34 Common Market Law Review, Issue 6, pp. 1389-1412.

Katner 2006
Katner W., in Wlodyka S. (edt.), Prawo umów handlowych, Tom 5, Warszawa: C.H. Beck 2006.

Keane and McKeown 2014
Keane A., McKeown P., The Modern Law of Evidence, Oxoforf University Press 2014.

Klik/*diss.* 2008
Klik P., Conformiteit bij koop, Deventer: Kluwer 2008.

Klik 2011
Klik P., Koop en consumentenkoop, Deventer: Kluwer 2011.

Klöhn 2007
Klöhn L., Beweislastumkehr beim Verbrauchsgüterkauf (§ 476 BGB), NJW 2007, pp. 2811-2812.

Kokott 1998
Kokott J., The Burden of Proof in Comparative and International Human Rights Law: Civil and Common Law Approaches with Special Reference to the American and German Legal Systems, Brill Academic Publishers 1998.

Kołodziej 2006
Kołodziej A., Konsumenckie prawo odstąpienia od umowy sprzedaży rzeczy, Warszawa 2006.

Kołodziej 2010
Kołodziej A., in Jezioro J., Ustawa o szczególnych warunkach sprzedaży konsumenckiej. Komentarz, Warszawa: C.H. Beck 2010.

Koszowski 2012
Koszowski M, Ciężar dowodu w przypadku niezgodności towaru konsumpcyjnego z umową, Przedgląd legislacyjny, 2012, nr. 4, pp. 36-46.

Koszowski 2013 (SIT)
Koszowski M., Oczekiwania konsumentów odnośnie do oferowanych im towarów oparte na zapewnieniach publicznych pochodzących od sprzedawcy, producenta, osoby, która sie za producenta podaje, importera i dystrybutora towaru oraz ich przedstawicieli, Studia Iuridica Toruniensia nr. 1/2013, pp. 113-149.

Koszowski 2013
Koszowski M., Ocena rozwiązań prawnych zawartych w ustawie o szczególnych warunkach sprzedaży konsumenckiej oraz zmianie Kodeksu cywilnego implementującej dyrektywę Parlamentu Europejskiego i Rady nr 1999/44/WE, Przedląd Sądowy 6/2013, pp. 9-28.

Kmiecik 2008
Kmiecik Z.R., Incjatywa dowodowa w postępowaniu administracyjnym, Prokuratura i Prawo 6, 2008.

Krans 2010
Krans H.B., Nederlands burgerlijk procesrecht en materieel EU recht, Deventer: Kluwer 2010.

Kurowska 2008
Kurowska A., Wydanie towaru innego niż umówiony (*aliud pro alio*) na gruncie ustawy o sprzedaży konsumenckiej, Monitor Prawniczy 20/2008.

Lasok 1994
Lasok K.P.E., The European Court of Justice: Practice and Procedure, London: Butterworths 1994.

Laumen 2007
Laumen H.W., in Laumen H.W., Kessen M., Handbuch der Beweislast, Bürgerliches Gesetzbuch Algemeiner Teil, Köln: Carl Heymans Verlag 2007.

Law and Martin 2009
Law J., and Martin E. A., Oxford Dictionary of Law, Oxford University Press 2009.

Law Commissions 2009
Law Commission for England and Wales and the Scottish Law Commission (2009), Consumer Remedies for Faulty Goods, Nr. 217 and 216, 2002.

Leible 2010
Leible S., in Gebauer M., Wiedmann T., Zivilrecht unter europäischem Einfluss. Die richtlinienkonforme Auslegung des BGB und anderer Gesetze Kommentierung der wichtigsten EU-Verordnungen, Stuttgart: Boorberg 2010.

Lenaerts and Arts 2003
Lenaerts K., Arts D., Europees Procesrecht, Antwerpen-Apeldoorn: Maklu 2003.

Liepold 2008
Liepold D., Neuere Entwicklungen der Beweislast und der Beweiserleichterungen nach deutchem und europäischen Zivilprozessrecht, Ritsumeiken Law Review, 25/2008, pp. 77-99.

Loos 2003
Loos M., Consumentenkoop en garanties volgens het herziene consumentenkooprecht, 9 Nederlands Tijdschrift voor Europees Recht 6, pp. 155-161.

Loos 2004
Loos M., Consumentenkoop (Mon. Nieuw BW nr. B65b), Deventer: Kluwer 2004.

Loos 2005
Loos M., Privaatrecht Actueel. Het begrip consument in het Europese en Nederlands privaatrecht, WPNR 2005, pp. 771-772.

Loos 2009
Loos M., Consumer sales law in the proposal for a consumer rights directive, Centre for the Study of European Contract Law, Working Paper Series No. 2009/07.

Loos 2009 (de Geschillencommissie)
Loos M., de Geschillencommissie Voertuigen 2 april 2009 (Noot), Tijdschrift voor Consumentenrecht & handelspraktijken, 2009/6, pp. 256-257.

Looschelders 2003
Looschelders D., in Dauner-Lieb B., Konzen H., Schmidt K., Das neue Schuldrecht in der Praxis, Cologne: Heymans 2003.

Loranc-Borkowska 2006
Loranc-Borkowska J. Sprzedaż konsumencka – uwagi ogólne do ustawy, Zeszyty Naukowe Akademii Ekonomicznej w Krakowie nr. 725.

Lorenz 2004
Lorenz S., Sachmangel und Beweislastumkehr im Verbrauchsgüterkauf – Zur Reichweite der Vermutungsregelung in § 476 BGB, NJW 2004, 3020.

Lorenz 2006
Lorenz S., Anmerkung, NJW (2006), 3201, 3202.

Lorenz 2008
Lorenz S., Münchener Kommentar zum BGB, 5. Auflage 2008.

Lorenz 2012
Lorenz S., Münchener Kommentar zum BGB, 6. Auflage 2012, BGB § 476 Beweislastumkehr, at http://beck-online.beck.de/?vpath=bibdata/komm/MuekoBGB_6_Band3/BGB/cont/MuekoBGB.BGB.p476.glII.gl2.htm

Löwisch 2003
Löwisch M., New Law of Obligations in Germany, Ritsumeiken Law Review, 20/2003, pp. 141-156.

Łętowska 1978
Łętowska E., Ochrona konsumenta z punktu widzenia polityki prawa, PiP 1978, z. 4.

Łętowska 2004
Łętowska E., Europejskie prawo umów konsumenckich, Warszawa: CH Beck 2004.

Łętowska, Jagielska, Lis, Miklaszewicz and Wiewiórkowska-Domagalska 2007
Łętowska E., Jagielska M., Lis K., Miklaszewicz P., Wiewiórkowska-Domagalska A., Implementation of the Consumer Law in Poland, (2007) Eurpean Review of Private Law, Issue 6, pp. 873-889.

Macdonald 1999
Macdonald E., 'In the course of business'- a fresh examination, Web Journal of Current Legal Issues, Blackstone Press Ltd, 1999 at http://webjcli.ncl.ac.uk/1999/issue3/macdonald3.html

Machnikowski 2011
Machnikowski P., in Gniewek (edt.), Komentarz do kodeksu cywinego, Warszawa: C.H. Beck 2011.

Macleod 2007
Macleod J.K., Consumer Sales Law, London- New York: Routledge-Cavendisch 2007.

Maliszewska-Nienartowicz 2002
Maliszewska-Nienartowicz J., Sprzedaż konsumencka – wybrane problemy prawne, Glosa 12/2002.

Mangold/*diss.* 2008
Mangold S., Verbraucherschutz und Kunstkauf im deutschen en europäischen Recht, Frankfurt: Peter Lang 2008.

Mankowski 2003
Mankowski P., Beweislastumkehr beim Verbrauchsgüterkauf, EWiR 2003, pp. 465-466.

Martis 2010
Martis R., Aktuelle Entwicklungen im Kaufrecht – Die Beweisvermutung des § 476 BGB, MDR 15/2010, pp. 841 *et seq.*

Massimo Bianca and Grundmann 2002
Massimo C. Bianca, Grundmann S., EU Sales Directive. Commentary, Antwerp-Oxford-New York: Intersentia 2002.

Maultzsch 2006
Maultzsch F., Der Ausschluss der Beweislastumkehr gem. § 476 BGB a. E., NJW 2006, pp. 3091-3097.

Mckendrick 2013
Mckendrick E., Contract Law, Text Cases and Materials, Oxford: Palgrave Macmillan 2013.

Micklitz 1999
Micklitz H.-W., Die Verbrauchsgüterkauf-Richtlinie, Europïsches Zeitschrift für Wirtschaftsrecht 10 (1999), pp. 485-493.

Micklitz 2002
Micklitz H.-W., The New German Sales Law: Changing Patterns in the Regulation of Product Quality, Journal of Consumer Policy 2002, Volume 25, Issue 3-4, pp. 379-401.

Micklitz 2012
Micklitz H.-W., Münchener Kommentar zum Bürgerlichen Gesetzbuch: BGB, Band 1: Allgemeiner Teil, §§ 1-240, ProstG, AGG, 6 Auflage 2012.

Micklitz, Reich and Rott 2009
Micklitz H.W., Reich N., Rott P., Understanding EU Consumer Law, 2009.

Miller 2007
Miller L., The Common Frame of Reference and the Feasibility of a Common Contract Law in Europe, Journal of Business Law 2007 (Jun), pp. 378-411.

Miller 2011
Miller L., The Emergence of EU Contract Law. Exploring Europeanization, Oxford 2011.

Möllers 2002
Möllers T.M.J, European Directives on Civil Law, The German Approach: Towards the Re-codification and New Foundation of Civil Law Principles, RabelsZ 6/2002, pp. 777-798.

Morawski 1992
Morawski L., Ciężar dowodu – niektóre problemy dowodowe, Studia cywilistyczne 1982, 32, pp. 189 *et seq.*

Morgan-Taylor and Naidoo 2002
Morgan-Taylor M., Naidoo A., The Draft Regulations to Adopt the Directive on Certain Aspects of the Sale of Consumer Goods and Associated Guarantees – Problems of the Time of Conformity for the Quality Obligation, 2002 3 Web JCLI at http://webjcli.ncl.ac.uk/2002/issue3/taylor3.html

Müller 2003
Müller M., Die Umgehung des Rechts des Verbrauchsgüterkaufs im Gebrauchtwagenhandel, NJW 2003, pp. 1975-1980.

Munday 2013
Munday R., Evidence, Oxford University Press 2013.

Murray and Stürner 2004
Murray P.L., Stürner R., German Civil Justice, Durham North California: Carolina Academic Press 2004.

Musielak 1975
Musielak H.-J., Die Grundlagen der Beweislast im Zivilprozeß, Berlin: De Gruyter 1975.

Musielak/Bearbeiter 2013
Musielak H.-J., Kommentar zur Zivilprozessordnung, München: Verlag Franz Vahlen 2013.

Musielak and Heinrich 2011
Musielak H.-J., Heinrich Ch., Kommentar zur Zivilprozessordnug: ZPO, München: Verlag Franz Vahlen 2011.

Naidoo 2011
Naidoo A., Consumer Remedies following the sale of faulty goods, Journal of Business Law 8/2011, pp. 804-815.

National Consumer Council 2004
National Consumer Council (NCC) Seeking Resolution Report, January 2004.

Neumann/*diss.* 2006
Neumann L., Das Pferdekaufrecht nach der Schuldrechtmodernisierung, Berlin: FN Verlag 2006.

Nowakowski 1967
Nowakowski K., Ochrona nabywcy rzeczy z wadami, RPEiS 1967, z. 2, pp. 1-29.

OFT 2010
OFT, Mapping UK consumer redress. A summary guide to dispute resolution systems, May 2010.

Olczyk 2006
Olczyk M., Sprzedaż konsumencka, Warszawa: Lexis Nexis 2006.

Osajda 2006
Osajda K., Kiedy sprzedawca nieruchomości jest również konsumentem?, Rzeczpospolita, wydanie internetowe 27-12-2006. http://www.rp.pl/artykul/57237_Kiedy_sprzedawca_nieruchomosci_jest_rowniez_konsumentem.html.

Oughton and Willett 2002
Oughton D., Willett Ch., Quality Regulation in European Private Law, (2002) 25 Journal of Consumer Policy, pp. 299-328.

Parisi 2004
Parisi F., The Harmonisation of Legal Warranties in European Sales Law: An Economic Analysis, The American journal of comparative law Vol. 52, No. 2 (2004), pp. 403-432.

Pecyna 2003
Pecyna M., Komentarz do ustawy z dnia 27 lipca 2002 r. o szczególnych warunkach sprzedaży konsumenckiej oraz o zmianie Kodeksu cywilnego (Dz.U.02.141.1176). LEX/el. 2003.

Pecyna 2012
Pecyna M., Sprzedaż konsumencka *de lege ferenda*, Transformacje Prawa Prywatnego 2/2012, pp. 145-166.

Pfeiffer 2002
Pfeiffer T., Kommentierung der Verbrauchsgüterkauf-Richtlinie, in: Dauner-Lieb B., Heidel T., Anwaltskommentar zum neuen Schuldrecht, Bonn: Deutscher AnwaltVerlag 2002.

Piasecki 2010
Piasecki K., System dowodów i postępowanie dowodowe w sprawach cywilnych, Warszawa: Lexis Nexis 2010.

Pisulinski 2004
Pisulinski J., in Rajski J. (edt.), System Prawa Prywatnego, 7/2004.

Prütting 1983
Prütting S., Gegenwartsprobleme der Beweislast, München: C.H. Beck 1983.

Prütting, Wegen and Weinreich 2014
Prütting H., Wegen G., Weinreich G., BGB Kommentar, 9 Auflage, Luchterhand Verlag 2014.

Radwański 2003
Radwański Z., Podmioty Prawa Cywilnego w świetle zmian przeprowadzonych ustawą z dnia 14 lutego 2003, Przegląd Sądowy 2003, nr 7-8.

Radwański 2006
Radwański Z. (edt.), Zielona Księga. Optymalna wizja Kodeksu Cywilnego w Rzeczypospolitej Polskiej, Ministerstwo Sprawiedliwości, Warszawa 2006.

T.M., Parl. gesch. NBW (Inv. Boeken 3, 5 en 6), Boek 7 (Reehuis and Slob 1991)
Reehuis W.H.M., Slob E.E., Parlementaire geschiedenis van het nieuwe Burgerlijk Wetboek, Invoering Boeken 3, 5 en 6. Boek 7. Bijzondere overeenkomsten, Titels 1, 7, 9 en 14, Deventer: Kluwer 1991.

Reich 1992
Reich N., Diverse Approaches to Consumer Protection Philosophy, Journal of Consumer Policy 1991-1992, Volume 14, Issue 3, pp. 257-292.

Reich and Micklitz 2003
Reich N., Micklitz H-W., Europäisches Verbraucherrecht, 2003.

Reich, Micklitz, Rott and Tonner 2014
Reich N., Micklitz H-W., Rott P., Tonner K., European Consumer Law, Cambridge-Antwerp-Portland: Intersentia 2014.

Reinicke and Tiedtke 2009
Reinicke D., Tiedtke K., Kaufrecht, München: Carl Heymanns Verlag 2009.

Reinking 2004
Reinking, Umkehr der Beweislastumkehr durch den BGH, AnwBl 2004, pp. 607-611.

Reynolds 2003
Reynolds F.M.B., Loss of the right to reject, (2003) 199 Law Quarterly Review, pp. 544-545.

Rosenberg 1965
Rosenberg L., Die Beweislast, 5 Auflage, München: CH Beck 1965.

Rosenberg, Schwab and Gottwald 2010
Rosenberg L., Schwab K.H., Gottwald P., Zivilprozessrecht, München: Verlag C.H. Beck 2010.

Van Rossum 2012
Van Rossum M.M., Bijzondere overeenkomsten, Groene Serie, Burgerlijk Wetboek Boek 7, Artikel 18, Deventer: Kluwer 2012.

Roth 2004
Roth H., Beweislastumkehr beim Verbrauchsguterkauf, ZIP 2004, pp. 2025-2027.

Rott 2004
Rott P., German Sales Law Two Years After the Implementation of Directive 1999/44/EC, 5/2004 German Law Journal, pp. 237-255.

Rott 2005
Rott. P., What is the role of the ECJ in the EC Private Law? A comment on the ECJ judgments in Oceano Grupo, Freiburger Kommunalbauten, Leitner and Veedfald, Hanser Law Review 2005, Vol. 1, No. 1, pp. 6-17.

Rott 2008
Rott P., 17 April 2008, Case C-404/06 *Quelle AG v. Bundesverband der Verbraucherzentralen und Verbraucherverbände*, C-404/06. The Quelle case and the potential of and limitations to interpretation in the light of the relevant Directive, ERPL 6/2008, pp. 1119-1130.

Rudnicki and Trzaskowski/Kodeks Cywilny 2014
Rudnicki S., Trzaskowski R., Gudowski J. (edt), Kodeks Cywilny, Komentarz, Czesc Ogolna I, Warszawa: Lexis Nexis 2014.

Rutgers and Krans 2014
Rutgers G.R., Krans H.B., Bewijs, PITLO Het Nederlands burgerlijk recht, Deel 7, Deventer: Kluwer 2014.

Rühl 2009
Rühl G., Zur Vermutung der Mangelhaftigkeit beim Verbrauchsgüterkauf. Die Rechtsprechung des BGH in rechtsvergleichender Perspektive, Rabels Nr. 4 2009, 73, pp. 912-934.

Saenger and Schultze (Hk BGB) 2010
Saenger I., Schultze R. u.a., Bürgerliches Gesetzbuch: BGB. Handkommentar, 6 Auflage, Nomos 2010.

Saueressig 2008
Saueressig Ch., Die Anwendungsvoraussetzungen der vorschrift des § 476 BGB, NJOZ 2008, p. 2075.

Schafer and Pfeiffer 1999
Schafer P., Pfeiffer K., Die EG-Richtlinie über den Verbrauchsgüterkauf, ZIP 1999, p. 1829.

Bijzondere overeenkomsten (Schelhaas) 2013
Schelhaas H.N., in Wessels B., Verheij A.J. (edt.), Bijzondere oveereenkomsten, Deventer: Kluwer 2013.

Schermaier 2003
Schermaier M.J., Verbraucherkauf in Europa: altes Gewährleistungsrecht und die Umsetzung der Richtlinie 1999/44/EG, München: Sellier, European law publishers 2003.

Schinkels 2007
Schinkels B., BGH: Vermutung des § 476 BGB bei nicht erkennbaren Tierinfekten, LMK 2007, 240778, beck-online.

Schlechtriem 2002
Schlechtriem P., The German Act to Modernize the Law of Obligations in the Context of Common Principles and Structures of the Law of Obligations in Europe, 2002 Oxford U Comparative L Forum 2 at ouclf.iuscomp.org

Schulte-Nölke 2002
Schulte-Nölke H., The New German Law of Obligations: an Introductuion, 2002, p. 1, at http://www.iuscomp.org/gla/index.html

Schulte-Nölke, Twigg-Flesner and Ebers 2008
Schulte-Nölke H., Twigg-Flesner Ch., Ebers M.,The EC Consumer Law Compendium Comparative Analysis, February 2008.

Schulze/Wendehorst 2012
Wendehorst in Schultze R., Common European Sales Law. Commentary, C.H. Beck/Nomos/Hart 2012.

Schürnbrand 2008
Schürnbrand J., Beweislastumkehr nach § 476 BGB, 2008, at http://www.jura.uni-mainz.de/habersack/Dateien/Kurzskript_476_BGB.pdf.

Schwartze 2000
Schwartze A., Europaische Sachmangelggewahrleistung beim Warenkauf, 2000.

Sejm RP 2014
Sejm RP 17.01.2014, Druk nr. 2076, Statute justification.

Sengayen 2002
Sengayen M., Consumer Sales Law in Poland: Changing the Law, Changing Attitudes, Journal of Consumer Policy, Volume 25, Number 4, 2002, pp. 403-437.

Shears 2000
Shears P., It will be the biggest change to consumer rights for 20 years, The Journal of Business Law, May 2000, pp.262-277.

Sikorska (A.) 2005
Sikorska A., Ciężar dowodu w przypadku odstąpienia od umowy sprzedaży przez kupującego z powodu wad rzeczy lub niezgodności towaru z umową, Radca Prawny 1/2005, pp. 59 *et seq.*

Sirks 2003
Sirks A.J.B., Die Umsetzung der Richtlinie 1999/44/EG in den Niederlanden, in Schermaiera M., Verbraucherkauf in Europa. Altes Gewährleistungsrecht und die Umsetzung der Richtlinie 1999/44/EG, München: European Law Publishers Sellier 2003.

Sivesand 2005
Sivesand H., The Buyer's remedies for non-conforming goods. Should there be Free Choice or are Restrictions Necessary?, München: European Law Publishers Sellier 2005.

Slomski/*diss.* 2011
Slomski M., Die geschichtliche Entwicklung des polnischen Verbraucherkaufrechtes und die Umsetzung der Verbrauchsgüterkaufrichtlinie in Polen, Verlag Dr. Kovac 2011.

Smits 2001
Smits J.M., De voorgenomen implementatie van de richtlijn consumentenkoop: een gebrekkig wetvoorstel, WPRN 6470 (2001), pp. 1047-1049.

Smits 2003
Smits J., De richtlijn consumentenkoop en het Nederlandse recht, in De richtlijn consumentenkoop in perspectief pp.1-27, Den Haag: BJu 2003.

Snijders, Klaassen and Meijer 2011
Snijders H.J., Klaassen C.J.M. and Meijer G.J., Nederlands burgerlijk procesrecht, Deventer: Kluwer 2011.

Sokołowski 2012
Sokołowski T., in Kidyba A. (edt.) Kodeks Cywilny. Komentarz. Tom I. Część Ogólna, Wolters Kluwer Polska 2012.

Sołtysiński 1970
Sołtysiński S., Odpowiedzialność producenta wobec konsumenta za szkody wyrządzone wprowadzeniem do obrotu rzeczy z wadami, Studia Cywilistyczne, t. XV, Kraków 1970.

Spencer and Spencer 2007
Spencer M., Spencer J., Evidence, Oxford University Press 2007.

Staudenmayer 2000
Staudenmayer D., The Directive on the Sale of the Consumer Goods and Associated Guarantees – A Milestone in the European Consumer and Private Law, European Review of Private Law, 4/2000, pp. 547-564.

Staudenmayer 2004
Staudenmayer D., The Place of Consumer Contract Law Within the Process on European Contract Law, Journal of Consumer Policy 27/2004, pp. 269-287.

Staudinger 2004
Staudinger J., Kommentar zum Bürgerlichen Gesetzbuch – Buch 2: Recht der Schuldverhältnisse §§ 433-487 (Kaufrecht und Leasingrecht), Sellier – de Gruyter 2004.

Stefaniak 1973
Stefaniak A., *Onus probandi* w procesie cywilnym, Lublin: Tow. Nauk Organizacji i Kierownictwa 1973.

Stefanicki 2004
Stefanicki R., Sprzedaż konsumencka w świetle ustawy o szczególnych warunkach sprzedaży, Monitor Prawniczy 7/2004.

Stefanicki 2006
Stefanicki R., Ochrona konsumenta w świetle ustawy o szczególnych warunkach sprzedaży konsumenckiej, Kraków: Wolters Kluwer Polska, Zakamycze 2006.

Stefanicki 2009
Stefanicki R., Arbitraż w sprawach konsumenckich – zagadnienia wybrane (glos w dyskusji), Kwartalnik ADR, Nr 2 (6) 2009, pp. 65-72.

Storskrubb 2008
Storskrubb E., Civil Procedure and EU Law. A Policy Area Uncovered, Oxford University Press 2008.

Szczotka 2007
Szczotka J., Sprzedaż konsumencka w prawie Polskim i Unii Europejskiej, Komentarz, Lublin: Verba 2007.

Thoe Schwartzenberg 2013
Thoe Schwartzenberg H.W.B., Civiel bewijsrecht voor de rechtspraktijk, Apeldoorn-Antwerpen: Maklu 2013.

Tims 2011
Tims A., Are you entitled to a refund when the item you've bought is faulty? The Observer, 17 April 2011, on http://www.guardian.co.uk/money/2011/apr/17/consumer-rights-refunds (14.10.2014).

Torbus 2009
Torbus A., Ochrona konsumenta jako strony zapisu na zagraniczny sąd polubowny, Kwartalnik ADR, Nr 2 (6) 2009, pp. 93-100.

Tuil 2010
Tuil M.L., in Hodges C., Vogenauer S., Tulibacka M., The Costs and Funding of Civil Litigation. A comparative Perspective, Oxford: Hart Publishing 2010.

Tulibacka 2012
Tulibacka M., in Hodges Ch., Benöhr I., Creutzfeldt-Banda N. (edt.), Consumer ADR in Europe, Oxford: Hart Publishing 2012.

Twigg-Flesner and Bradgate 2000
Twigg-Flesner Ch., Bradgate R., The EC Directive on Certain Aspects of the Sale of Consumer Goods and Associated Guarantees – All Talk and No Do?, 2000 2 Web JCLI.

Usowicz 2005
Usowicz E., Reklamacje. UOKiK ostrzega, Gazeta Prawna 1.2.2005.

Valk 2010
Valk W.L., Stellen en bewijzen in gevallen van dwaling en non-conformiteit, part I and part II, WPNR 2010/6867and 2010/6868.

Warendorf, Thomas and Curry-Sumner 2009
Warendorf H., Thomas R., Curry-Sumner I., The Civil Code of the Netherlands, Wolters Kluwer Law & Business 2009.

Watterson 2001
Watterson S., Consumer Sales Directive 1999/44 EC – The impact on English law, (2001) 9 European Review of Private Law, Issue 2-3, pp. 197-221.

Wendehorst 2014
Wendehorst Ch., Das neue Gesetz zur Umsetzung der Verbraucherrechterichtlinie, NJW 2014, pp. 577-584.

Wessels 2010
Wessels B., Koop: algemeen (Monografieën BW nr. B65a), Deventer: Kluwer 2010.

Welser and Jud 2000
Welser R., Jud B., Zur Reform des Gewährleistungsrechts, Vienna 2000.

Wertenbruch 2012
Wertenbruch J., Die besonderheiten des Tierkaufs bei Sachmängelgewährleistung, NJW 2012, pp. 2065-2070.

Westermann 2012
Westermann H.P., Münchener Kommentar zum BGB, 6. Auflage, München: Verlag C.H. Beck 2012.

Whittaker 2005
Whittaker S., Liability for products, English law, French law and European Harmonisation, Oxford University Press 2005.

Whittaker 2007
Whittaker S., Form and Substance in the Reception of EC Directives into English Contract Law, (2007) 3 European Review of Contract Law, pp. 381-409.

Whittaker 2008
Whittaker S., Burden of Proof in the Consumer *Acquis* and in the Draft Common Frame of Reference: Law, Fact and Things in Between' (2008) European Review of Contract Law, pp. 411-444.

Willett 2000
Willett, The Role of Contract Law in Product Liability, in Howells G., The Law of Product Liability, London: Lexis Nexis Butterworths 2000.

Willett and Morgan-Taylor 2013
Willett Ch., Morgan-Taylor M., Consumer protection, in Furmston M., Chauh J. (edt.), Commercial Law, Pearson 2013.

Willett, Morgan-Taylor and Naidoo 2004
Willett Ch., Morgan-Taylor M., Naidoo A., The Sale and Supply of Goods to Consumers Regulations, Journal of Business Law 2004, pp. 94-120.

Wissink/*diss.* 2001
Wissink M.H., Richtlijnconforme interpretatie van burgerlijk recht, Deventer: Kluwer 2001.

Verbintenissenrecht 2014
De Jong G.T., Krans H.B., Wissink M.H., Verbintennisrecht algemeen, Deventer: Kluwer 2014.

Witte and Micklitz 2011
de Witte B, Micklitz H.-W., The European Court of Justice and Autonomy of the Member States, Intersentia 2011.

Włodarska-Dziurzyńska 2009
Włodarska-Dziurzyńska K., Sankcje w prawie konsumenckim na przykładzie wybranych umów, Warszawa: Lexis Nexis 2009.

Woodroffe and Lowe 2013
Woodroffe G., Lowe R., Consumer Law and Practice, London: Sweet and Maxwell 2013.

Zerres 2007
Zerres T., Die Bedeutung der Verbrauchsgüterkaufrichtlinie für die Europäisierung des Vertragsrechts. Eine rechtsvergleichende Untersuchung am Beispiel des deutschen und englischen Kaufrechts, European Law Publishers Selier 2007.

Zimmermann 2004
Zimmermann R., Liability for non-conformity: the system of remedies in German sales law and its historical context, The Irish Jurist New Series 2004, 39, pp. 1-50.

Zimmermann 2005
Zimmermann R., The new German Law of Obligations. Historical and Comparative Perspectives, Oxford University Press 2005.

Zuckerman 2013
Zuckerman A., Zuckerman on Civil Procedure. Principles of Practice, Sweet & Maxwell 2013.

Żuławska 1977
Żuławska C., Ochrona interesów prawnych konsumenta w dzialalności spółdzielni spożywców, Warszawa 1977.

Żuławska 2005
Żuławska Cz., in Nowicka A. (edt), O niektórych zmianach w regulacjach stosunku klienteli, Prawo prywatne czasu przemian. Księga pamiątkowa dedykowana Profesorowi Stanisławowi Sołtysińskiemu, Poznań 2005.

Żuławska/Bieniek 2007
Żuławska Cz., in Bieniek G. (edt) Komentarz do Kodeksu Cywilnego, Warszawa 2007.

Żuławska and Trzaskowski 2013/Kodeks Cywilny
Żuławska Cz., Trzaskowski R., Gudowski J. (edt), Kodeks Cywilny, Komentarz, Zobowiązania III, Warszawa: Lexis Nexis 2013.

Legislation

EU

Consumer Sales Directive

Recital 8	221, 278
Recital 14	373
Recital 15	149
Recital 17	399
Art. 1 (2)	195, 202, 205
Art. 2 (1)	219, 275
Art. 2 (2)	14, 101, 202, 218-221, 250, 257, 259, 276, 277, 280, 282, 285, 286, 288, 292-295, 297-299, 303, 304, 306, 310, 322, 326, 329, 330, 334, 350, 355, 356, 358, 361, 362, 372, 376, 377, 438, 644
Art. 2 (3)	252, 253, 287, 324, 351, 352
Art. 2 (5)	222, 283, 316, 317, 345
Art. 3	101, 119, 153, 154, 219, 367
Art. 5 (1)	176
Art. 5 (3)	3, 5, 14, 19, 101, 176, 207, 259, 364-369, 371, 375, 376, 379, 381-384, 387, 388, 414, 418, 423, 429, 435, 440, 444, 448, 451, 456, 461, 464, 468, 484, 489, 492, 494, 506, 512, 514, 516, 524, 525, 544, 546, 552, 582, 588-592, 599, 610, 615, 618, 622, 631, 632, 635, 642
Art. 6	367

Regulation (EEC, Euratom) No. 1182/71 of the Council of 3 June 1971

Art. 3 (1)	374, 541
Art. 3 (2)	457

Treaty on European Union (Maastricht Treaty 1992)

Art 3 (s)	100

Poland

Civil Code

Article	Pages
Art. 6	23, 25, 27, 30, 32, 33, 35, 40, 94, 114, 116, 262, 265, 266, 268, 273, 384, 389, 407, 416, 429, 430
Art. 22^{1}	108
Art. 111 (2)	403
Art. 112	403, 404, 605
Art. 114	404
Art. 169	230
Art. 348	401
Art. 544	401
Art. 556 (1)*	224, 229
Art. 556 (2)*	230
Art. 556^{1}**	224-227, 244-246, 256, 261, 267, 273, 388, 595
Art. 556^{2}**	116, 256, 262, 383, 384, 398, 402, 407, 408, 422, 424, 428, 432, 583, 605, 621
Art. 557**	245, 255, 272
Art. 556^{3}**	230, 242, 245, 593
Art. 559*	114-116
Art. 560 (1)*	117
Art. 561^{5}**	395, 411, 596, 612

* before the implementation of the Consumer Sales Directive

** amended/introduced in 2014

Consumer Sale Act

Article	Pages
Art. 1 (1)	108
Art. 1 (4)	111, 232
Art. 3	266
Art. 4	228, 230, 231, 234, 235, 248
Art. 4 (1)	115, 116, 256, 262, 383-387, 398, 402-404, 407, 408, 410, 415, 423-425, 428, 429, 583, 605, 611, 621
Art. 4 (2)	224-226, 230, 232, 233, 235, 236, 239, 243, 256-260, 263, 264, 267, 268, 273, 377, 388, 390, 391, 410

Art. 4 (3) 224-226, 230, 232, 233, 235, 238, 240-243, 245, 256-260, 263, 264, 267, 268, 273, 377, 388, 390, 391, 410
Art. 5 242
Art. 6 234, 243, 248, 260, 265
Art. 7 251-253, 266
Art. 8 (3) 395, 411, 596, 612
Art. 9 (1) 395, 398, 408
Art. 10 (1) 116

Kodeks postepowania cywilnego (k.p.c.)

Art. 3 27
Art. 87 (5) 126
Art. 126 29
Art. 130 29
Art. 187 29
Art. 210 34
Art. 231 37
Art. 232 27, 28, 30
Art. 234 35
Art. 398[2] 122

Rozporządzenie Ministra Gospodarki, Pracy i Polityki Społecznej z dnia 30 stycznia 2003 r. w sprawie terminów zawiadomienia sprzedawcy o stwierdzeniu niezgodności towaru żywnościowego z umową, Dz. U. Nr 31 poz. 258

Art. 1 399

Germany

German Constitution

Art. 20 (3) 150

BGB

§ 13 292
§ 90a 472, 480
§ 187 (1) 456, 457, 463, 606
§ 187 (2) 456

§ 188 (2) 457, 606
§ 188 (3) 457
§ 193 458
§ 294 452
§ 295 452
§ 296 452
§ 309 (12) 466
§ 363 289, 292, 435, 489
§ 433 137, 142, 275, 286, 290, 292, 295
§ 434 274-278, 280, 281, 285, 286, 288, 290, 292-295, 343, 360, 438, 440-442, 444, 445, 447, 462, 474, 475, 478, 481, 482, 491, 492, 597, 508
§ 434 (1) 277-279, 291, 285, 293
§ 434 (2) 283
§ 434 (3) 291
§ 435 274, 276, 284, 286, 288, 293-295, 438
§ 437 153, 156
§ 439 151, 153, 156, 217
§ 439 (4) 149, 150, 156
§ 442 287, 291, 294
§ 459* 275, 435
§ 446 448, 452
§ 447 453, 466
§ 474 137, 138, 141, 443, 455, 474, 482
§ 475 138, 141
§ 476 138, 141, 148, 283, 290, 435, 436, 438-440, 442-452, 454, 458, 460-466, 468, 472-479, 481, 483-489, 491, 493, 584, 587, 597-599, 622, 630
§ 477 138, 141
§ 478 138, 141

* before the implementation of the Consumer Sales Directive

ZPO

§ 130 (3) 46
§ 130 (5) 46
§ 139 (1) 46

§ 286 54
§ 292 52, 465, 488, 613

England and Wales

Sale of goods Act 1979

Section 12 317
Section 13 175, 303, 305
Section 14 301, 302, 309-312, 315, 317, 318, 625
Section 15 306, 318
Section 32 507
Section 35 170
Section 48A 299, 321, 361, 497, 498, 500, 504, 512, 515, 516, 518, 607, 614, 632
Section 48B 172
Section 48C 172
Section 48D 174
Section 48F 175, 299, 321, 326, 391

Consumer Rights Bill

Section 3 182
Section 9 302, 309, 315, 325
Section 10 311
Section 11 305
Section 13 307
Section 14 308
Section 19 (3) 505, 600
Section 19 (14) 500, 505, 509, 512, 600, 607
Section 19 (15) 517, 614, 632
Section 20 173
Section 29 (2) 508

UCTA

Section 6 167

SSGCR 2002

Part 5A s. 48A 497
Part 5A s. 48F 175

Supply of Goods and Services Act 1982

Part 1B 182

Limitation Act 1980

Section 5 176

The Netherlands

BW

Art. 3:40 198
Art. 6:99 84
Art. 7:1 333
Art. 7:5 (1) 195, 204, 205
Art. 7:5 (3) 195, 202
Art. 7:5 (5) 204
Art. 7:6 198, 197, 204, 524
Art. 7:7 204
Art. 7:9 204, 333, 347, 540, 608
Art. 7:10 540, 608
Art. 7:11 198, 204, 540
Art. 7:15 347
Art. 7:16 347
Art. 7:17 198, 202, 205, 332, 334, 343, 349, 362, 532, 536
Art. 7:17 (1) 333
Art. 7:17 (2) 200, 338-342, 348, 350, 352, 357, 528, 536, 549, 559, 556, 602
Art. 7:17 (3) 200, 335, 343
Art. 7:17 (4) 200, 335, 344
Art. 7:17 (5) 335, 351, 352, 536
Art. 7:17 (6) 335
Art. 7:18 (1) 200, 335

Art. 7:18 (2)	86, 89, 197, 202, 205, 207, 353, 369, 524-532, 535, 536, 539, 540, 544, 546-549, 551, 552, 556, 558, 560, 562, 564, 566, 568, 569, 574, 576-578, 581, 586, 615, 635
Art. 7:18 (3)	335, 336, 345
Art. 7:19a	204
Art. 7:21 (4)	196
Art. 7:21 (5)	196
Art. 7:23	198, 200, 205, 346, 362, 543, 574, 608
Art. 7:24	196
Art. 7:25	196
Art. 7:900-906	209

Rv

Art. 21	82
Art. 22	82
Art. 149	75, 91
Art. 150	77-79, 81, 83-85, 92, 94, 362, 525, 529, 530
Art. 151 (1)	90
Art. 151 (2)	89, 90
Art. 152	90

OBW

Art. 196 (2)	197

Algemene Termijnenwet

Art. 1 (1)	542
Art. 4a	542

Table of Cases

ECJ/CJEU

ECJ 10.04.1983, C-14/83, *Sabine von Colson and Elisabeth Kamann v Land Nordrhein Westfalen*, ECR (1983) I-1891

ECJ 09.11.1983, *Amministrazione delle Finanze dello Stato v SpA San Giorgio*, C-199/82, ECR (1983) I-03595

ECJ 19.01.1993, C-89/91, *Shearson Lehman Hutton v TVB Treuhandgesellschaft für Vermögensverwaltung und Beteiligungen mbH*, ECR (1993) I-0139

ECJ 14.03.1991, C-361/89, *France v Patrice Di Pinto*, ECR (1991) I-1213

ECJ 30.05.1991, C-361/88, *Commission v Germany*, ECR (1991) I-2567

ECJ 15.06.1995, C-220/94, *Commission v Luxembourg*, ECR (1995) I-1589

ECJ 03.07.1997, C-269/95, *Benincasa v Dentalkit Srl.*, ECR (1997) I-3793

ECJ 13.01.2000, C-220/98, *Estee Lauder cosmetics GmbH & Co. OHG v Lancester Group GmbH*, ECR (2000) I-0117

ECJ 16.07.1998, C-210/96, *Gut Springenheide GmbH v Oberkreisdirektor des Kreises Steinfurt*, ECR (1998) I-4657

ECJ 18.01.2001, C-162/99, *Commission v Italy*, ECR (2001) I-00541

ECJ 22.11.2001, Joined Cases C-541/99 and C-542/99, *Cape Snc v Idealservice Srl* and *Idealservice MN RE Sas v OMAI Srl*, ECR (2001) I-9059

ECJ 05.10.2004, C-397/01 - C-401/0, 1 *Bernhard Pfeiffer and Others v Deutsches Rotes Kreuz, Kreisverband Waldschut eV*, ECR (2004) I-8835

ECJ 05.06.2005 Joined Cases C-11/03, C-299/03 and C-316/03 to C-318/03 *HLH Warenvertrieb, Orthica v Bundesrepublik Deutschland*, ECR (2005) I-5141

ECJ 25.10.2005, C-350/03, *Elisabeth Schulte v Deutsche Bausparkasse Badenia AG*, ECR (2005) I-9215.

ECJ 04.07.2006, C-212/04, *Konstantinos Adeneler and Others v Ellinikos Organismos Galaktos (ELOG)*, ECR (2006) I-6057

ECJ 26.10.2006, C-168/05, *Mostaza Claro v Centro Móvil Milenium SL*, ECR (2006) I-10421

ECJ 18.07.2007, C-119/05, *Lucchini* ECR(2007) I-6199

ECJ 17.04.2008, C-404/06 *Quelle AG v Bundesverband der Verbraucherzentralen und Verbraucherverbände*, ECR (2008) I-2713

ECJ 08.05.2008, *Danske Svineproducenter v Justitsministeriet*, ECR (2008) I-3343

ECJ 16.06.2011, C-65/09, *Gebr. Weber GmbH v J. Wittmer and I. Putz v Medianess Electronics GmbH*, ECR (2011) I-2567

ECJ 30.05.2013, C-397/11, *E. Joros v Aegon Magyarorszag Hitel Zrt.*, not yet published

ECJ 03.10.2013, C-32/12 *Soledad Duarte Hueros v Atoiciba et al.*, not yet published
ECJ 05.12.2013, C-413/12, *Associacion de Consumidores Independedienties de Castilla y Leon v Anuntis Segundamano Espana S.L.*, not yet published
ECJ 27.02.2014, C-470/12, *Pohotovost s.r.o. v M. Vasuta*, not yet published

Poland

SN 20.12.1933, C III 67/33
SN 13.06.1947, C III 1054/45
SN 03.10.1969, II PR 313/69
SN 28.06.1972, II CR 218/72
SN 10.07.1980, II UZP 10/80
SN 30.12.1988, III CZP 48/88
SN 20.04.1994, I CRN 44/94
SN 03.10.2000, I CK 308/00
SN 24.10.2000, V CKN 132/00
SN 26.10.2000, II CKN 305/00
SN 02.04.2003, I CKN 244/01
SN 08.11.2006, III CSK 174/2006
SN 20.12.2006, IV CSK 299/06
SN 03.12.2008, V CSK 293/08
SN 14.10.2011, III CZP 50/2011
SN 05.07.2012, IV CSK 75/2012

SO Poznań 25.08.2006, II Ca 1031/06
SO Białystok 17.01.2013, II Ca 996/12
SO Warszawa 27.01.2011, XVII AmC 452/10
SO Wrocław 30.01.2013, II Ca 1425/12
SO Szczecin 13.02.2013, II Ca 1268/12
SO Świdnica 12.03.2013, II Ca 44/13
SO Elbląg 08.04.2013, I Ca 55/13
SO Wrocław 28.05.2013, II Ca 259/13
SO Słupsk 07.06.2013, IV Ca 262/13
SO Lublin 08.08.2013, II Ca 438/13
SO Białystok 29.08.2013, II Ca 567/13
SO Sieradz 09.10.2013, I Ca 369/13
SO Tarnów 05.11.2013, I C 288/13
SO Słupsk 20.12.2013, IV Ca 608/13

SR Lubań 07.11.2012, I C 388/12
SR Złotoryja 28.12.2012, I C 413/12
SR Zgorzelec 14.01.2013, I C 842/12
SR Wrocław-Fabryczna 23.01.2013, XI C 695/12
SR Oleśnica 05.02.2013, I C 100/12
SR Wrocław Fabryczna 11.02.2013, XI C 695/12
SR Wrocław-Śródmieście 08.03.2013, VIII C 170/12
SR Złotoryja 23.04.2013, I C 461/12
SR Świdnica 04.06.2013, I C 741/11
SR Kłodzk 14.03.2013, I C 203/12
SR Wrocław-Krzyków 20.06.2013, I C 846/11
SR Wrocław-Śródmieście 01.10.2013, VII C 318/13
SR Wrocław-Śródmieście 23.10.2013, VIII C 797/13
SR Wrocław-Śródmieście 29.10.2013, VIII C 1030/13

Consumer Arbitration
Decision 26/2006 Consumer Arbitration

Germany

BGH 17.02.1970, III ZR 139/67, BGHZ 53, 245
BGH 24.11.1976, VIII ZR 137/75, BGHZ 67, 359
BGH 21.09.1982, VI ZR 302/80, BGHZ 85, 212
BGH 13.12.1984, III ZR 20/83, NJW 1985, 1774
BGH 30.04.1991, VI ZR 178/90, BGHZ 114, 284
BGH 27.09.2001, IX ZR 281/00, NJW 2002, 825
BGH 23.10.2001, XI ZR 63/01, BGHZ 149, 80
BGH 02.06.2004, VIII ZR 329/03, BGHZ 159, 215
BGH 22.11.2004, VIII ZR 21/04, NJW 2005, 283
BGH 14.09.2005, VIII ZR 363/04, NJW 2005, 3490
BGH 23.11.2005, VIII ZR 43/05, NJW 2006, 434
BGH 29.03.2006, VIII ZR 173/05, BGHZ 167, 40
BGH 11.07.2007, VIII ZR 110/06, NJW 2007, 2619
BGH 18.07.2007, VIII ZR 259/06, NJW 2007, 2621
BGH 10.10.2007, VIII ZR 330/06, NJW 2008, 53
BGH 08.11.2007, VII ZR 183/05, BGHZ 174, 110
BGH 11.11.2008, VIII ZR 265/07, NJW 2009, 580
BGH 26.11.2008, VIII ZR 200/05, BGHZ 179, 27
BGH 14.01.2009, VIII ZR 70/08, NJW 2009, 1660

BGH 24.02.2010, VIII ZR 71/09, NJW 2010, 8
BGH 17.10.2012, VIII ZR 226/11 NJW 2013, 220
BGH 16.04.2013, VIII ZR 375/11, Beck RS 2013, 15325

OLG Braunschweig 04.02.2003, 8 W 83/02, NJW 2003, 1053
OLG Köln 11.11.2003, 22 U 88/03, NJW-RR 2004, 268
OLG Bremen 11.03.2004, 2 U 99/03, JurionRS 2004, 17711
OLG Koblenz Hinweisbeschluss 08.01.2013, 2 U 1066/12, JurionRS 2013, 35008
OLG Stuttgart 18.01.2005, 10 U 179/04, ZGS 2005, 276
OLG Hamm 03.05.2005, 19 U 123/04, NJW-RR 2005, 1369
OLG Nürnberg 23.08.2005, 3 U 991/05, NJW 2005, 3000
OLG Celle 31.05.2006, 7 U 252/05, OLGReport Celle 2006, 577
OLG Hamm 04.08.2006, 11 U 142/05, Beck RS 2007, 04385
OLG München 06.09.2006, 20 U 1860/06, Beck RS 2006, 10640
OLG Saarbrücken 24.05.2007, 8 U 328/06, OLGReport Frankfurt 2007, 645
OLG Köln 08.08.2007, 11 U 23/7, VersR 2012, 1008
OLG Düsseldorf 23.06.2008, 1 U 264/07, Beck RS 2008, 15373
OLG Celle 22.11.2010, 20 U 8/10, NJW 2011, 132
OLG Saarbrücken, 25.10.2011, 4 U 540/10, NJW-RR 2012, 285
OLG Naumburg 11.10.2012, 1 U 2/12, Beck RS 2013, 05532

AG Marsberg 09.10.2002, 1 C 143/02, Beck RS 2002, 14584
AG Aachen 10.12.2003, 14 C 161/03, Beck RS 2005, 06814
AG Berlin-Charlottenburg 10.10.2008, 232 C 196/07, Beck RS 2009, 12941
AG Schorndorf 25.02.2009, 2 C 818/08, Beck RS 2009, 88603
AG Hamburg 25.03.2009, 7c C53/08, Beck RS 2008, 12681
AG Schleswig 18.06.2010, 2 C 21/10, NJW 2010, 2893
AG Schwäbisch Hall 20.12.2011, 5 C 557/11, Beck RS 2012, 12524

LG Ellwangen 13.12.2002, 3 O 219/02, NJW 2003, 517
LG Düsseldorf 22.04.2003, 24 S 548/02, Beck RS 2003, 12280
LG Luneburg 28.10.2003, 4 O 28/03
LG Bonn 27.02.2004, 10 O 618/03
LG Halle/Saale 18.10.2012, 4 O 1417/10

England and Wales

Drummond v Van Ingen (1887) 12 App Cas 284, HL at 297
Donoghue v Stevenson (1932) All ER Rep. 1, (1932) AC 562

Joseph Constantine Steamship Line Ltd v Imperial Smelting Corp Ltd (1942) AC 154, HL
Judge Hilbery J. in the R v Murtagh and Kennedy (1955) 39 cr App Rep 72
R v Murtagh and Kennedy (1955) 39 cr App Rep 72
Mash and Murrell v Joseph I Emmanuel Ltd (1962) 1 WLR 16
Ashington Piggeries Ltd v Christopher Hill Ltd (1972) AC 441, HL
Lee v York Coach (1977) RTR 35
Levison v Patent Steam Carpet Cleaning Co Ltd (1978) QB 69, AC
Hummingbird Motors v Hobbs (1986) R.T.R. 278
Aswan Engineering Co v Lupdine Ltd (1987) I W.R.L.I
Bernstein v Pamson Motors (Golders Green) Ltd (1987) 2 All ER 220
Brady v Group Lotus Car Companies plc (1987) All ER 1050
R & B Customs Brokers Co Ltd v United Dominions Trust Ltd (1988) WLR 321
Graanhandel T Vink BV v European Grain & Shipping, Ltd (1989) 2 Lloyd's Rep. 531
John Thorburn & Sons v Border Harvesters Ltd (1991), 1992 S.L.T. 549
Pickford v Imperial Chemical Industries (1998) 1 WLR 1189
Stevenson v Rogers (1999) QB 1028
Truk (UK) Ltd v Tokmakidis GmbH (2000) 1 LL Rep 543
Clegg v Andersson T/A Nordic Marine (2003) EWCA Civ 320
Jewson Ltd v Boyhan (2003) EWCA Civ 1030
The London Borough of Newham v Kathu, Zeb and Iqbal, and the Office of Fair Trading (Interested Party) (2004) EWCA Civ 55
Jones v Gallagher (2004) EVCA 10
Bramhill v Edwards (2004) EWCA Civ 403
Stephens v Cannon (2005) EWCA Civ 222
Domsalla (t/a Domsalla Building Services) v Dyason (2007) Adj.L.R 05/04
Fiat Auto Financial Services v Conelly (2007) S.L.T. (Sh ct) 111
Whitecap v John H Rubdle Ltd (2008) 2 Loyd's Rep 216 at 45
Macdonald v Pollock (2012) CSIH 12

The Netherlands

HR 13.03.1981, ECLI:NL:HR:1981:AG4158, NJ 1981/635 m.nt. CJHB (Haviltex)
HR 31.01.1992, ECLI:NL:HR:1992:ZC0491, NJ 1992/319 (Dijks/Delta Lloyd)
HR 23.10.1992, ECLI:NL:HR:1992:ZC0727 (Van der Pasch/Van der Velden)
HR 31.10.1997, ECLI:NL:HR:1997:ZC2476, NJ 1998/85
HR 04.12.1998, ECLI:NL:HR:1998:ZC2796, NJ 1999/549
HR 29.06.2001, ECLI:NL:HR:2001:AB2432, NJ 2001/476 (Industromontaza)
HR 29.11.2002, ECLI:NL:HR:2002:AE7345, NJ 2004/304 (TFS c.s/NS c.s.)

HR 29.11.2002, ECLI:NL:HR:2002:AE7351, NJ 2004/305 (Kastelijn/Gemeente Achtkarspelen)
HR 25.02.2005, ECLI:NL:HR:2005:AR5383 (Fabels/Meenderink)
HR 08.07.2005, ECLI:NL:HR:2005:AT3097, NJ 2006/22 (Kousedghi/Westminster Rental)
HR 09.09.2005, ECLI:NL:HR:2005:AT8238, NJ 2006/99
HR 15.12.2006, ECLI:NL:HR:2006:AZ1083, NJ 2007/203 (NNEK/Mourik)
HR 29.06.2007, ECLI:NL:HR:2007:AZ7617, NJ 2008/606 (Pouw/Visser)
HR 23.11.2007, ECLI:NL:HR:2007:BB3733, NJ 2008/552
HR 21.05.2010, ECLI:NL:HR:2010:BL8295, NJ 2010/275

Hof Arnhem 02.05.2006, ECLI:NL:GHARN:2006:AX6541
Hof Amsterdam 01.03.2007, ECLI:GHAMS:2007:BA9978
Hof Arnhem 06.11.2007, ECLI:NL:GHARN:2007:BC2967
Hof Leeuwarden 12.03.2008, ECLI:NL:GHLEE:2008:BC8175
Hof Leeuwarden 18.05.2010, ECLI:NL:GHLEE:2010:BM6766
Hof Amsterdam 23.11.2010, NJF 2011/80
Hof Amsterdam 21.12.2010, RCR 2011/36
Hof 's-Hertogenbosch 02.08.2011, ECLI:NL:GHSHE:2011:BR5909
Hof Amsterdam 17.04.2012, ECLI:NL:GHAMS:2012:BW3101
Hof Arnhem 17.07.2012, ECLI:NL:GHARN:2012:BX2358
Hof Leeuwarden 25.09.2012, ECLI:NL:GHLEE:2012:BX9126
Hof 's-Hertogenbosch 18.10.2012, ECLI:NL:GHSHE:2012:BY6857
Hof Arnhem-Leeuwarden 19.03.2013, ECLI:NL:GHARL:2013:BZ4794
Hof Den Haag 19.03.2013, ECLI:NL:GHDHA:2013:BZ6596
Hof Arnhem-Leeuwarden 09.04.2013, ECLI:NL:GHARL:2013:BZ6346
Hof Arnhem-Leeuwarden 13.08.2013, ECLI:NL:GHARL:2013:5954
Hof Arnhem-Leeuwarden 10.09.2013, ECLI:NL:GHARL:2013:6635
Hof Arnhem-Leeuwarden 26.11.2013, ECLI:NL:GHARL:2013:8982
Hof Den Haag 03.12.2013, ECLI:NL:GHDHA:2013:4492
Hof Arnhem-Leeuwarden 25.02.2014, ECLI:NL:GHARL:2014:1388

Rb Zutphen 18.07.2002, ECLI:NL:RBZUT:2002:AE6846
Rb Zwolle 21.05.2003, ECLI:NL:RBZWO:2003:AH8762
Rb Arnhem 24.05.2004, ECLI:NL:RBARN:2004:AP4372
Rb Arnhem 06.09.2006, ECLI:NL:RBARN:2005:AT2927
Rb Arnhem 11.10.2006, ECLI:NL:RBARN:2006:AZ2929
RB Haarlem 24.01.2007, ECLI:NL:RBHAA:2007:AZ7480
Rb Arnhem 07.03.2007, ECLI:NL:RBARN:2007:BA1777
Rb Zutphen 15.02.20008, ECLI:NL:RBZUT:2008:BC4965

Rb Haarlem 21.05.2008, ECLI:NL:RBHAA:2008:BD2453
Rb Breda 04.06.2008, ECLI:NL:RBBRE:2008:BD5195
Rb 's-Gravenhage 04.06.2008, ECLI:NL:RBSGR:2008:BE8794
Rb Rotterdam 28.01.2009, ECLI:NL:RBROT:2009:BH3367
Rb Utrecht 18.03.2009, ECLI:NL:RBUTR:2009:BH6552
Rb Utrecht 25.03.2009, ECLI:NL:RBUTR:2009:BI1714
Rb Arnhem 10.06.2009, ECLI:NL:RBARN:2009:BJ4349
Rb Haarlem 10.06.2009, ECLI:RBHAA:2009:BJ2323
Rb Groningen 19.08.2009, ECLI:NL:RBGRO:2009:BJ6974
Rb Alkmaar 19.08.2009, ECLI:NL:RBALK:2009:BJ5668
Rb Haarlem 17.02.2010, ECLI:NL:RBHAA:2010:BM3339
Rb Groningen 10.03.2010, ECLI:NL:RBGRO:2010:BL8009
Rb Haarlem 12.05.2010, ECLI:NL:RBHAA:2010:BN1607
Rb Haarlem 19.05.2010, ECLI:NL:RBHAA:2010:BN0550
Rb Alkmaar 09.06.2010, ECLI:NL:RBALK:2010:BN7766
Rb Maastricht 20.07.2010, ECLI:NL:RBMAA:2010:BQ6158
RB Rotterdam 06.10.2010, ECLINL:RBROT:2010:BO4071
Rb Arnhem 10.11.2010, ECLI:NL:RBARN:2010:BO4047
Rb Dordrecht 12.01.2011, ECLI:NLRBDOR:2011:BP0723
Rb Leeuwarden 26.04.2011, ECLI:NL:RBLEE:2011:BQ3070
Rb Alkmaar 20.06.2011, ECLI:NL:RBALK:2011:BR1997
Rb Breda 29.06.2011, ECLI:NL:RBBRE:2011:BR1086
Rb Amsterdam 09.11.2011, ECLI:NL:RBAMS:2011:BV2833
Rb Groningen 21.12.2011, ECLI:NL:RBGRO:2011:BU9714
Rb Arnhem 09.01.2012, ECLI:NL:RBARN:2012:BV3827
Rb Almelo 14.02.2012, ECLINL:RBALM:2012:BV9721
Rb Arnhem 18.01.2012, ECLI:NL:RBARN:2012:BV3590
Rb Haarlem 15.02.2012, ECLI:NL:RBHAA:2012:BV8727
Rb Dordrecht 16.05.2012, ECLI:NL:2012:BW6760
Rb Almelo 10.10.2012, ECLI:NL:RBALM:2012:BE0677
Rb Assen 16.10.2012, ECLI:NL:RBASS:2012:BY1448
Rb Almelo 05.12.2012, ECLI:NL:BRALM:2012:BY812 4
Rb Midden-Nederland 09.01.2013, ECLI:NL:RBMNE:2013:BY8341
Rb Noord-Holland 13.05.2013, ECLI:NL:RBNHO:2013:10061
Rb Midden-Nederland 10.07.2013, ECLI:NL:RBMNE:2013:3233
Rb Limburg 07.08.2013, ECLI:NL:RBLIM:2013:4796

Index

ADR 125, 127, 154, 186, 187, 209, 210, 212, 216
Animals 421, 472, 477-480, 484, 526, 535, 548, 554-558, 561, 569, 570, 572, 573, 576, 580, 586, 597, 598, 600, 602, 620, 623, 627, 636, 637, 639, 642
B2B 111, 112, 153, 338
B2C 111, 112, 338, 346
Conforming interpretation 147-153, 156, 197, 205, 318, 350, 360
Conformiteitvereiste 333, 356
Consumer protection 2, 4, 12, 19, 100-103, 115, 116, 120, 128, 130, 131, 134, 148, 153, 158, 159, 165-167, 188, 191, 193, 194, 202, 205, 208, 212, 213, 216, 217, 279, 322, 345, 356, 368, 382, 383, 386, 411, 428, 433, 439, 444, 483, 548, 551, 575, 582, 583, 587-589, 594, 599, 603, 609, 615, 621
C2C 111, 112, 153, 338
Durability 241, 300, 301, 313, 321, 328, 330, 340, 361, 460, 504, 511, 515, 520, 606, 607
Duty to inform 198, 200, 207, 351, 362, 396, 408, 543, 608
Duty to investigate 170, 200, 338, 352
Evidence to the contrary 52, 69, 86, 89, 380, 382, 415, 417, 419, 422, 427, 430, 465, 467, 485, 488, 515, 519, 547, 548, 565, 575, 576, 578, 580, 583, 586, 611, 613, 615-617, 638, 640, 641, 643
Ex officio 53, 203, 205-207, 213, 214, 217
Folgemangel 14, 442, 444, 447, 462, 486, 491, 598, 603, 629
Factual presumption 36, 37, 69, 87, 95, 115, 116, 268, 288, 301, 328, 354, 361, 407, 444, 447, 499, 520, 598, 607, 611, 643
Grundmangel 14, 442-444, 461, 462, 479, 486, 500, 598, 603, 629
Implementation duty 19, 196, 213, 329, 386

Implied terms 167, 179, 221 297-299, 321, 326, 330, 331, 361, 497, 519, 585, 560

Internal market 1, 2, 15, 101

Know-how 394, 436, 592, 595

Limitation period 116, 137, 138, 141, 143, 177, 178, 190, 230, 249, 382, 409, 538, 585, 607

Luchtzuigen 548, 555, 563, 639

Mandatory application 103, 110, 196, 198, 524

Minimum harmonisation 100, 284, 386, 423, 456, 501

Nature of the goods 335, 338, 353, 381, 418, 421, 423, 431, 442, 469, 471-477, 516-518, 552-554, 556-562, 561, 574, 576, 618, 620, 624-627, 631-633, 637-639

Nature of the non-conformity (defects) 419, 421, 431, 477-483, 518, 562-570, 572, 573, 576, 620

Non liquet 26, 40, 44, 47, 62, 78, 379, 382, 447, 611, 613, 616

Non-performance 79, 143, 198, 289, 292, 435, 489, 507

Normentheorie 50, 76

Perishable goods 301, 399, 471, 516, 527, 554-556, 570, 576, 586, 605, 620, 624, 633, 636, 637, 642

Prima facie 37, 94, 465, 485, 488, 498, 499, 520, 548, 613, 615, 643

Procedural autonomy 18

Public policy 52, 67, 98

Reasonable expectations 120, 242, 335, 337-342, 348, 350, 352-355, 574, 602

Reasonable time 171, 172, 175, 177, 180, 198, 200, 325, 346, 362

Redelijkheid en billijkheid 77, 83, 85, 200, 351, 529

Remedies 116, 117, 168, 170-175, 177, 180-182, 303, 321, 346, 351, 395, 409, 413, 499-501, 505, 511, 522, 585, 601, 608

Reversed burden of proof 52, 77, 85, 95, 473, 495, 522, 600, 643

Second-hand goods 141, 142, 249, 266, 278, 384, 421, 438, 447, 473, 474, 477, 481, 485, 492, 528, 570, 576, 580, 625, 628, 642

Summary proceedings 34, 121

Weaker party 21, 40, 124, 126, 160, 200
Wear and tear 321, 421, 442, 445, 447, 449, 452, 474, 481, 486, 491, 515, 598, 614